VOL. 23
Action Edition

Story and Art by
RUMIKO TAKAHASHI

English Adaptation by Gerard Jones

Translation/Mari Morimoto
Touch-Up Art & Lettering/Bill Schuch
Cover and Interior Graphic Design/Yuki Ameda
Editor/Urian Brown

Managing Editor/Annette Roman
Director of Production/Noboru Watanabe
Vice President of Publishing/Alvin Lu
Sr. Director of Acquisitions/Rika Inouye
VP of Sales & Marketing/Liza Coppola
Publisher/Hyoe Narita

Printed in Canada.

Published by VIZ Media, LLC.
P.O. Box 77010
San Francisco, CA 94107

Action Edition
10 9 8 7 6 5 4 3 2 1
First printing, August 2005

www.viz.com

store.viz.com

InuYasha

VOL. 23   Action Edition

STORY AND ART BY
RUMIKO TAKAHASHI

CONTENTS

Long ago, in the "Warring States" era of Japan's Muromachi period (*Sengoku-jidai*, approximately 1467-1568 CE), a legendary dog-like half-demon called "Inu-Yasha" attempted to steal the Shikon Jewel—or "Jewel of Four Souls"—from a village, but was stopped by the enchanted arrow of the village priestess, Kikyo. Inu-Yasha fell into a deep sleep, pinned to a tree by Kikyo's arrow, while the mortally wounded Kikyo took the Shikon Jewel with her into the fires of her funeral pyre. Years passed.

Fast-forward to the present day. Kagome, a Japanese high school girl, is pulled into a well one day by a mysterious centipede monster, and finds herself transported into the past—only to come face to face with the trapped Inu-Yasha. She frees him, and Inu-Yasha easily defeats the centipede monster.

The residents of the village, now 50 years older, readily accept Kagome as the reincarnation of their deceased priestess Kikyo, a claim supported by the fact that the Shikon Jewel emerges from a cut on Kagome's body. Unfortunately, the jewel's rediscovery means that the village is soon under attack by a variety of demons in search of this treasure. Then, the jewel is accidentally shattered into many shards, each of which may have the fearsome power of the entire jewel.

Although Inu-Yasha says he hates Kagome because of her resemblance to Kikyo, the woman who "killed" him, he is forced to team up with her when Kaede, the village leader, binds him to Kagome with a powerful spell. Now the two grudging companions must fight to reclaim and reassemble the shattered shards of the Shikon Jewel before they fall into the wrong hands....

THIS VOLUME Naraku's minion kidnaps Lord Sesshômaru's tiny human companion, Rin. When Sesshômaru comes to the rescue he tries to strike a bargain and convince him to kill Inuyasha. However, Naraku finds out the hard way that Sesshômaru will not do his bidding. But, Naraku has known this all along and has laid another

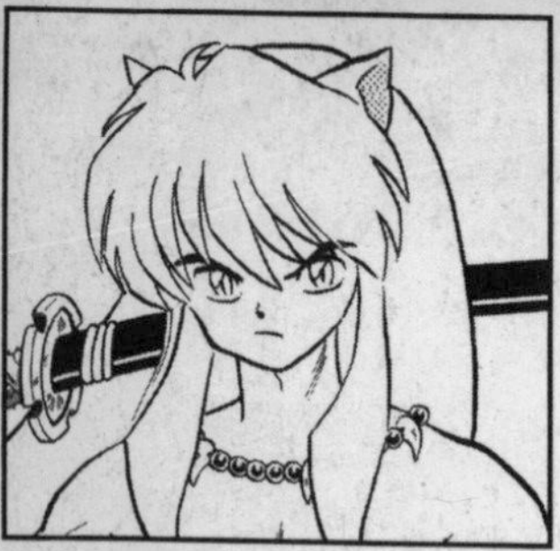

INU-YASHA
Half-demon hybrid, son of a human mother and demon father. His necklace is enchanted, allowing Kagome to control him with a word.

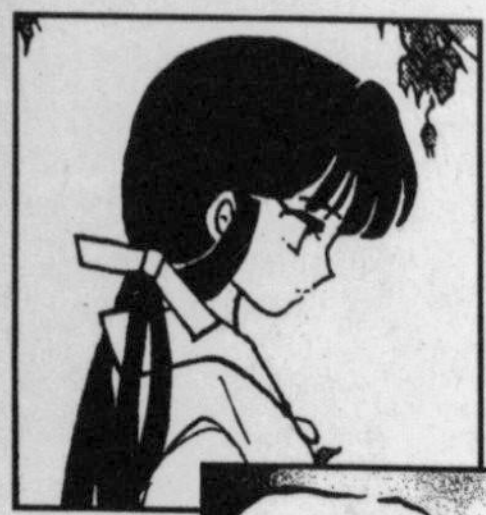

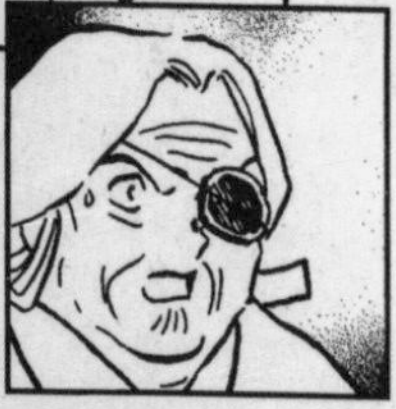

KIKYO and KAEDE
Once older and younger sisters, Kikyo's initial death and Kaede's long, human life have put them half a century apart.

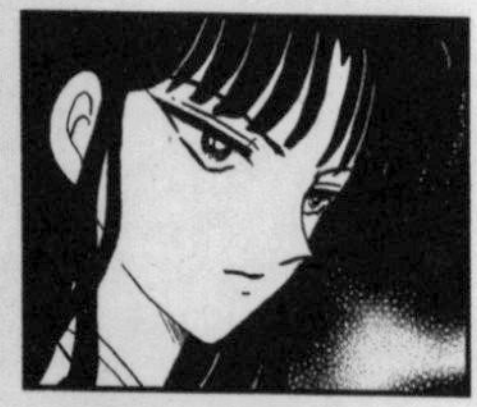

NARAKU
Enigmatic demon-mastermind behind the miseries of nearly everyone in the story.

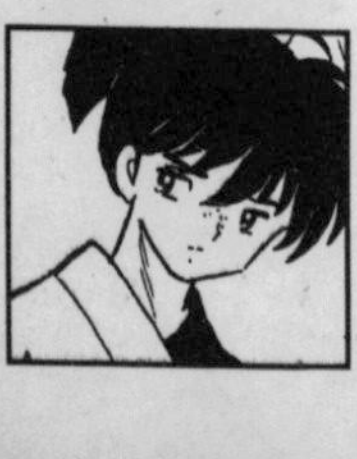

KOHAKU
Killed by Naraku—but not before first slaying both his own and Sango's father—now he's back again in a newer...if somewhat *slower*...form.

KAGOME
Modern-day Japanese schoolgirl who can travel back and forth between the past and present through an enchanted well.

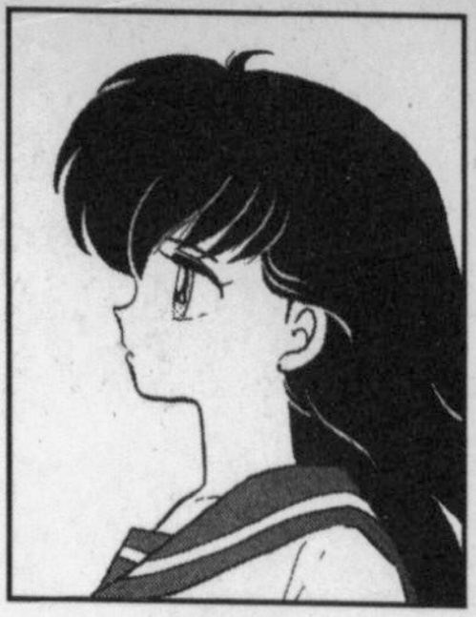

MIROKU
Lecherous Buddhist priest cursed with a mystical "hellhole" in his hand that's slowly killing him.

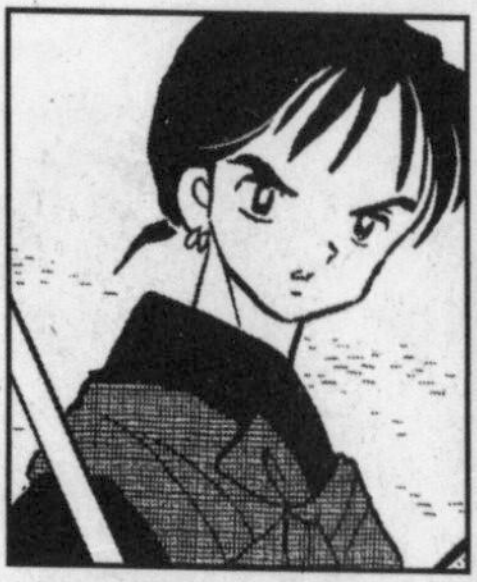

SANGO
"Demon Exterminator" or slayer from the village where the Shikon Jewel was first born.

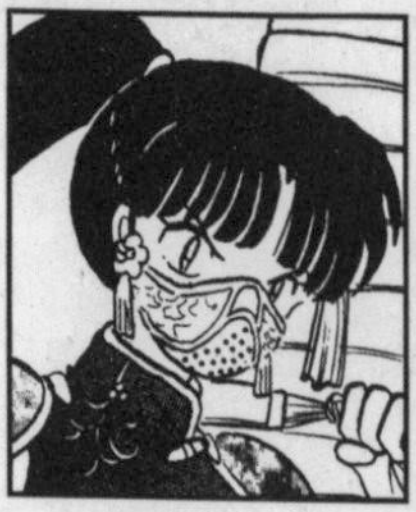

KAGURA
A demon created by Naraku from parts of his body, Kagura—the Wind Demon—is Naraku's second incarnation. Unlike others, however, Kagura resents Naraku's control over her and aids him only for her own survival.

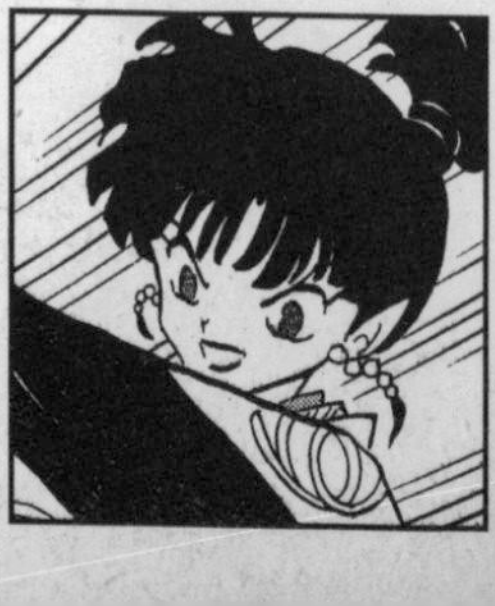

SCROLL ONE
KIDNAPPED

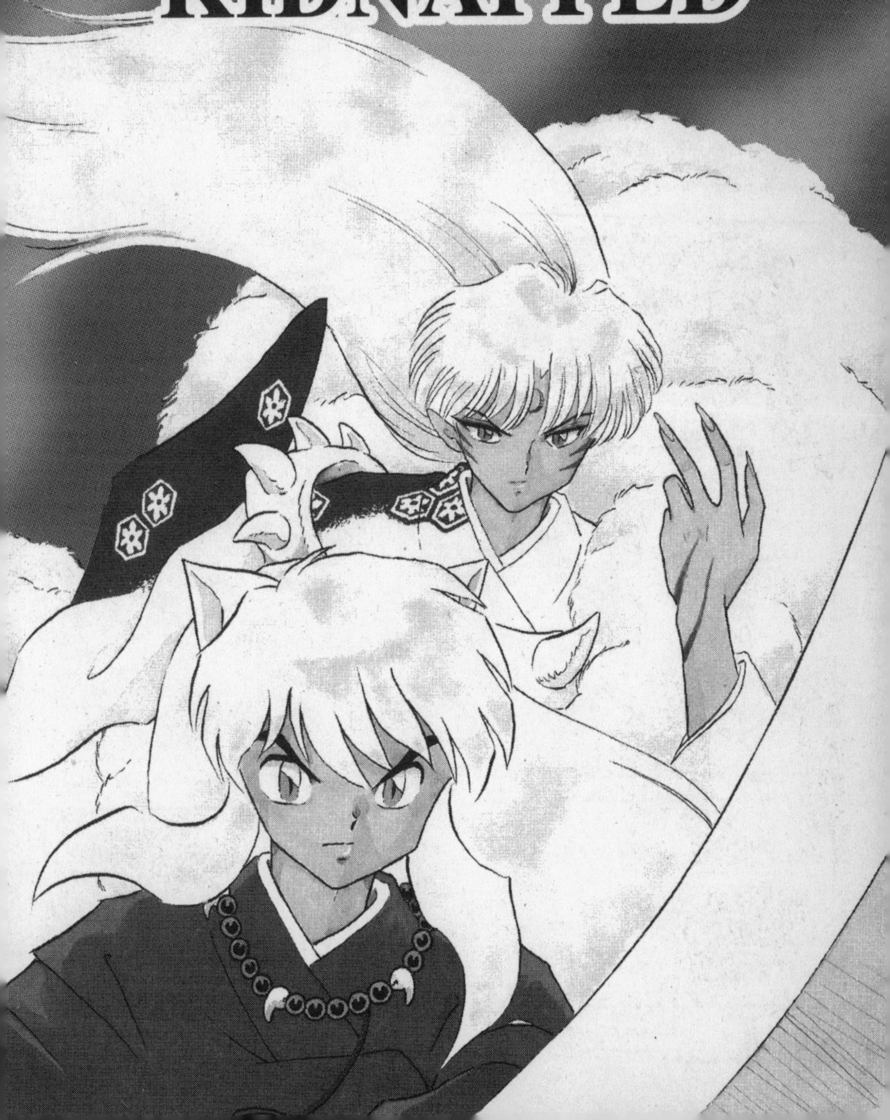

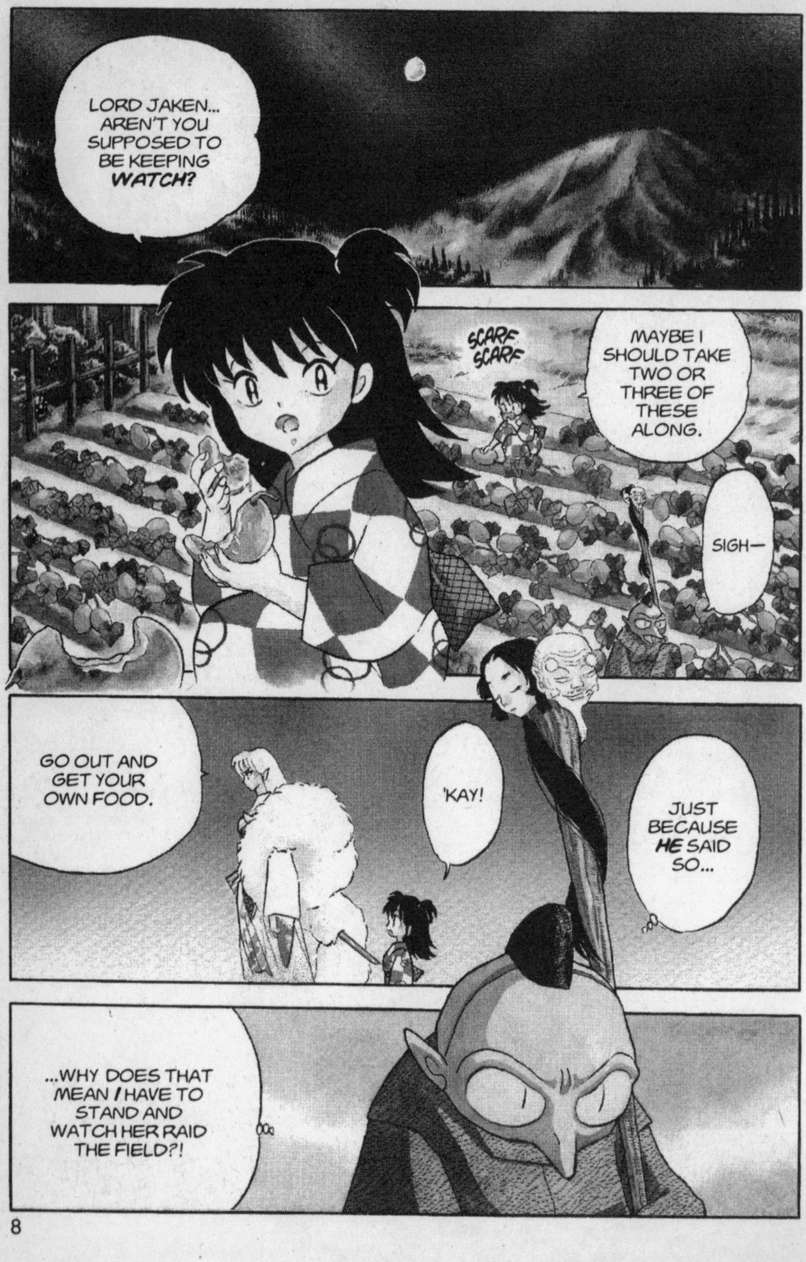
LORD JAKEN... AREN'T YOU SUPPOSED TO BE KEEPING WATCH?
SCARF SCARF
MAYBE I SHOULD TAKE TWO OR THREE OF THESE ALONG.
SIGH—
GO OUT AND GET YOUR OWN FOOD.
'KAY!
JUST BECAUSE HE SAID SO...
...WHY DOES THAT MEAN I HAVE TO STAND AND WATCH HER RAID THE FIELD?!

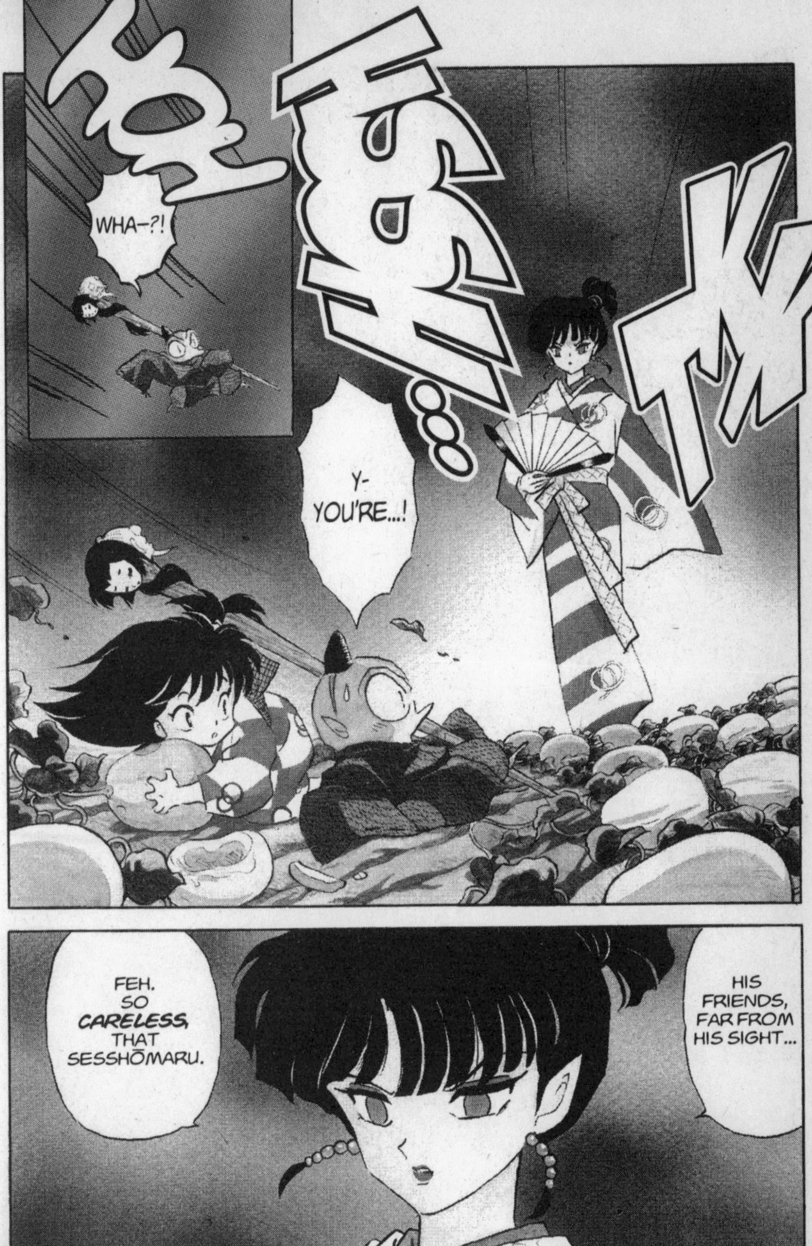
WHA-?!
Y-YOU'RE...!
FEH. SO *CARELESS,* THAT SESSHŌMARU.
HIS FRIENDS, FAR FROM HIS SIGHT...

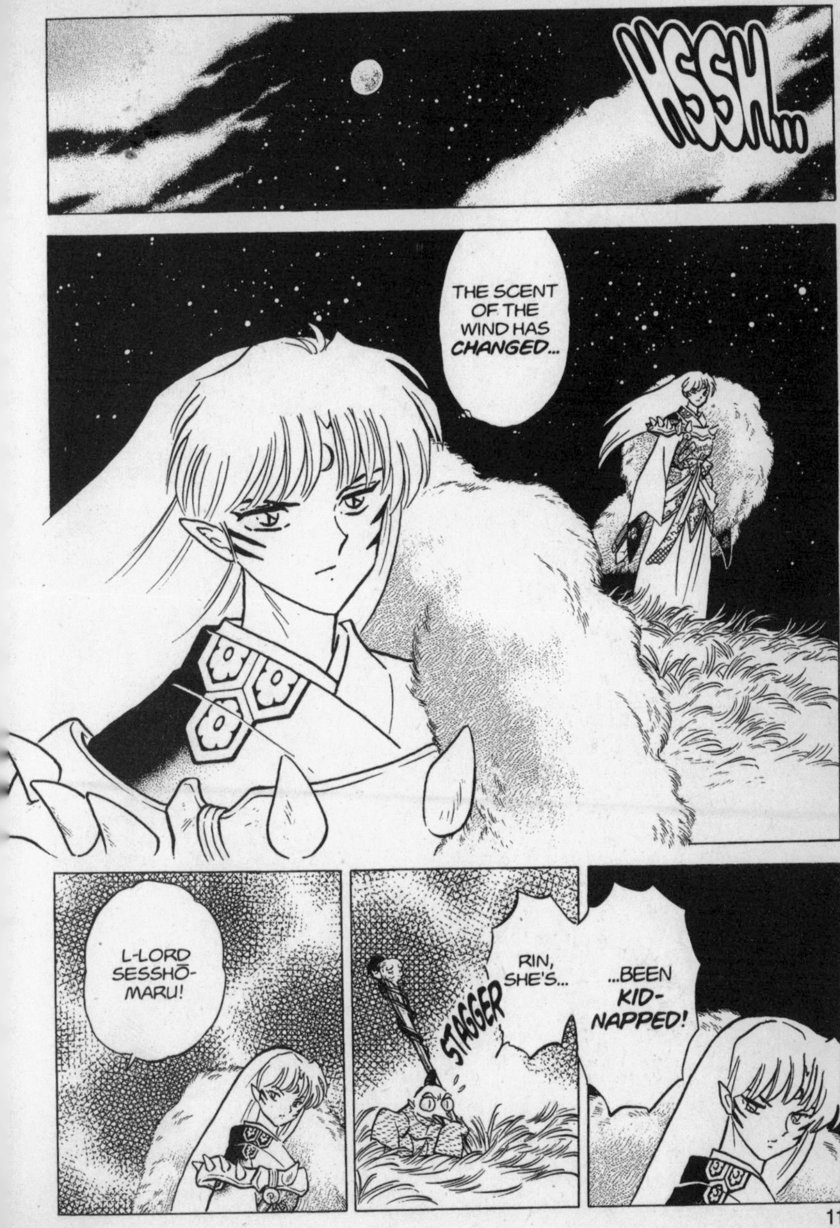
HSSH...
THE SCENT OF THE WIND HAS CHANGED...
L-LORD SESSHŌMARU!
STAGGER
RIN, SHE'S...
...BEEN KIDNAPPED!

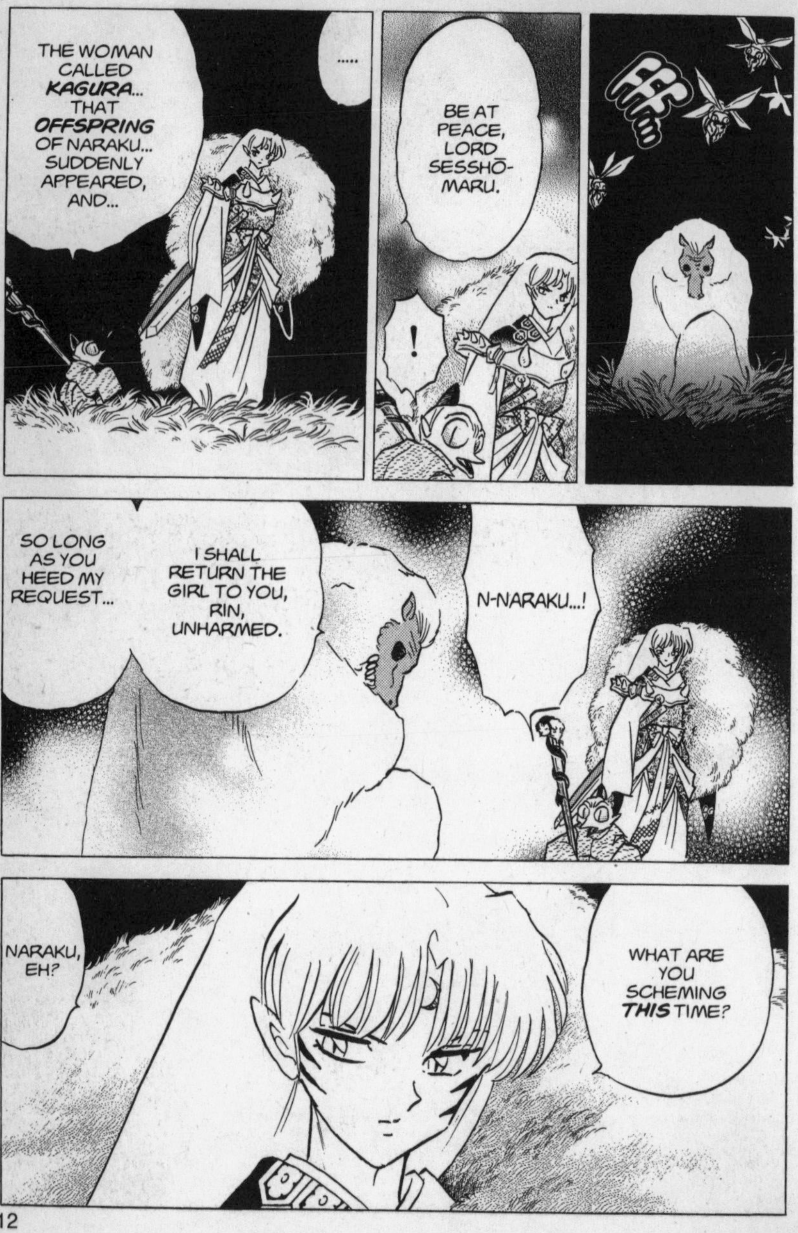
THE WOMAN CALLED KAGURA... THAT OFFSPRING OF NARAKU... SUDDENLY APPEARED, AND...
.....
BE AT PEACE, LORD SESSHŌ-MARU.
!
SO LONG AS YOU HEED MY REQUEST...
I SHALL RETURN THE GIRL TO YOU, RIN, UNHARMED.
N-NARAKU...!
NARAKU, EH?
WHAT ARE YOU SCHEMING THIS TIME?

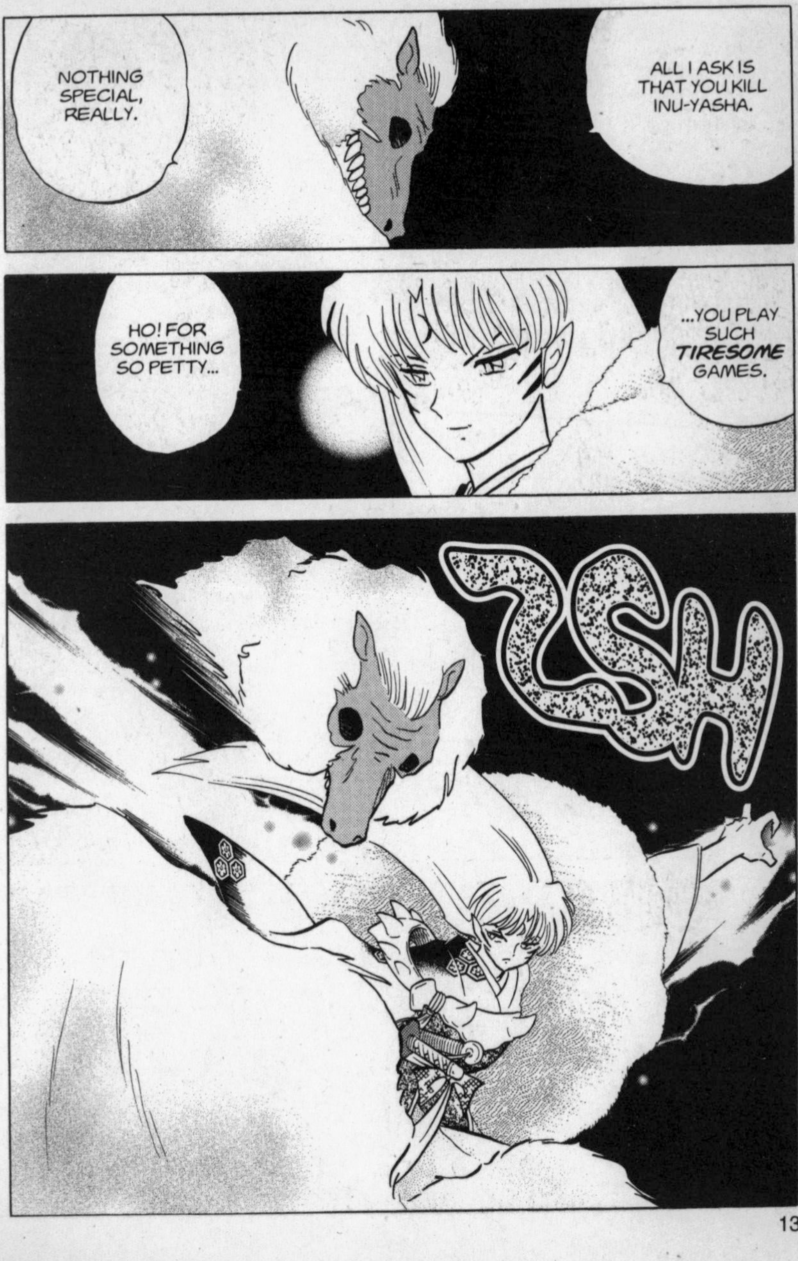
NOTHING SPECIAL, REALLY.
ALL I ASK IS THAT YOU KILL INU-YASHA.
HO! FOR SOMETHING SO PETTY...
...YOU PLAY SUCH *TIRESOME* GAMES.
ZSH

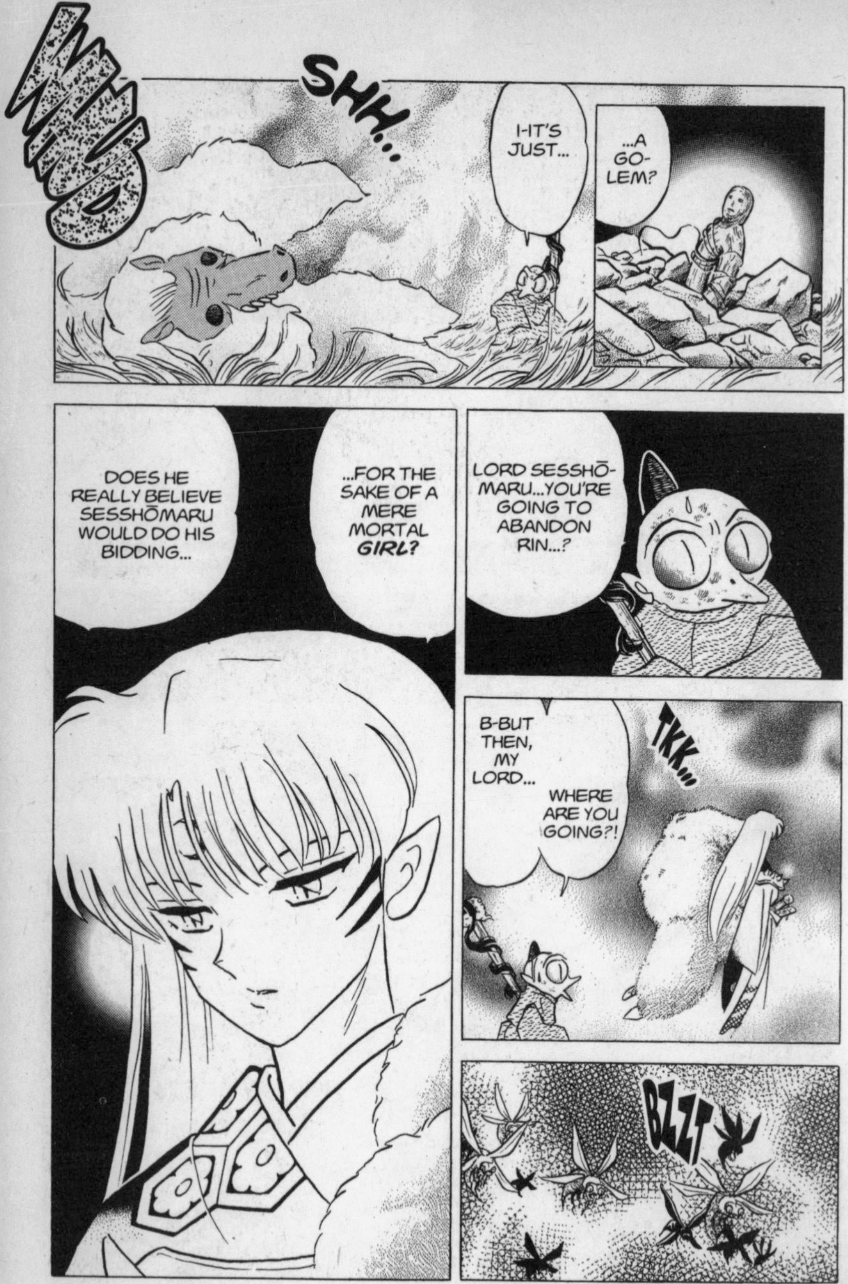
SHH...
I-IT'S JUST...
...A GO-LEM?
DOES HE REALLY BELIEVE SESSHŌMARU WOULD DO HIS BIDDING...
...FOR THE SAKE OF A MERE MORTAL GIRL?
LORD SESSHŌ-MARU...YOU'RE GOING TO ABANDON RIN...?
B-BUT THEN, MY LORD...
TKK...
WHERE ARE YOU GOING?!
BZZT

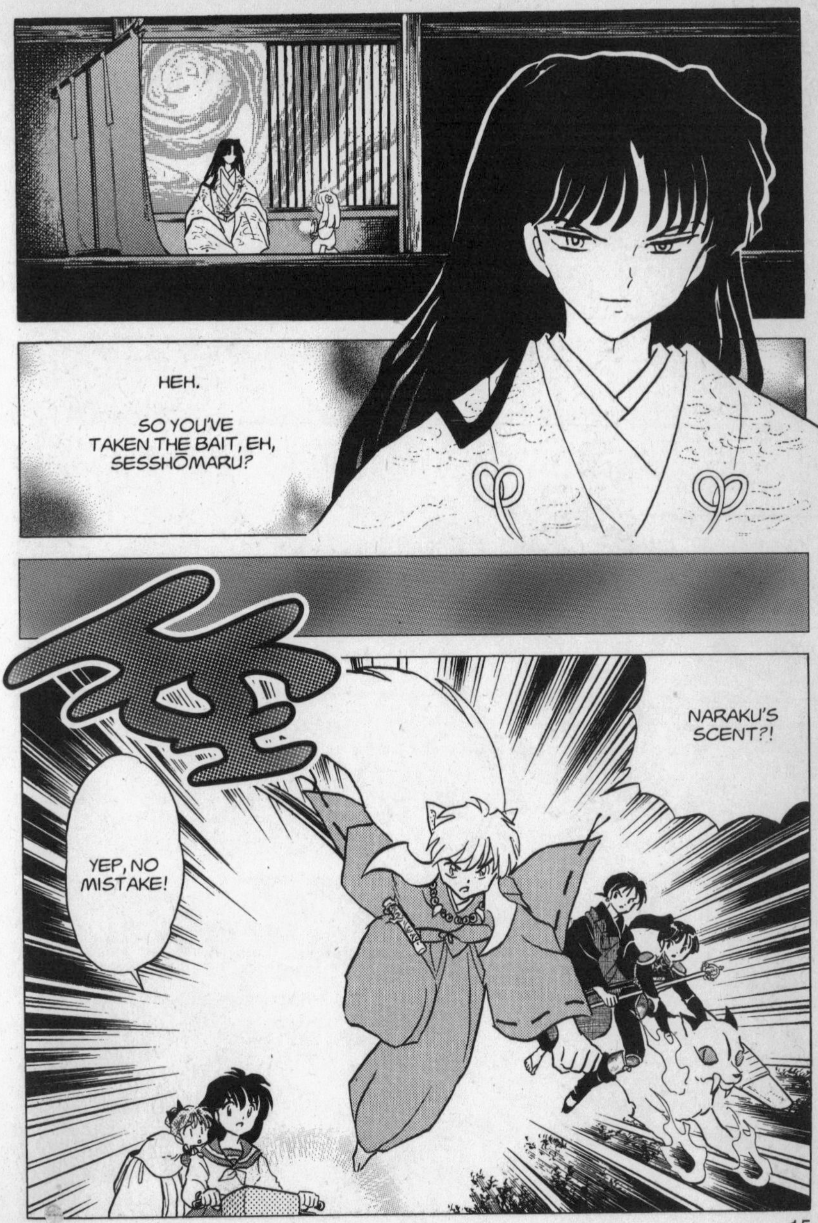
HEH.
SO YOU'VE TAKEN THE BAIT, EH, SESSHŌMARU?
NARAKU'S SCENT?!
YEP, NO MISTAKE!

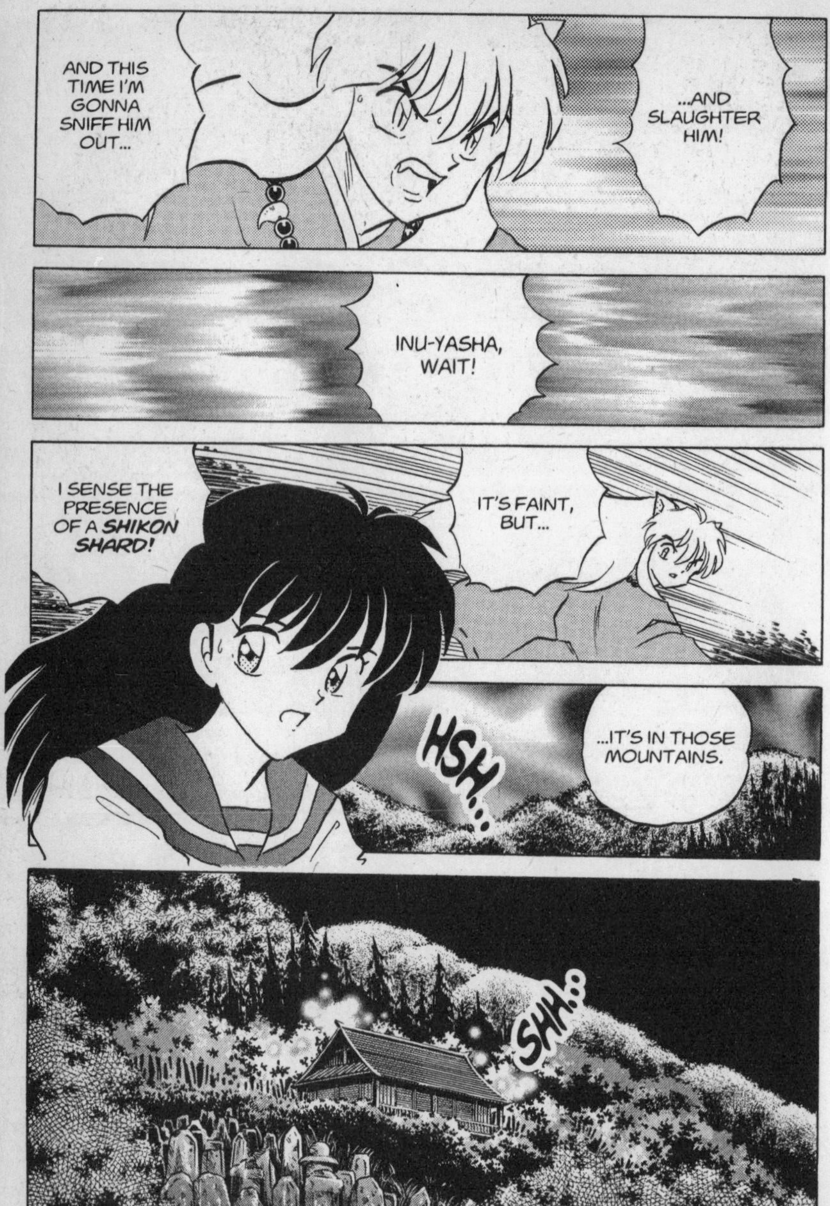

AND THIS TIME I'M GONNA SNIFF HIM OUT...
...AND SLAUGHTER HIM!
INU-YASHA, WAIT!
I SENSE THE PRESENCE OF A **SHIKON SHARD!**
IT'S FAINT, BUT...
HSH...
...IT'S IN THOSE MOUNTAINS.
SHH...

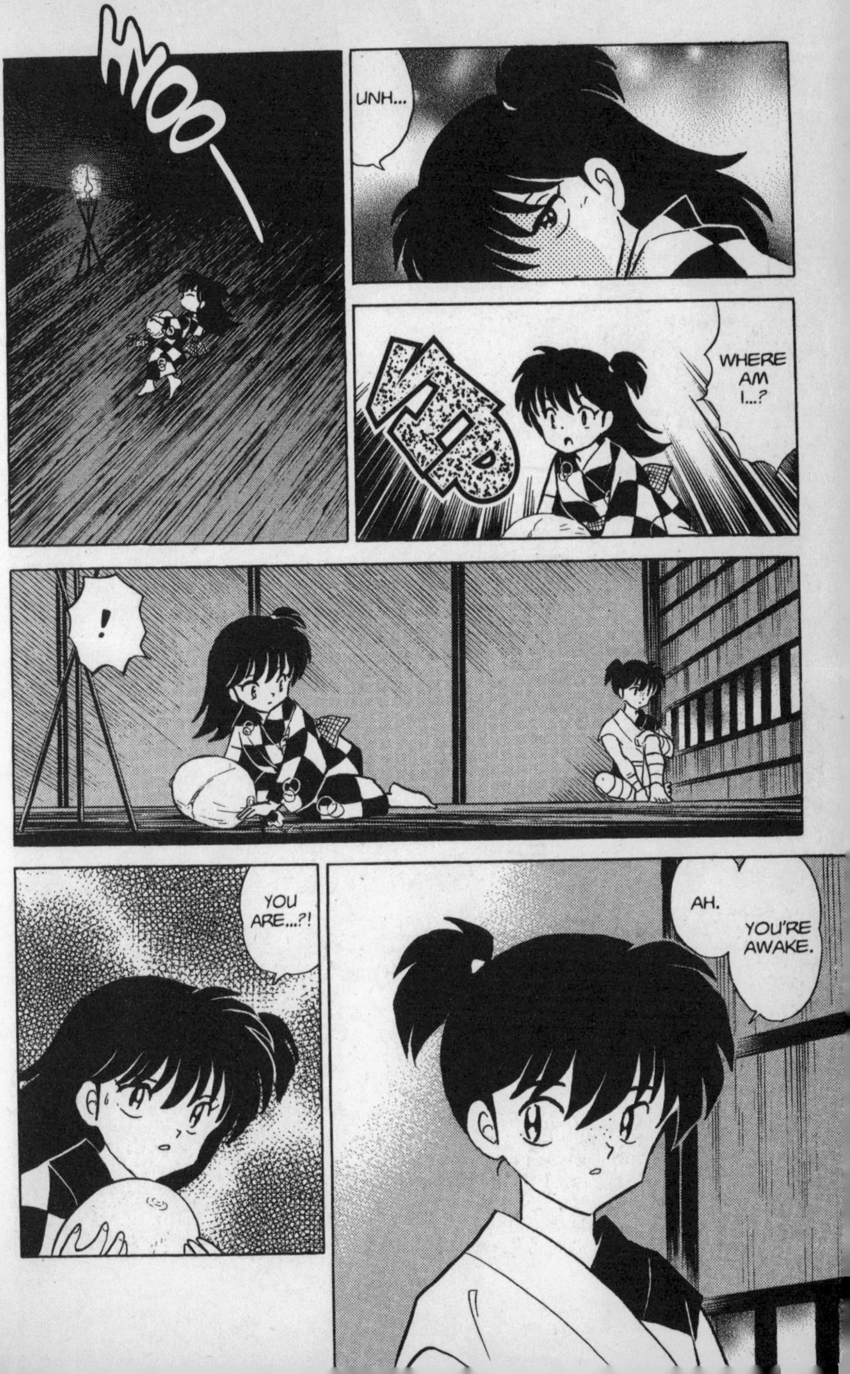
HYOO
UNH...
YEP
WHERE AM I...?
!
YOU ARE...?!
AH.
YOU'RE AWAKE.

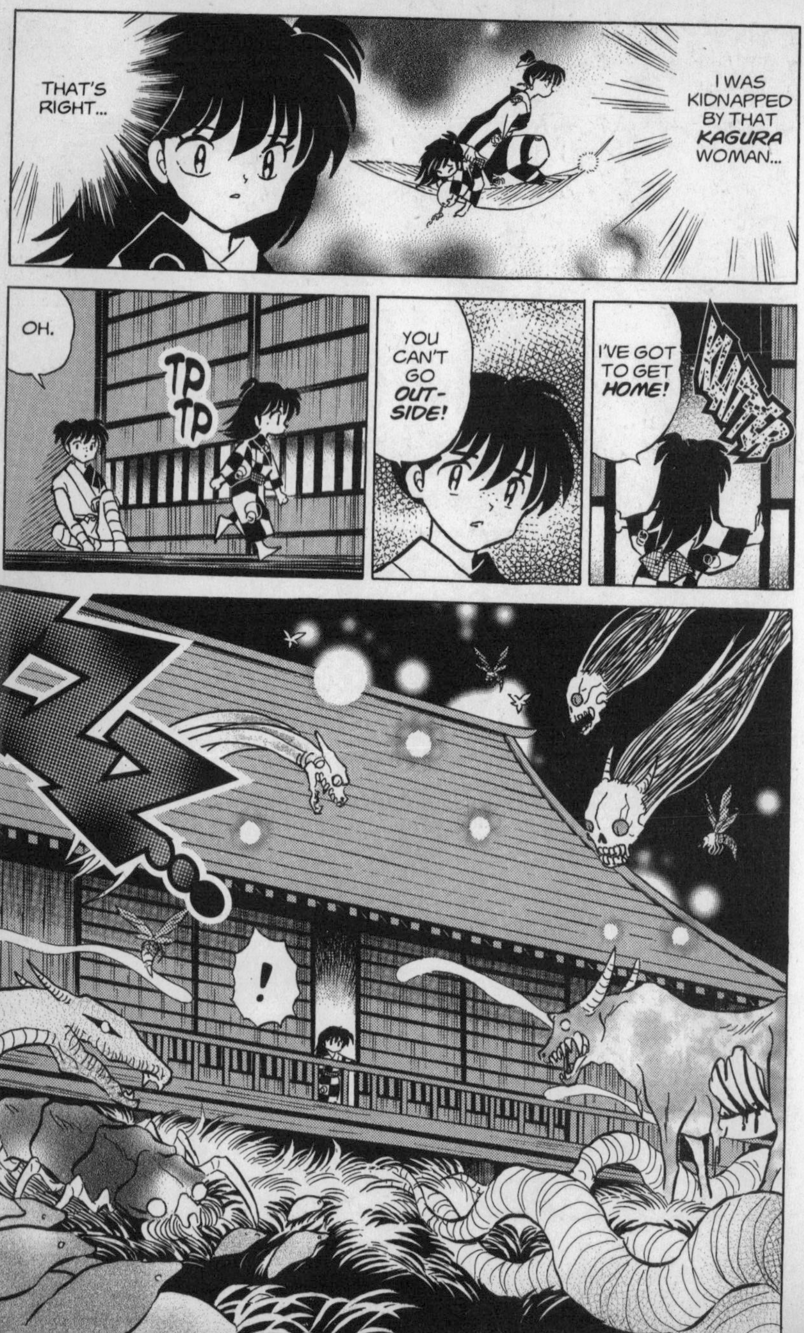
THAT'S RIGHT...
I WAS KIDNAPPED BY THAT **KAGURA** WOMAN...
OH.
TP TP
YOU CAN'T GO **OUT-SIDE!**
I'VE GOT TO GET **HOME!**
!

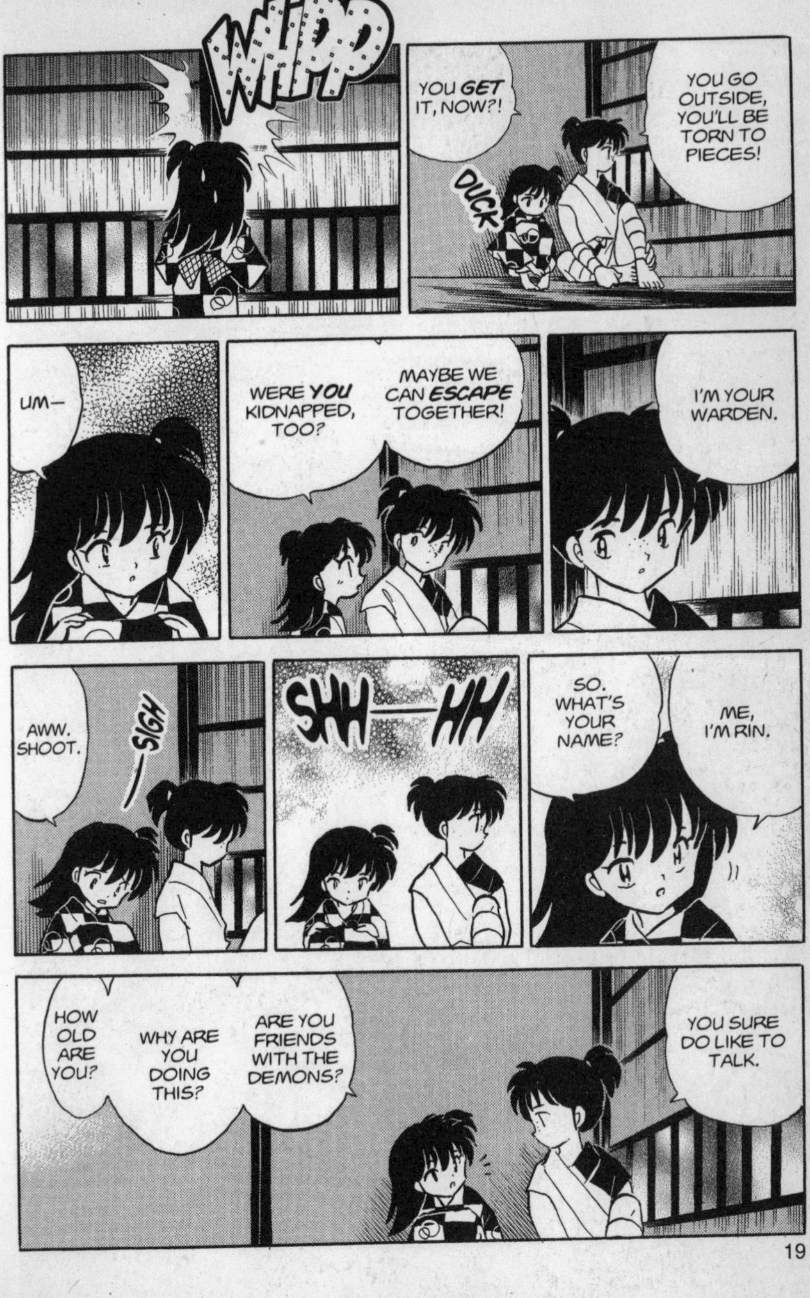

WHPP
YOU **GET** IT, NOW?!
DUCK
YOU GO OUTSIDE, YOU'LL BE TORN TO PIECES!
UM—
WERE **YOU** KIDNAPPED, TOO?
MAYBE WE CAN **ESCAPE** TOGETHER!
I'M YOUR WARDEN.
AWW. SHOOT.
—SIGH
SHH—HH
SO. WHAT'S YOUR NAME?
ME, I'M RIN.
HOW OLD ARE YOU?
WHY ARE YOU DOING THIS?
ARE YOU FRIENDS WITH THE DEMONS?
YOU SURE DO LIKE TO TALK.

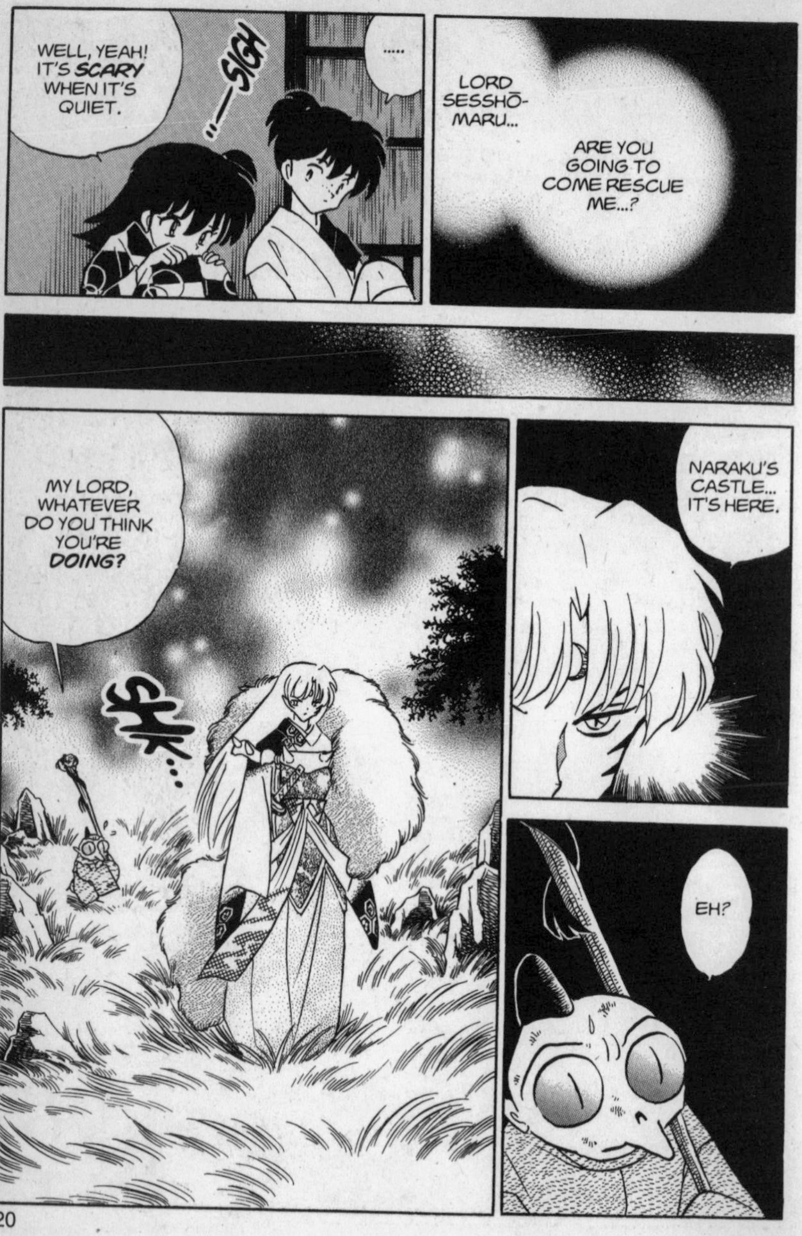
WELL, YEAH! IT'S SCARY WHEN IT'S QUIET.
SIGH--!!
.....
LORD SESSHŌ-MARU...
ARE YOU GOING TO COME RESCUE ME...?
MY LORD, WHATEVER DO YOU THINK YOU'RE DOING?
SHK...
NARAKU'S CASTLE... IT'S HERE.
EH?

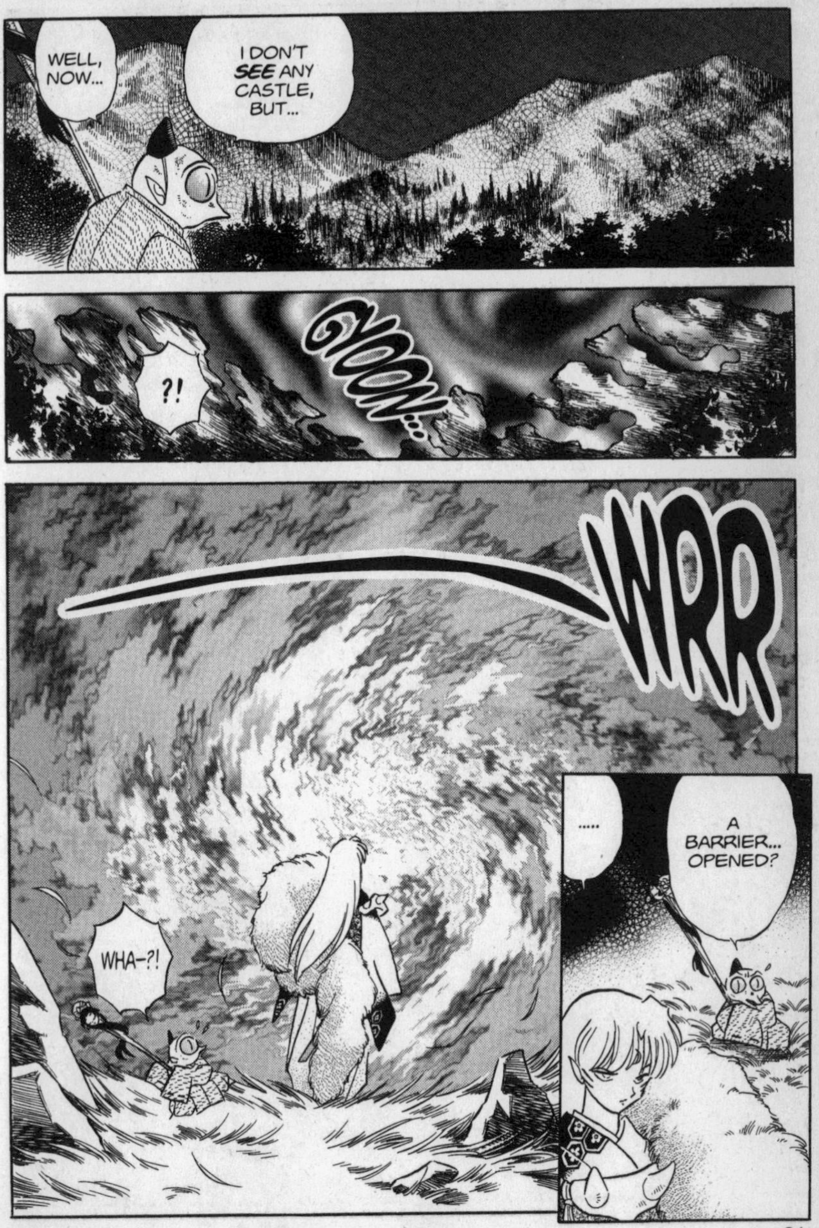
WELL, NOW...
I DON'T **SEE** ANY CASTLE, BUT...
?!
GYOON...
WRR
WHA-?!
.....
A BARRIER... OPENED?

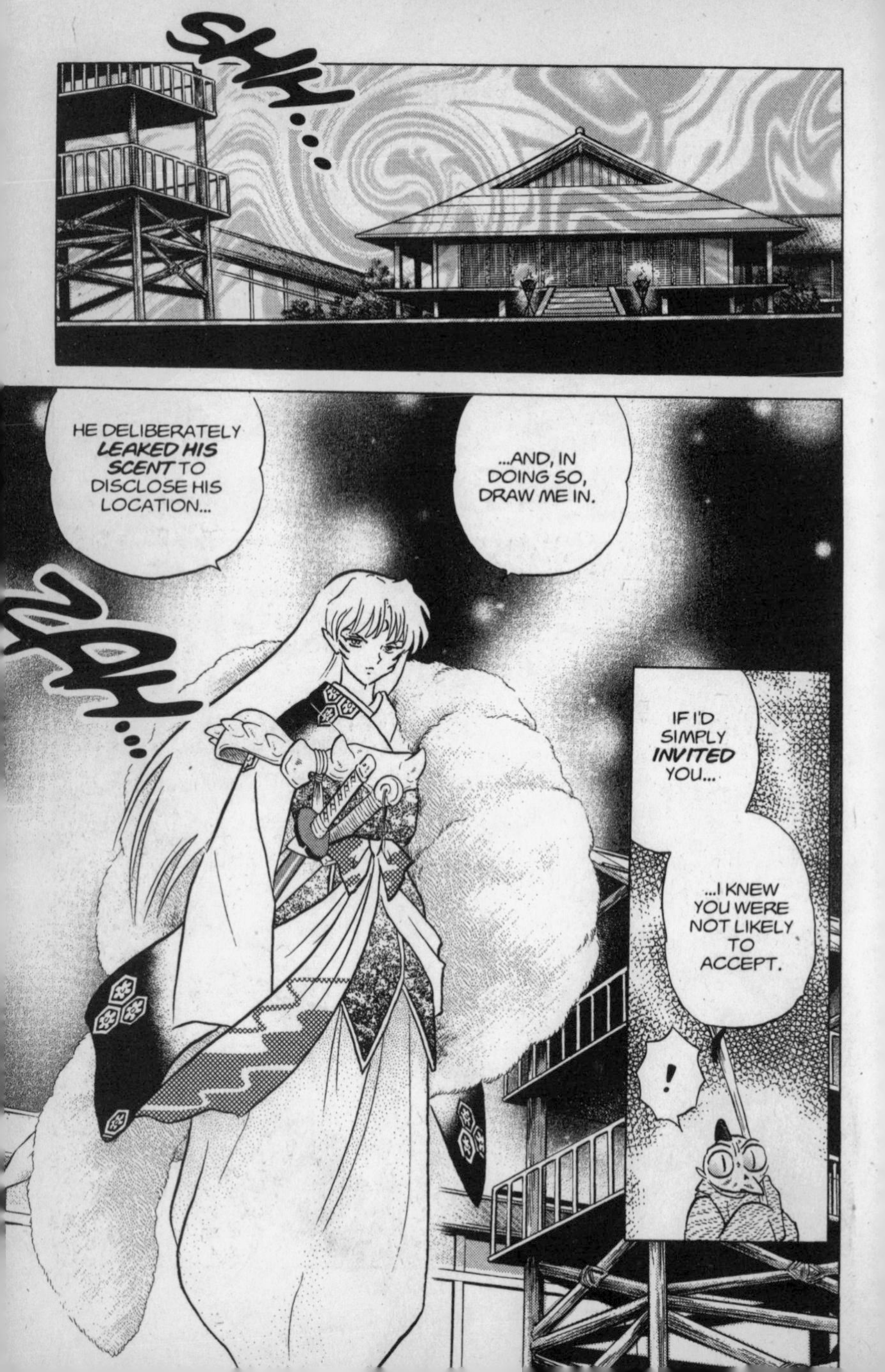
SHH...
ZAH...
HE DELIBERATELY LEAKED HIS SCENT TO DISCLOSE HIS LOCATION...
...AND, IN DOING SO, DRAW ME IN.
IF I'D SIMPLY INVITED YOU...
...I KNEW YOU WERE NOT LIKELY TO ACCEPT.
!

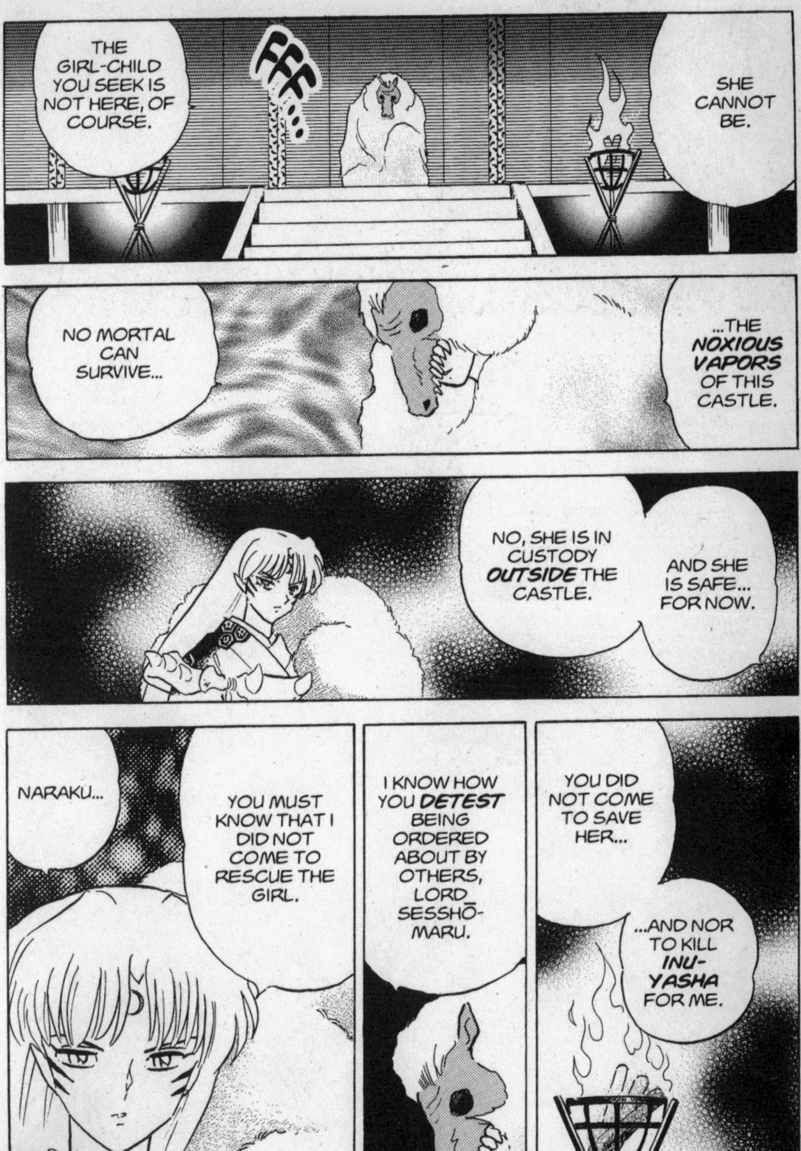
THE GIRL-CHILD YOU SEEK IS NOT HERE, OF COURSE.
FFF...
SHE CANNOT BE.
NO MORTAL CAN SURVIVE...
...THE NOXIOUS VAPORS OF THIS CASTLE.
NO, SHE IS IN CUSTODY OUTSIDE THE CASTLE.
AND SHE IS SAFE... FOR NOW.
NARAKU...
YOU MUST KNOW THAT I DID NOT COME TO RESCUE THE GIRL.
I KNOW HOW YOU DETEST BEING ORDERED ABOUT BY OTHERS, LORD SESSHŌ-MARU.
YOU DID NOT COME TO SAVE HER...
...AND NOR TO KILL INU-YASHA FOR ME.

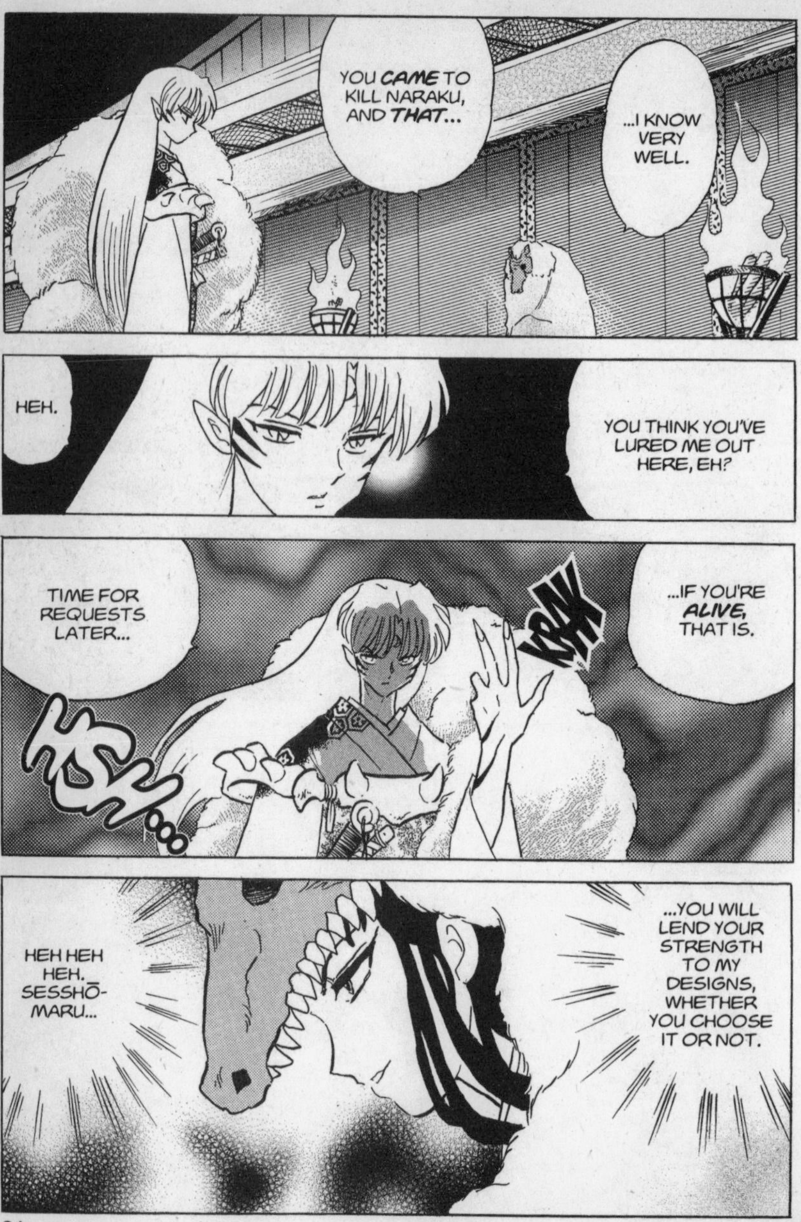
YOU CAME TO KILL NARAKU, AND THAT...
...I KNOW VERY WELL.
HEH.
YOU THINK YOU'VE LURED ME OUT HERE, EH?
TIME FOR REQUESTS LATER...
KRAK
...IF YOU'RE ALIVE, THAT IS.
HSSH...
HEH HEH HEH. SESSHŌMARU...
...YOU WILL LEND YOUR STRENGTH TO MY DESIGNS, WHETHER YOU CHOOSE IT OR NOT.

SCROLL TWO

NARAKU'S DESIGN

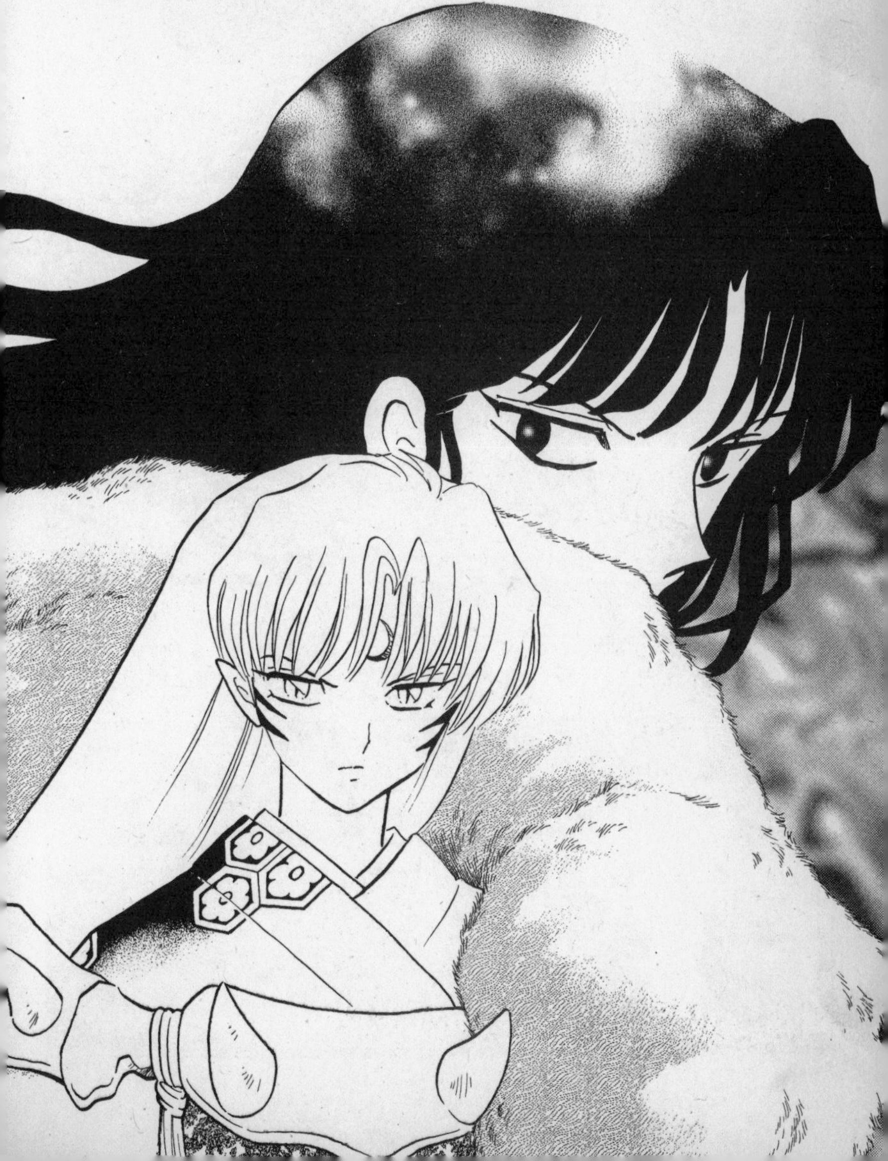

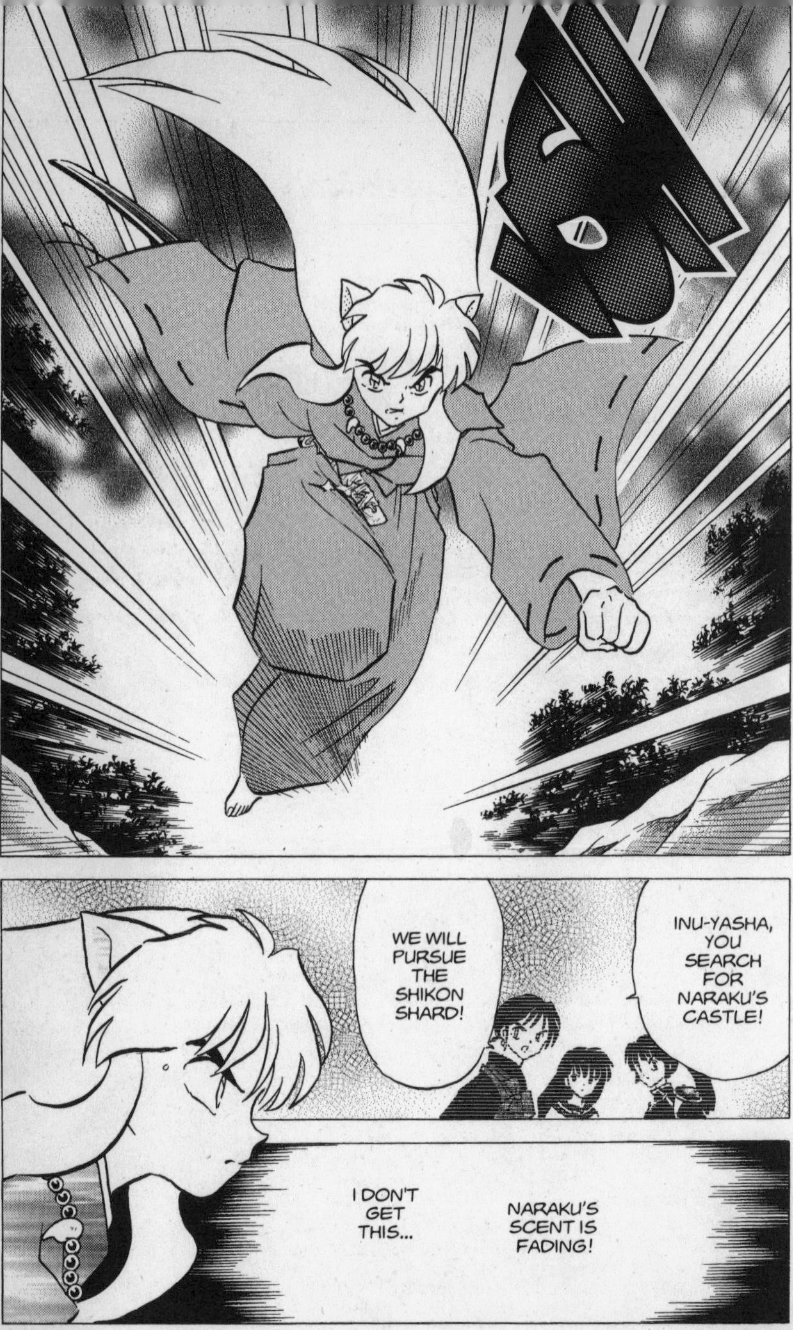
WE WILL PURSUE THE SHIKON SHARD!
INU-YASHA, YOU SEARCH FOR NARAKU'S CASTLE!
I DON'T GET THIS...
NARAKU'S SCENT IS FADING!

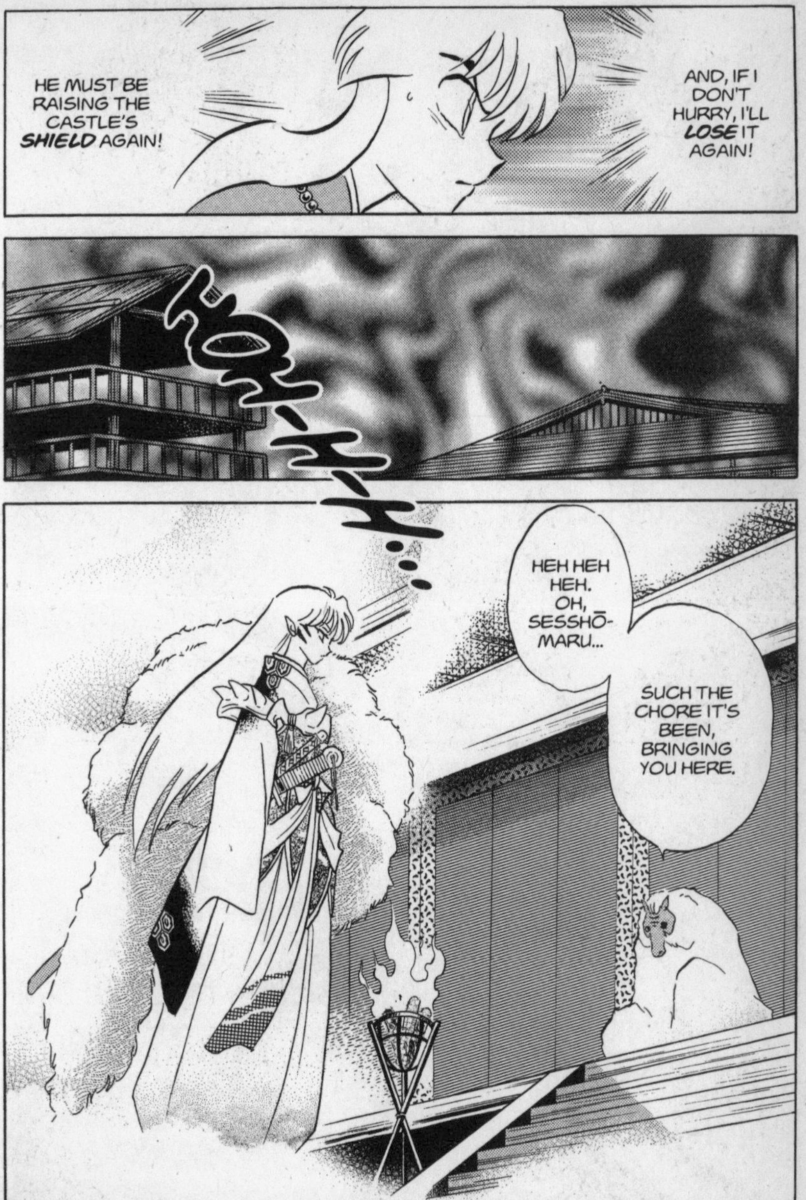
HE MUST BE RAISING THE CASTLE'S SHIELD AGAIN!
AND, IF I DON'T HURRY, I'LL LOSE IT AGAIN!
HOH-H-H...
HEH HEH HEH. OH, SESSHŌ-MARU...
SUCH THE CHORE IT'S BEEN, BRINGING YOU HERE.

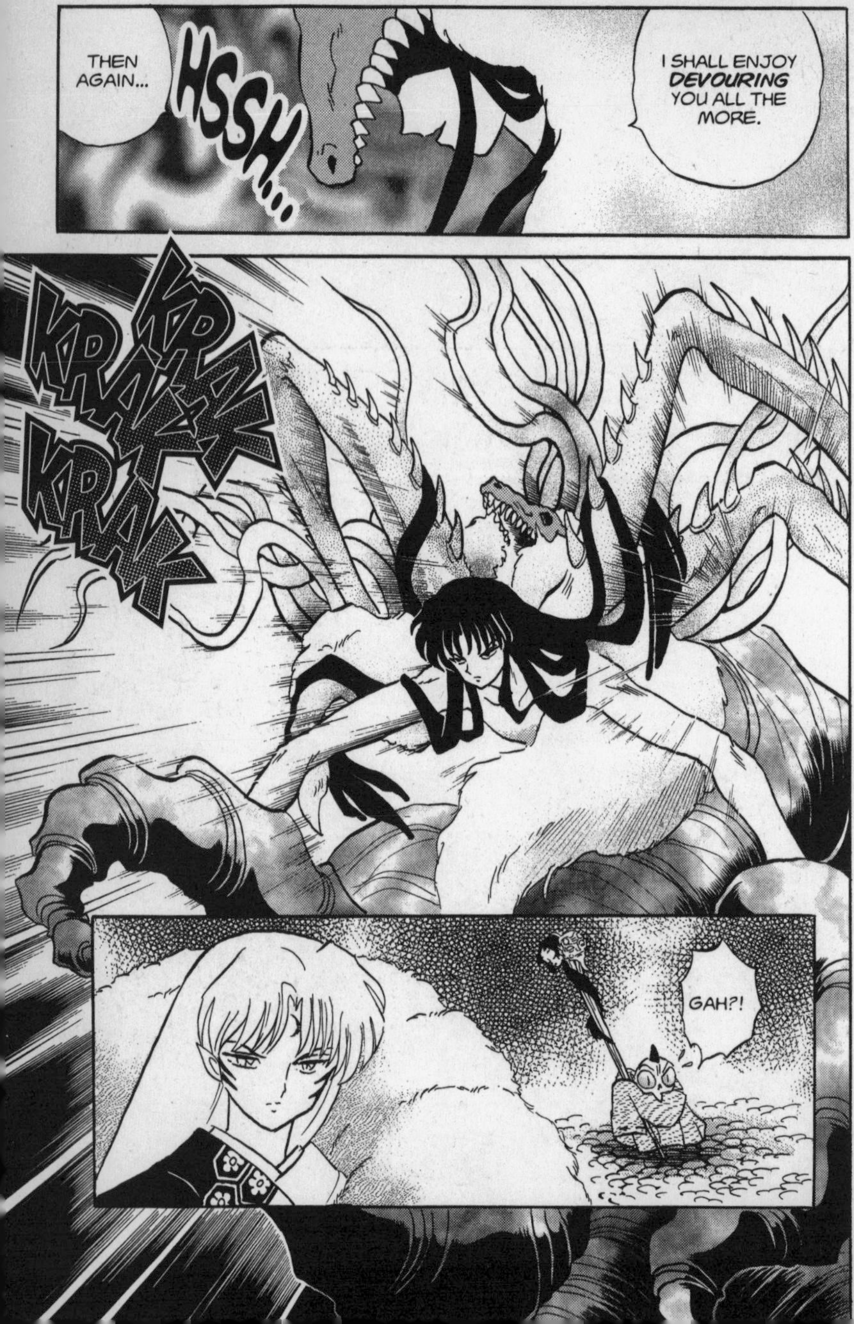
THEN AGAIN...
HSSH...
I SHALL ENJOY ***DEVOURING*** YOU ALL THE MORE.
KRAK KRAK KRAK
GAH?!

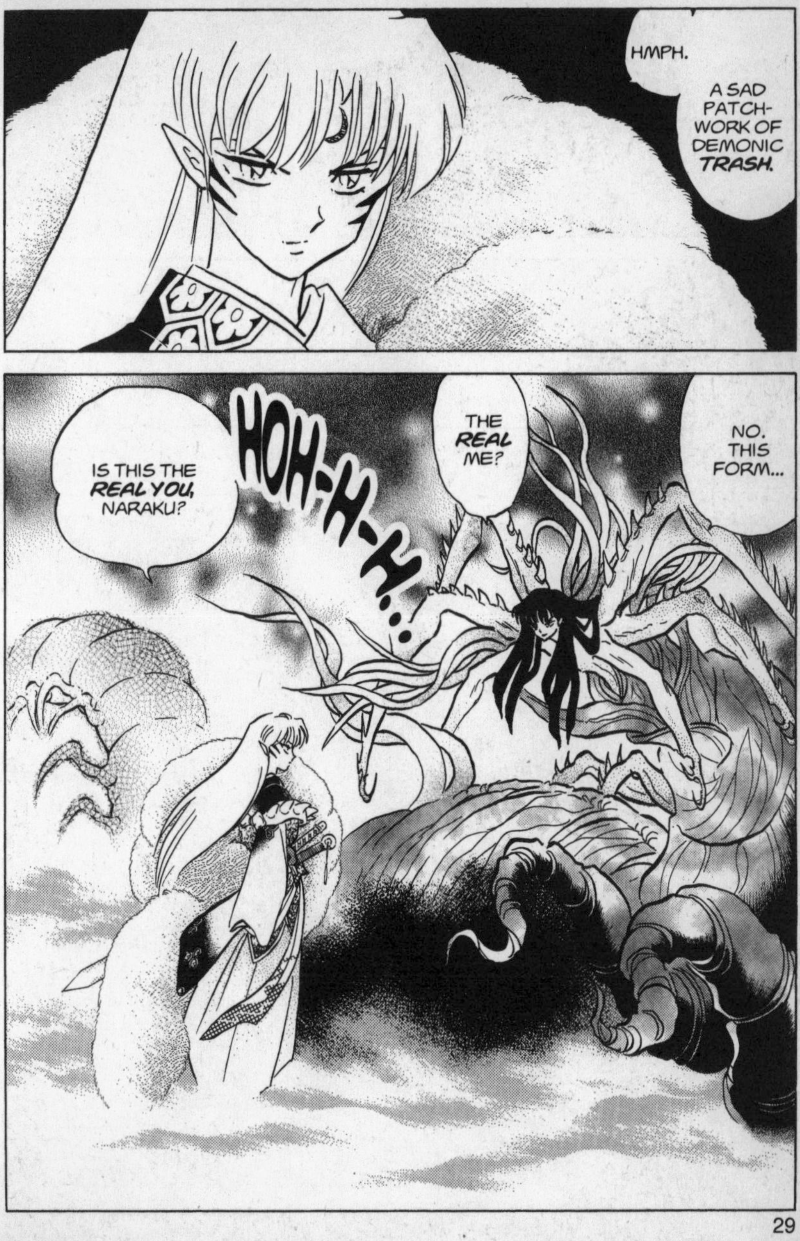
HMPH.
A SAD PATCH-WORK OF DEMONIC **TRASH.**
IS THIS THE **REAL YOU,** NARAKU?
HOH-H-H...
THE **REAL** ME?
NO. THIS FORM...

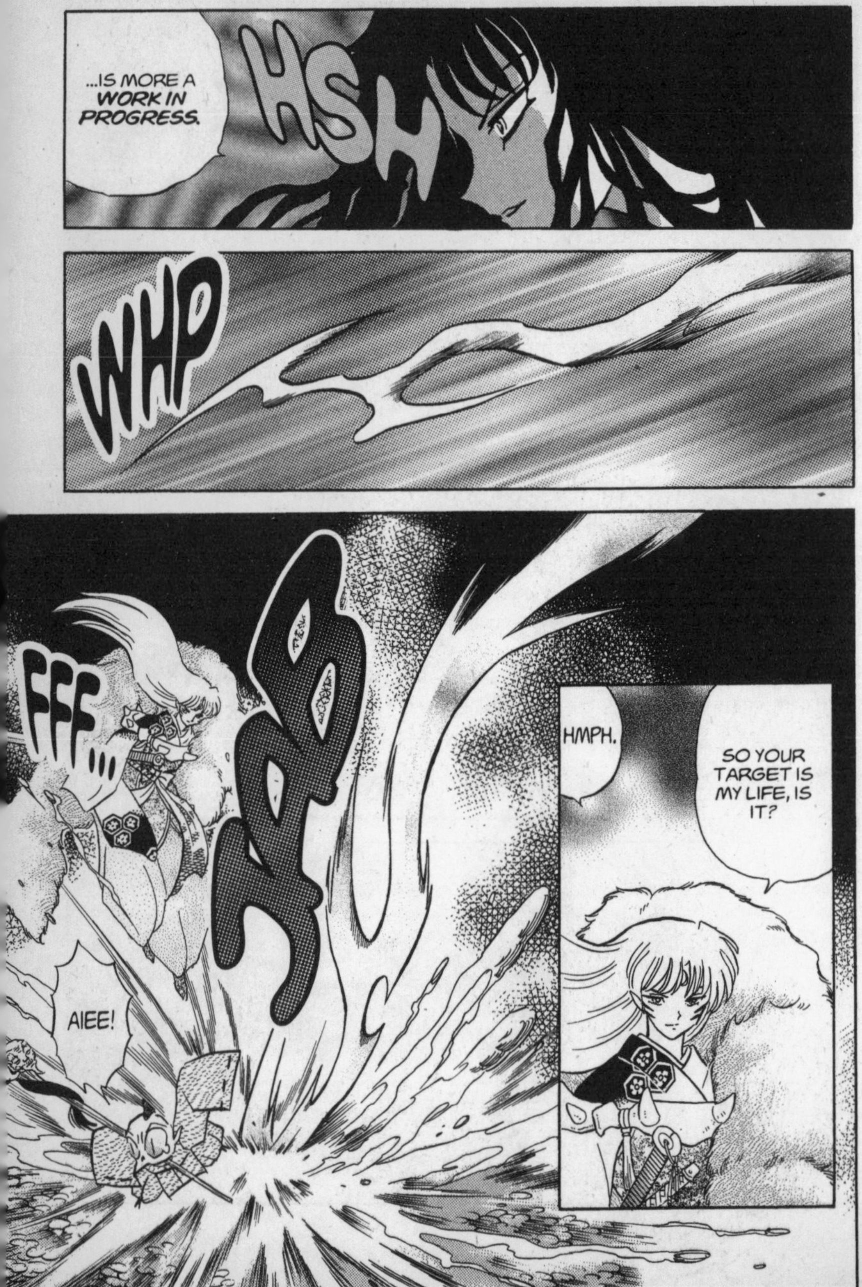
...IS MORE A WORK IN PROGRESS.
HSH
WHP
FFF...
AIEE!
HMPH.
SO YOUR TARGET IS MY LIFE, IS IT?

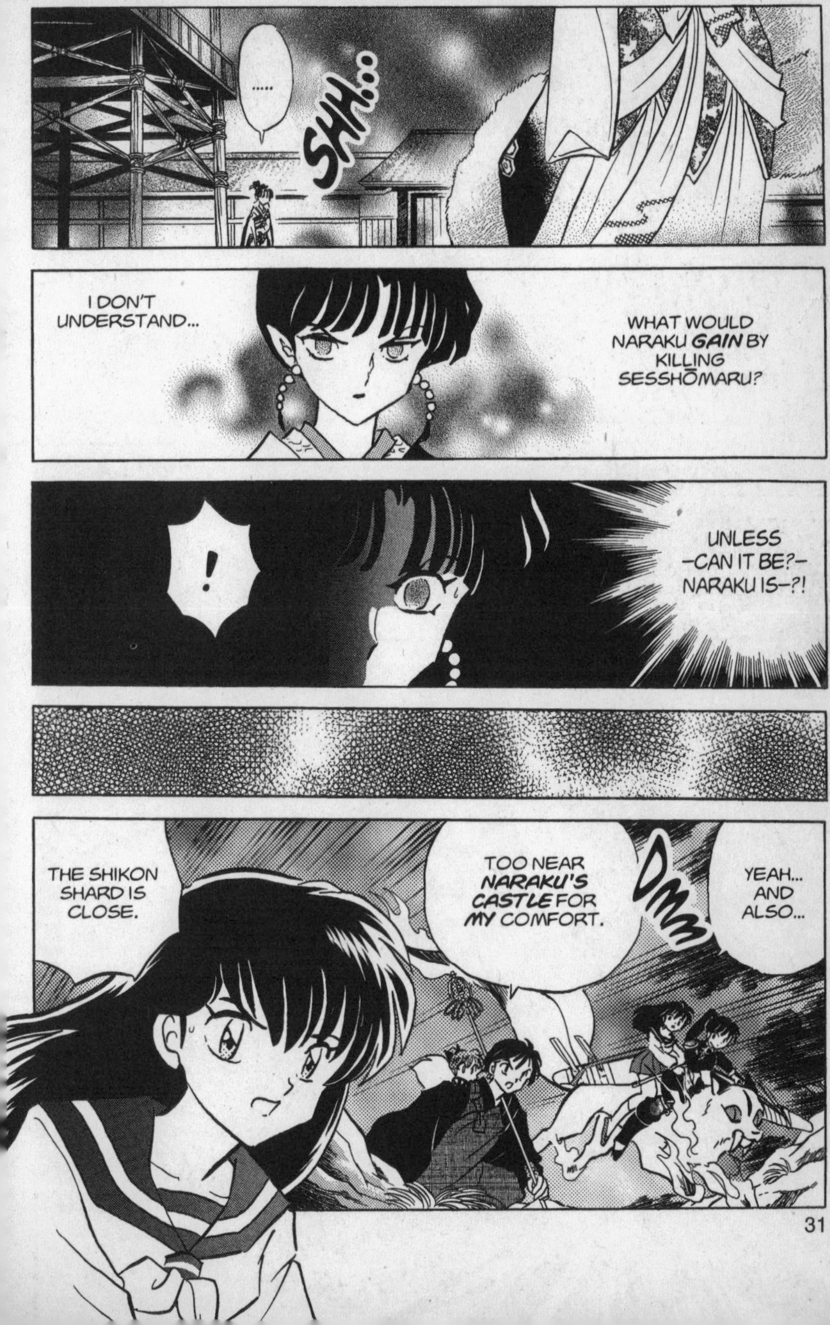
......
SHH...
I DON'T UNDERSTAND...
WHAT WOULD NARAKU GAIN BY KILLING SESSHŌMARU?
!
UNLESS -CAN IT BE?- NARAKU IS-?!
THE SHIKON SHARD IS CLOSE.
TOO NEAR NARAKU'S CASTLE FOR MY COMFORT.
DMM
YEAH... AND ALSO...

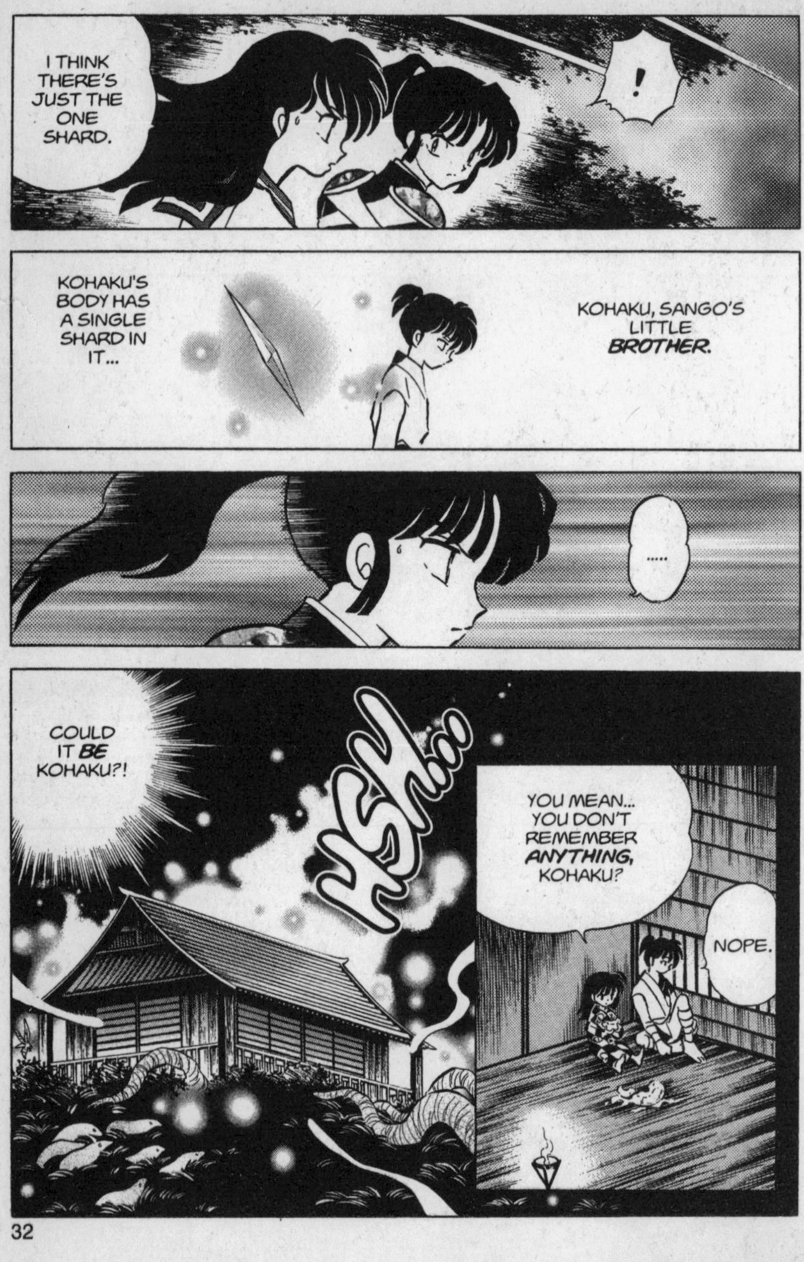
I THINK THERE'S JUST THE ONE SHARD.
!
KOHAKU'S BODY HAS A SINGLE SHARD IN IT...
KOHAKU, SANGO'S LITTLE **BROTHER**.
.....
COULD IT ***BE*** KOHAKU?!
HSH...
YOU MEAN... YOU DON'T REMEMBER ***ANYTHING***, KOHAKU?
NOPE.

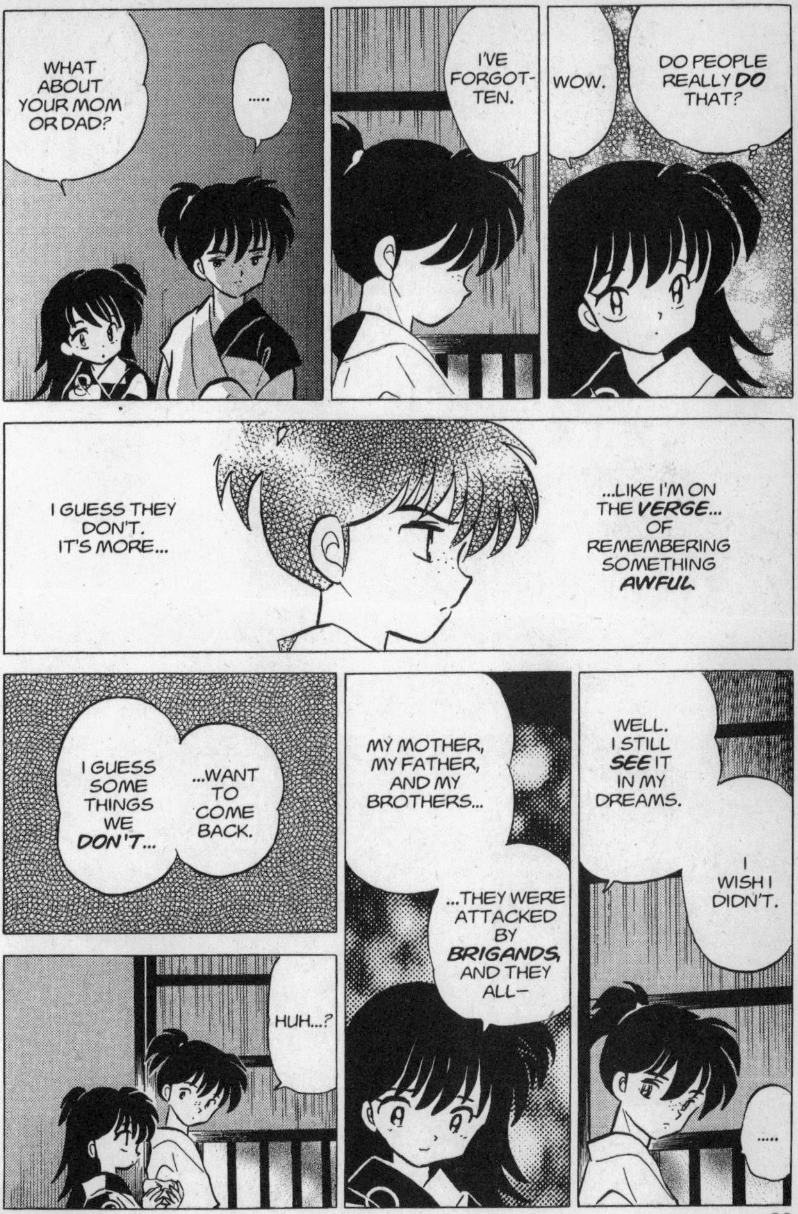
WHAT ABOUT YOUR MOM OR DAD?
.....
I'VE FORGOT-TEN.
WOW.
DO PEOPLE REALLY DO THAT?
I GUESS THEY DON'T. IT'S MORE...
...LIKE I'M ON THE VERGE... OF REMEMBERING SOMETHING AWFUL.
I GUESS SOME THINGS WE DON'T...
...WANT TO COME BACK.
HUH...?
MY MOTHER, MY FATHER, AND MY BROTHERS...
...THEY WERE ATTACKED BY BRIGANDS, AND THEY ALL—
WELL. I STILL SEE IT IN MY DREAMS.
I WISH I DIDN'T.
.....

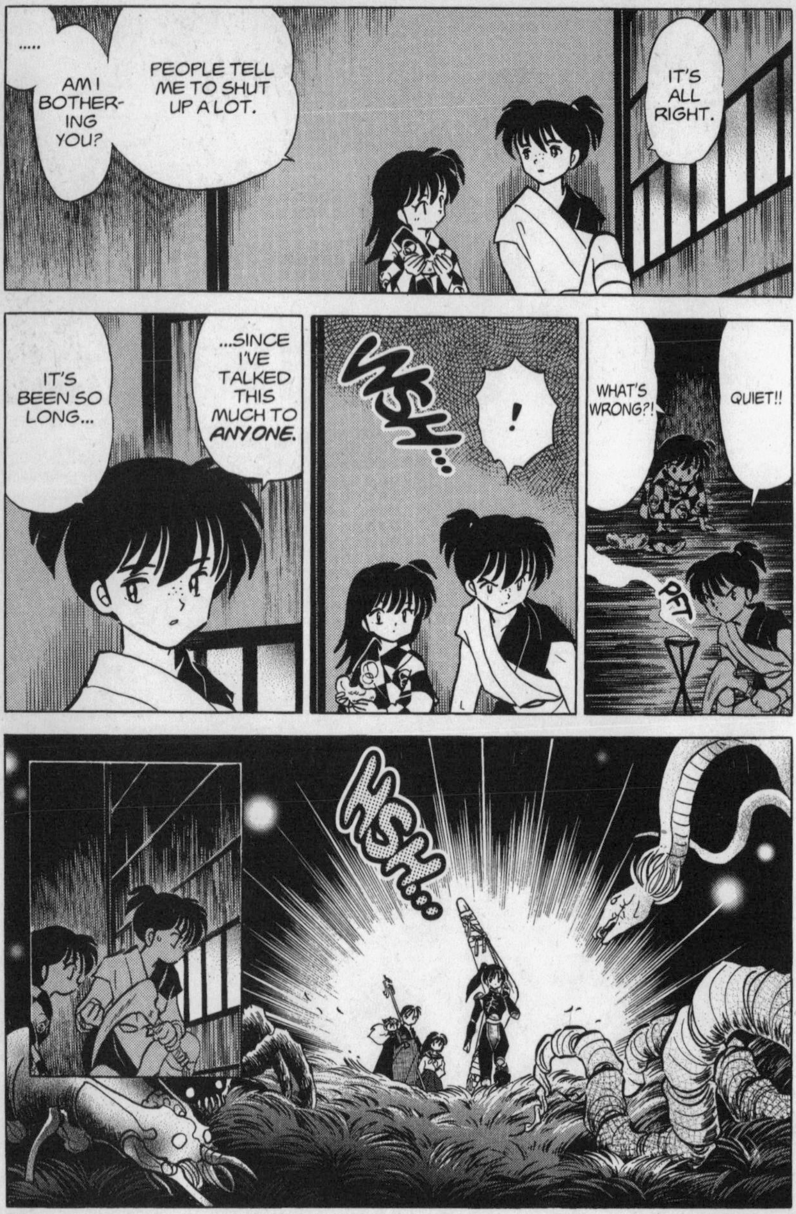
.....
AM I BOTHERING YOU?
PEOPLE TELL ME TO SHUT UP A LOT.
IT'S ALL RIGHT.
IT'S BEEN SO LONG...
...SINCE I'VE TALKED THIS MUCH TO ANYONE.
WSH...
!
WHAT'S WRONG?!
QUIET!!
PFT
HSH..

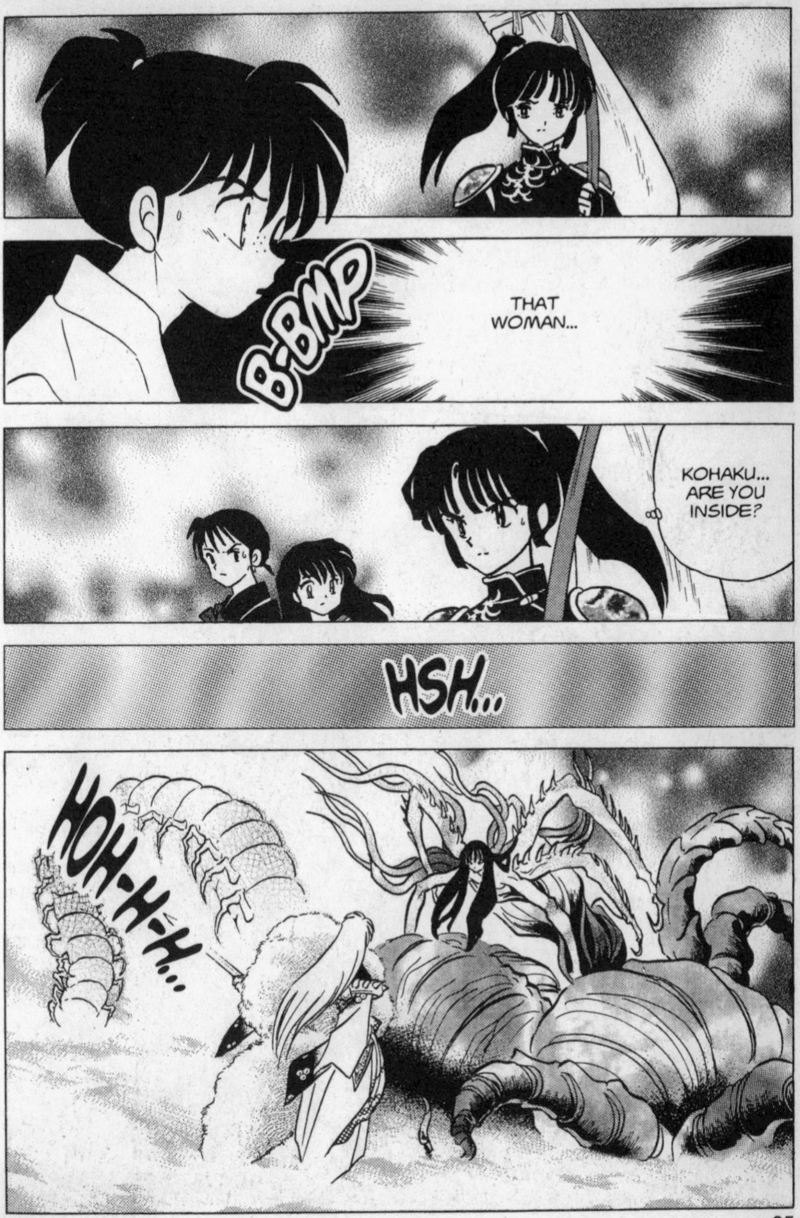
B-BMP
THAT WOMAN...
KOHAKU... ARE YOU INSIDE?
HSH...
HOH-H-H...

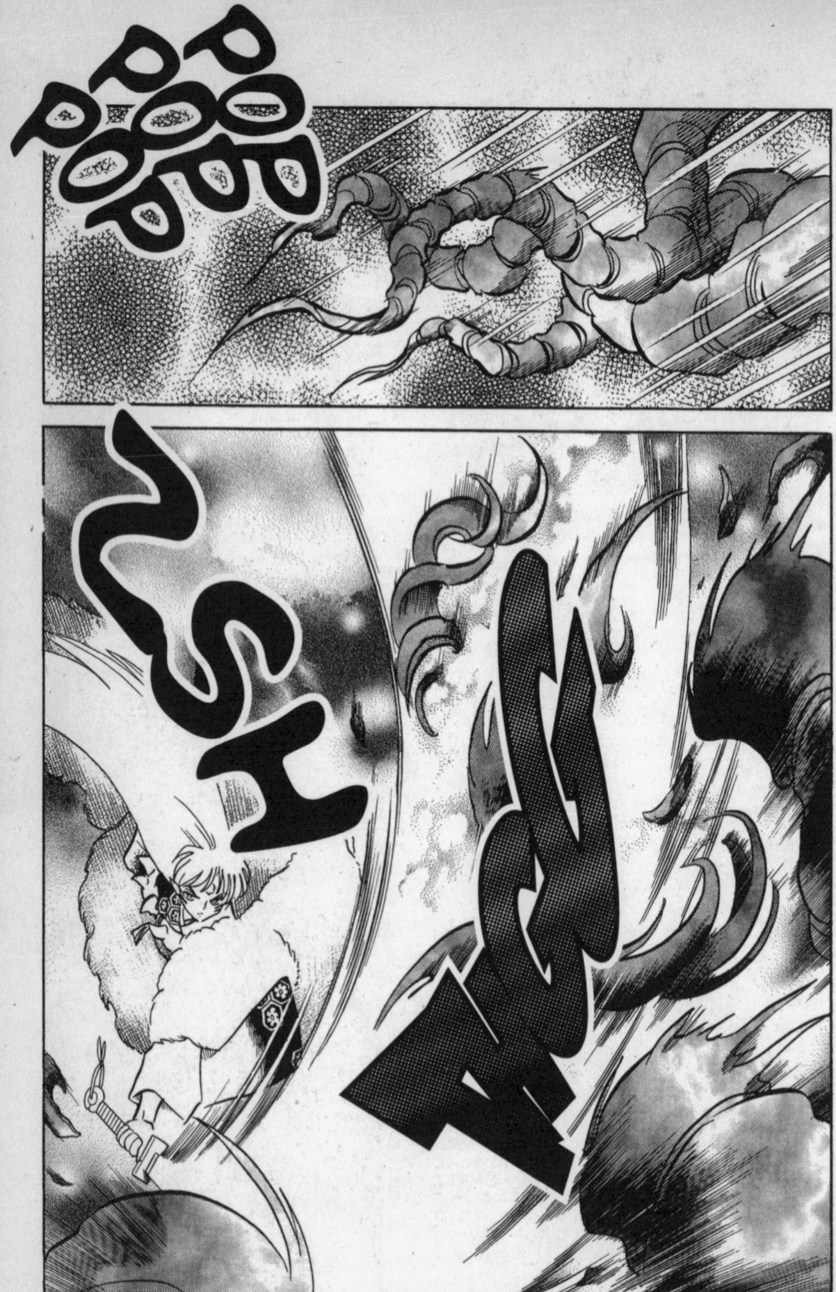
POP POP POP

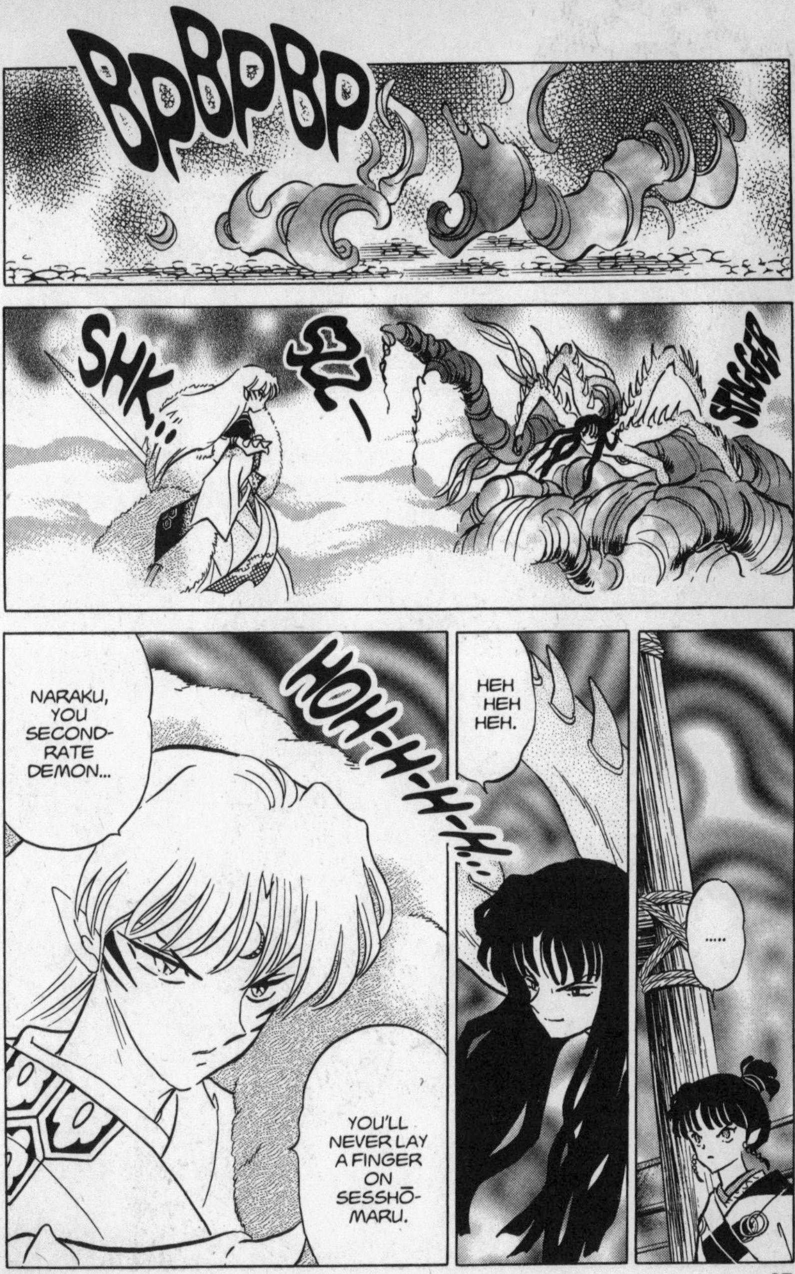
BDBPBP
SHK...
SQU-
STAGGER
NARAKU, YOU SECOND-RATE DEMON...
YOU'LL NEVER LAY A FINGER ON SESSHŌ-MARU.
HOH-H-H-H...
HEH HEH HEH.
.....

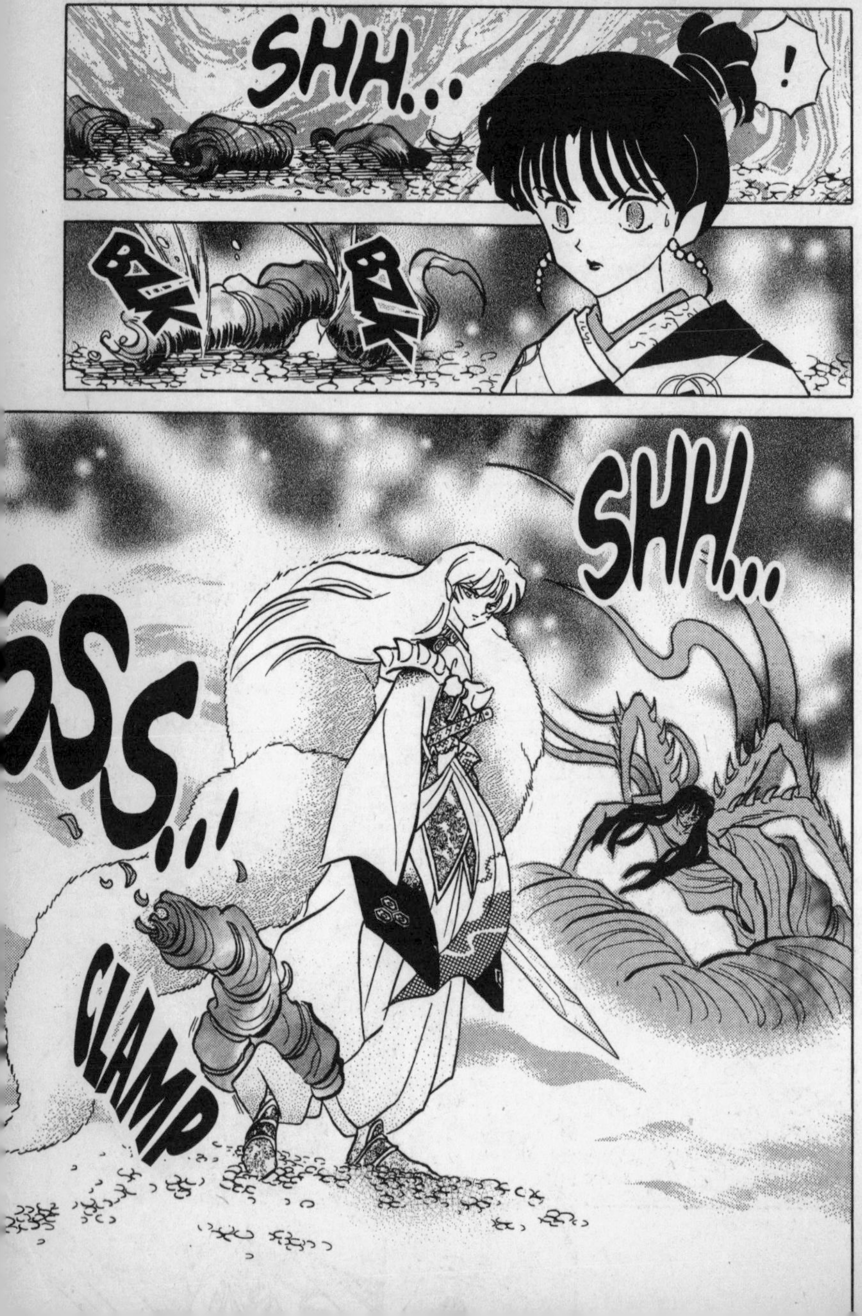
SHH...
!
BZK
BZK
SHH...
SSS...
CLAMP

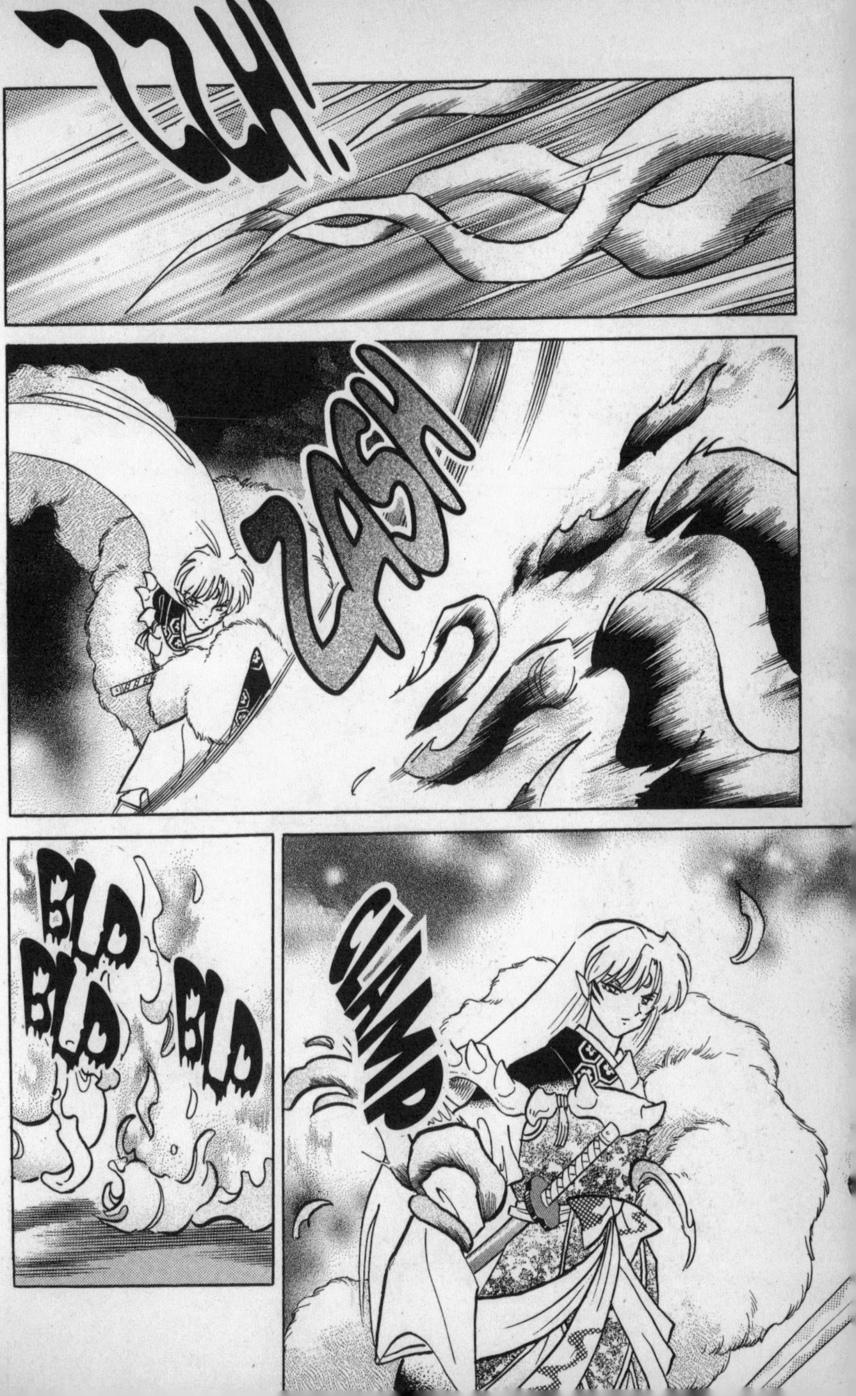
ZZZH!
ZASH
BLD BLD BLD BLD
CLAMP

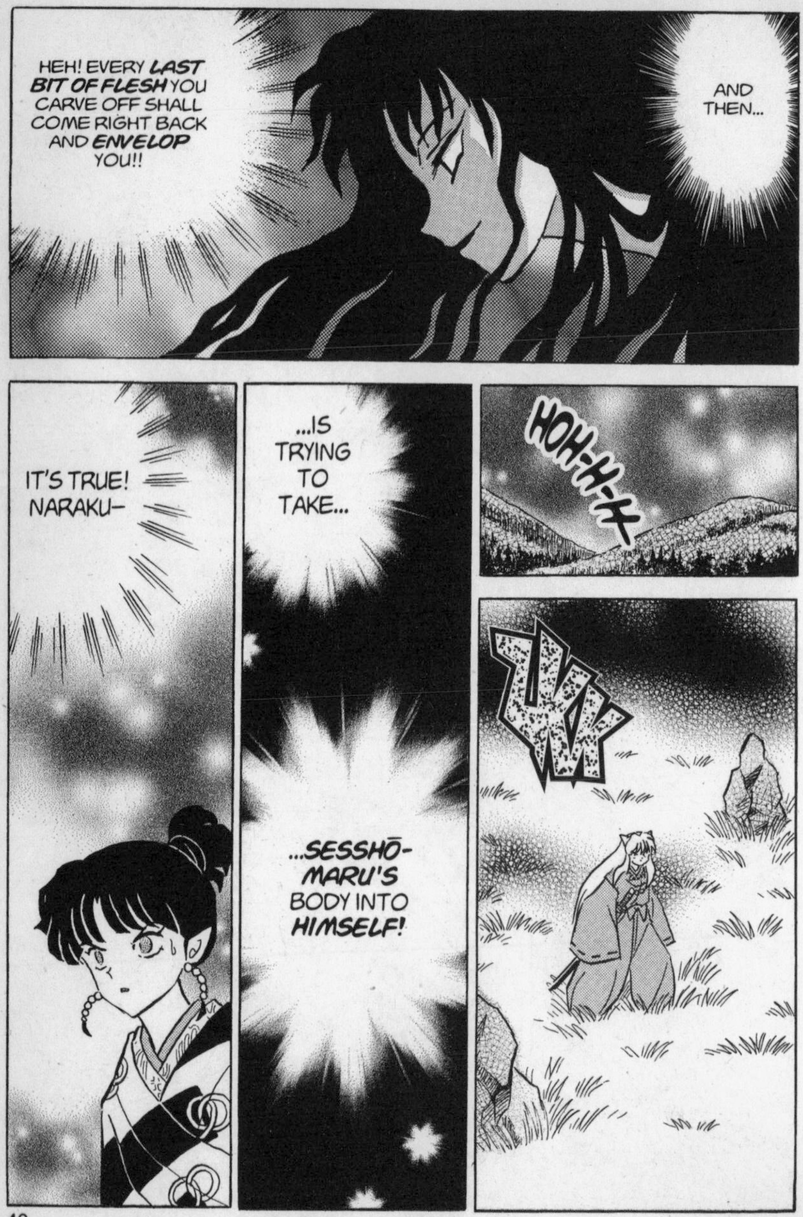

HEH! EVERY LAST BIT OF FLESH YOU CARVE OFF SHALL COME RIGHT BACK AND ENVELOP YOU!!
AND THEN...
IT'S TRUE! NARAKU-
...IS TRYING TO TAKE...
...SESSHŌ-MARU'S BODY INTO HIMSELF!
HOH-H-H

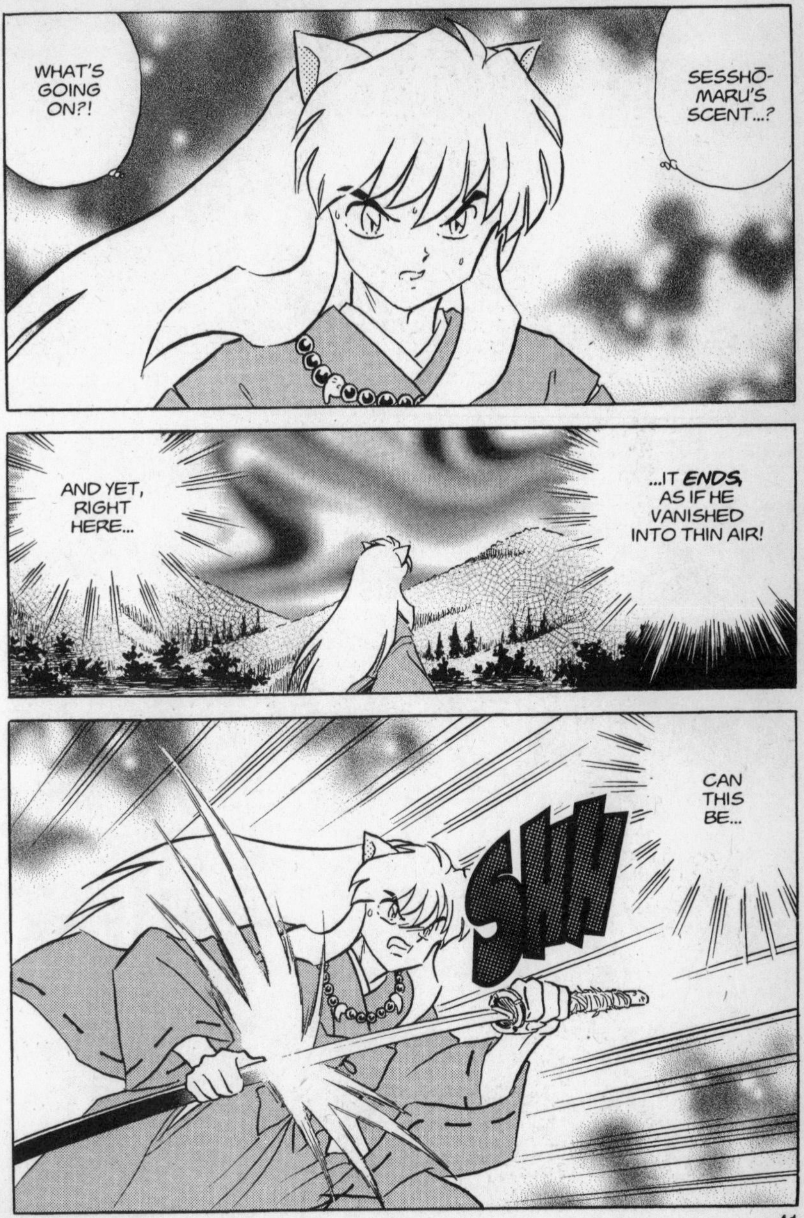
WHAT'S GOING ON?!
SESSHŌ-MARU'S SCENT...?
AND YET, RIGHT HERE...
...IT ***ENDS,*** AS IF HE VANISHED INTO THIN AIR!
CAN THIS BE...
SHH

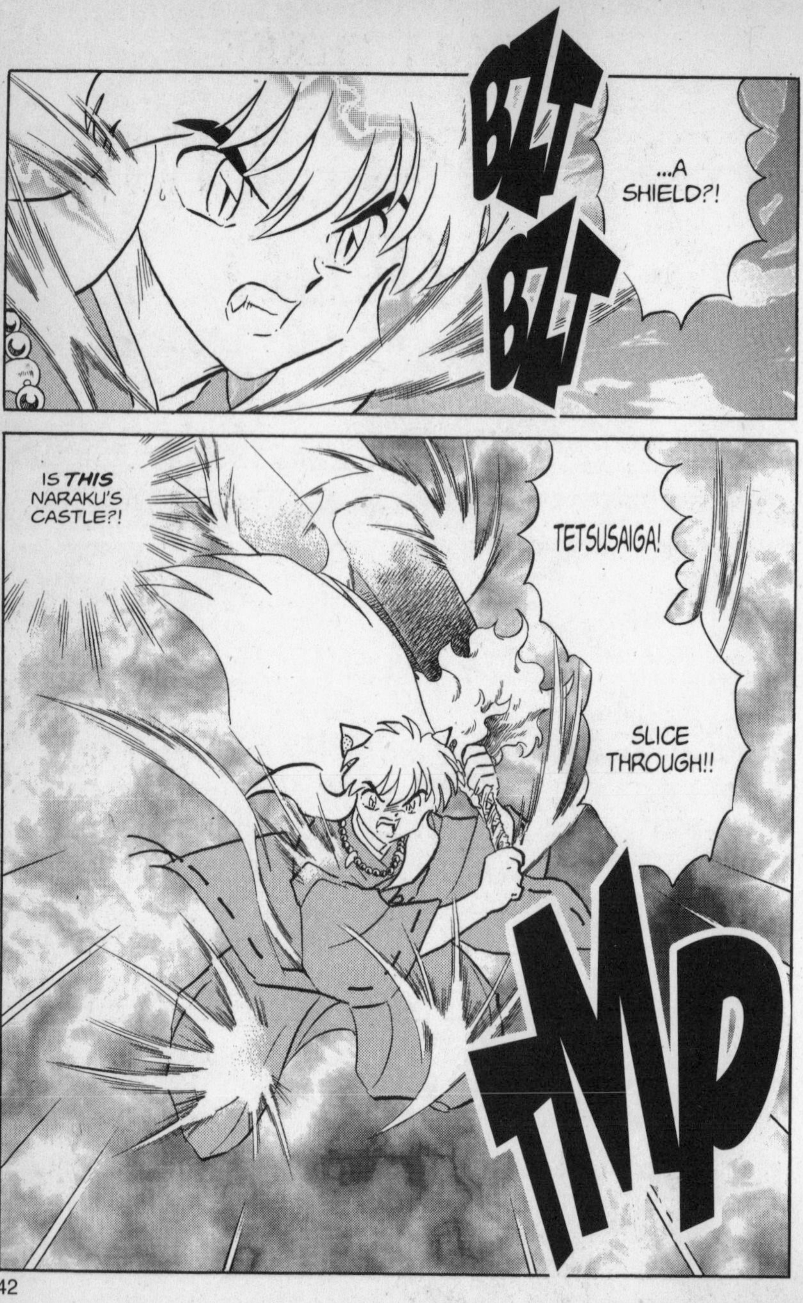
BZZT
BZZT
...A SHIELD?!
IS THIS NARAKU'S CASTLE?!
TETSUSAIGA!
SLICE THROUGH!!
TMP

SCROLL THREE

SLICING THE SHIELD

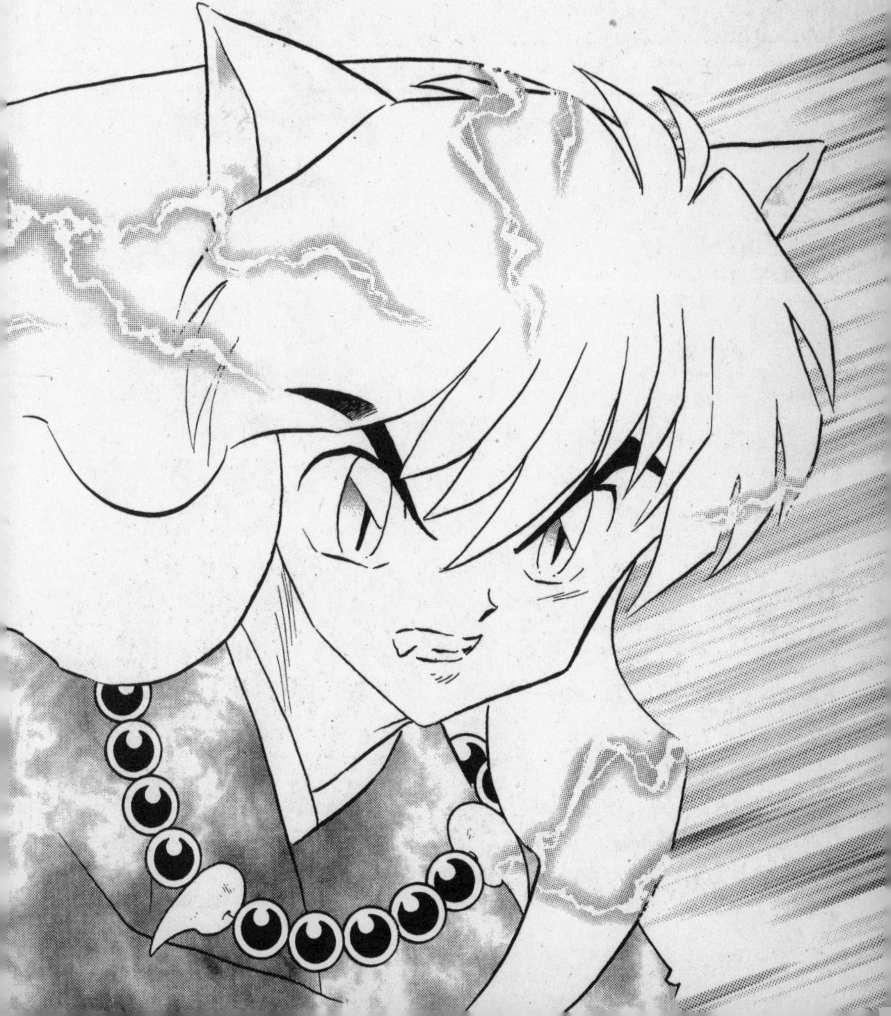

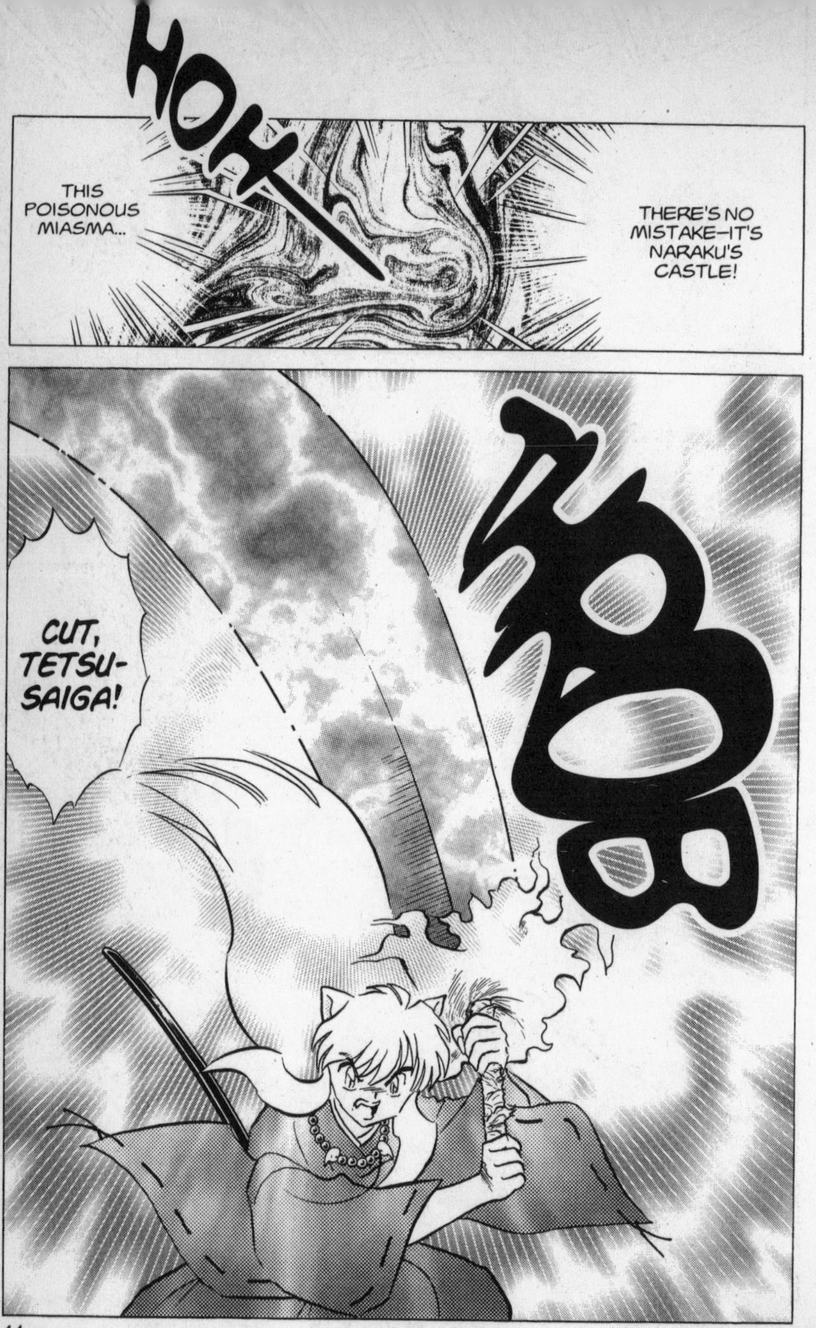
HOH
THIS POISONOUS MIASMA...
THERE'S NO MISTAKE—IT'S NARAKU'S CASTLE!
CUT, TETSU-SAIGA!
THROB

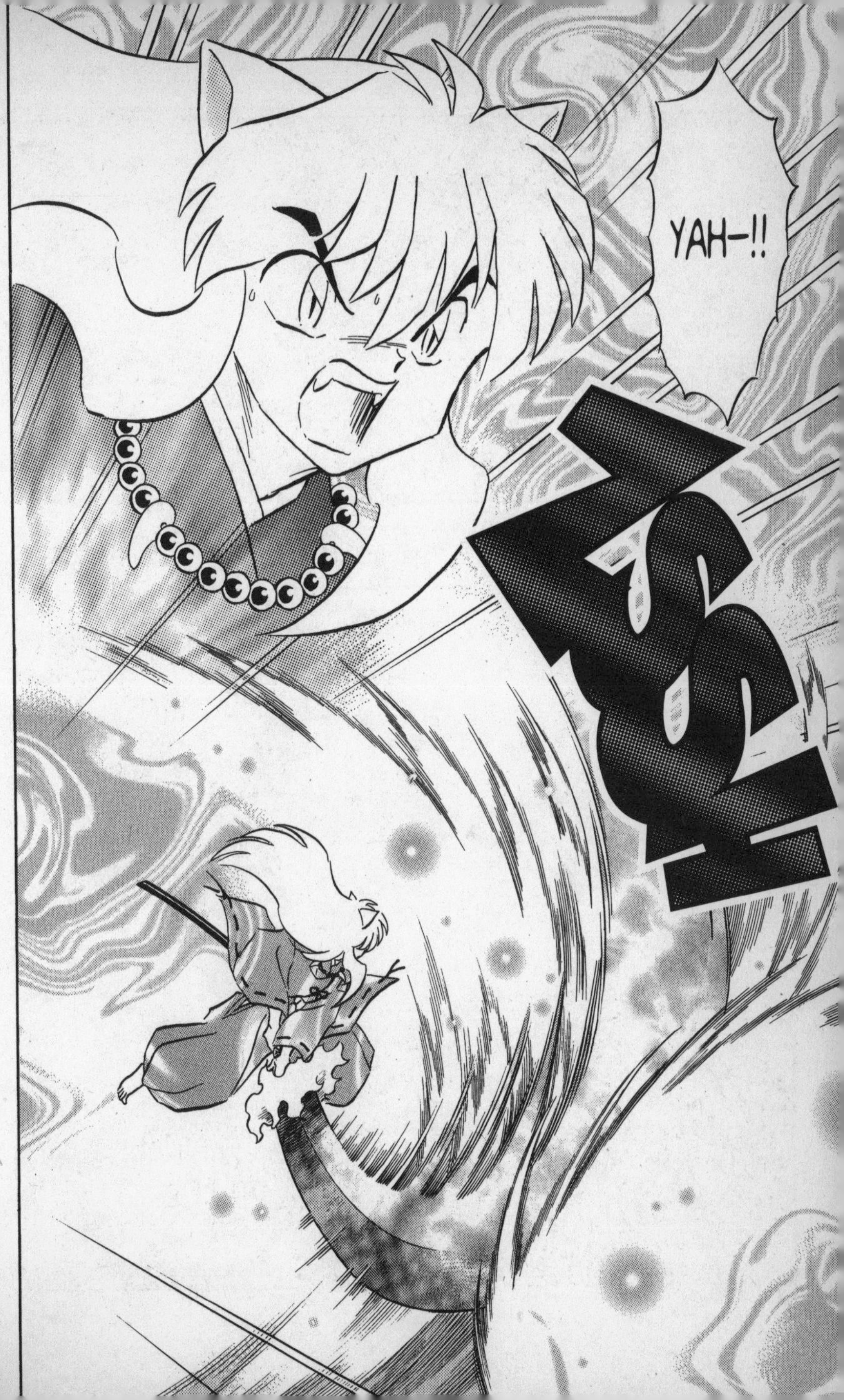
YAH-!!
ZSSH

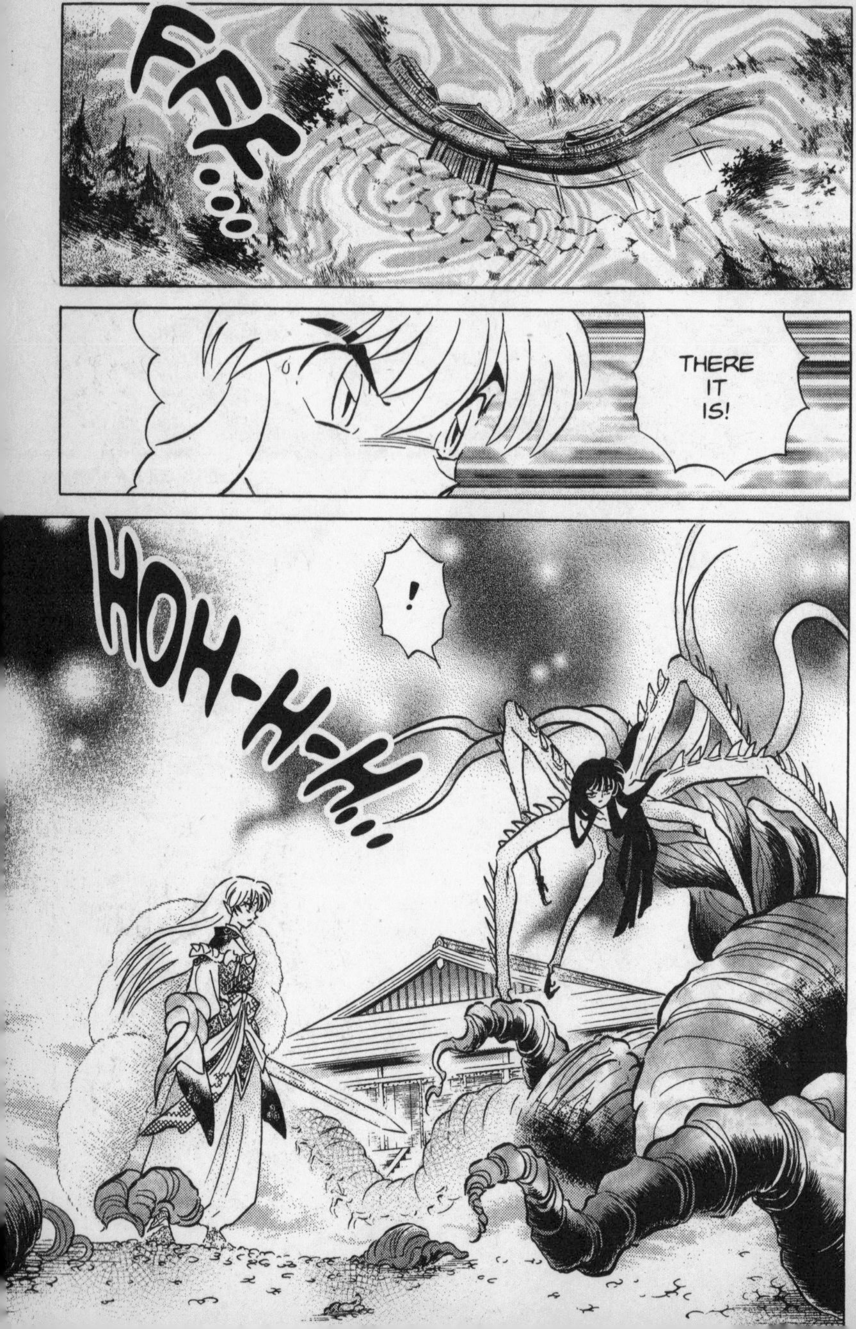
FFF...
THERE IT IS!
HOH-H-H-H...
!

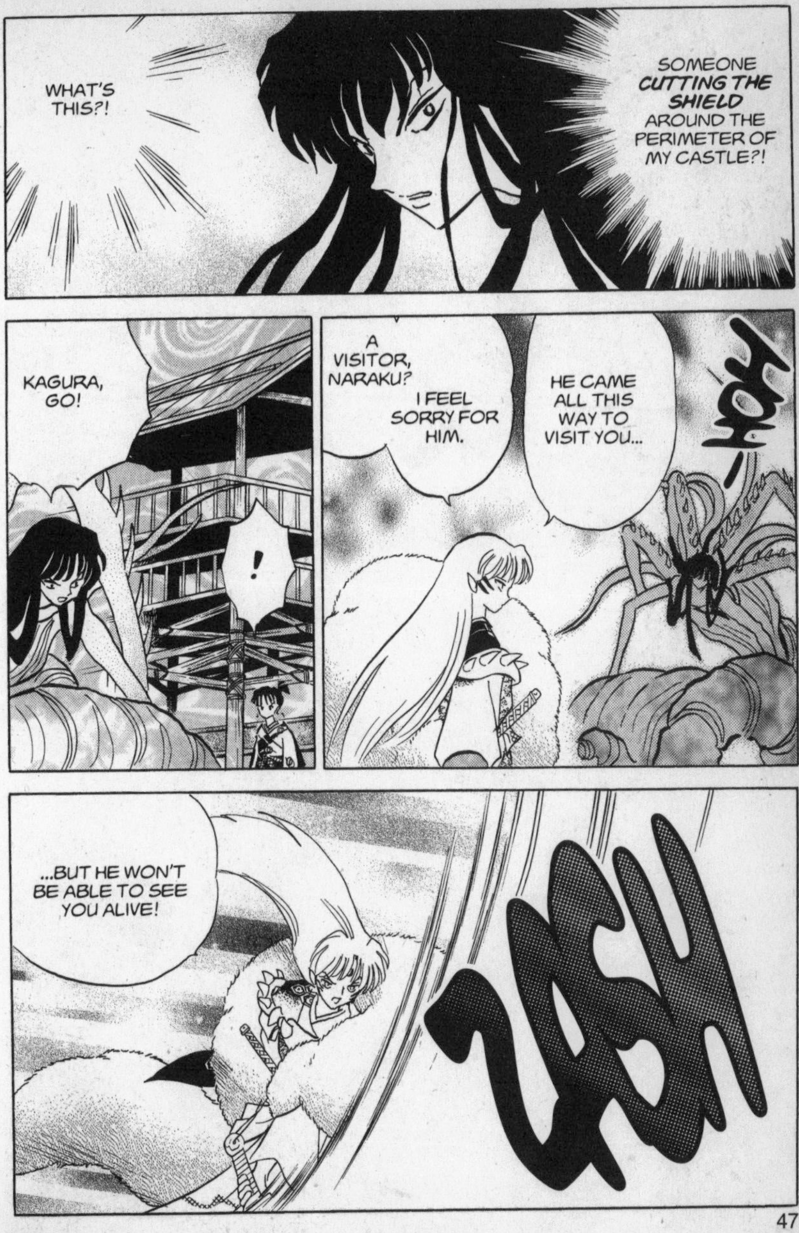
WHAT'S THIS?!
SOMEONE CUTTING THE SHIELD AROUND THE PERIMETER OF MY CASTLE?!
KAGURA, GO!
!
A VISITOR, NARAKU?
I FEEL SORRY FOR HIM.
HE CAME ALL THIS WAY TO VISIT YOU...
HOH
...BUT HE WON'T BE ABLE TO SEE YOU ALIVE!
ZASH

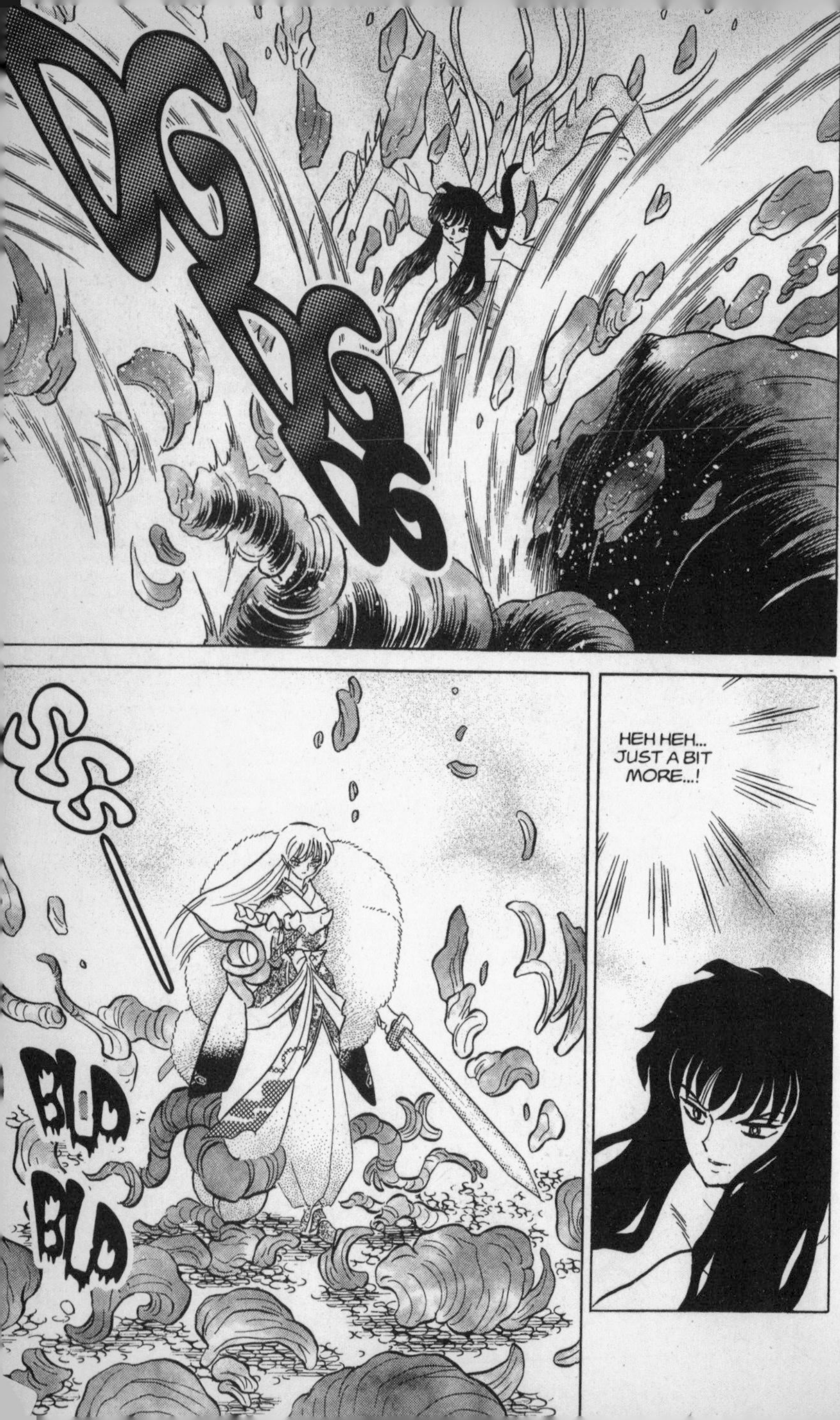
SSS
BLD BLD
HEH HEH... JUST A BIT MORE...!

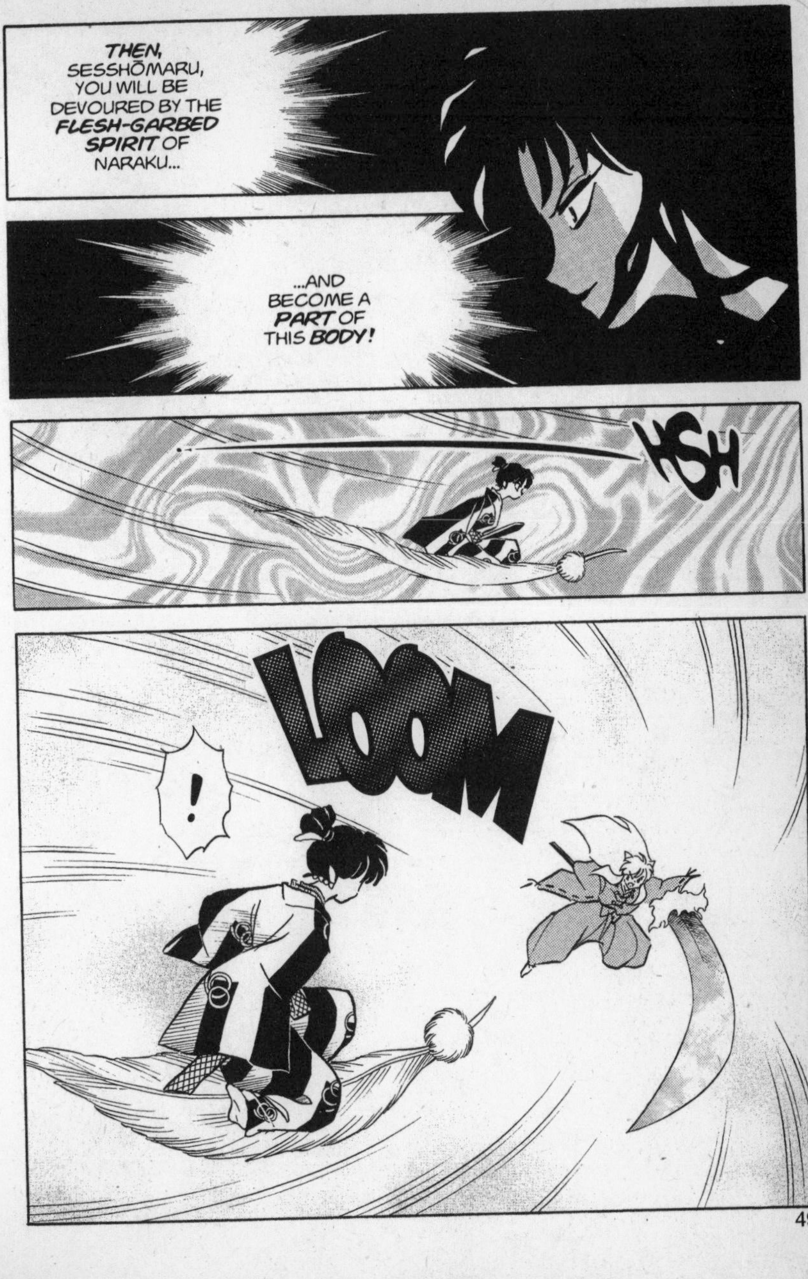
THEN, SESSHŌMARU, YOU WILL BE DEVOURED BY THE FLESH-GARBED SPIRIT OF NARAKU...
...AND BECOME A PART OF THIS BODY!
HSH
LOOM
!

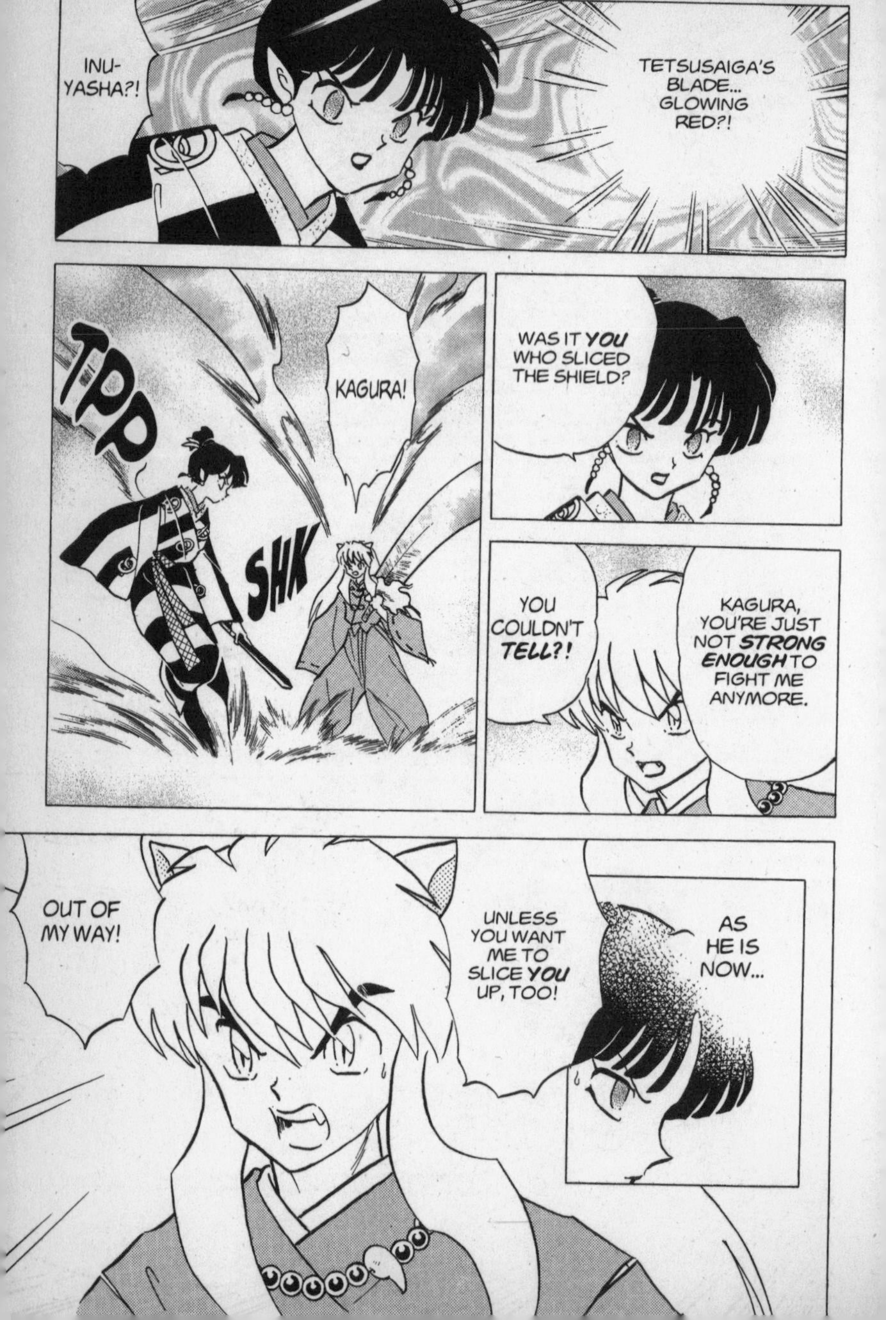
TETSUSAIGA'S BLADE... GLOWING RED?!
INU-YASHA?!
WAS IT *YOU* WHO SLICED THE SHIELD?
KAGURA, YOU'RE JUST NOT *STRONG ENOUGH* TO FIGHT ME ANYMORE.
YOU COULDN'T *TELL?!*
KAGURA!
TPP
SHK
AS HE IS NOW...
UNLESS YOU WANT ME TO SLICE *YOU* UP, TOO!
OUT OF MY WAY!

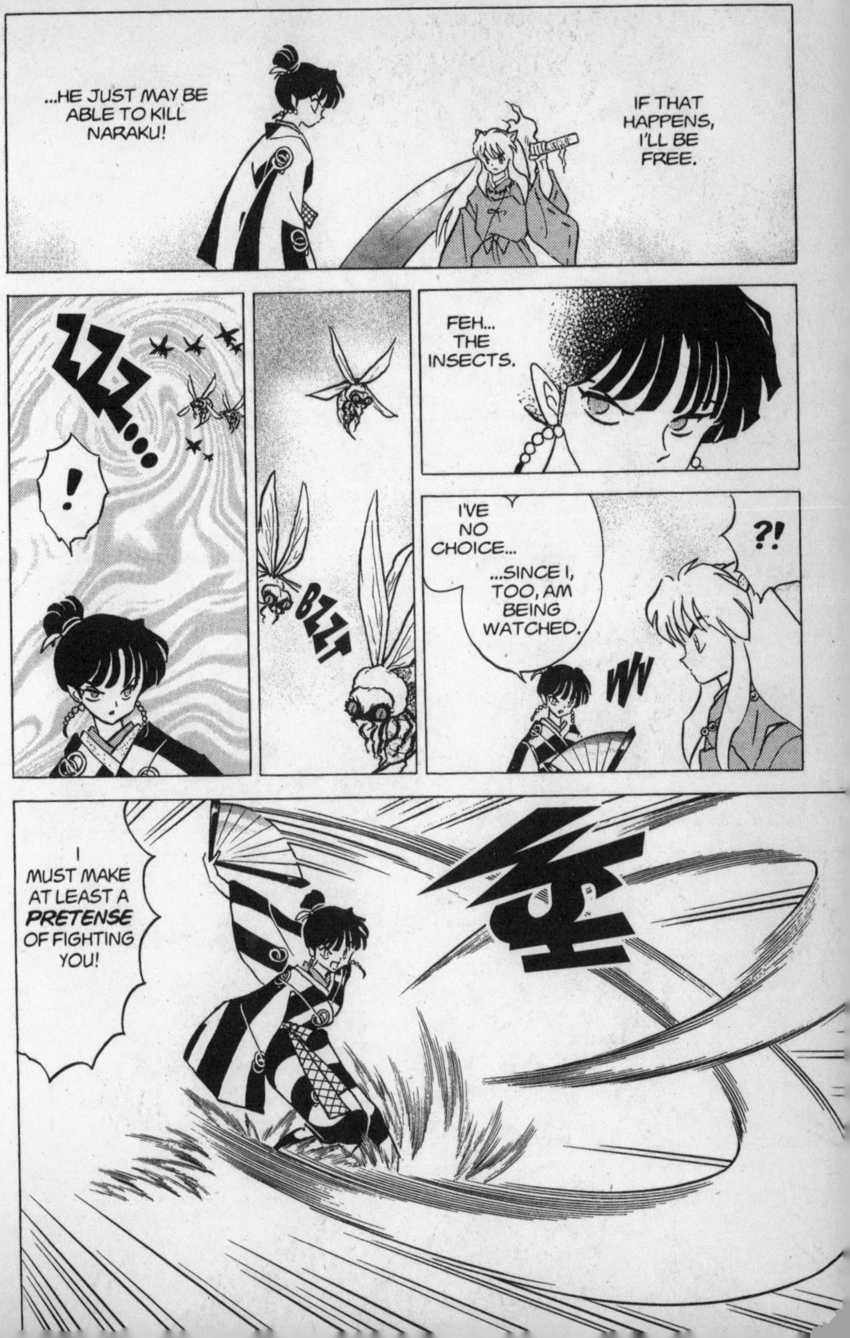
...HE JUST MAY BE ABLE TO KILL NARAKU!
IF THAT HAPPENS, I'LL BE FREE.
ZZZ...
!
BZZT
FEH... THE INSECTS.
I'VE NO CHOICE...
...SINCE I, TOO, AM BEING WATCHED.
?!
I MUST MAKE AT LEAST A **PRETENSE** OF FIGHTING YOU!

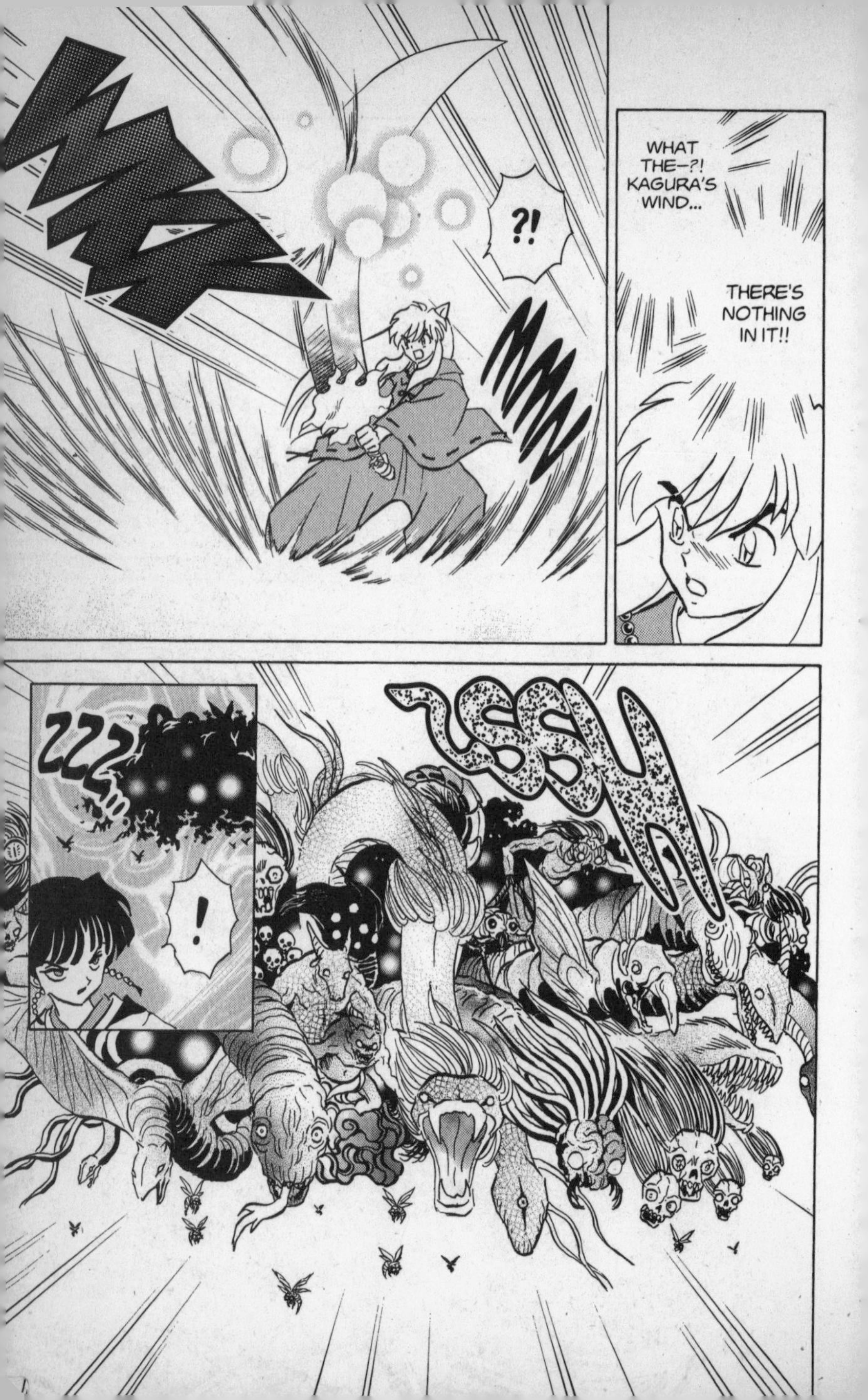
?!
WHAT THE–?! KAGURA'S WIND...
THERE'S NOTHING IN IT!!
ZZZ
!

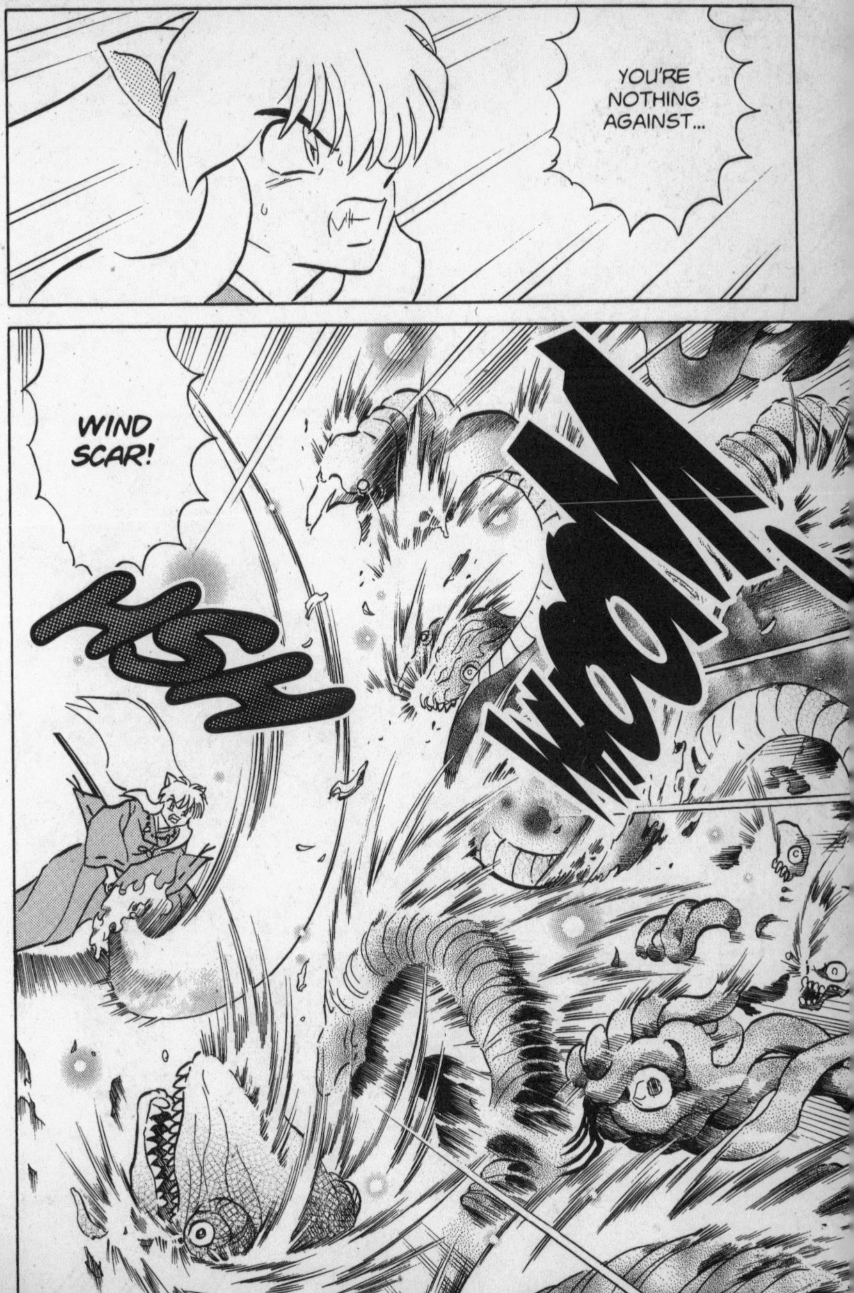
YOU'RE NOTHING AGAINST...
WIND SCAR!
WHOOM

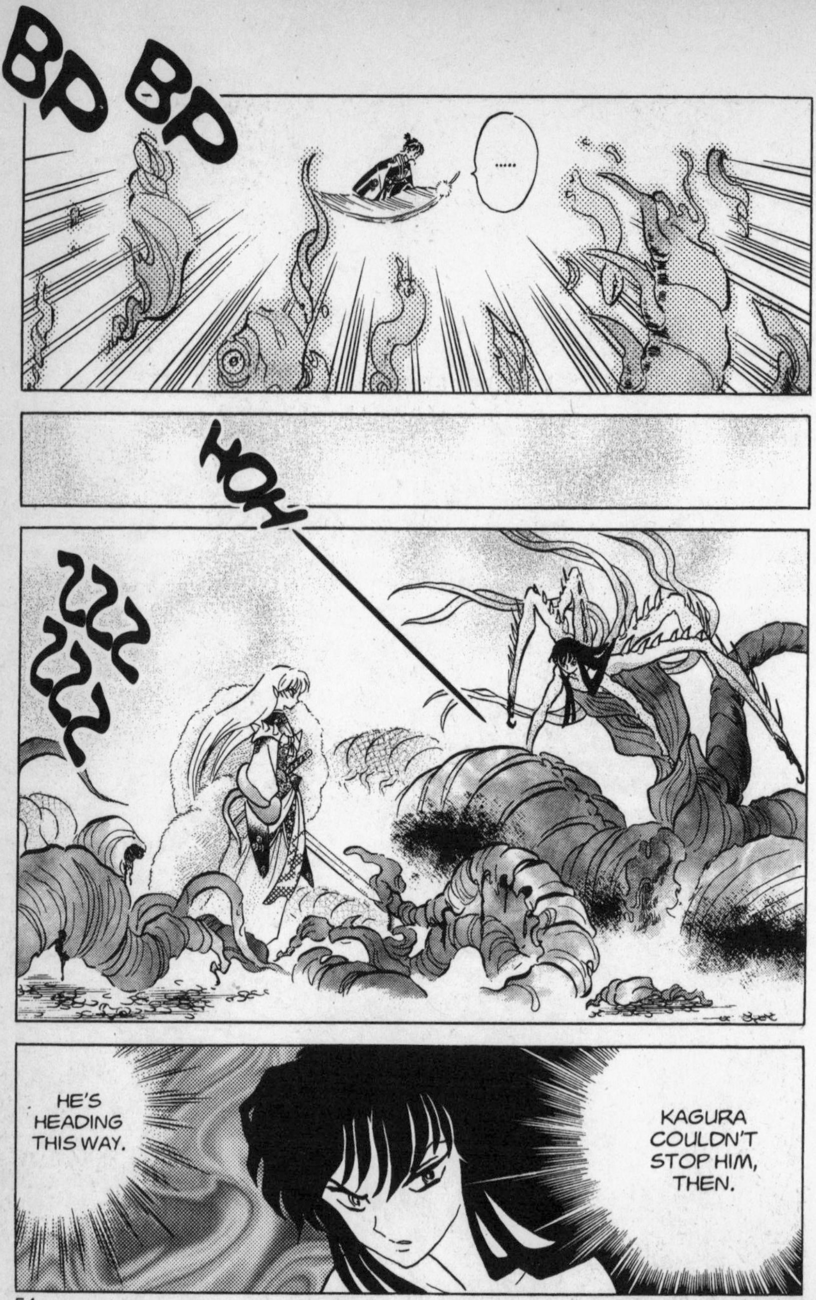
BP BP
......
HOH
ZZZ ZZZ
HE'S HEADING THIS WAY.
KAGURA COULDN'T STOP HIM, THEN.

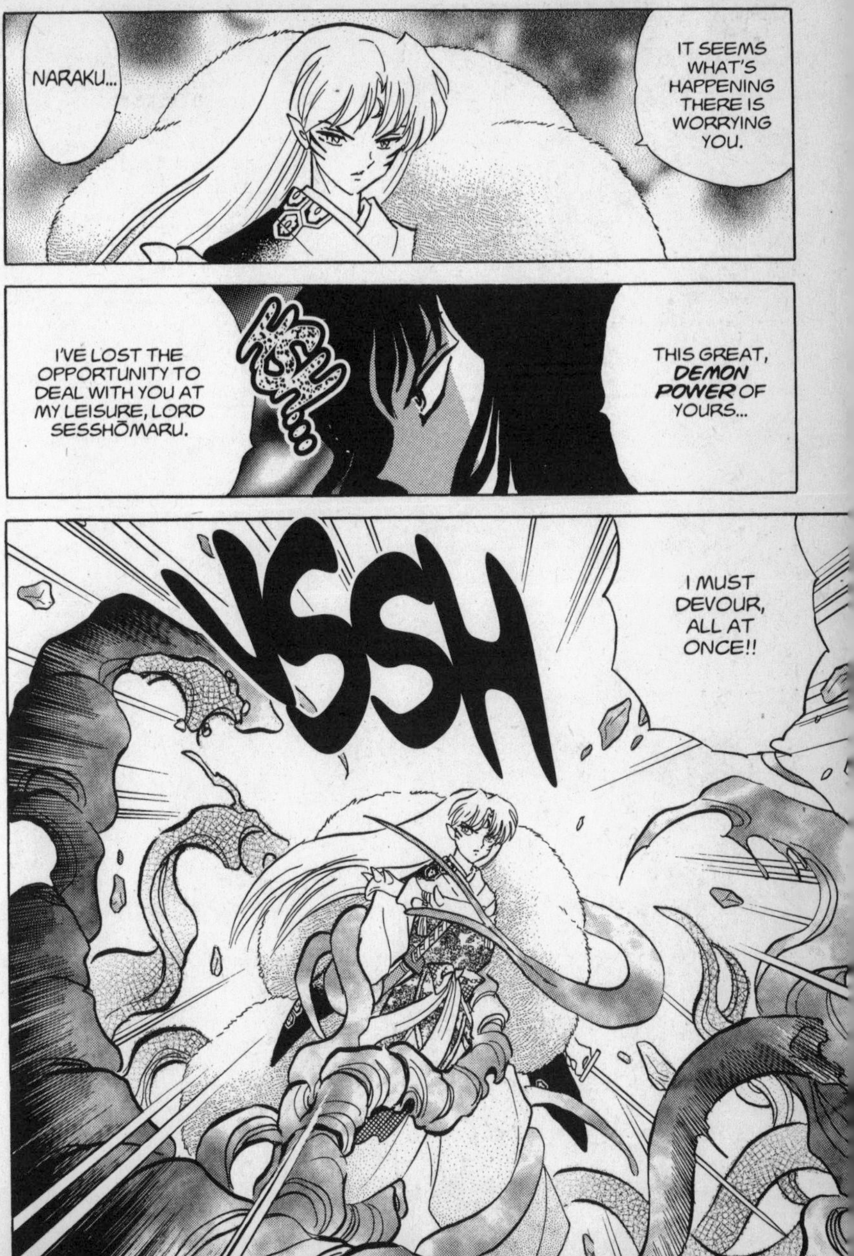
NARAKU...
IT SEEMS WHAT'S HAPPENING THERE IS WORRYING YOU.
I'VE LOST THE OPPORTUNITY TO DEAL WITH YOU AT MY LEISURE, LORD SESSHŌMARU.
THIS GREAT, DEMON POWER OF YOURS...
VSSH
I MUST DEVOUR, ALL AT ONCE!!

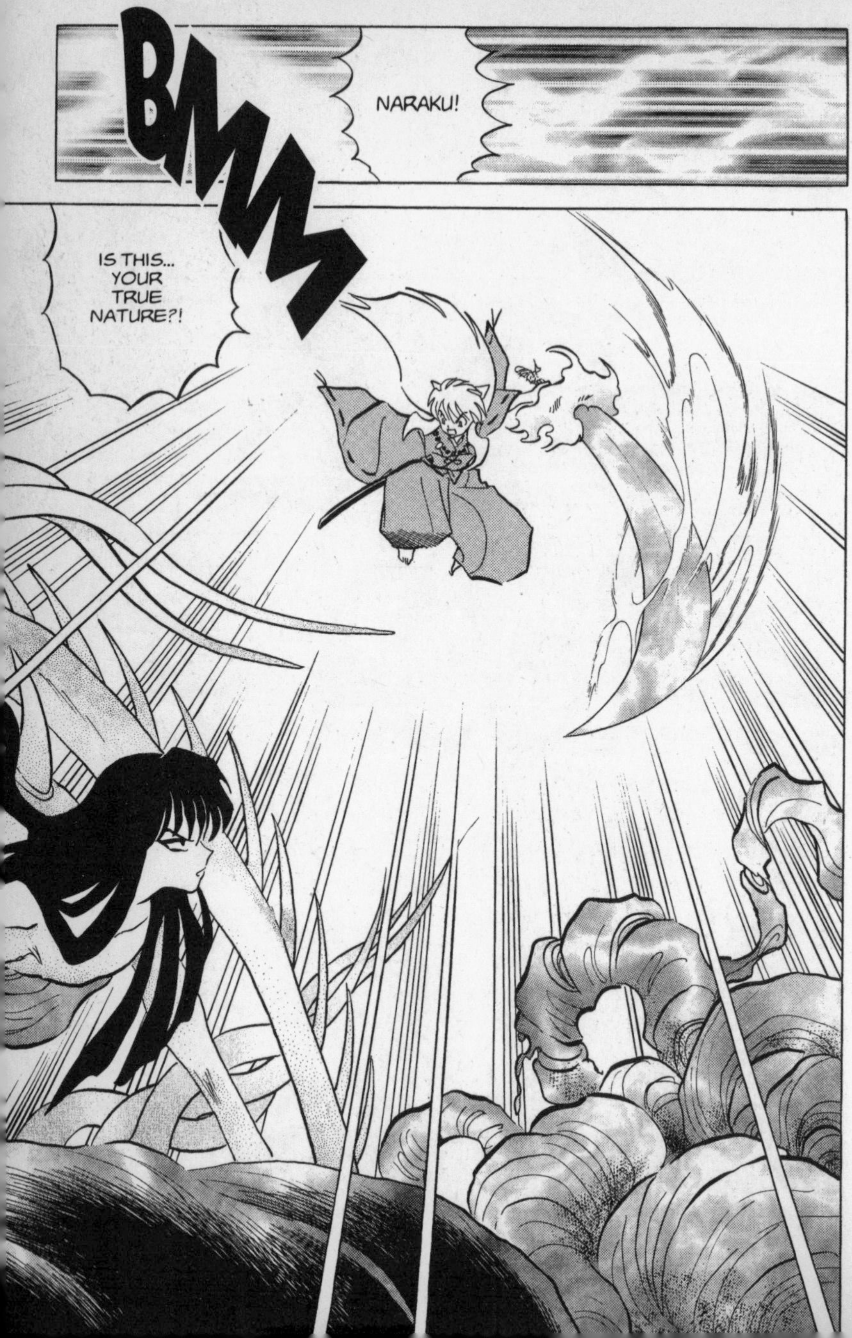
BMM
NARAKU!
IS THIS... YOUR TRUE NATURE?!

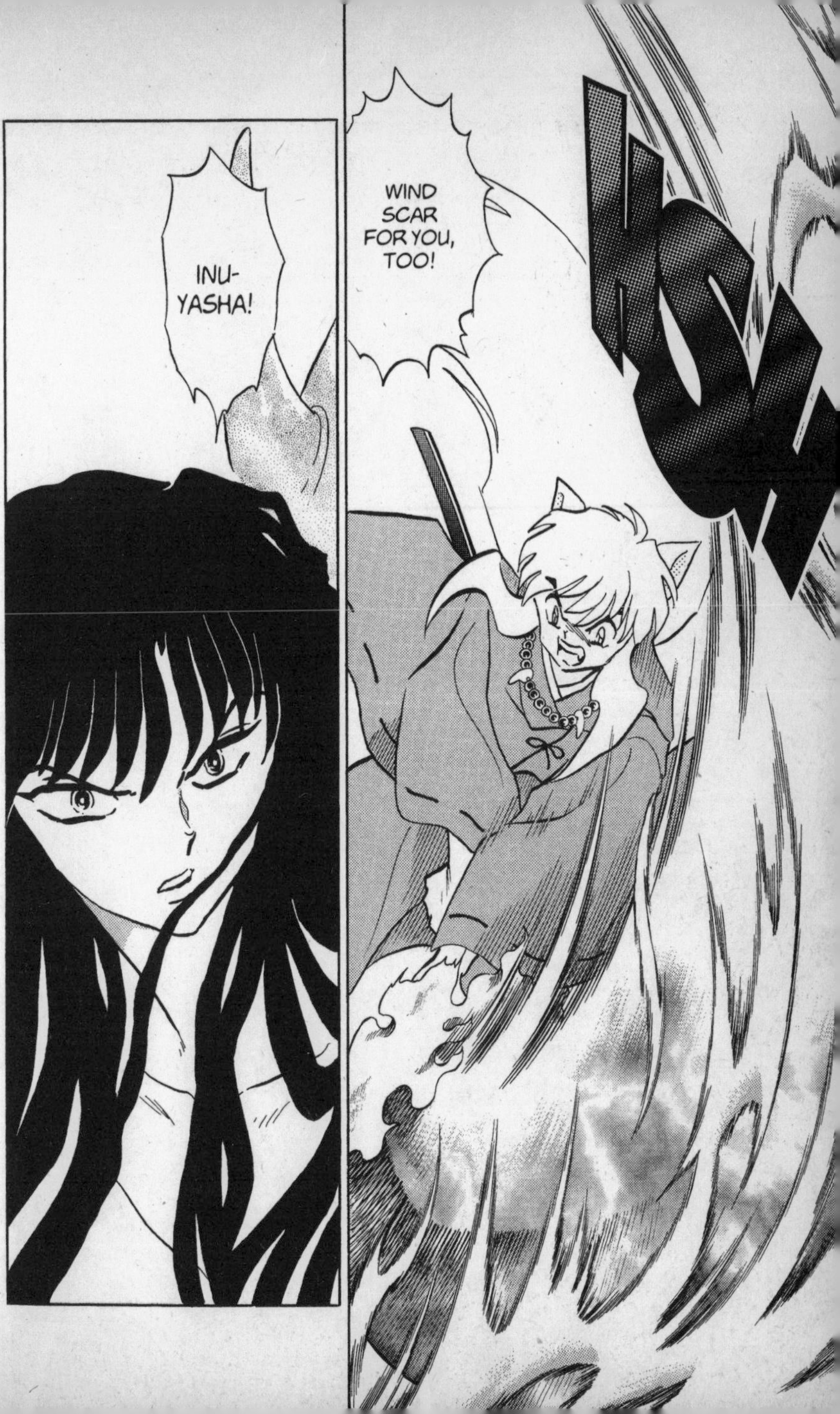
INU-YASHA!
WIND SCAR FOR YOU, TOO!
HSH!!

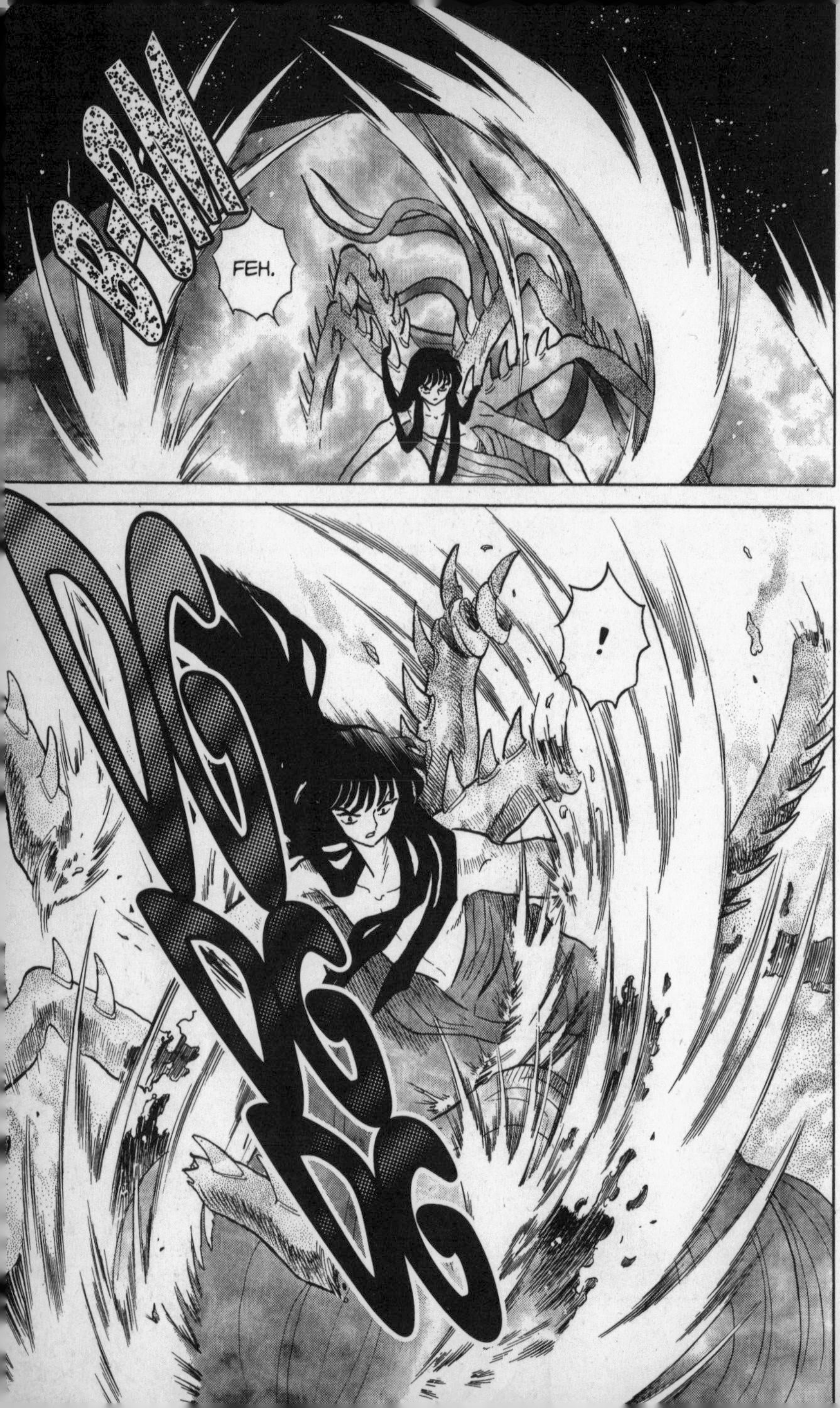
FEH.
!

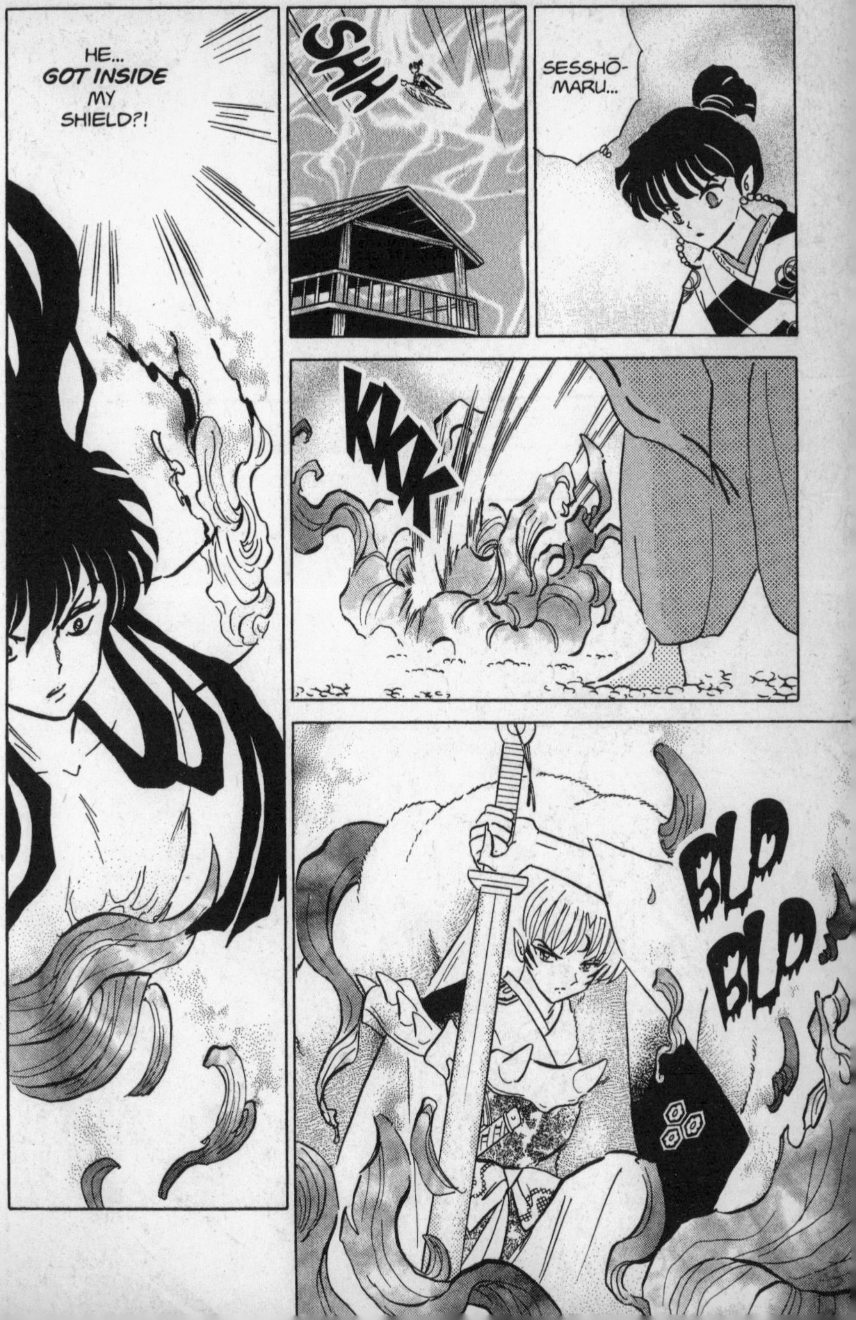
HE...
GOT INSIDE
MY
SHIELD?!
SHH
SESSHŌ-
MARU...
KKK
BLD
BLD

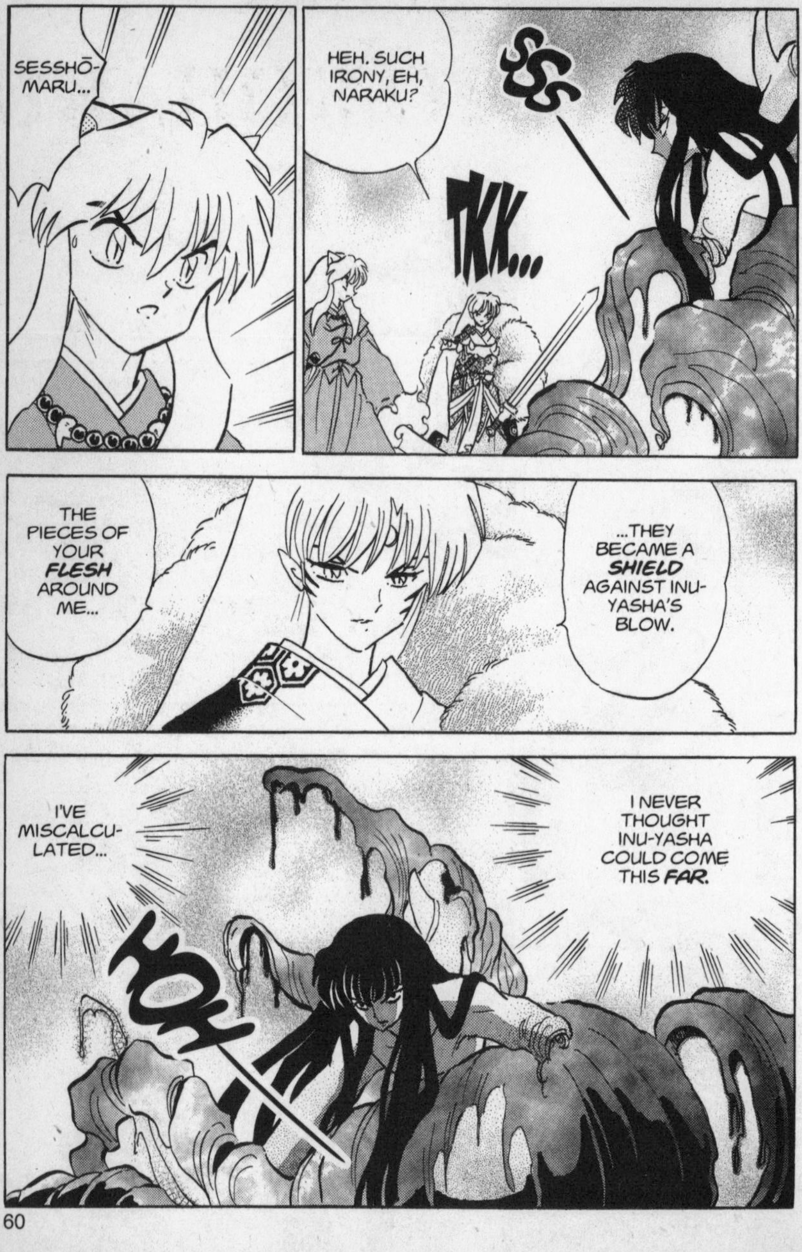

SESSHŌ-MARU...
HEH. SUCH IRONY, EH, NARAKU?
SSS
TKK...
THE PIECES OF YOUR **FLESH** AROUND ME...
...THEY BECAME A **SHIELD** AGAINST INU-YASHA'S BLOW.
I'VE MISCALCU-LATED...
I NEVER THOUGHT INU-YASHA COULD COME THIS **FAR**.

SCROLL FOUR

SIGNAL TO KOHAKU

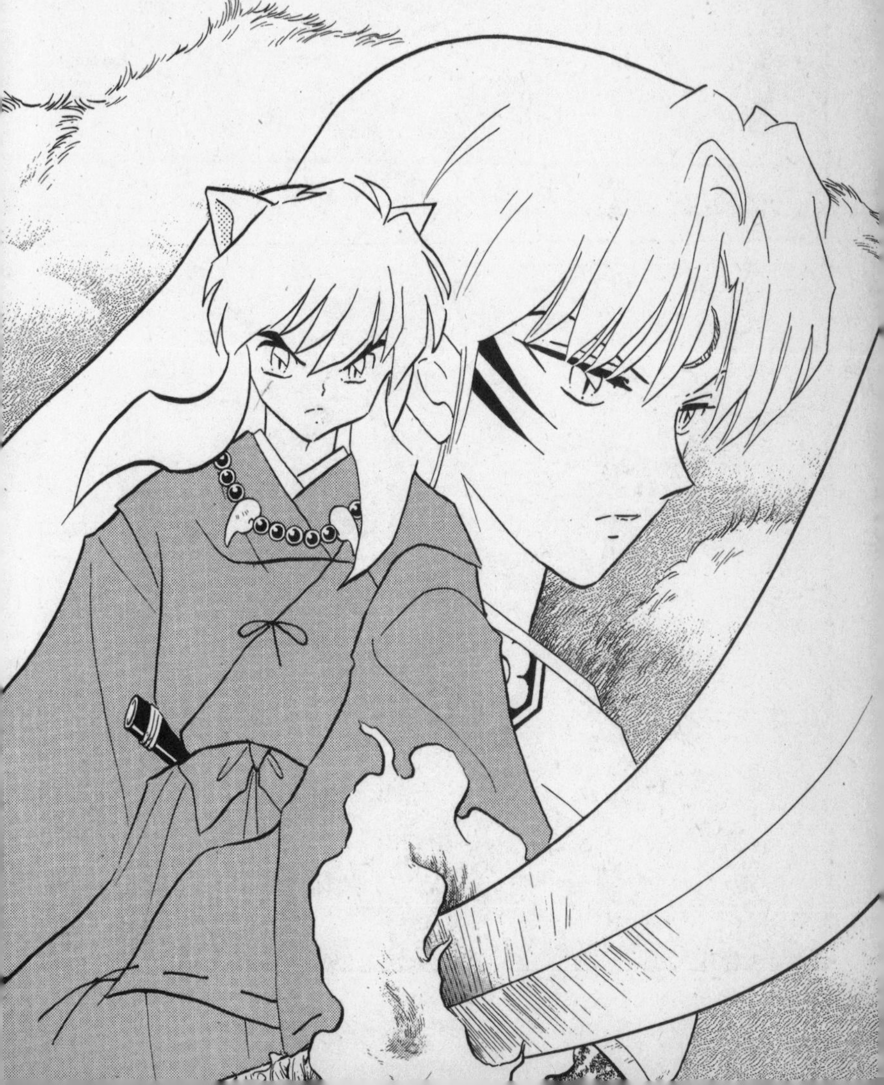

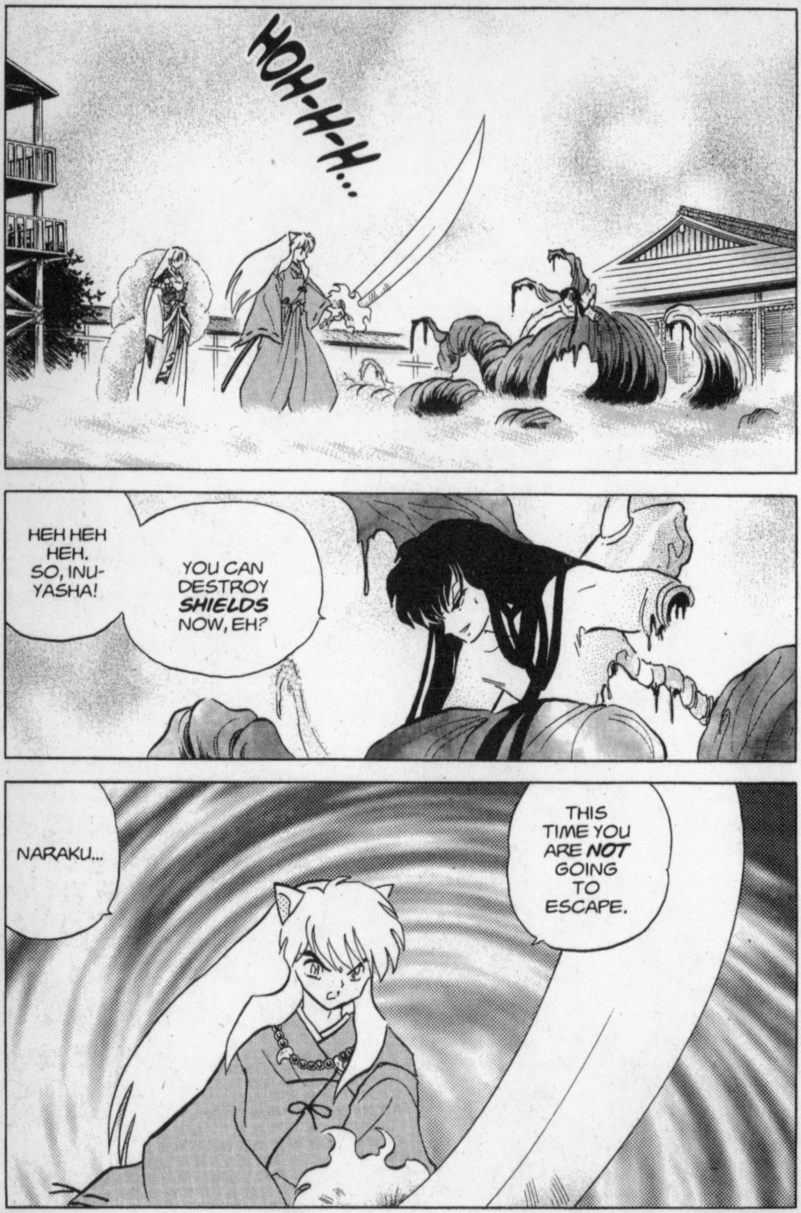
HOH-H-H...
HEH HEH HEH. SO, INU-YASHA!
YOU CAN DESTROY **SHIELDS** NOW, EH?
NARAKU...
THIS TIME YOU ARE **NOT** GOING TO ESCAPE.

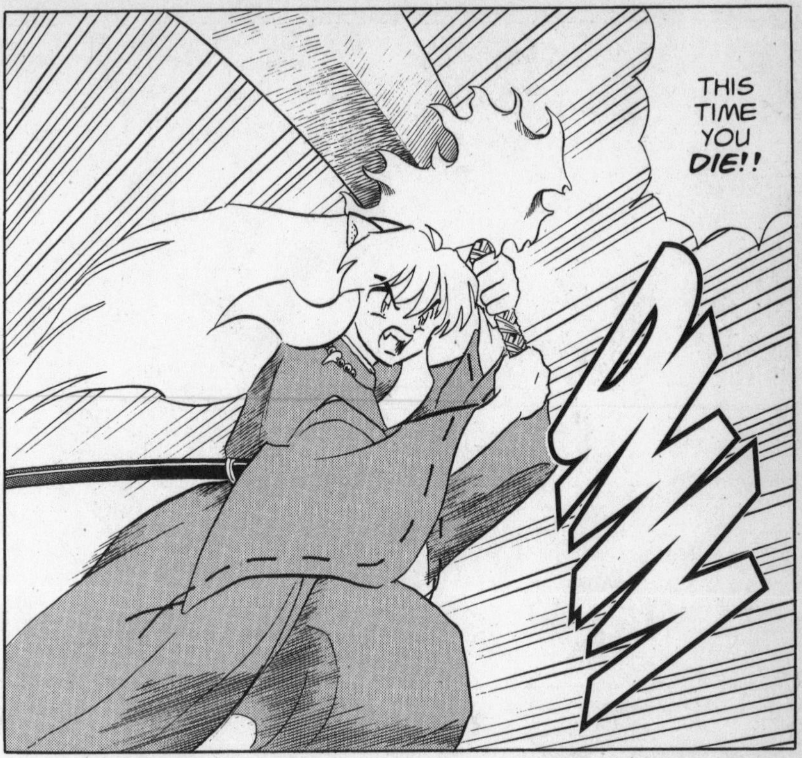
THIS TIME YOU DIE!!
SWING
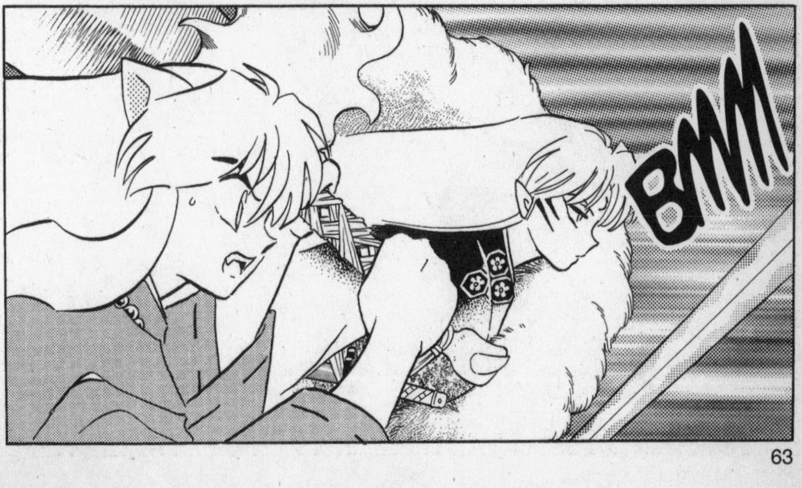
BAMM

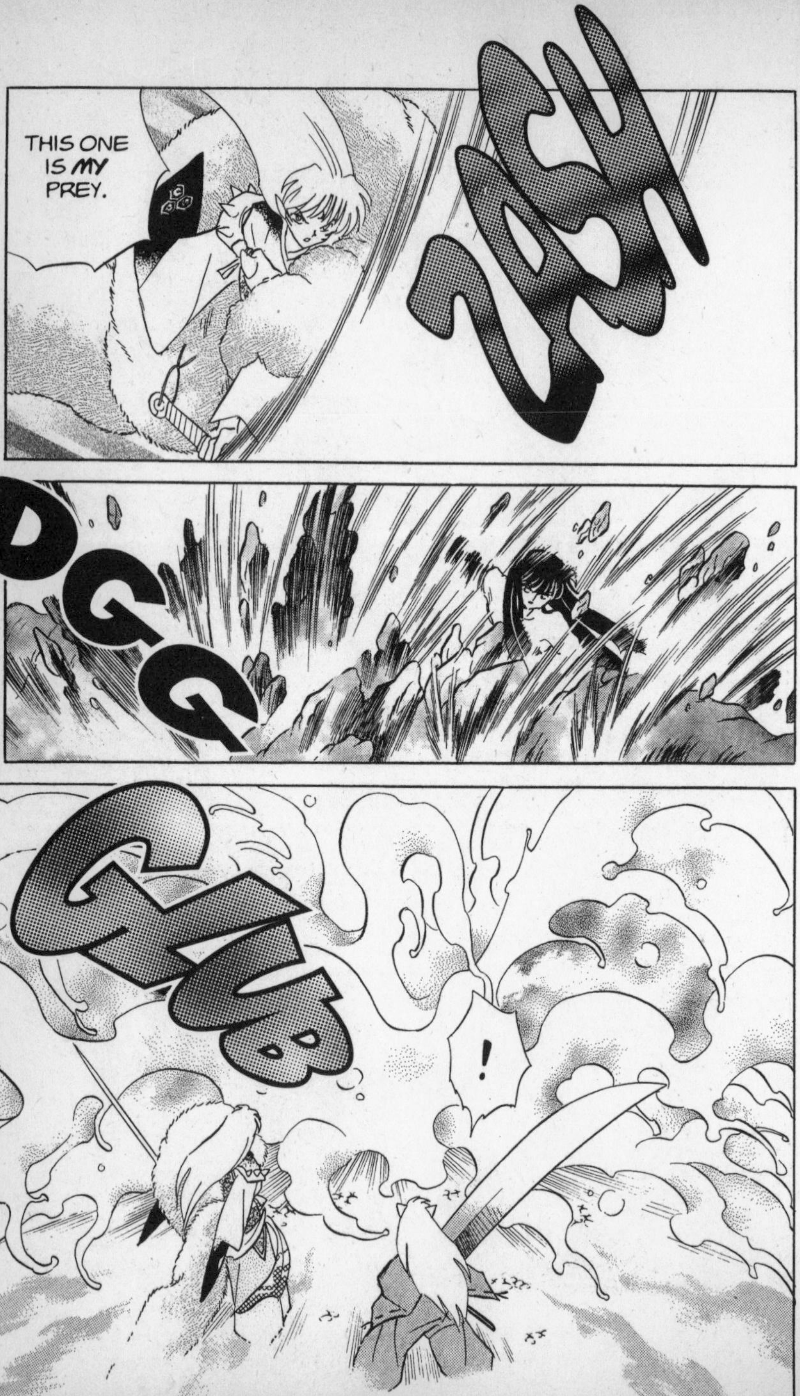
THIS ONE IS *MY* PREY.
ZASH
DGGG
GHUB
!

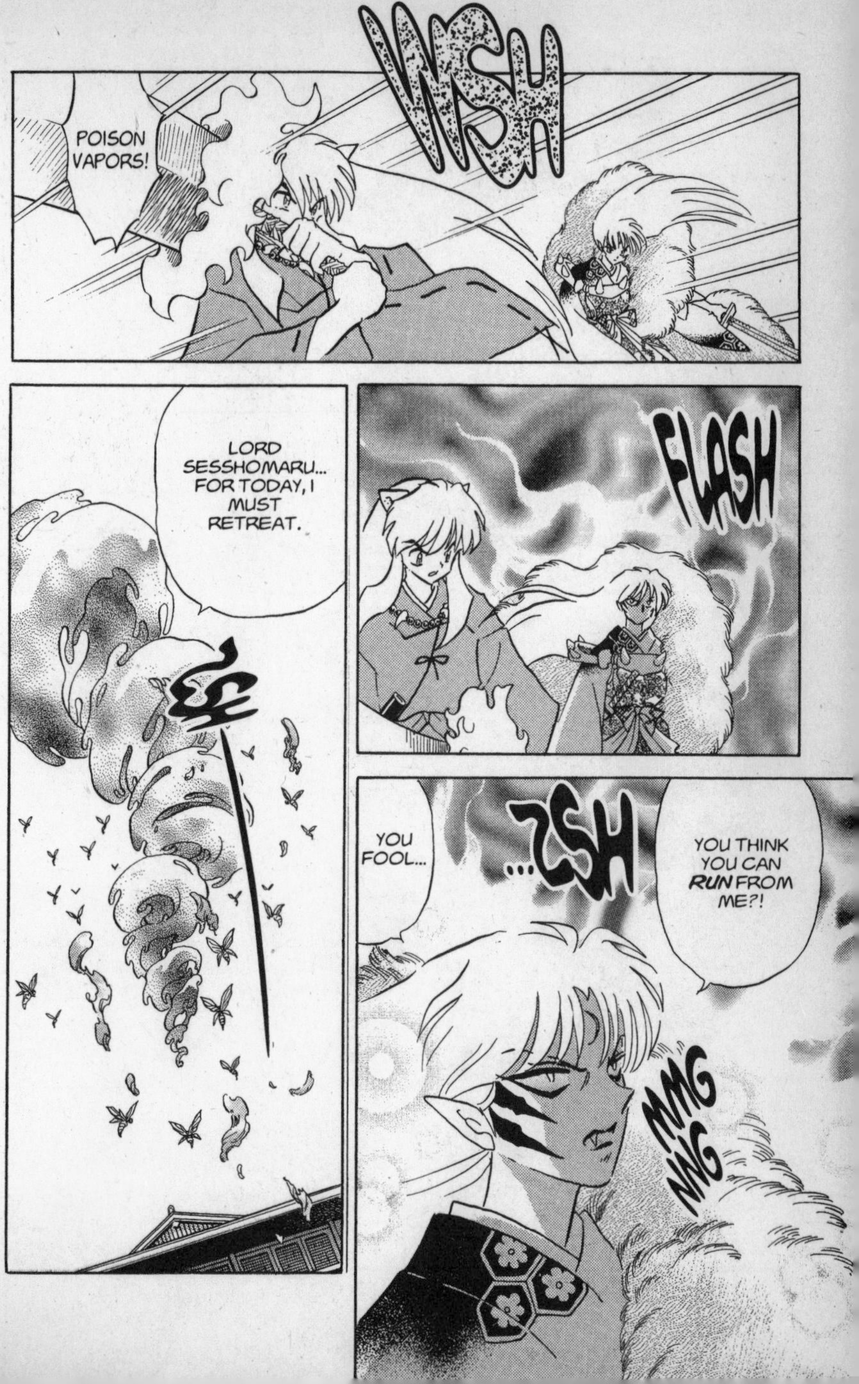

POISON VAPORS!
WSH
LORD SESSHOMARU... FOR TODAY, I MUST RETREAT.
ZSH
FLASH
YOU FOOL...
...ZSH
YOU THINK YOU CAN **RUN** FROM ME?!
MMG NNG

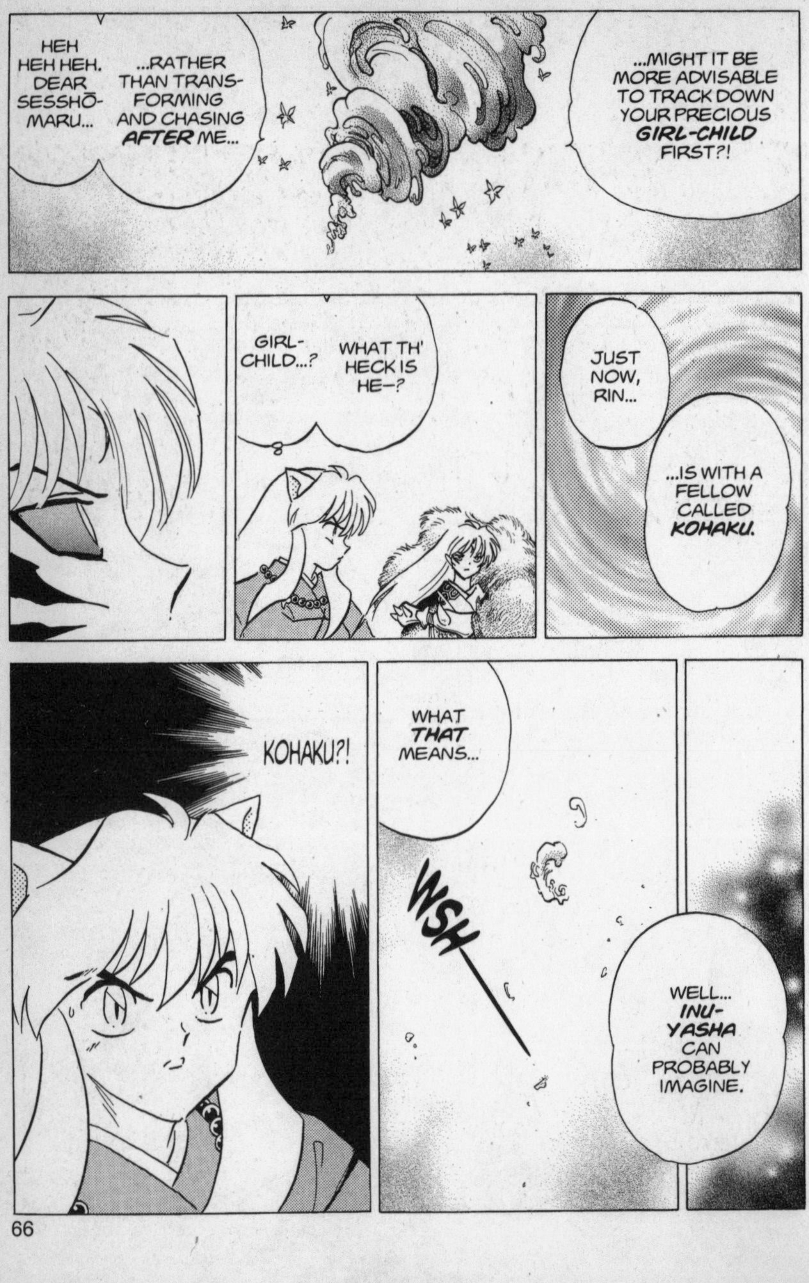
HEH HEH HEH. DEAR SESSHŌMARU...
...RATHER THAN TRANSFORMING AND CHASING AFTER ME...
...MIGHT IT BE MORE ADVISABLE TO TRACK DOWN YOUR PRECIOUS GIRL-CHILD FIRST?!
GIRL-CHILD...?
WHAT TH' HECK IS HE–?
JUST NOW, RIN...
...IS WITH A FELLOW CALLED KOHAKU.
KOHAKU?!
WHAT THAT MEANS...
WSH
WELL... INU-YASHA CAN PROBABLY IMAGINE.

HSH...

WHAT'S WRONG, KOHAKU?

.....

GLEEM

KOHAKU'S BEING CONTROLLED BY NARAKU...

...BECAUSE OF THE *SHIKON SHARD* IMPLANTED IN HIS BACK.

IF NARAKU SENDS THE ORDER...

...IT WON'T *MATTER* WHO THE OTHER PERSON IS—KOHAKU WILL *KILL* THEM!

HEY, SESSHŌMARU!

DID HE TAKE SOMEONE OF YOURS *HOSTAGE?!*

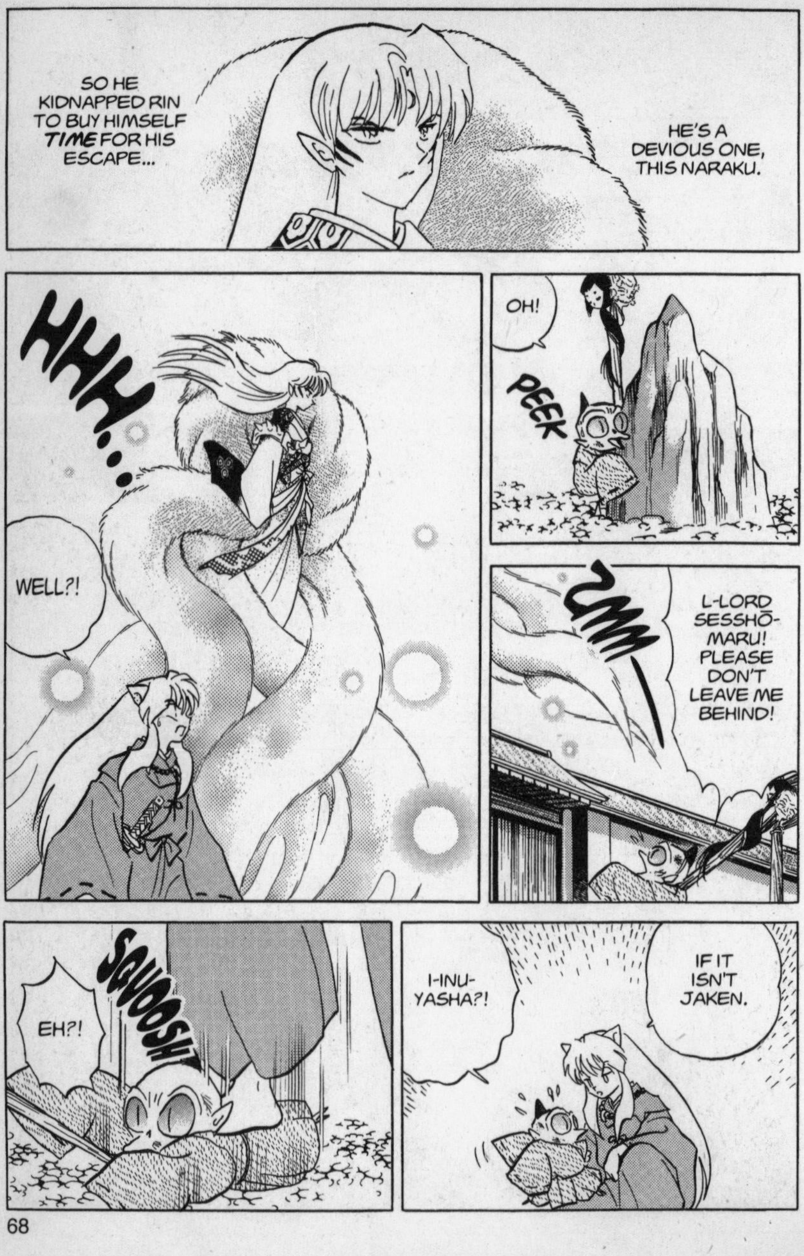
SO HE KIDNAPPED RIN TO BUY HIMSELF TIME FOR HIS ESCAPE...
HE'S A DEVIOUS ONE, THIS NARAKU.
HHH...
WELL?!
OH!
PEEK
ZMM
L-LORD SESSHŌMARU! PLEASE DON'T LEAVE ME BEHIND!
EH?!
SQUOOSH
I-INU-YASHA?!
IF IT ISN'T JAKEN.

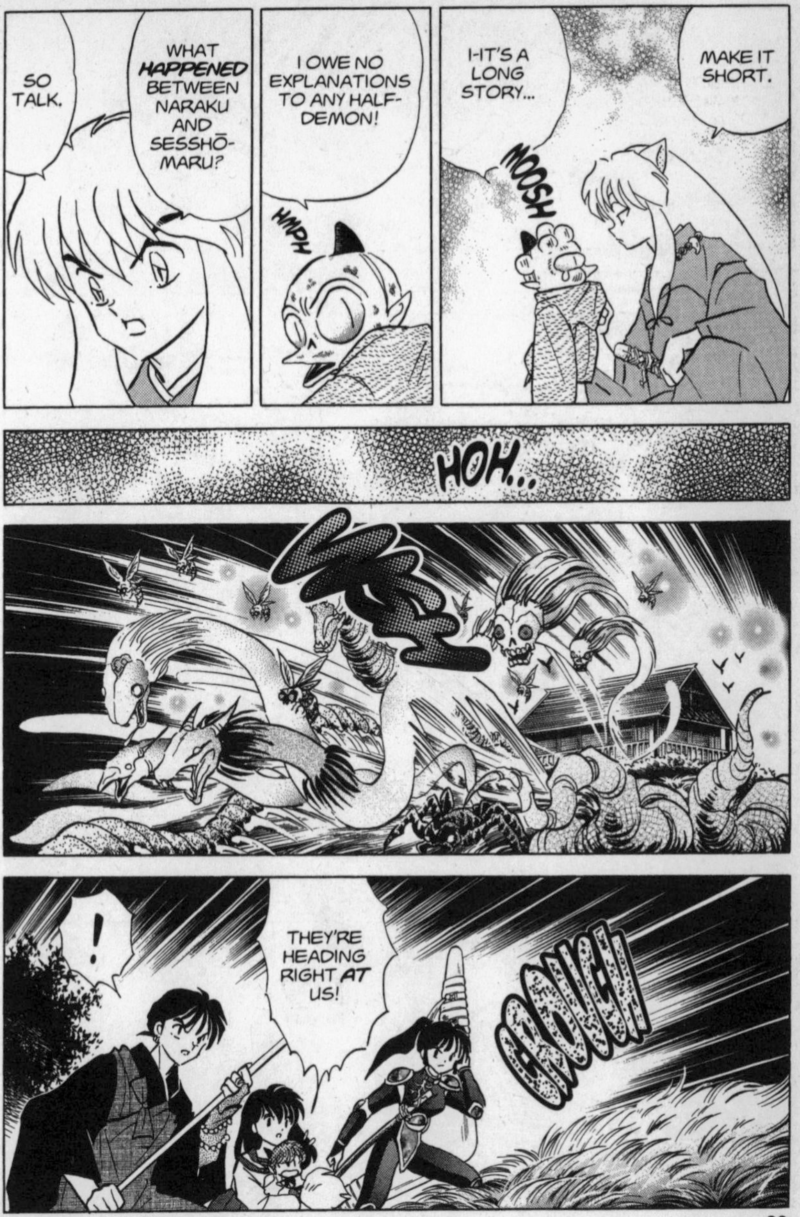
SO TALK.
WHAT HAPPENED BETWEEN NARAKU AND SESSHŌ-MARU?
I OWE NO EXPLANATIONS TO ANY HALF-DEMON!
HMPH
I-IT'S A LONG STORY...
MOOSH
MAKE IT SHORT.
HOH...
!
THEY'RE HEADING RIGHT AT US!

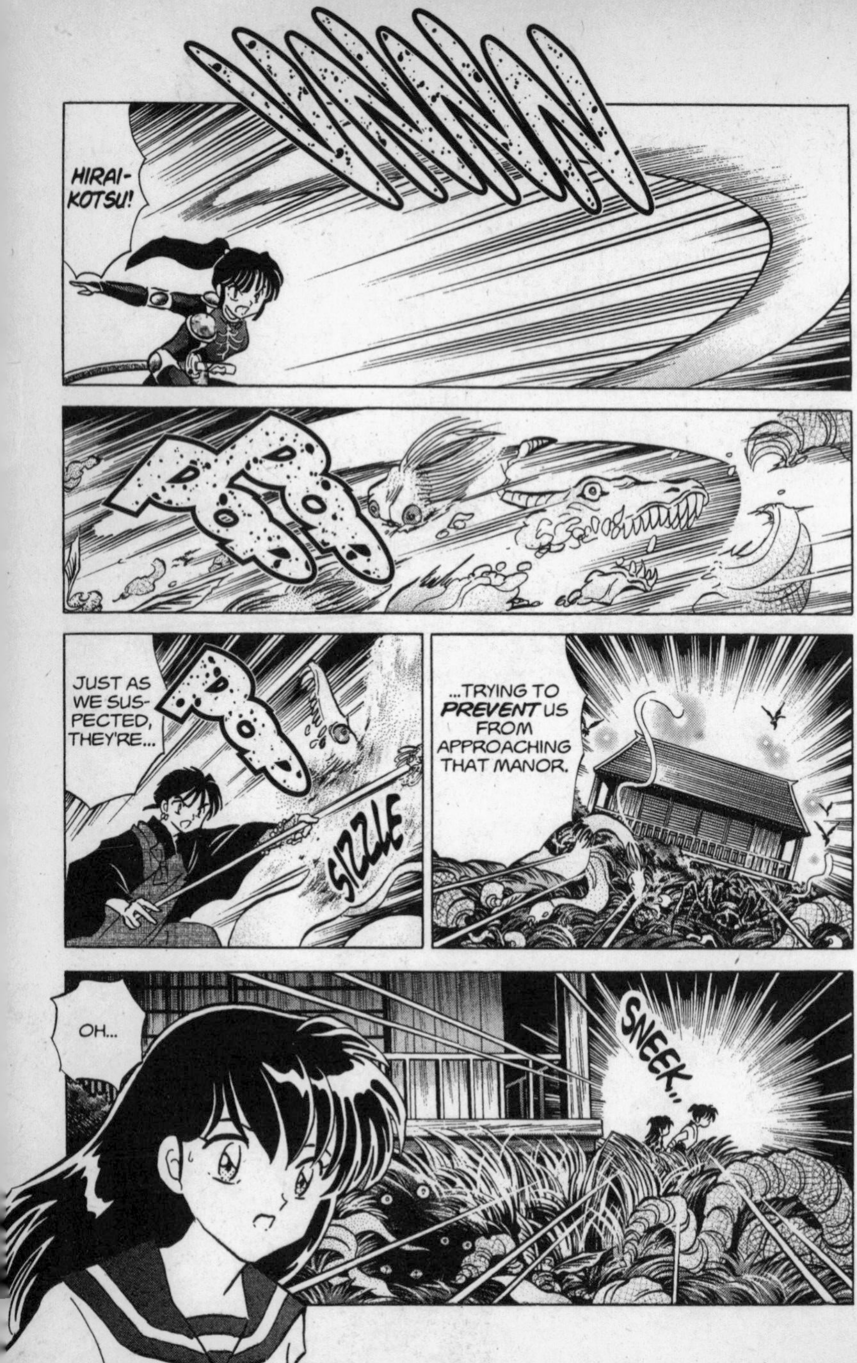
HIRAI-KOTSU!
JUST AS WE SUS-PECTED, THEY'RE...
SIZZLE
...TRYING TO **PREVENT** US FROM APPROACHING THAT MANOR.
OH...
SNEEK...

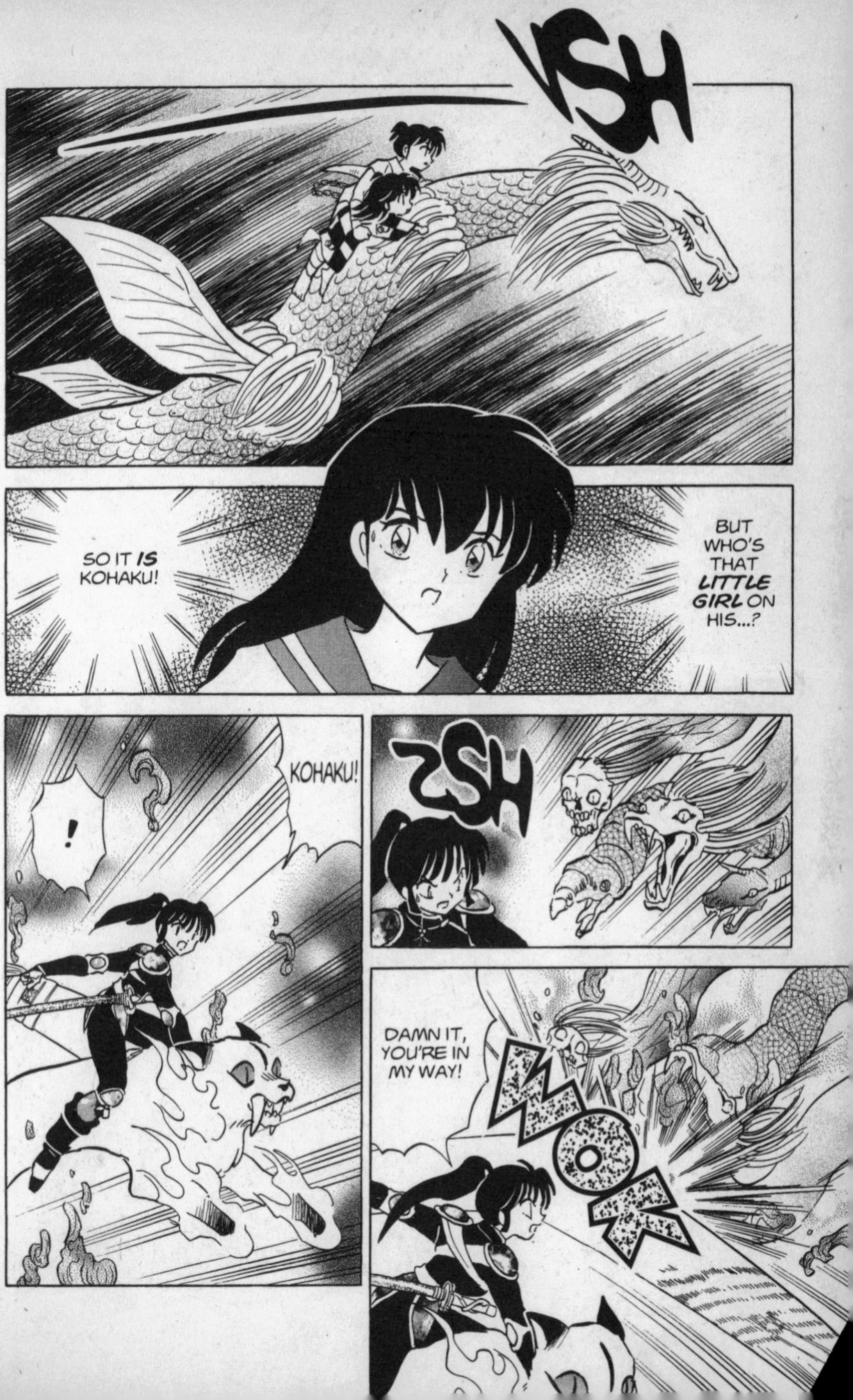
VSH
SO IT IS KOHAKU!
BUT WHO'S THAT LITTLE GIRL ON HIS...?
!
KOHAKU!
ZSH
DAMN IT, YOU'RE IN MY WAY!
WOK

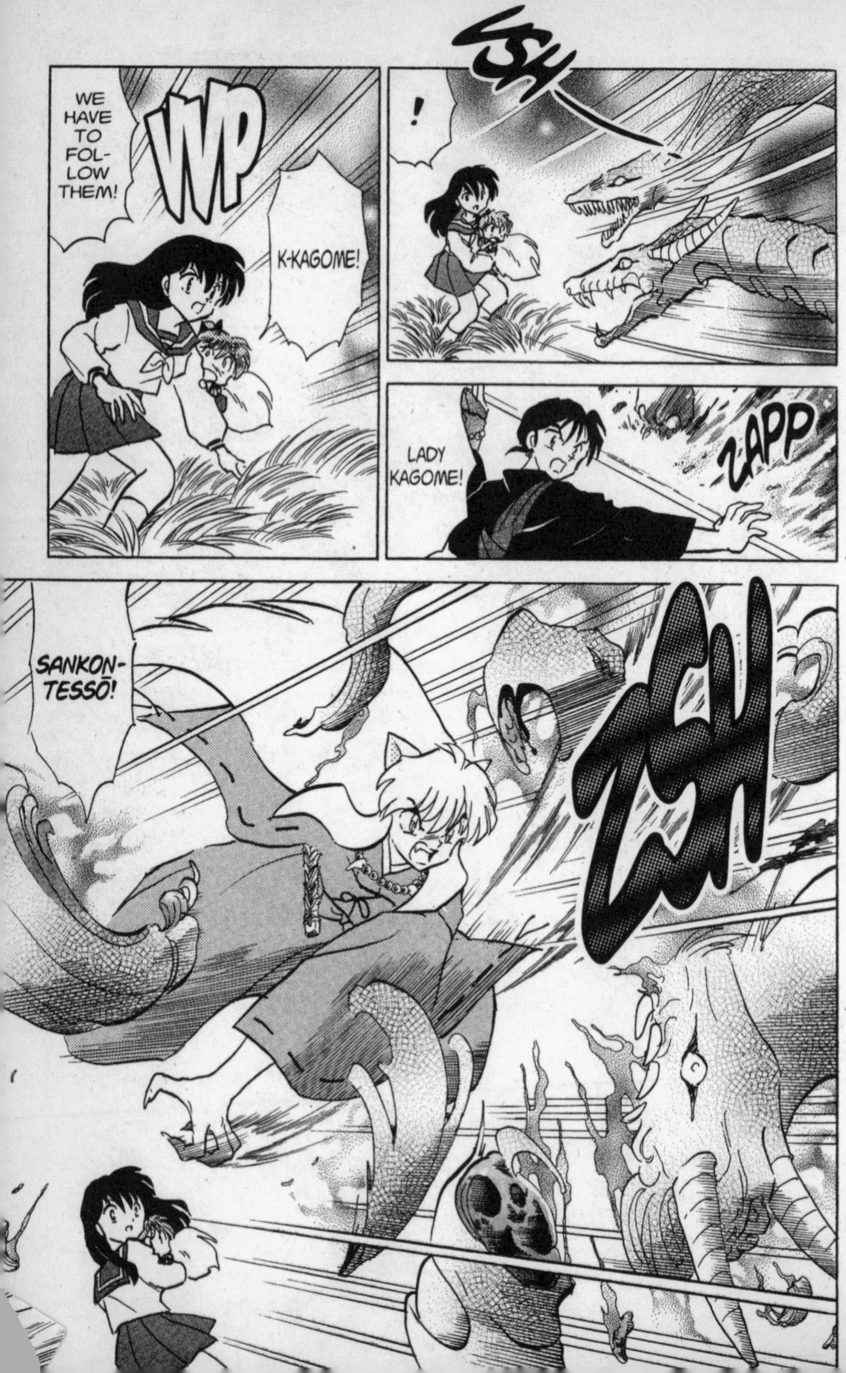
WE HAVE TO FOL-LOW THEM!
VWP
K-KAGOME!
VSH
!
LADY KAGOME!
ZAPP
SANKON-TESSŌ!
ZSH

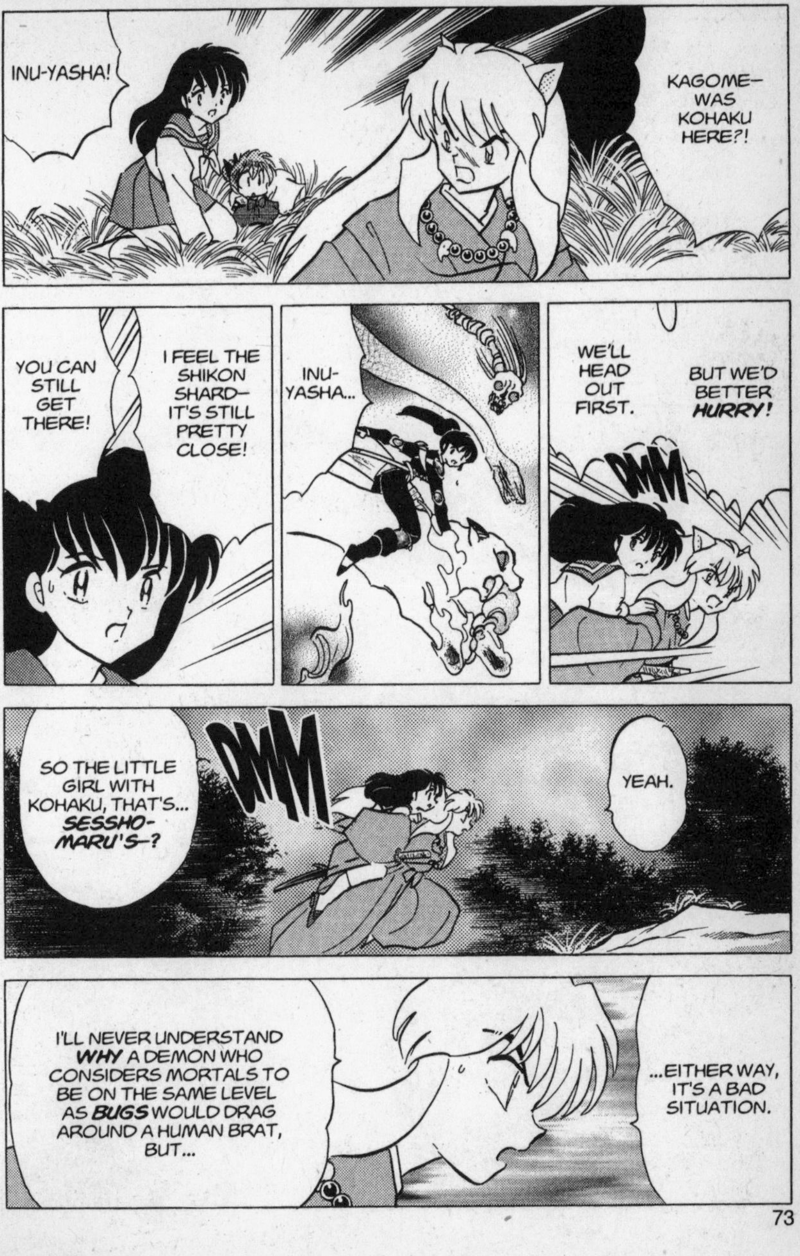
INU-YASHA!
KAGOME—WAS KOHAKU HERE?!
YOU CAN STILL GET THERE!
I FEEL THE SHIKON SHARD—IT'S STILL PRETTY CLOSE!
INU-YASHA...
WE'LL HEAD OUT FIRST.
BUT WE'D BETTER HURRY!
DMM
SO THE LITTLE GIRL WITH KOHAKU, THAT'S... SESSHO-MARU'S—?
DMM
YEAH.
I'LL NEVER UNDERSTAND WHY A DEMON WHO CONSIDERS MORTALS TO BE ON THE SAME LEVEL AS BUGS WOULD DRAG AROUND A HUMAN BRAT, BUT...
...EITHER WAY, IT'S A BAD SITUATION.

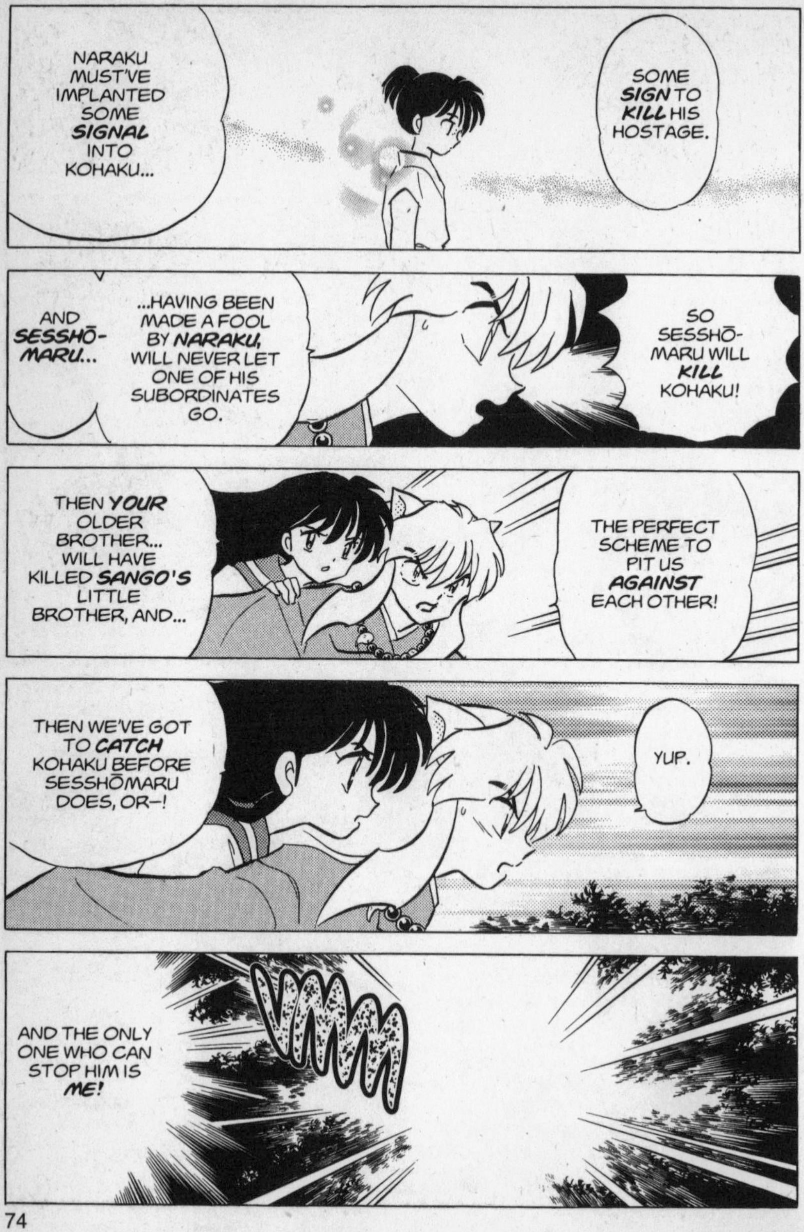
NARAKU MUST'VE IMPLANTED SOME SIGNAL INTO KOHAKU...
SOME SIGN TO KILL HIS HOSTAGE.
AND SESSHŌMARU...
...HAVING BEEN MADE A FOOL BY NARAKU, WILL NEVER LET ONE OF HIS SUBORDINATES GO.
SO SESSHŌMARU WILL KILL KOHAKU!
THEN YOUR OLDER BROTHER... WILL HAVE KILLED SANGO'S LITTLE BROTHER, AND...
THE PERFECT SCHEME TO PIT US AGAINST EACH OTHER!
THEN WE'VE GOT TO CATCH KOHAKU BEFORE SESSHŌMARU DOES, OR–!
YUP.
AND THE ONLY ONE WHO CAN STOP HIM IS ME!
VMM

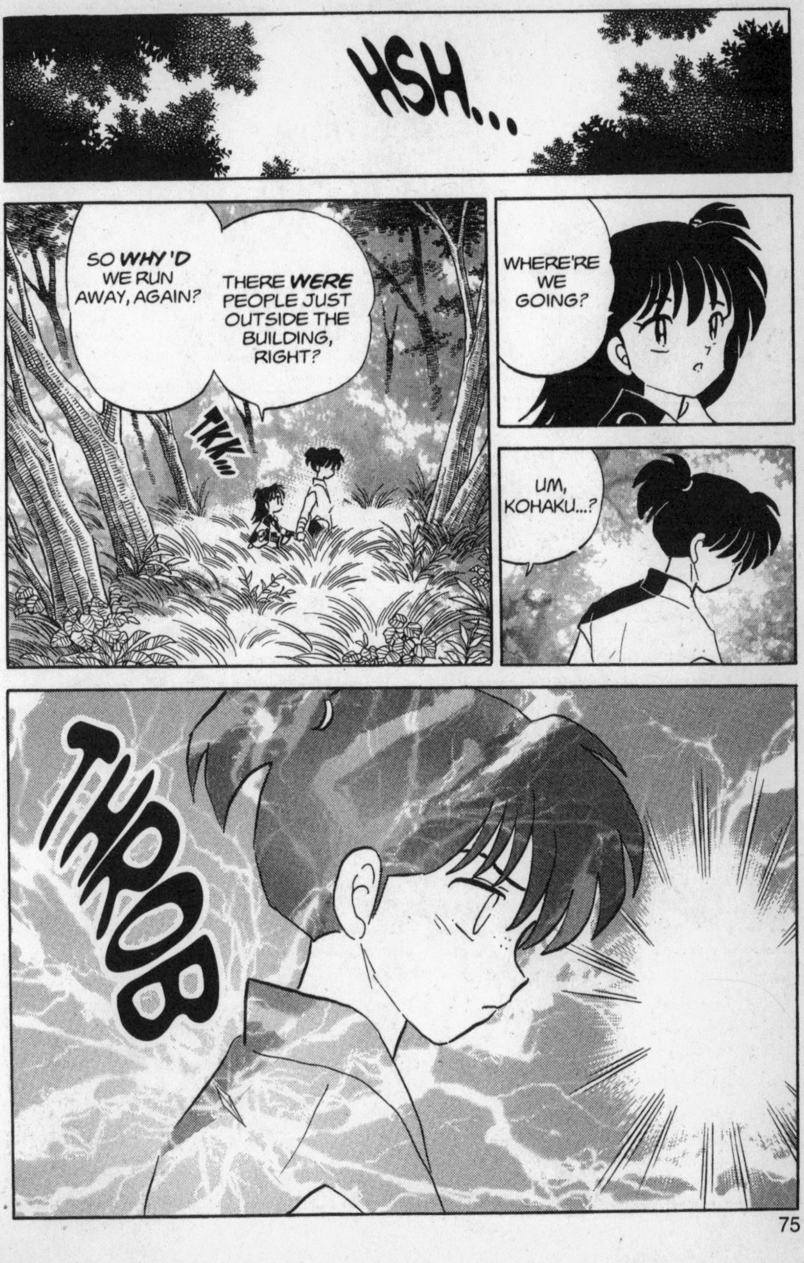
HSH...
SO WHY'D WE RUN AWAY, AGAIN?
THERE WERE PEOPLE JUST OUTSIDE THE BUILDING, RIGHT?
TKK...
WHERE'RE WE GOING?
UM, KOHAKU...?
THROB

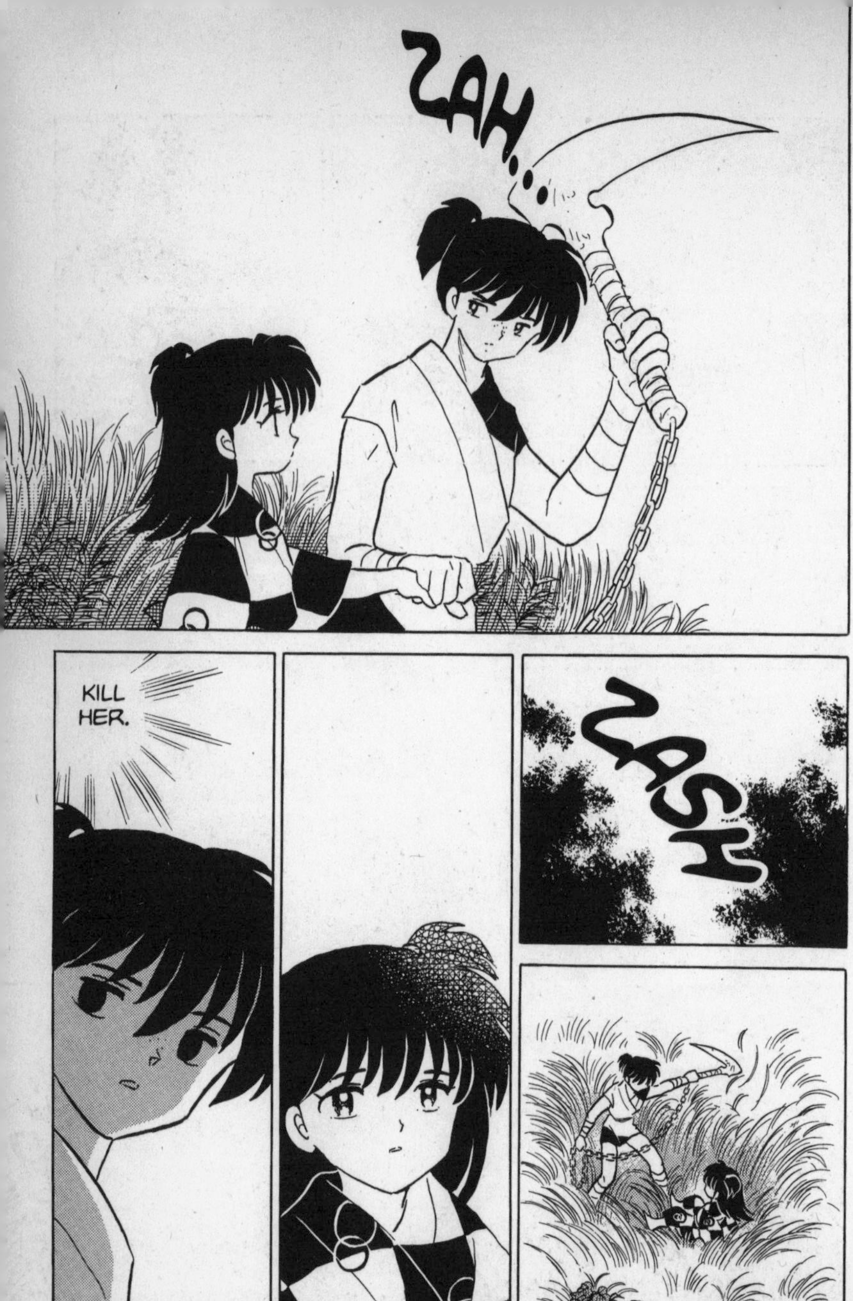
ZAH...
KILL HER.
ZASH

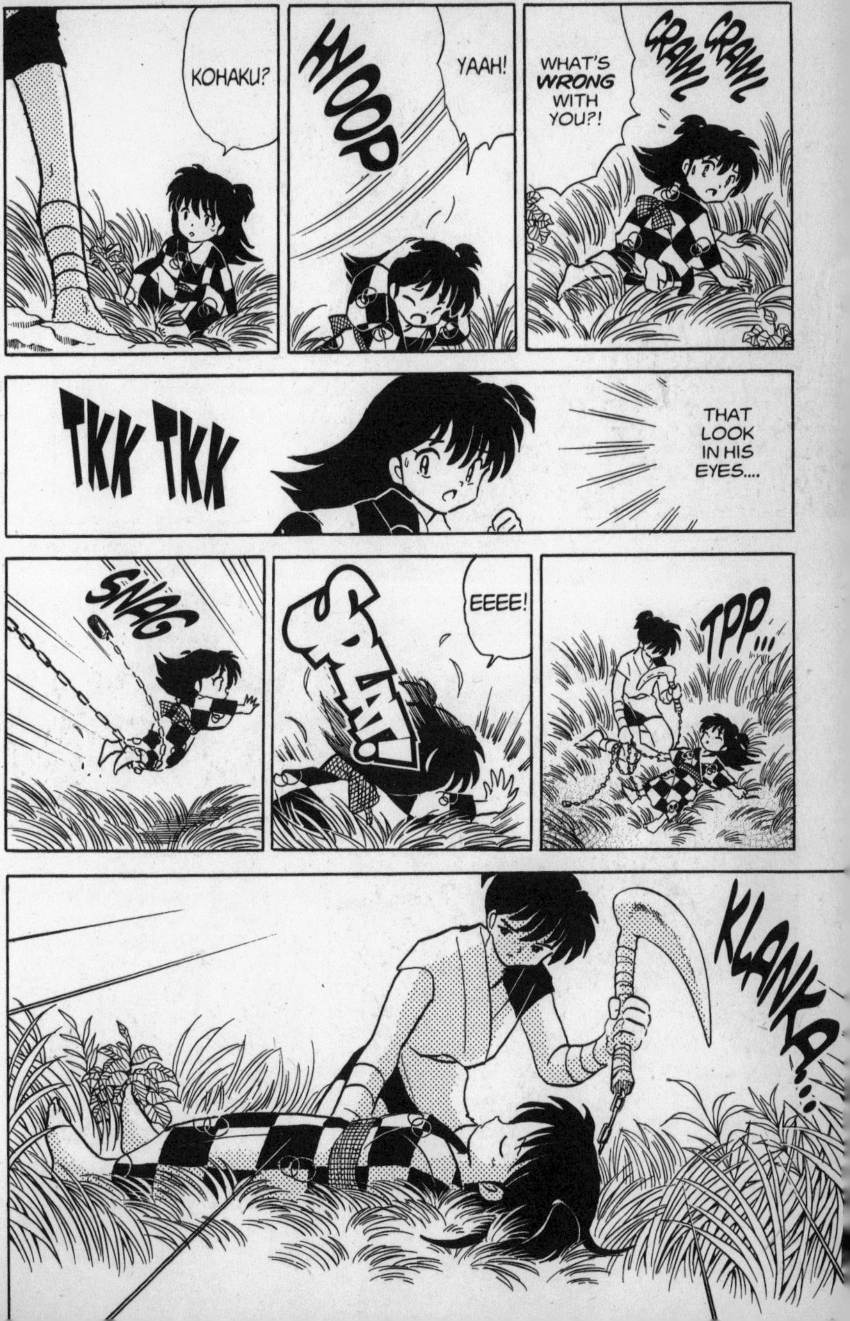
KOHAKU?
WHOOP
YAAH!
WHAT'S WRONG WITH YOU?!
CRAWL CRAWL
TKK TKK
THAT LOOK IN HIS EYES....
SNAG
SPLAT!
EEEE!
TPP...
KLANKA...

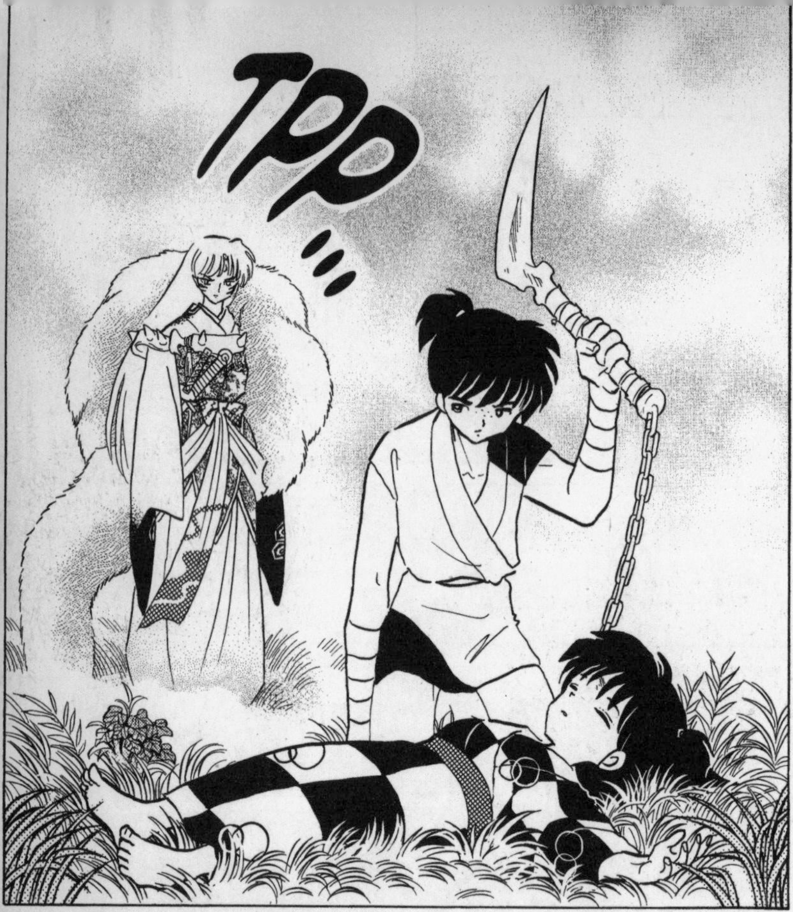
TPP...

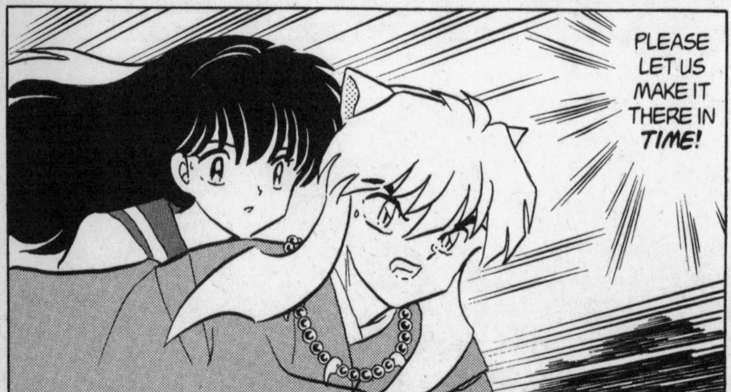
PLEASE LET US MAKE IT THERE IN *TIME!*

SCROLL FIVE
THE ABANDONED CASTLE

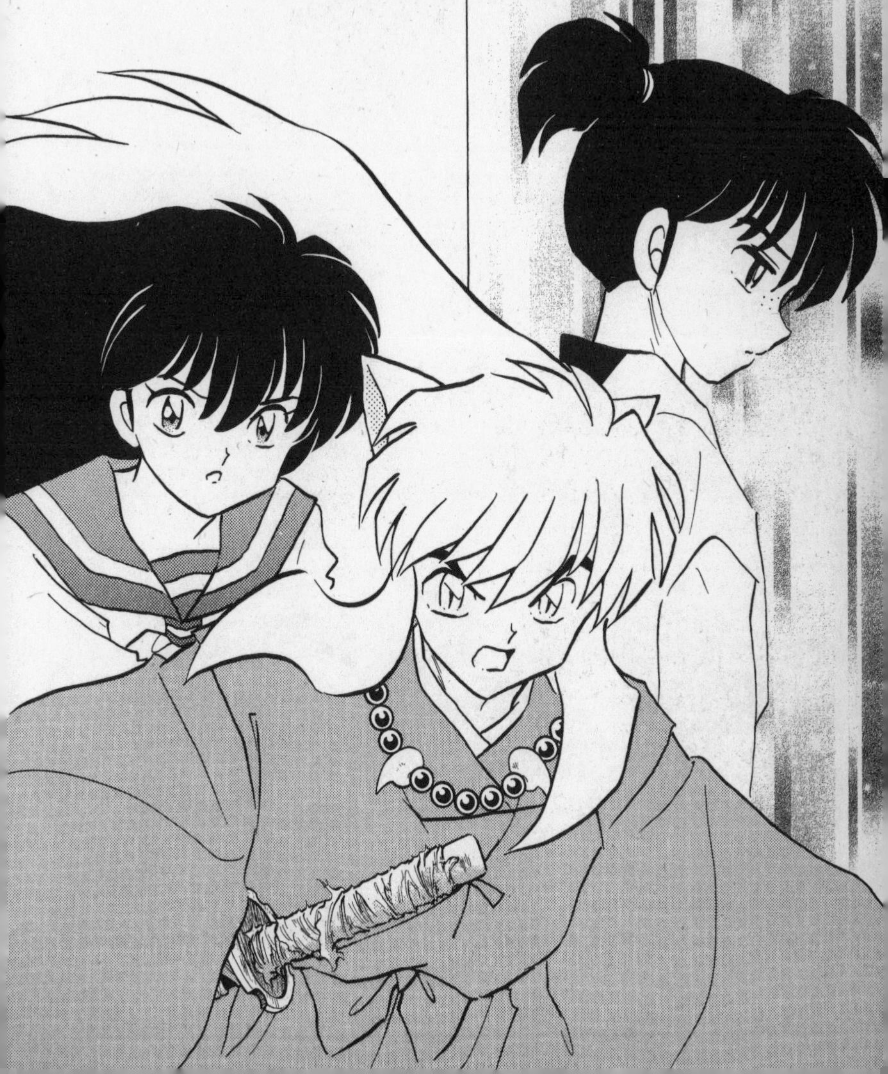

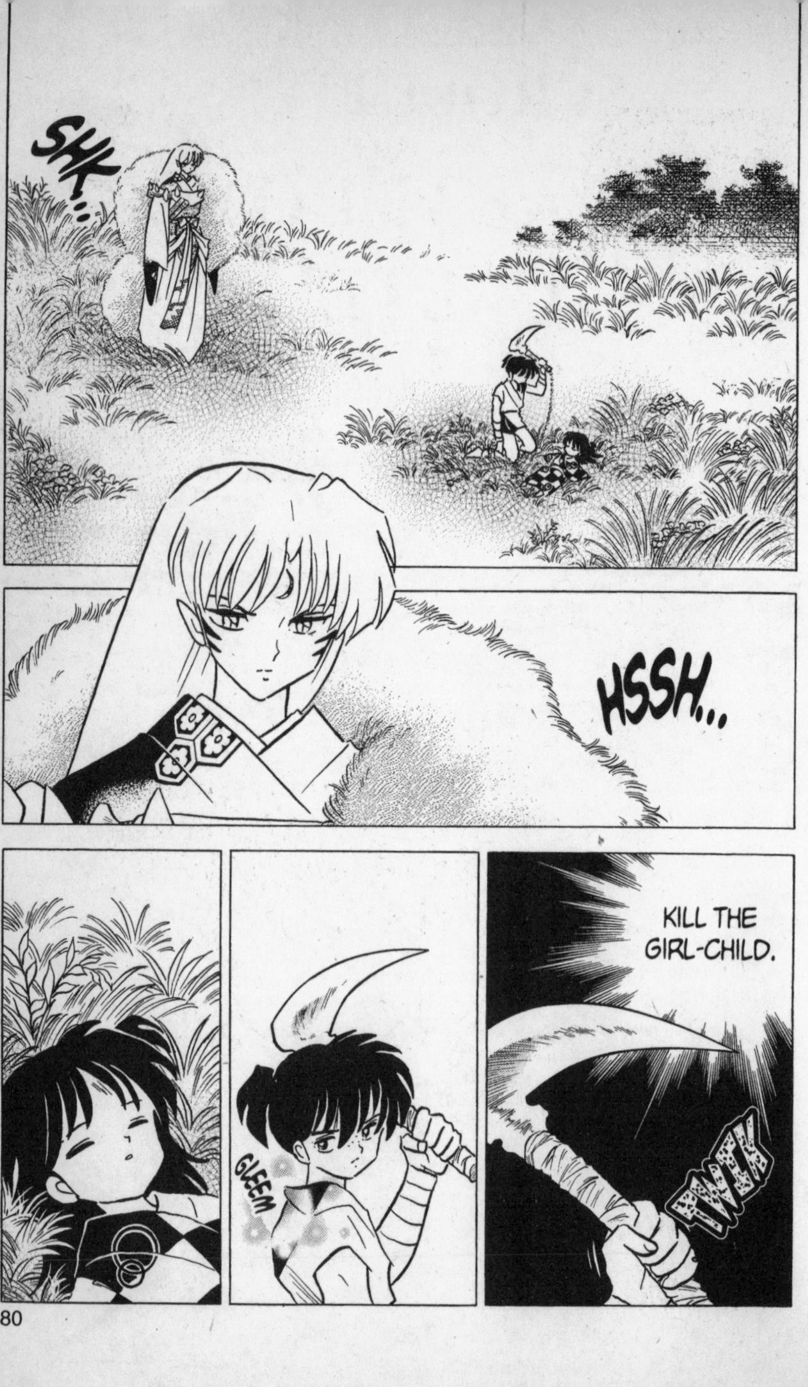
SHK!...
HSSH...
GLEEM
KILL THE GIRL-CHILD.
TWIK

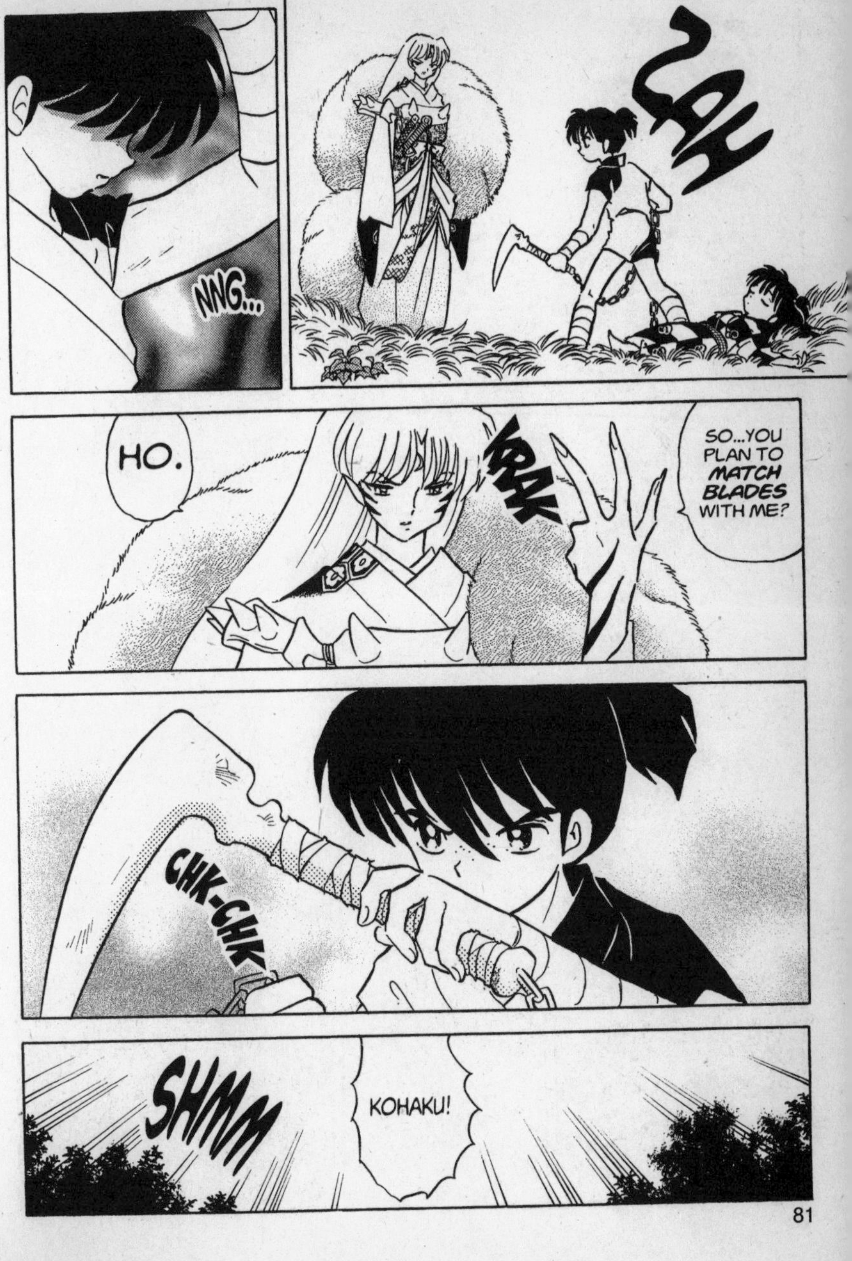
NNG...
ZAH
HO.
KRAK
SO...YOU PLAN TO *MATCH BLADES* WITH ME?
CHK-CHK
SHMM
KOHAKU!

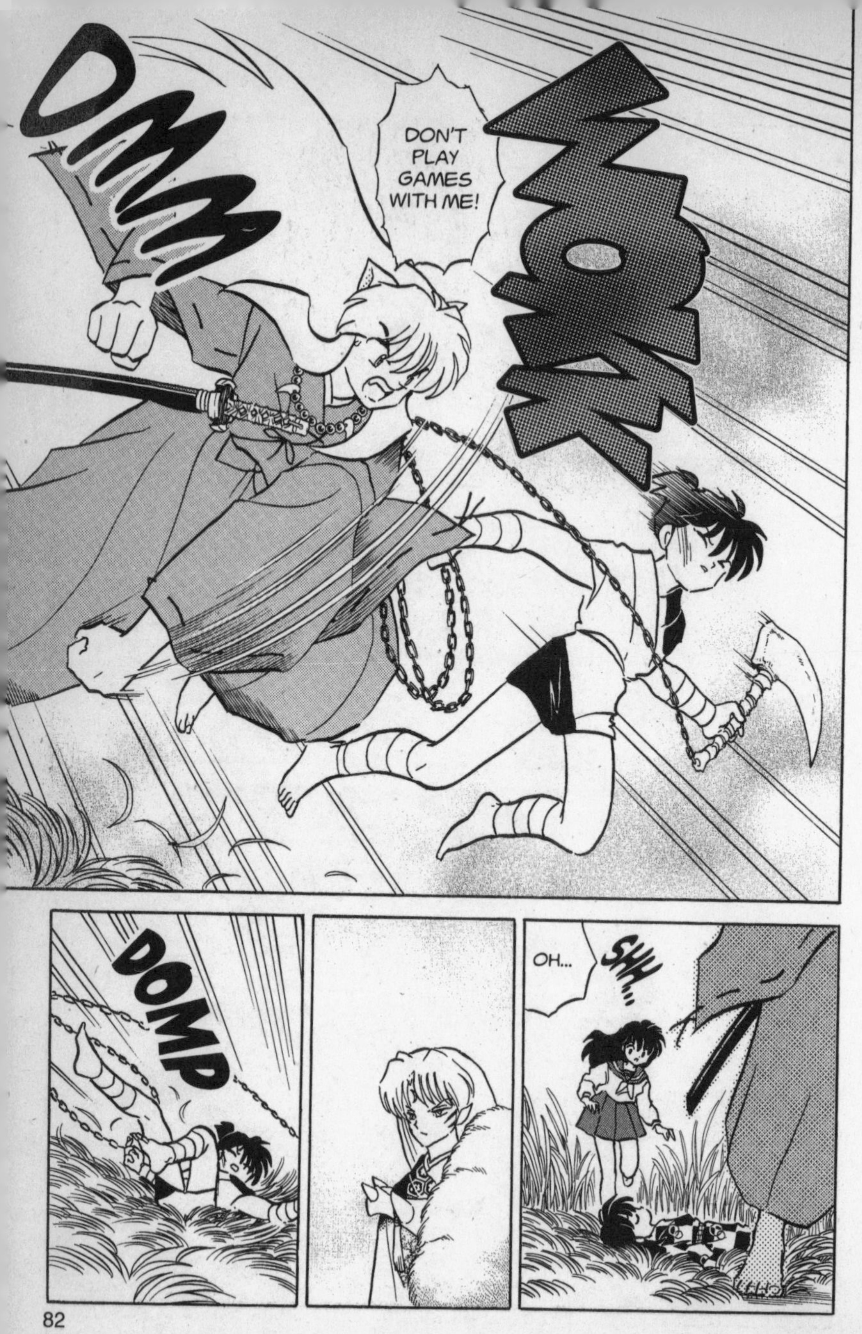
DON'T PLAY GAMES WITH ME!
DMM
OH...
SHH...
DOMP

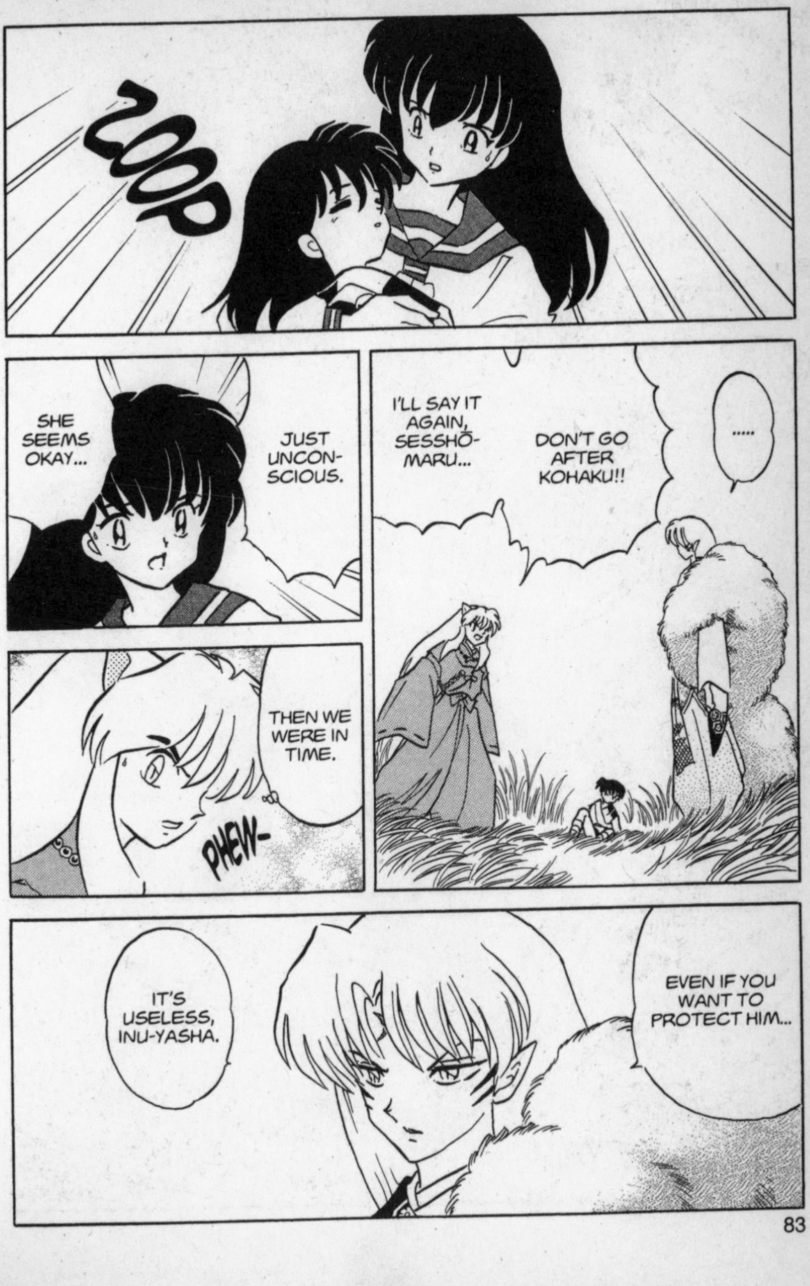
ZOOP
SHE SEEMS OKAY...
JUST UNCONSCIOUS.
THEN WE WERE IN TIME.
PHEW-
I'LL SAY IT AGAIN, SESSHŌMARU...
DON'T GO AFTER KOHAKU!!
.....
IT'S USELESS, INU-YASHA.
EVEN IF YOU WANT TO PROTECT HIM...

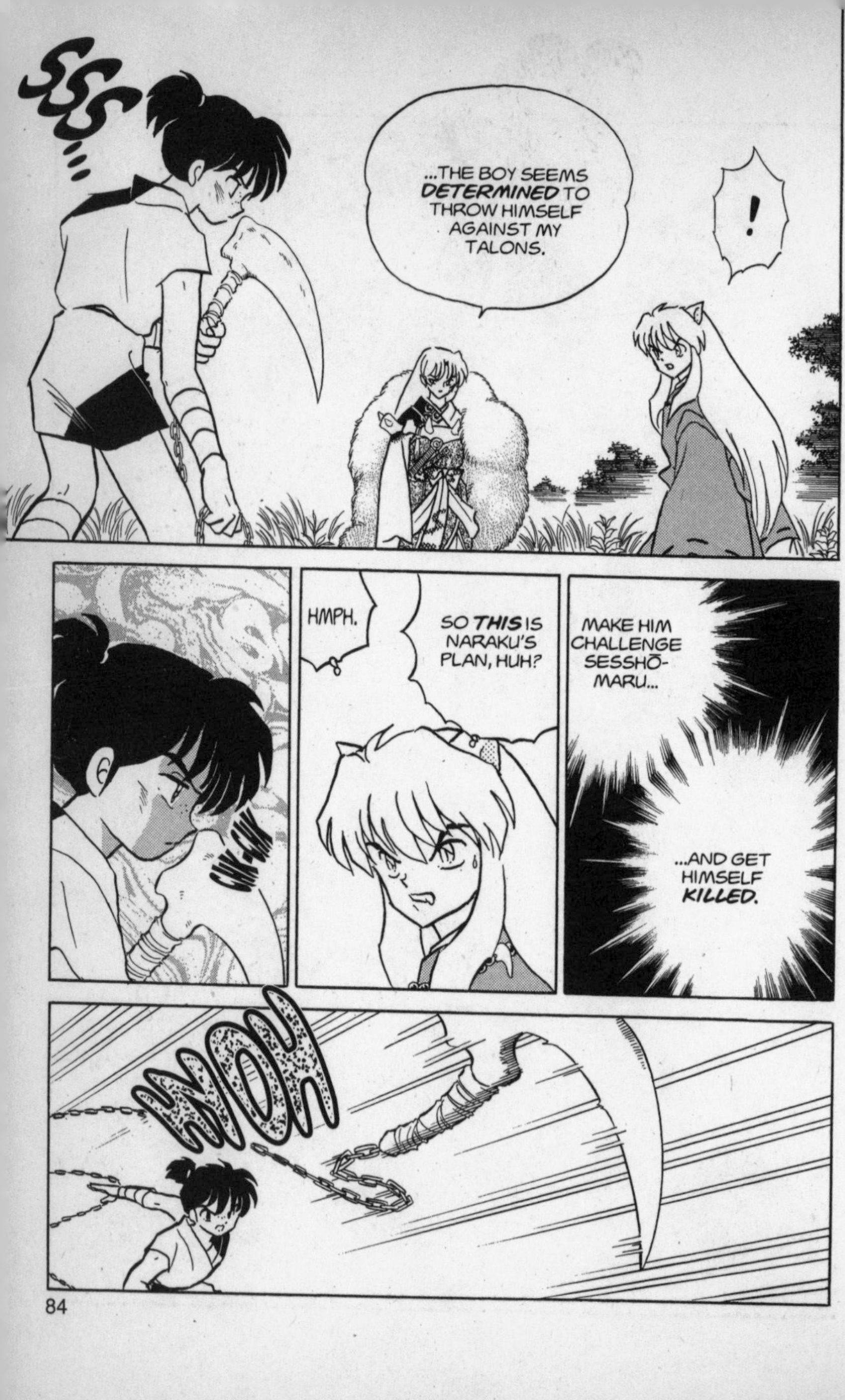
SSS...
...THE BOY SEEMS DETERMINED TO THROW HIMSELF AGAINST MY TALONS.
!
CHK-CHK
HMPH.
SO THIS IS NARAKU'S PLAN, HUH?
MAKE HIM CHALLENGE SESSHŌ-MARU...
...AND GET HIMSELF KILLED.

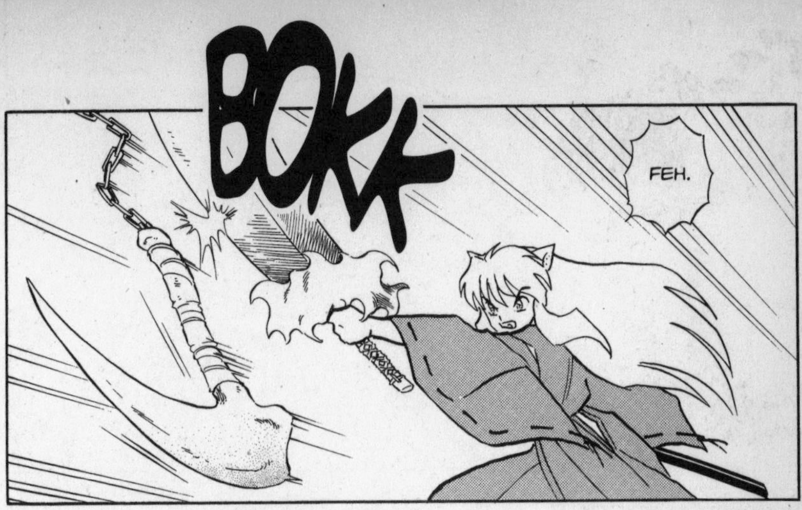
BOKA
FEH.

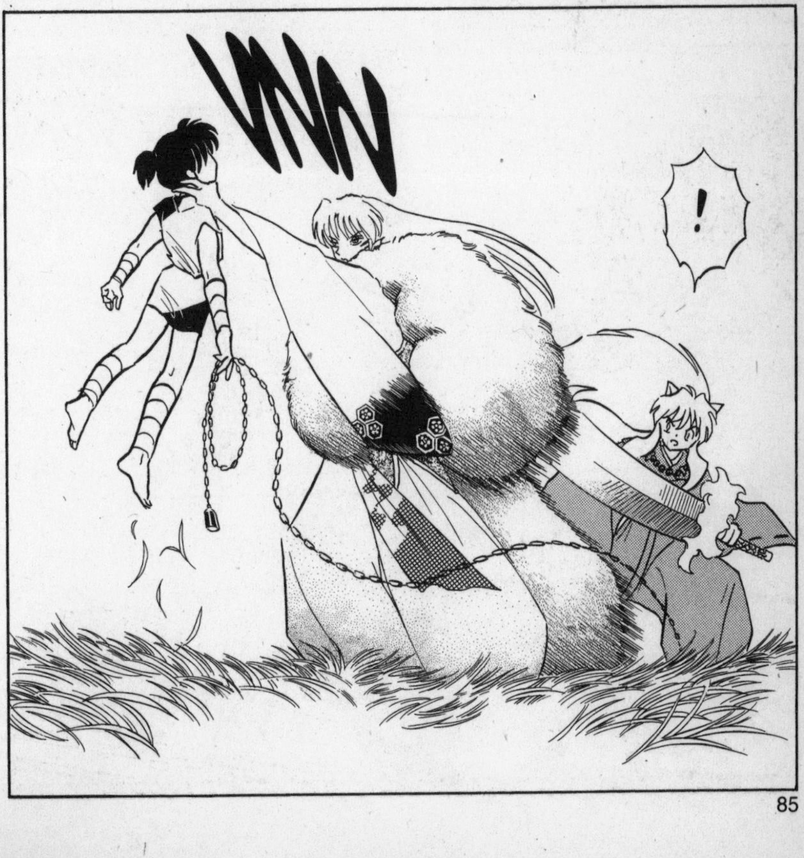
VMM
!

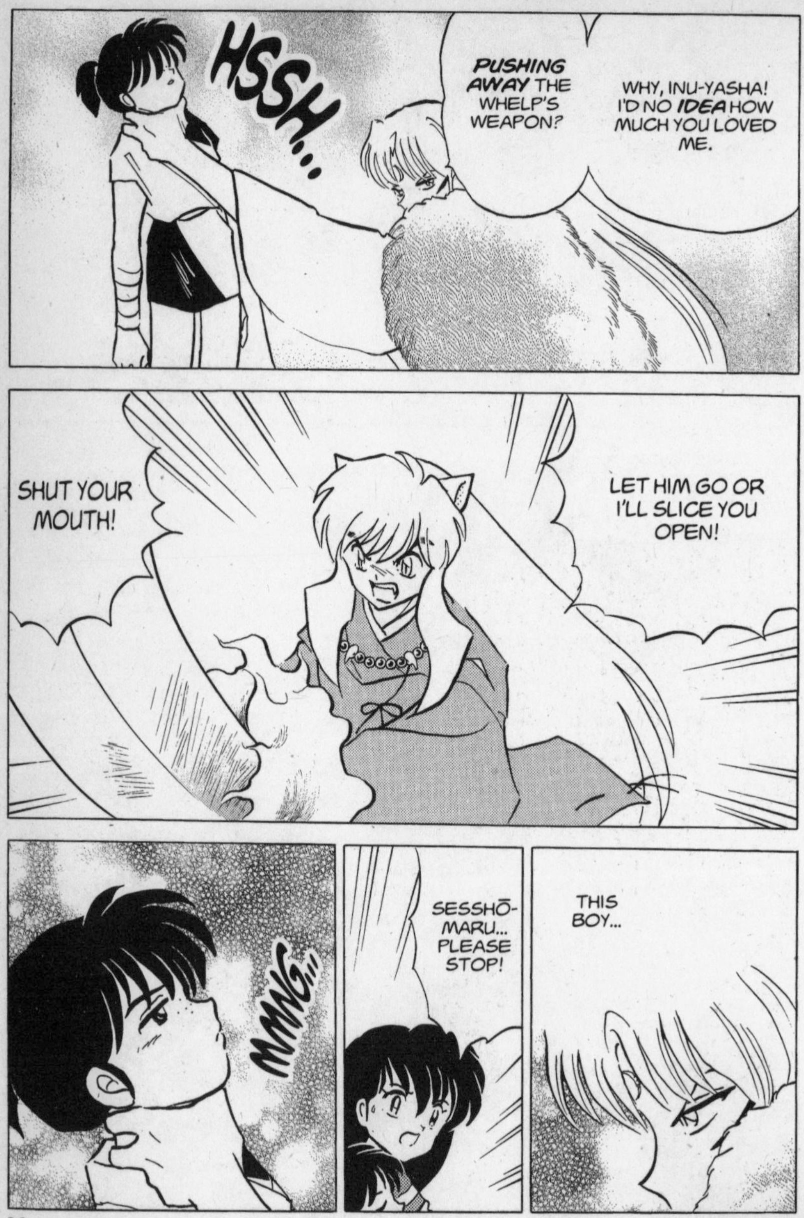
HSSH...
PUSHING AWAY THE WHELP'S WEAPON?
WHY, INU-YASHA! I'D NO IDEA HOW MUCH YOU LOVED ME.
SHUT YOUR MOUTH!
LET HIM GO OR I'LL SLICE YOU OPEN!
MMNG...
SESSHŌMARU... PLEASE STOP!
THIS BOY...

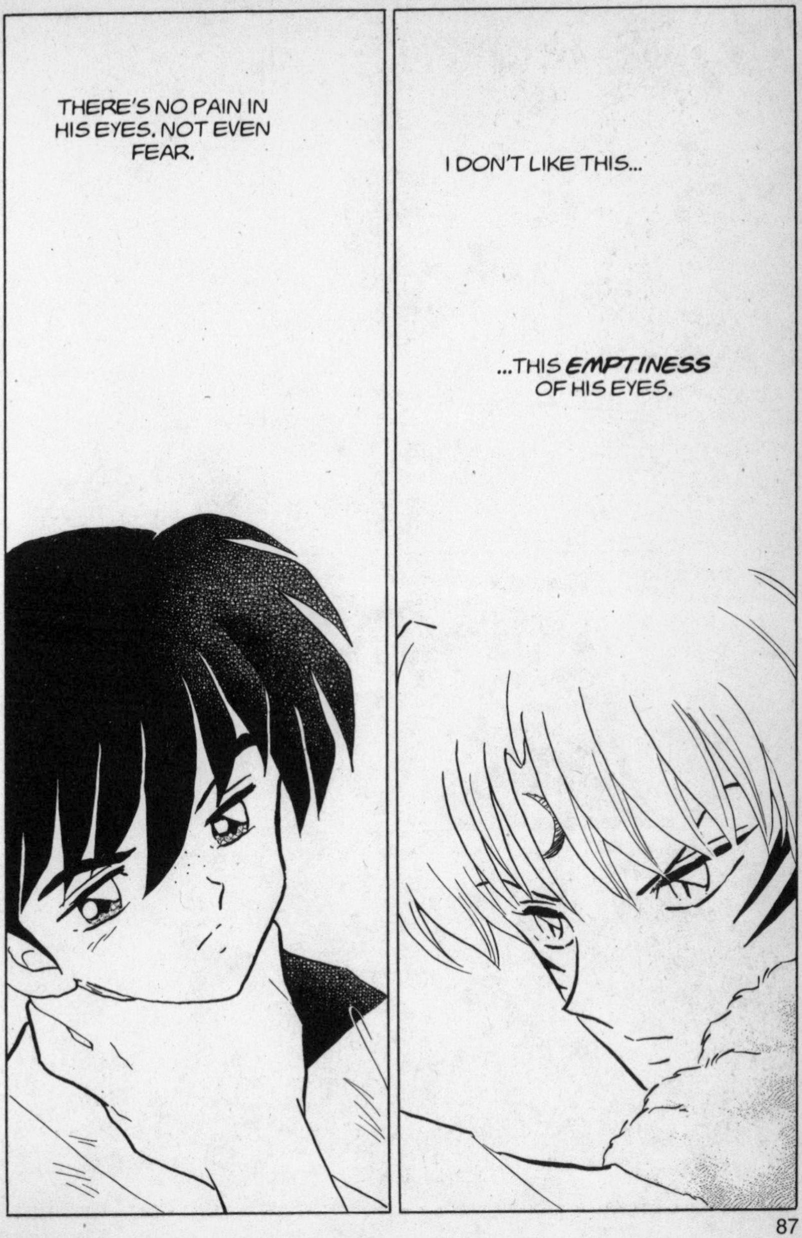
THERE'S NO PAIN IN HIS EYES. NOT EVEN FEAR.
I DON'T LIKE THIS...
...THIS *EMPTINESS* OF HIS EYES.

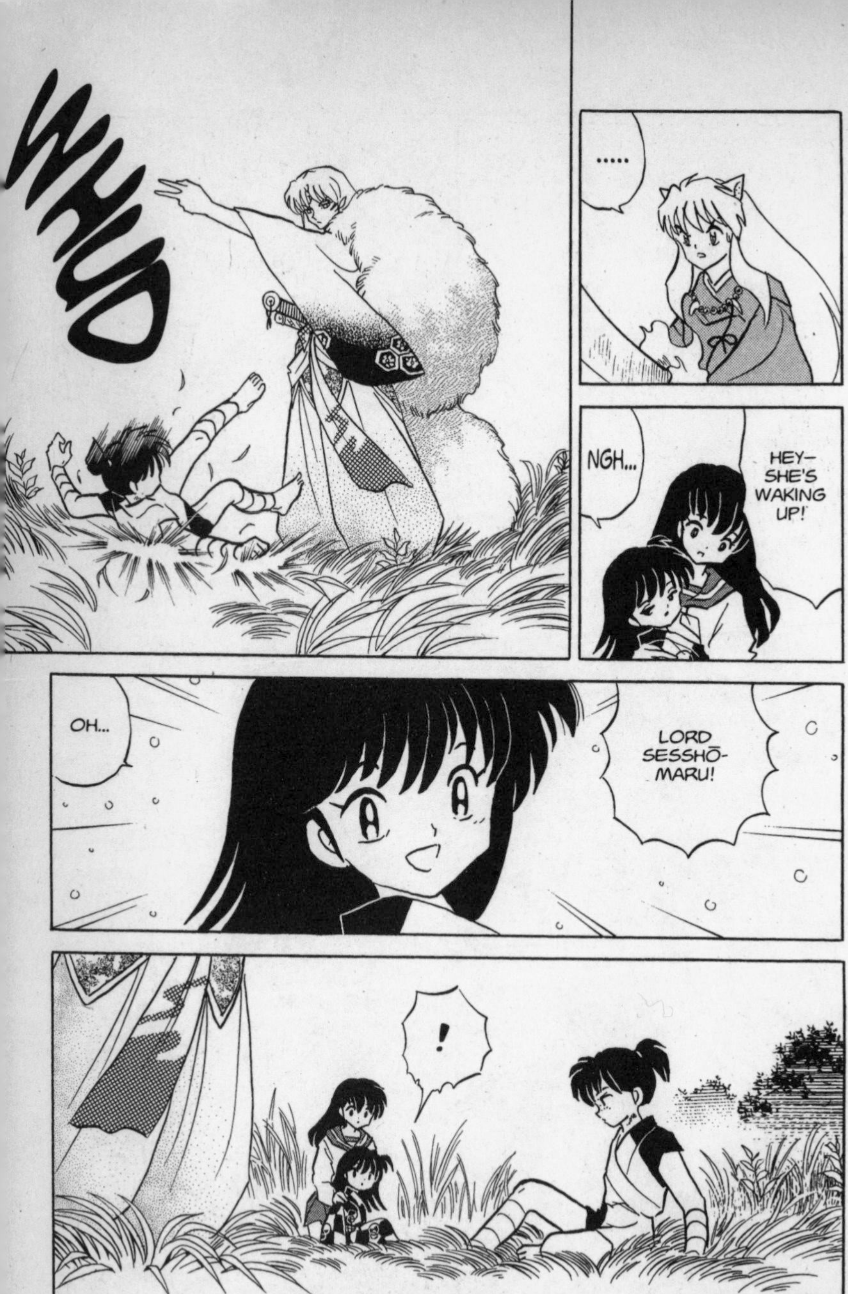
WHUD
......
NGH...
HEY— SHE'S WAKING UP!
OH...
LORD SESSHŌ-MARU!
!

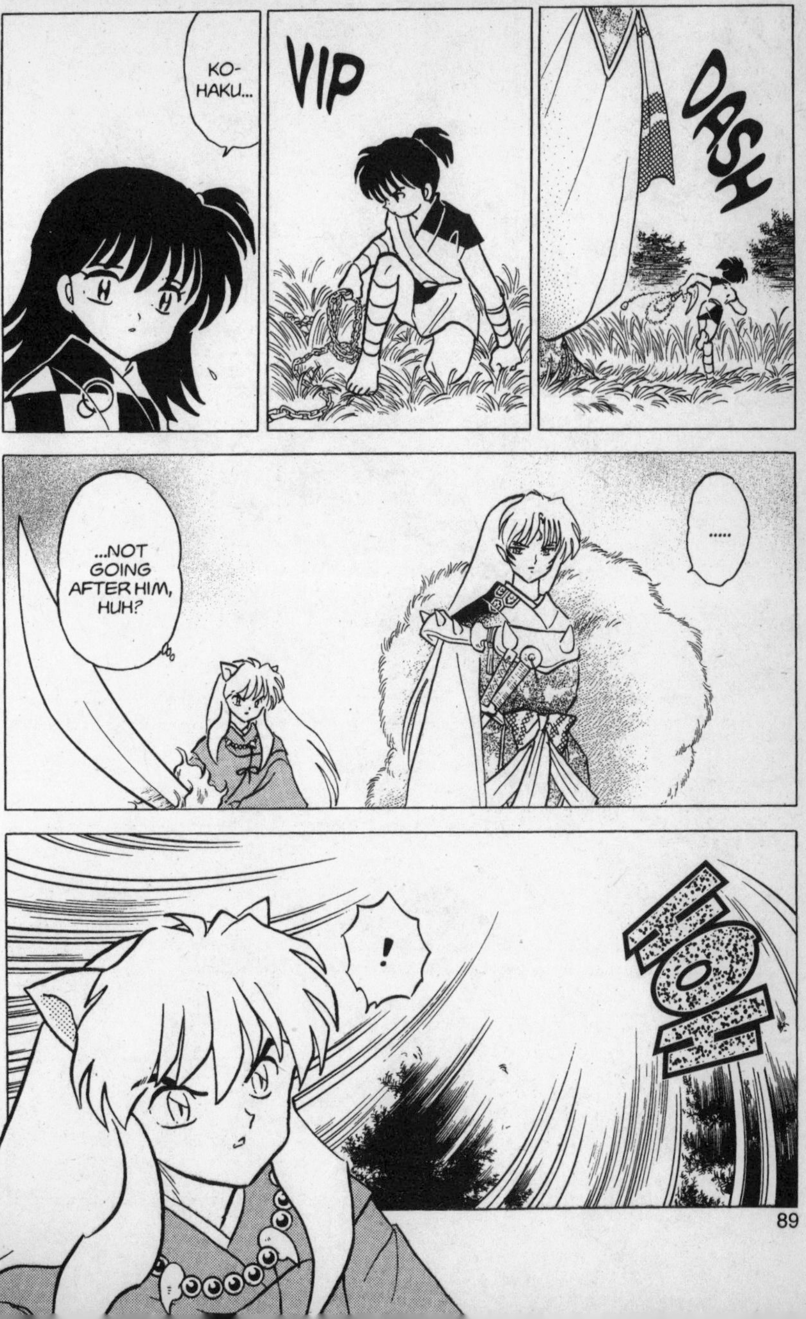

KO-HAKU...
VIP
DASH
...NOT GOING AFTER HIM, HUH?
.....
!
HOH

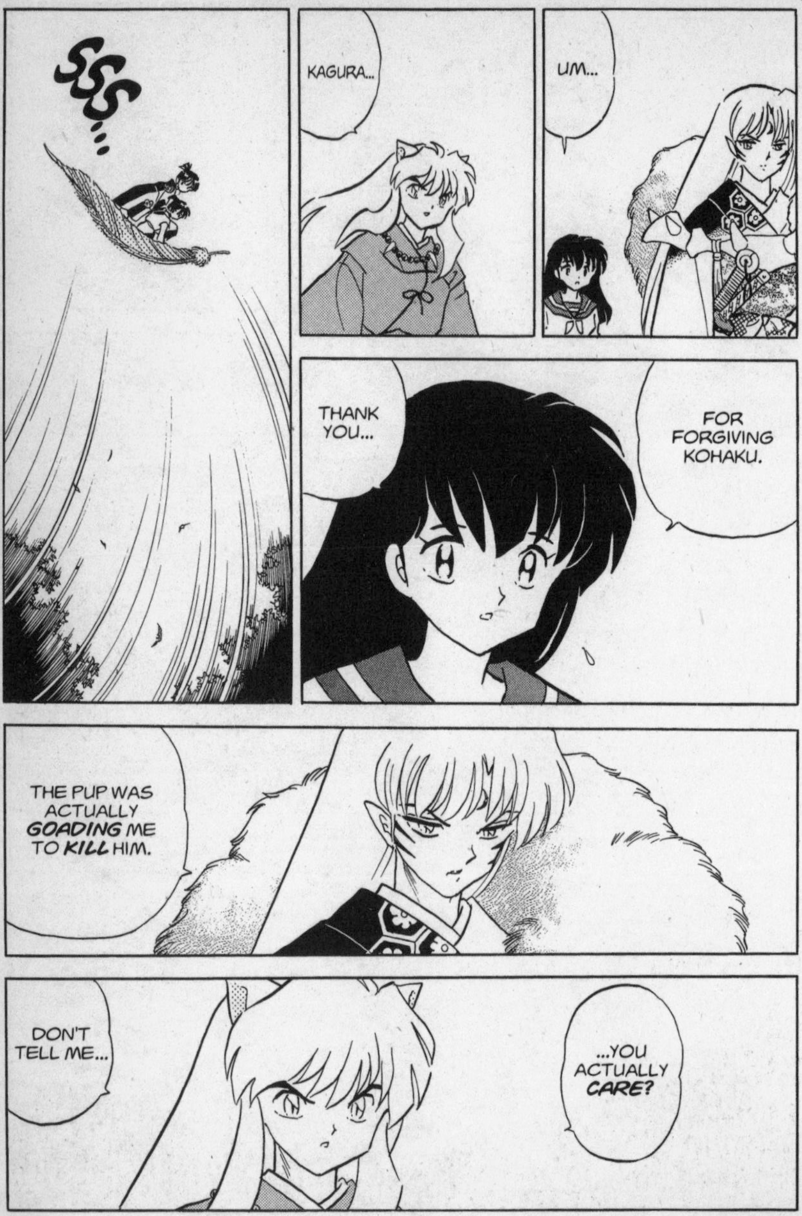
SSS...
KAGURA...
UM...
THANK YOU...
FOR FORGIVING KOHAKU.
THE PUP WAS ACTUALLY **GOADING** ME TO **KILL** HIM.
DON'T TELL ME...
...YOU ACTUALLY **CARE?**

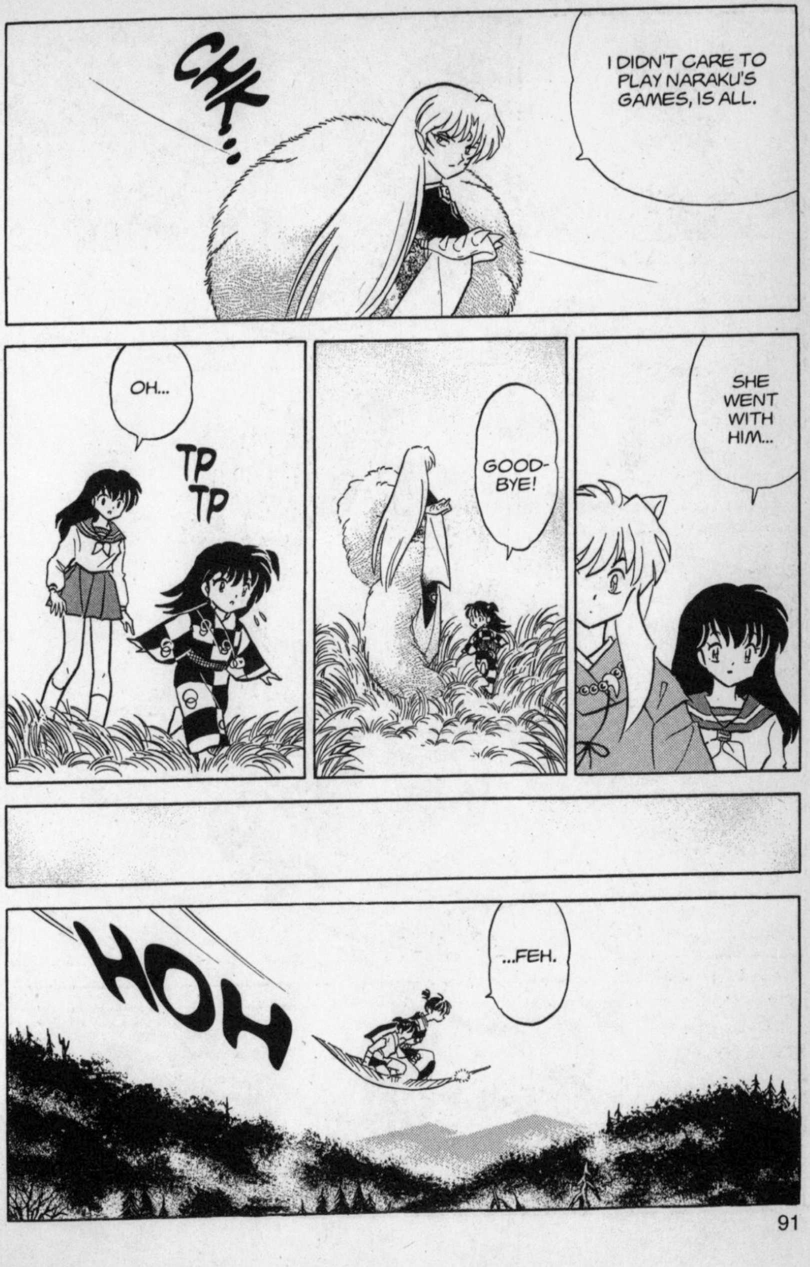
CHK...
I DIDN'T CARE TO PLAY NARAKU'S GAMES, IS ALL.
OH...
TP TP
GOOD-BYE!
SHE WENT WITH HIM...
HOH
...FEH.

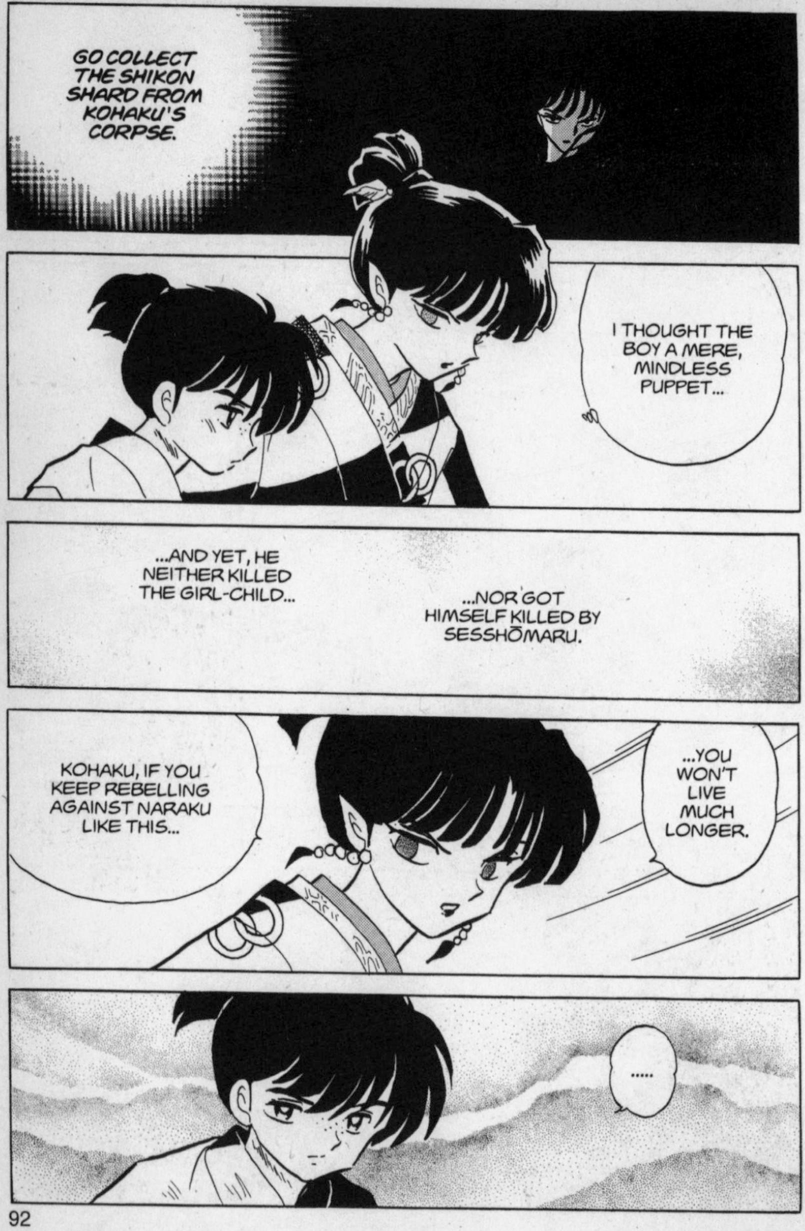
GO COLLECT THE SHIKON SHARD FROM KOHAKU'S CORPSE.
I THOUGHT THE BOY A MERE, MINDLESS PUPPET...
...AND YET, HE NEITHER KILLED THE GIRL-CHILD...
...NOR GOT HIMSELF KILLED BY SESSHŌMARU.
KOHAKU, IF YOU KEEP REBELLING AGAINST NARAKU LIKE THIS...
...YOU WON'T LIVE MUCH LONGER.
.....

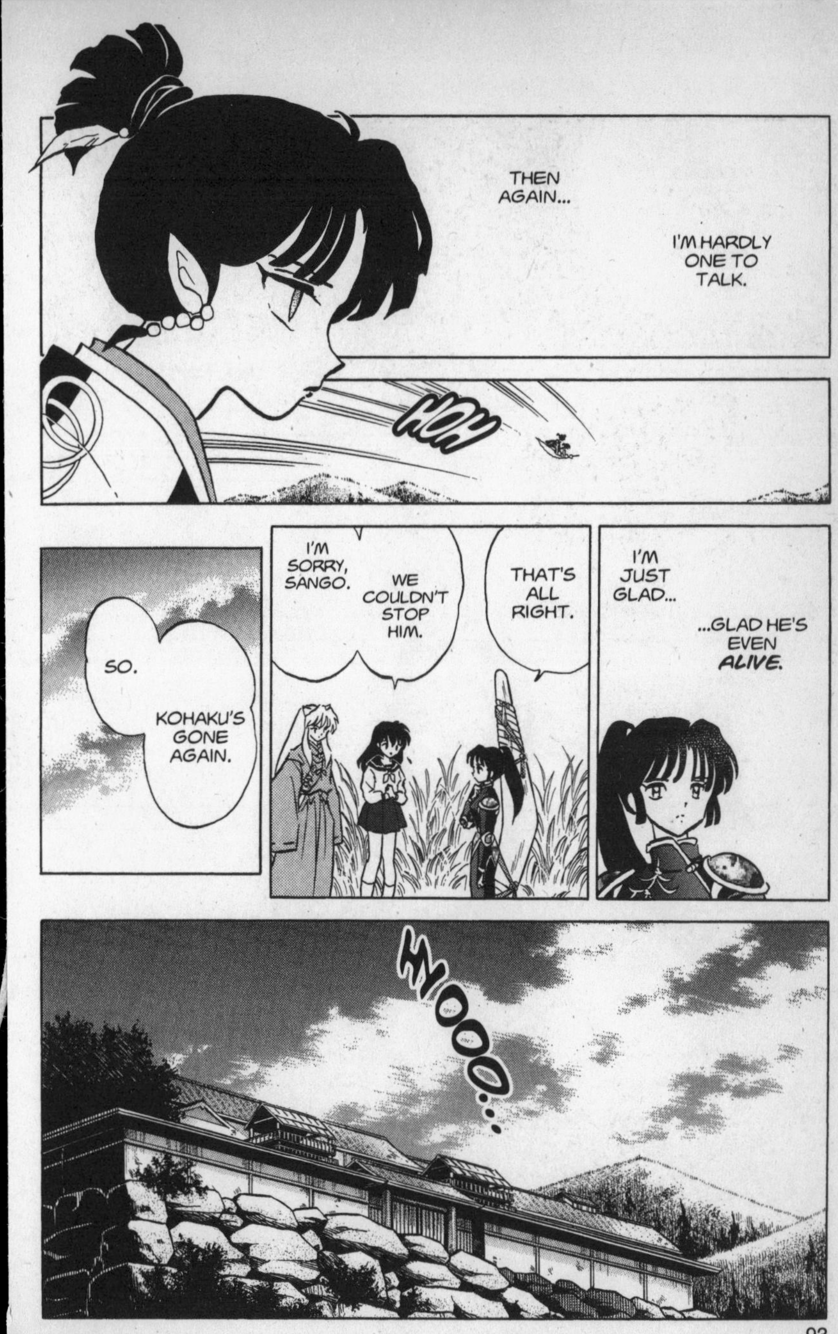
THEN AGAIN...
I'M HARDLY ONE TO TALK.
HOH
SO.
KOHAKU'S GONE AGAIN.
I'M SORRY, SANGO.
WE COULDN'T STOP HIM.
THAT'S ALL RIGHT.
I'M JUST GLAD...
...GLAD HE'S EVEN ALIVE.
HYOOO...

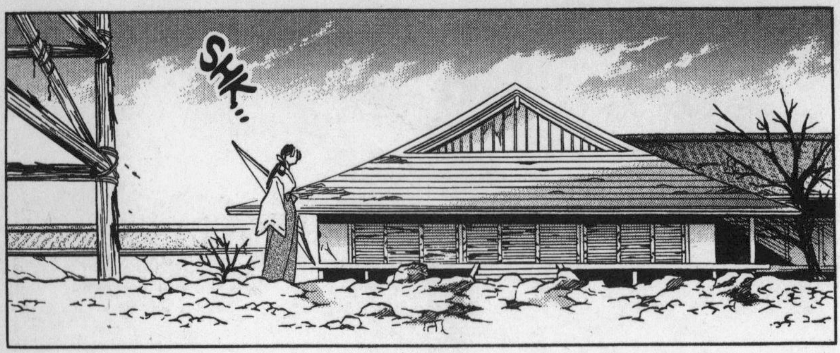
SHK...

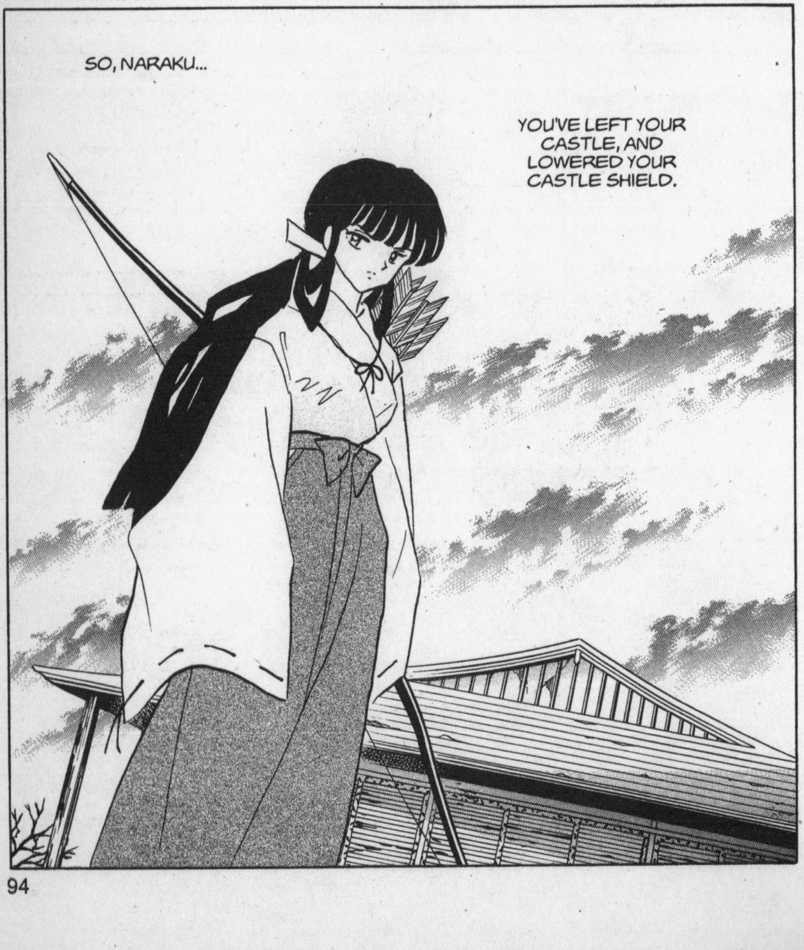
SO, NARAKU...
YOU'VE LEFT YOUR CASTLE, AND LOWERED YOUR CASTLE SHIELD.

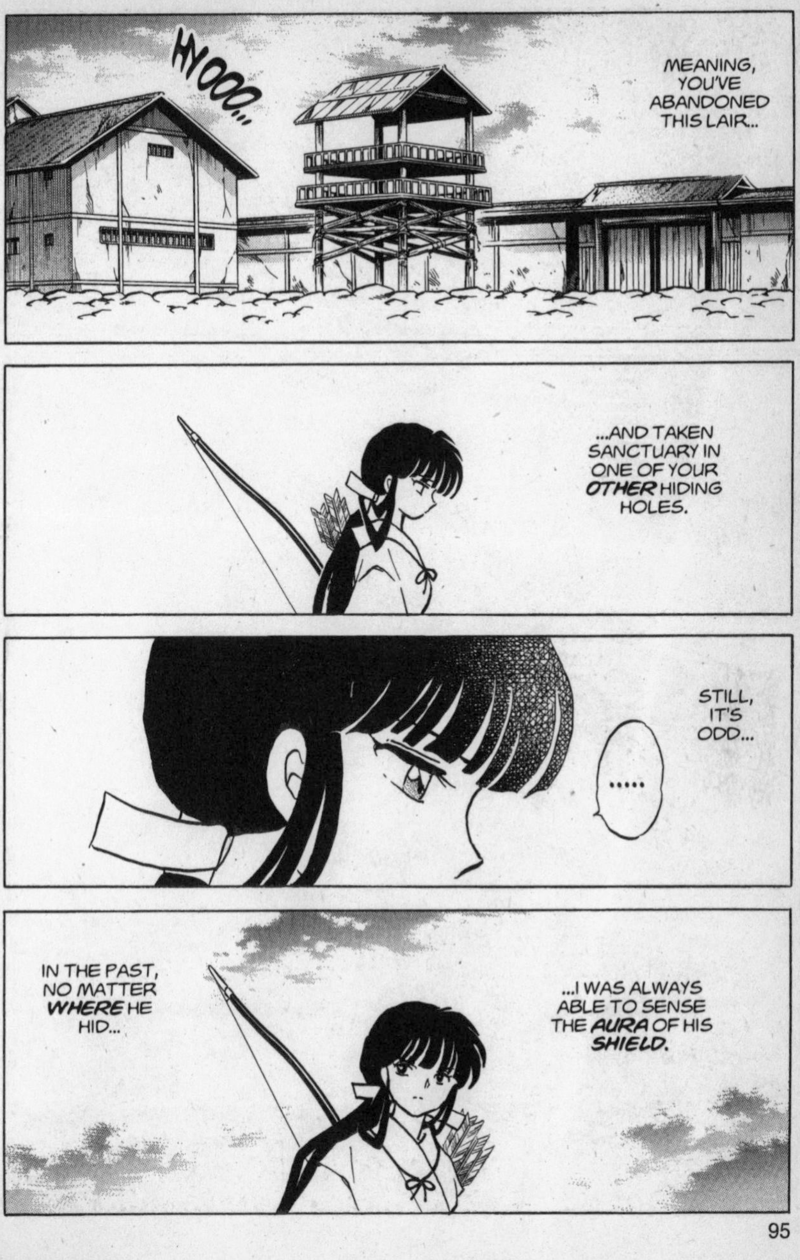
HYOOO...
MEANING, YOU'VE ABANDONED THIS LAIR...
...AND TAKEN SANCTUARY IN ONE OF YOUR OTHER HIDING HOLES.
STILL, IT'S ODD...
.....
IN THE PAST, NO MATTER WHERE HE HID...
...I WAS ALWAYS ABLE TO SENSE THE AURA OF HIS SHIELD.

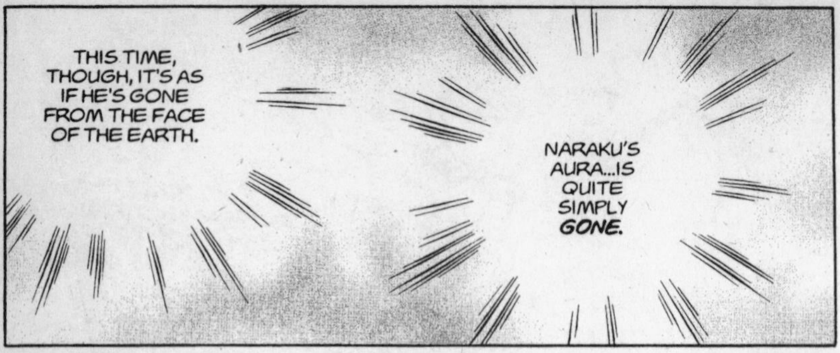
THIS TIME, THOUGH, IT'S AS IF HE'S GONE FROM THE FACE OF THE EARTH.
NARAKU'S AURA...IS QUITE SIMPLY *GONE.*

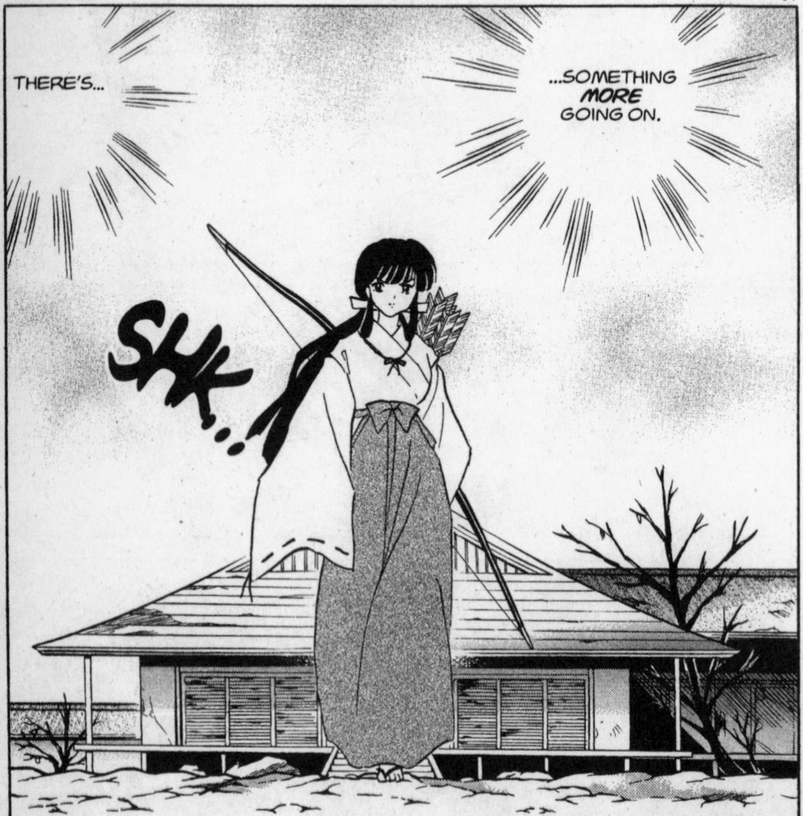
THERE'S...
...SOMETHING *MORE* GOING ON.
SHK...

SCROLL SIX
INTERMISSION

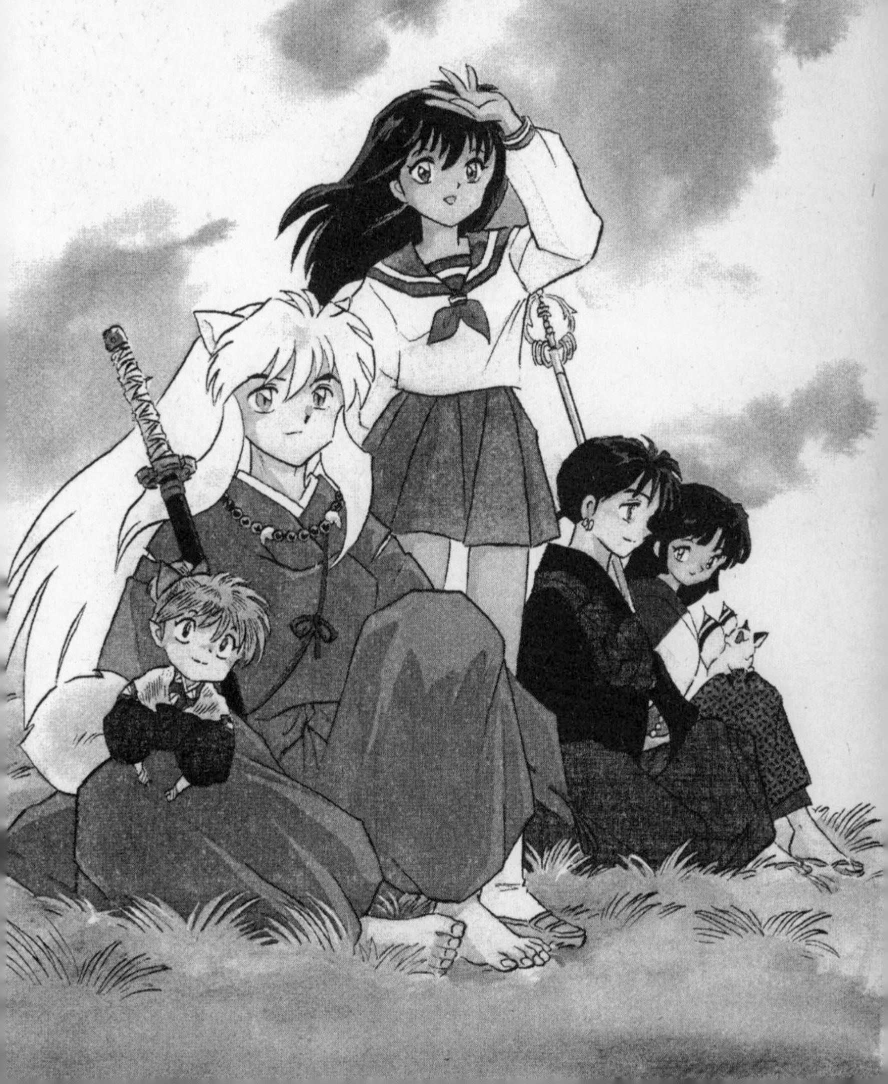

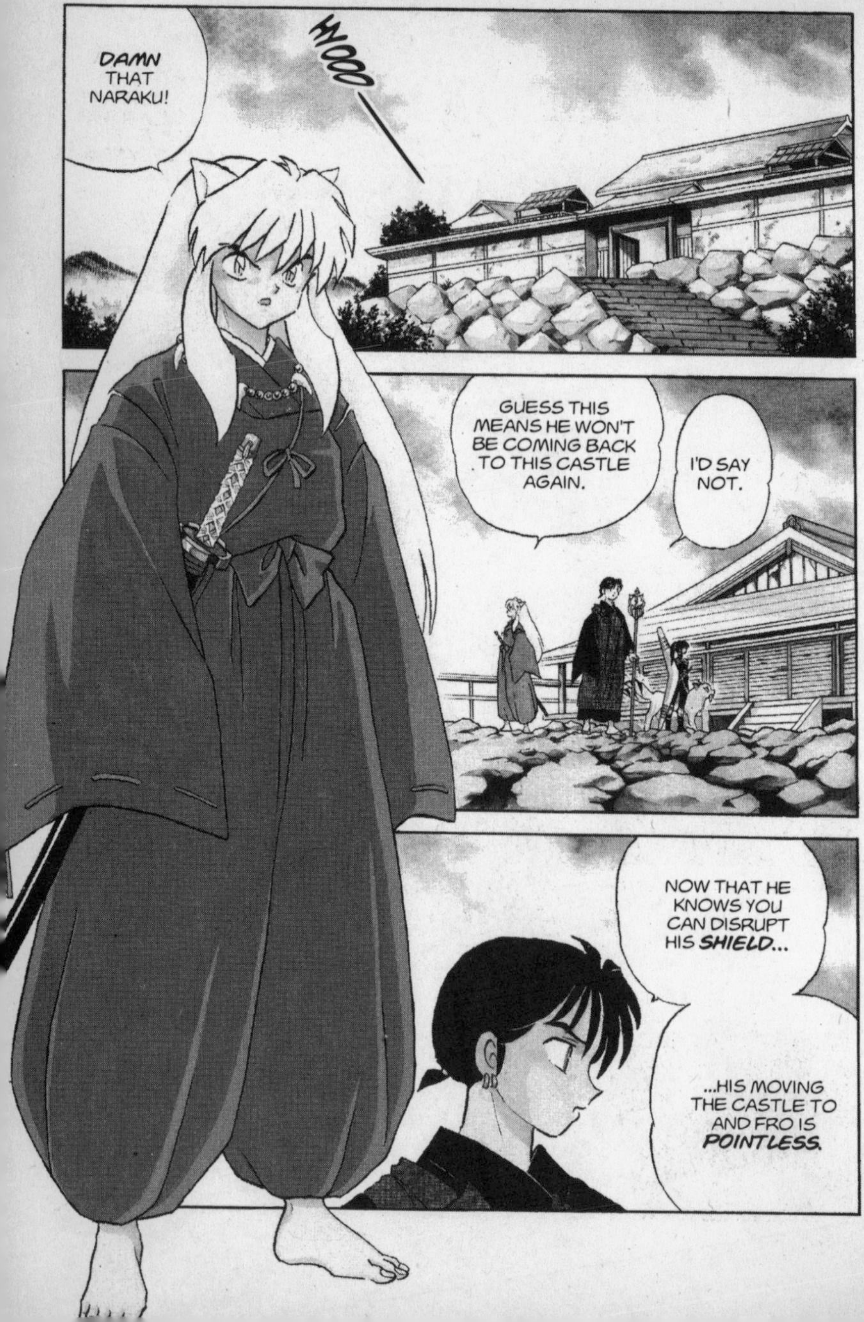
DAMN THAT NARAKU!
HYOOO
GUESS THIS MEANS HE WON'T BE COMING BACK TO THIS CASTLE AGAIN.
I'D SAY NOT.
NOW THAT HE KNOWS YOU CAN DISRUPT HIS SHIELD...
...HIS MOVING THE CASTLE TO AND FRO IS POINTLESS.

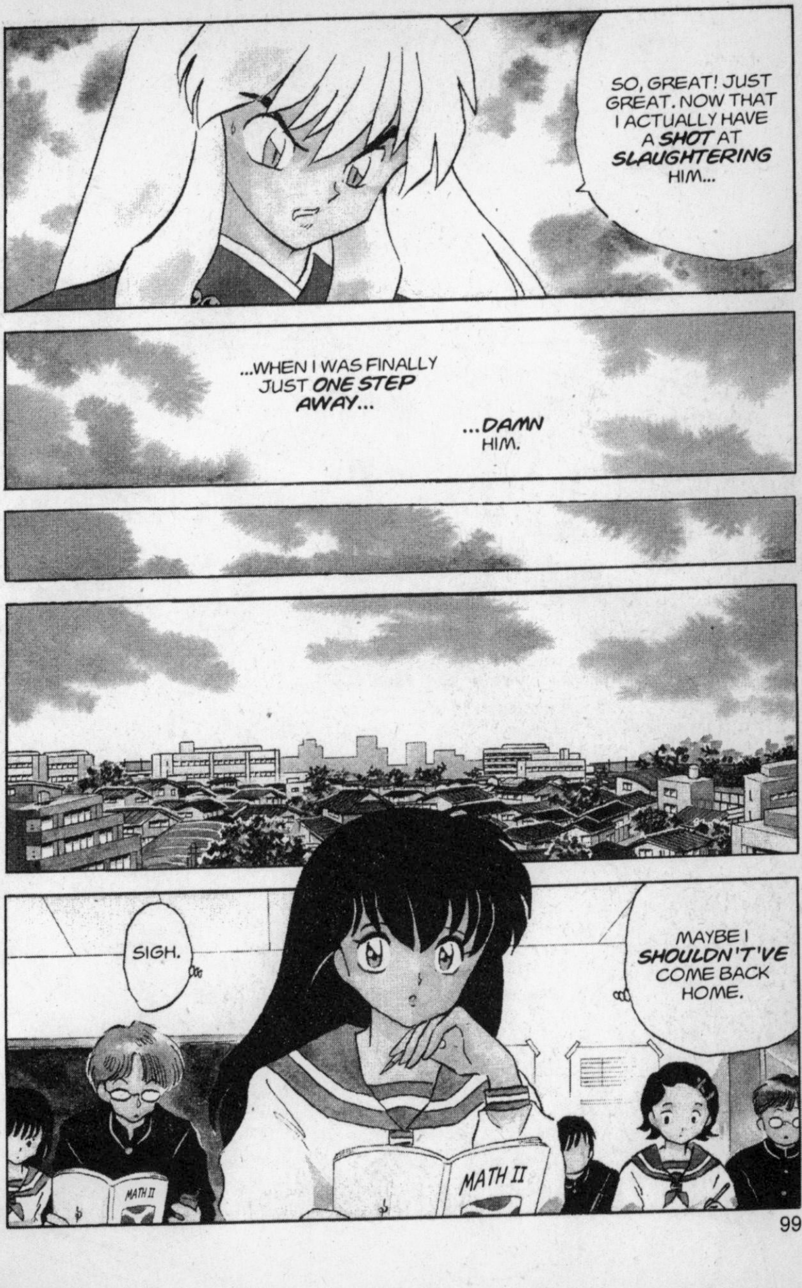
SO, GREAT! JUST GREAT. NOW THAT I ACTUALLY HAVE A **SHOT** AT **SLAUGHTERING** HIM...
...WHEN I WAS FINALLY JUST **ONE STEP AWAY**...
...**DAMN** HIM.
SIGH.
MAYBE I **SHOULDN'T'VE** COME BACK HOME.
MATH II
MATH II

I FEEL LIKE I'M *ABANDONING* INU-YASHA AND THE OTHERS...

THESE FORMULAS WILL BE ON THE MOCK EXAM THREE DAYS FROM NOW, SO LEARN THEM WELL.

$5. \left(-\frac{3}{4} x^2 Y\right) \times 4 XY\sim$

$6. \left(4 x^3 \pi -6 x^2 y\right)$

$7.$ BLANCH $\sqrt[3]{d}$

$N \infty a) -4\ell$ $(x^2 + 6x) -$

$4x^3 N \sim |k\Omega| 7$ $+5 \left(\frac{3}{5} \times Y\right)$

$D = \frac{1}{c} \frac{1}{c} \left(= \frac{1}{P} C\right.$

WHAT?!

MOCK EXAM?!

...KAGOME'S *LATE* AGAIN.

I *THOUGHT* SHE WAS COMING RIGHT BACK.

BUT SHE SAID SHE'D BE STAYING TWO TO THREE DAYS.

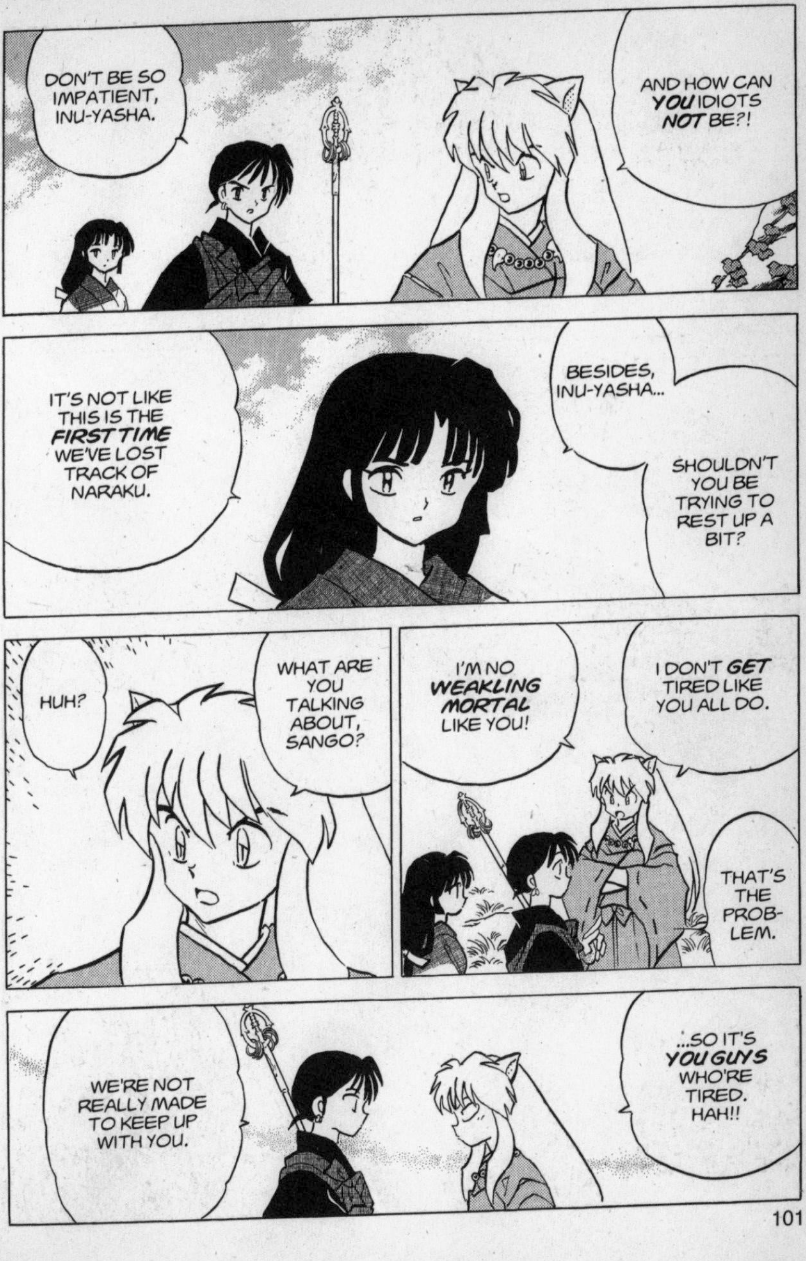
DON'T BE SO IMPATIENT, INU-YASHA.
AND HOW CAN **YOU** IDIOTS **NOT** BE?!
IT'S NOT LIKE THIS IS THE **FIRST TIME** WE'VE LOST TRACK OF NARAKU.
BESIDES, INU-YASHA...
SHOULDN'T YOU BE TRYING TO REST UP A BIT?
HUH?
WHAT ARE YOU TALKING ABOUT, SANGO?
I'M NO **WEAKLING MORTAL** LIKE YOU!
I DON'T **GET** TIRED LIKE YOU ALL DO.
THAT'S THE PROB-LEM.
WE'RE NOT REALLY MADE TO KEEP UP WITH YOU.
...SO IT'S **YOU GUYS** WHO'RE TIRED. HAH!!

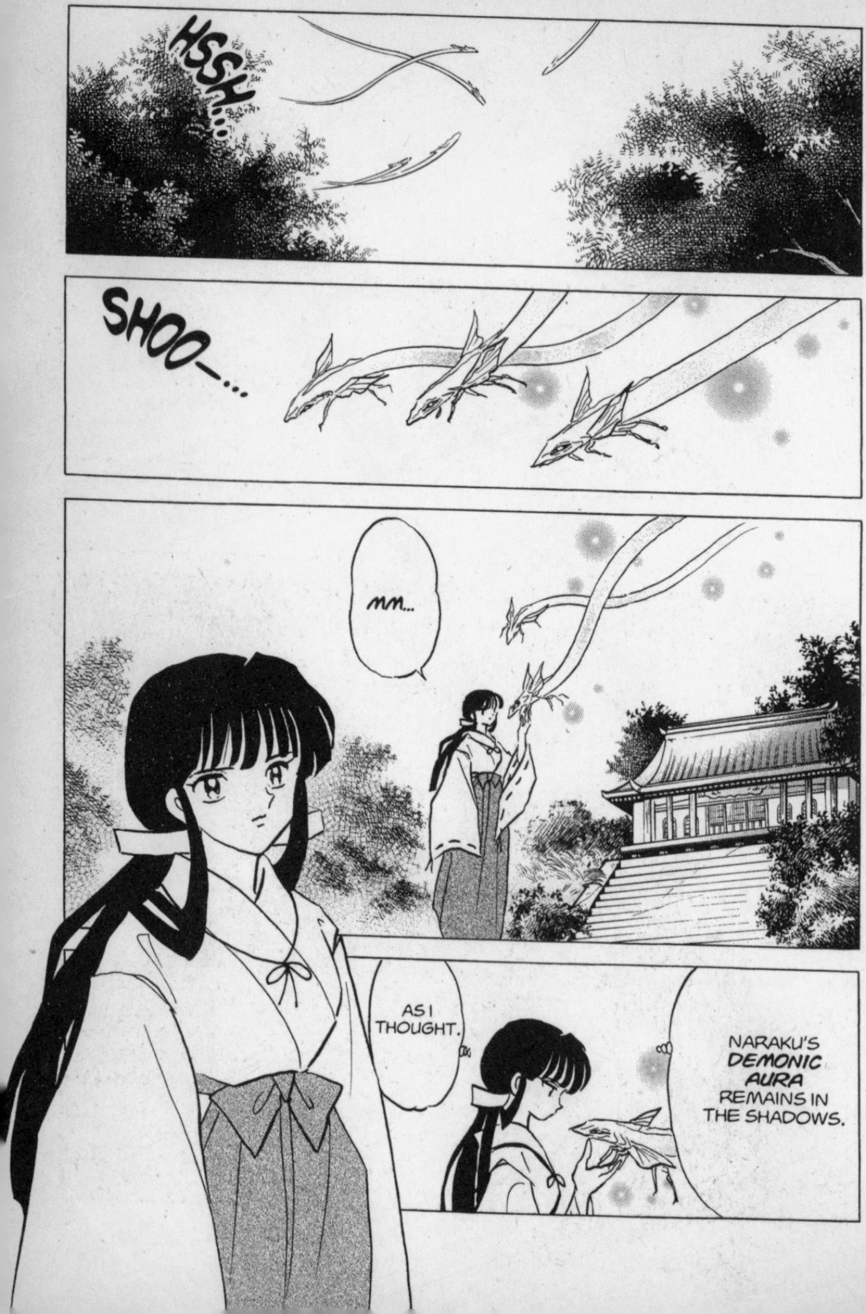
HSSH...
SHOO—...
mm...
AS I THOUGHT.
NARAKU'S **DEMONIC AURA** REMAINS IN THE SHADOWS.

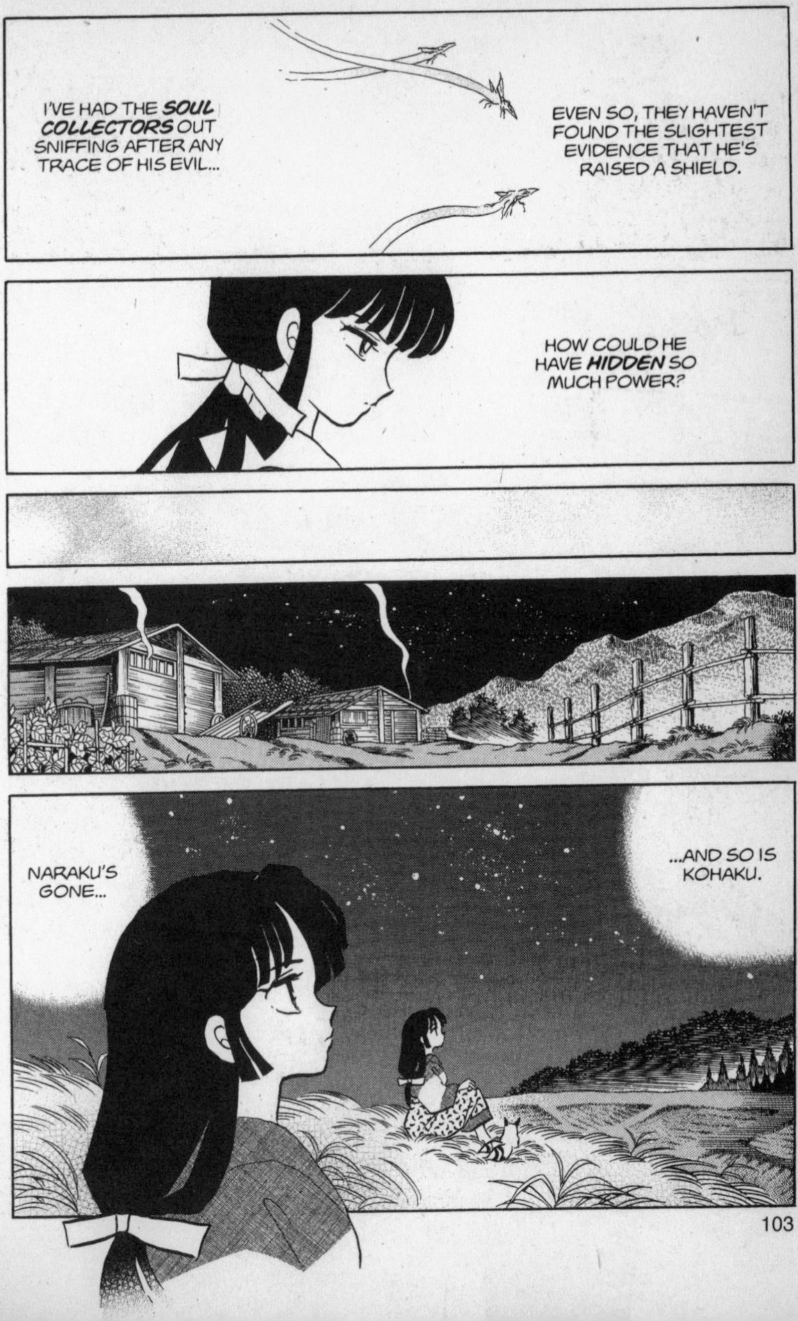
I'VE HAD THE SOUL COLLECTORS OUT SNIFFING AFTER ANY TRACE OF HIS EVIL...
EVEN SO, THEY HAVEN'T FOUND THE SLIGHTEST EVIDENCE THAT HE'S RAISED A SHIELD.
HOW COULD HE HAVE HIDDEN SO MUCH POWER?
NARAKU'S GONE...
...AND SO IS KOHAKU.

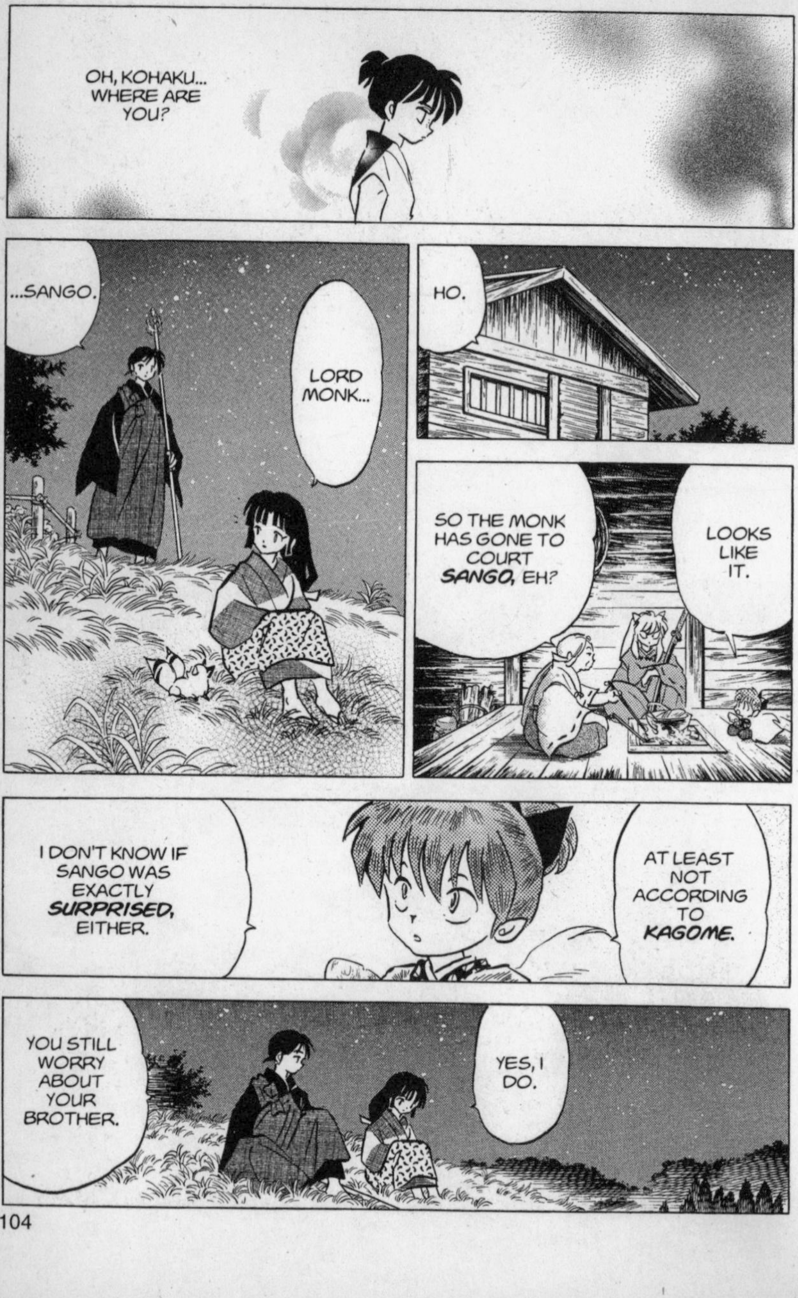
OH, KOHAKU... WHERE ARE YOU?
...SANGO.
LORD MONK...
HO.
SO THE MONK HAS GONE TO COURT SANGO, EH?
LOOKS LIKE IT.
I DON'T KNOW IF SANGO WAS EXACTLY SURPRISED, EITHER.
AT LEAST NOT ACCORDING TO KAGOME.
YOU STILL WORRY ABOUT YOUR BROTHER.
YES, I DO.

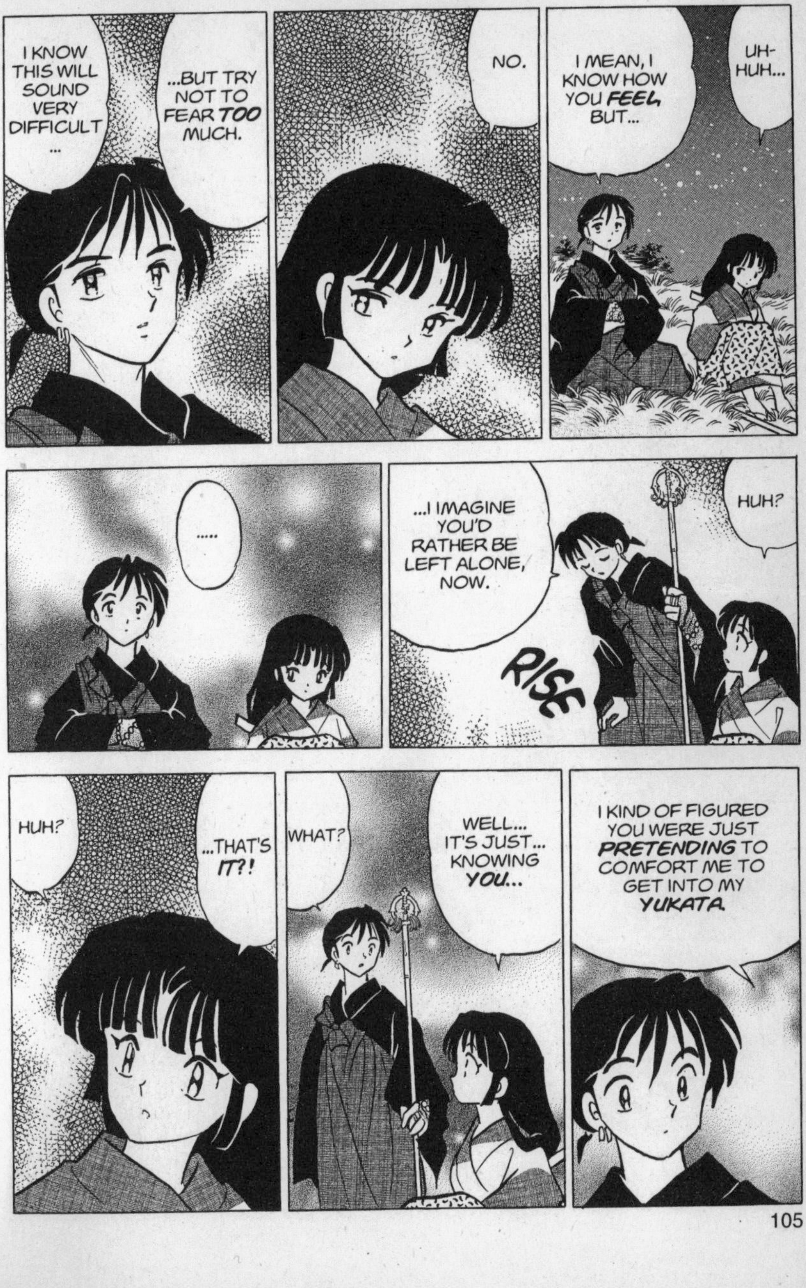
I KNOW THIS WILL SOUND VERY DIFFICULT ...
...BUT TRY NOT TO FEAR TOO MUCH.
NO.
I MEAN, I KNOW HOW YOU FEEL, BUT...
UH-HUH...
.....
...I IMAGINE YOU'D RATHER BE LEFT ALONE, NOW.
RISE
HUH?
HUH?
...THAT'S IT?!
WHAT?
WELL... IT'S JUST... KNOWING YOU...
I KIND OF FIGURED YOU WERE JUST PRETENDING TO COMFORT ME TO GET INTO MY YUKATA.

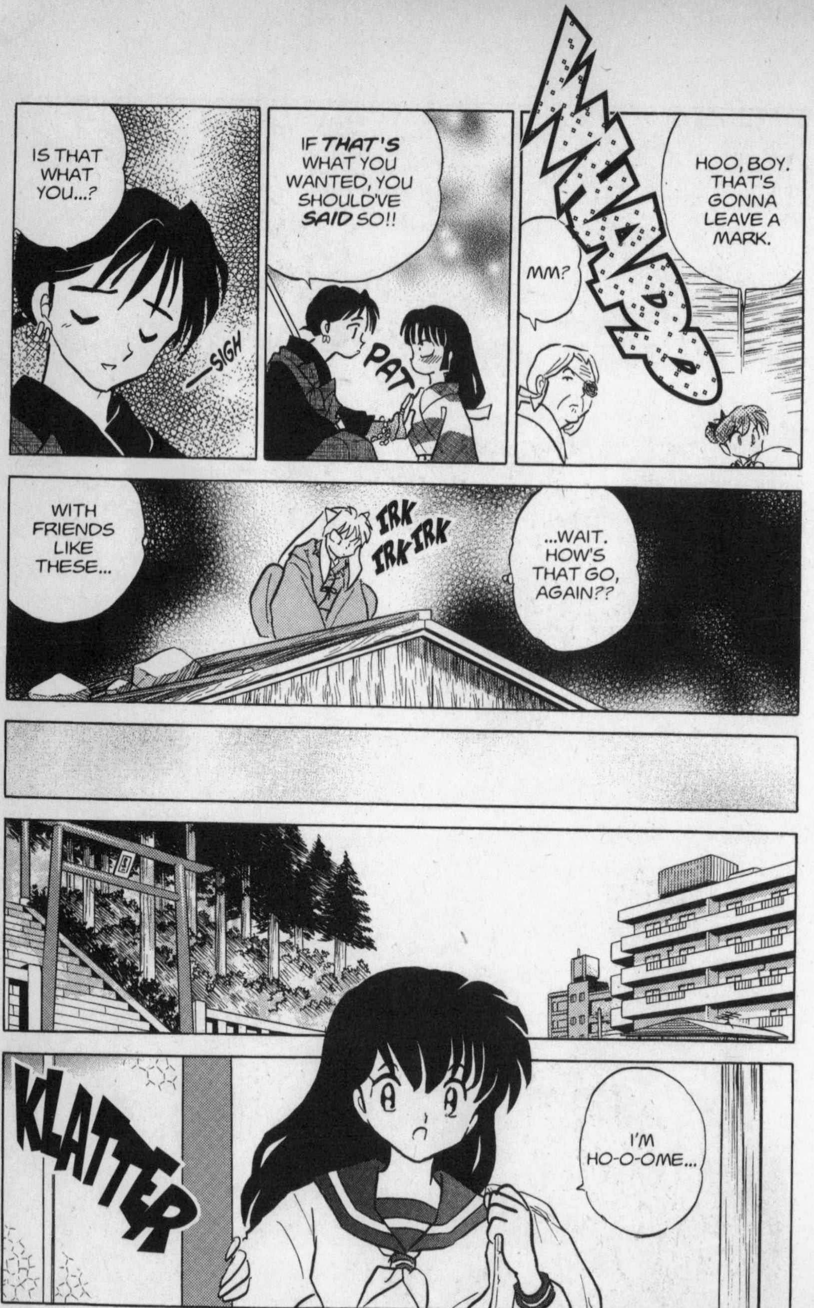
IS THAT WHAT YOU...?
—SIGH
IF **THAT'S** WHAT YOU WANTED, YOU SHOULD'VE **SAID** SO!!
PAT
WHAPP
MM?
HOO, BOY. THAT'S GONNA LEAVE A MARK.
WITH FRIENDS LIKE THESE...
IRK IRK-IRK
...WAIT. HOW'S THAT GO, AGAIN??
KLATTER
I'M HO-O-OME...

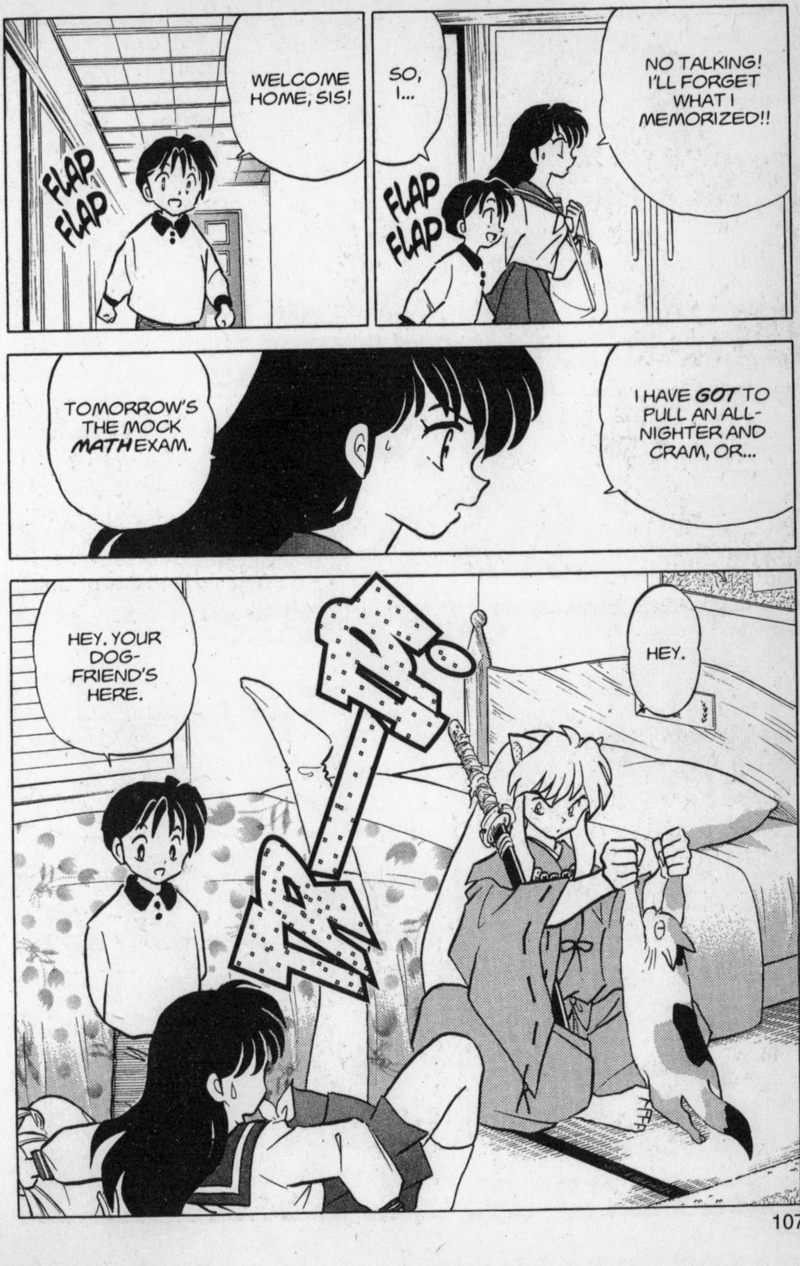
FLAP FLAP
WELCOME HOME, SIS!
SO, I...
FLAP FLAP
NO TALKING! I'LL FORGET WHAT I MEMORIZED!!
TOMORROW'S THE MOCK MATH EXAM.
I HAVE GOT TO PULL AN ALL-NIGHTER AND CRAM, OR...
HEY. YOUR DOG-FRIEND'S HERE.
HEY.

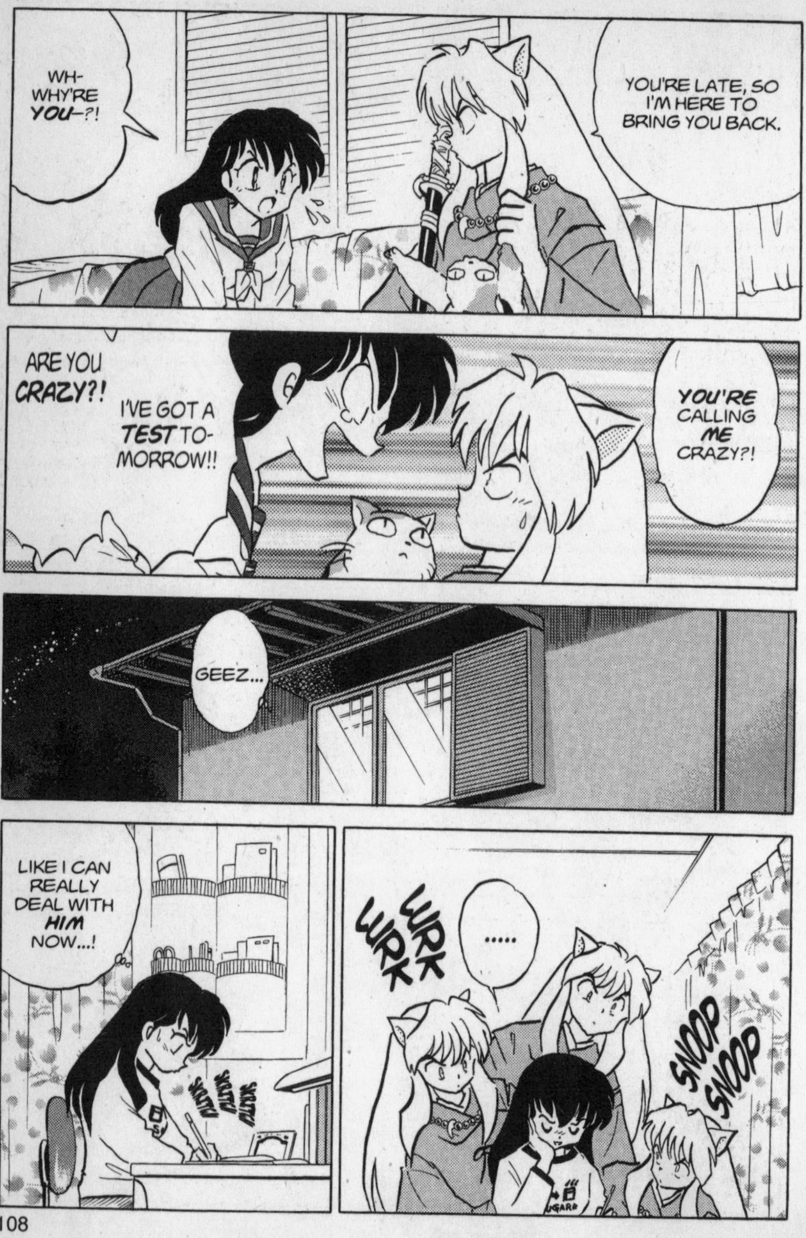
WH- WHY'RE **YOU**-?!
YOU'RE LATE, SO I'M HERE TO BRING YOU BACK.
ARE YOU **CRAZY?!**
I'VE GOT A **TEST** TO-MORROW!!
YOU'RE CALLING **ME** CRAZY?!
GEEZ...
LIKE I CAN REALLY DEAL WITH **HIM** NOW...!
SKRITCH SKRITCH SKRITCH
WRK WRK
.....
SNOOP SNOOP

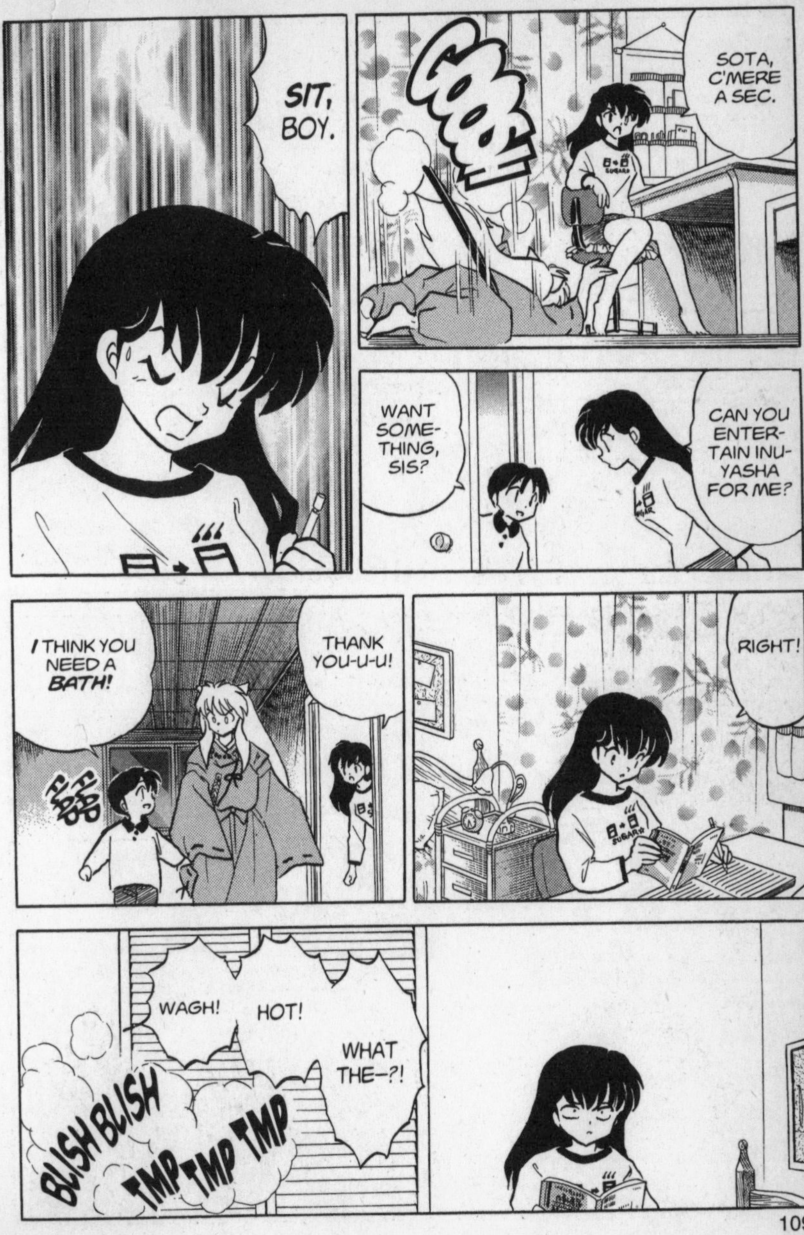
SIT, BOY.
GOOSH!
SOTA, C'MERE A SEC.
WANT SOME-THING, SIS?
CAN YOU ENTER-TAIN INU-YASHA FOR ME?
I THINK YOU NEED A BATH!
FLAP FLAP
THANK YOU-U-U!
RIGHT!
WAGH!
HOT!
WHAT THE-?!
BLISH BLISH
TMP TMP TMP

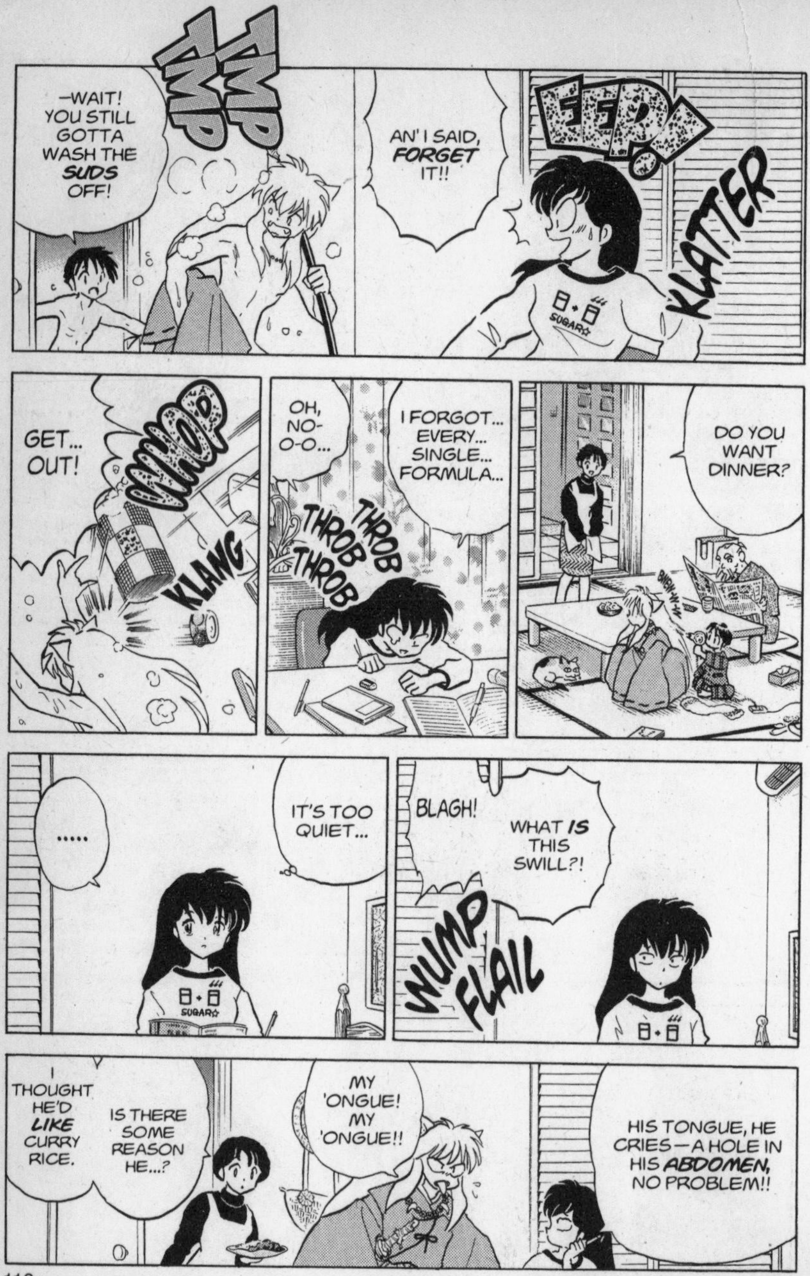

TMP TMP
—WAIT! YOU STILL GOTTA WASH THE SUDS OFF!
AN' I SAID, FORGET IT!!
EEP!
KLATTER
GET... OUT!
WHOP
KLANG
OH, NO-O-O...
I FORGOT... EVERY... SINGLE... FORMULA...
THROB THROB THROB
DO YOU WANT DINNER?
.....
IT'S TOO QUIET...
BLAGH!
WHAT IS THIS SWILL?!
WUMP FLAIL
I THOUGHT HE'D LIKE CURRY RICE.
IS THERE SOME REASON HE...?
MY 'ONGUE! MY 'ONGUE!!
HIS TONGUE, HE CRIES—A HOLE IN HIS ABDOMEN, NO PROBLEM!!

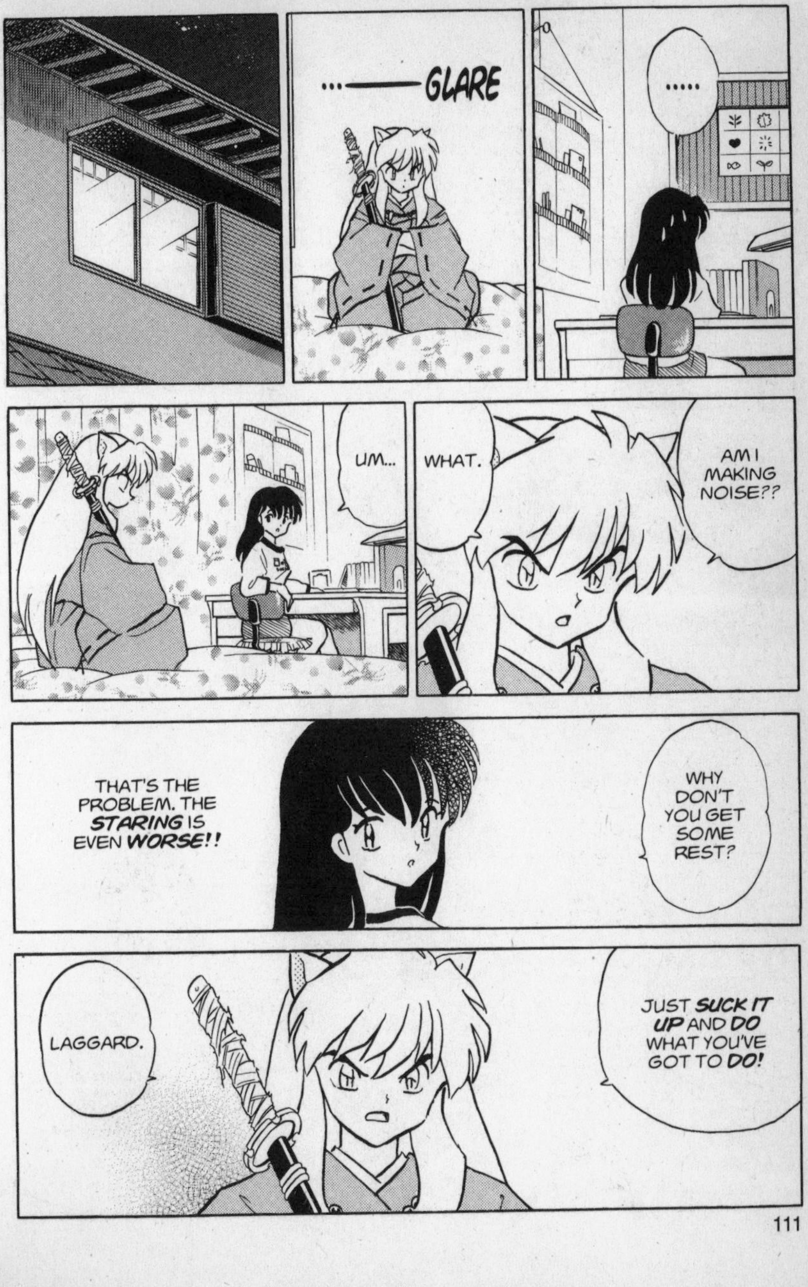
...——GLARE
.....
UM...
WHAT.
AM I MAKING NOISE??
THAT'S THE PROBLEM. THE **STARING** IS EVEN **WORSE!!**
WHY DON'T YOU GET SOME REST?
LAGGARD.
JUST **SUCK IT UP** AND **DO** WHAT YOU'VE GOT TO **DO!**

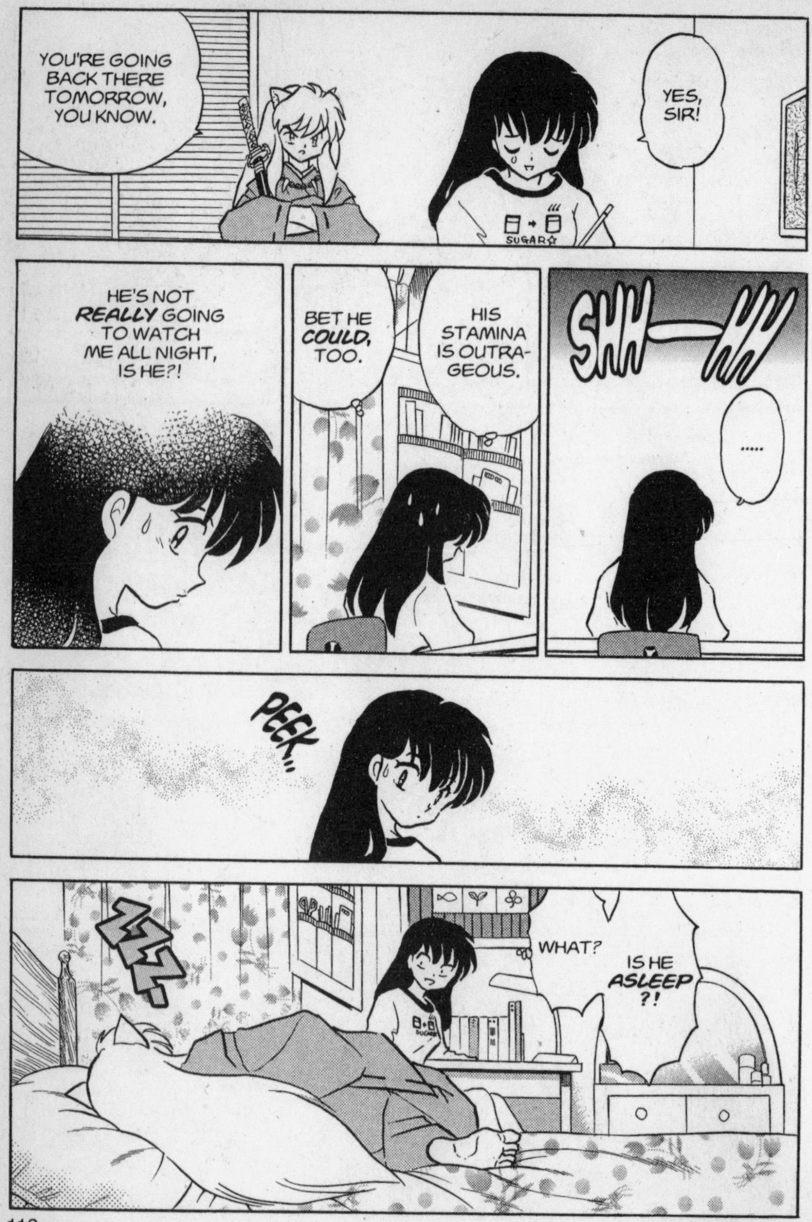
YOU'RE GOING BACK THERE TOMORROW, YOU KNOW.
YES, SIR!
SUGAR☆
HE'S NOT **REALLY** GOING TO WATCH ME ALL NIGHT, IS HE?!
BET HE **COULD,** TOO.
HIS STAMINA IS OUTRAGEOUS.
SHH—HH
......
PEEK...
ZZZ
WHAT?
IS HE **ASLEEP** ?!

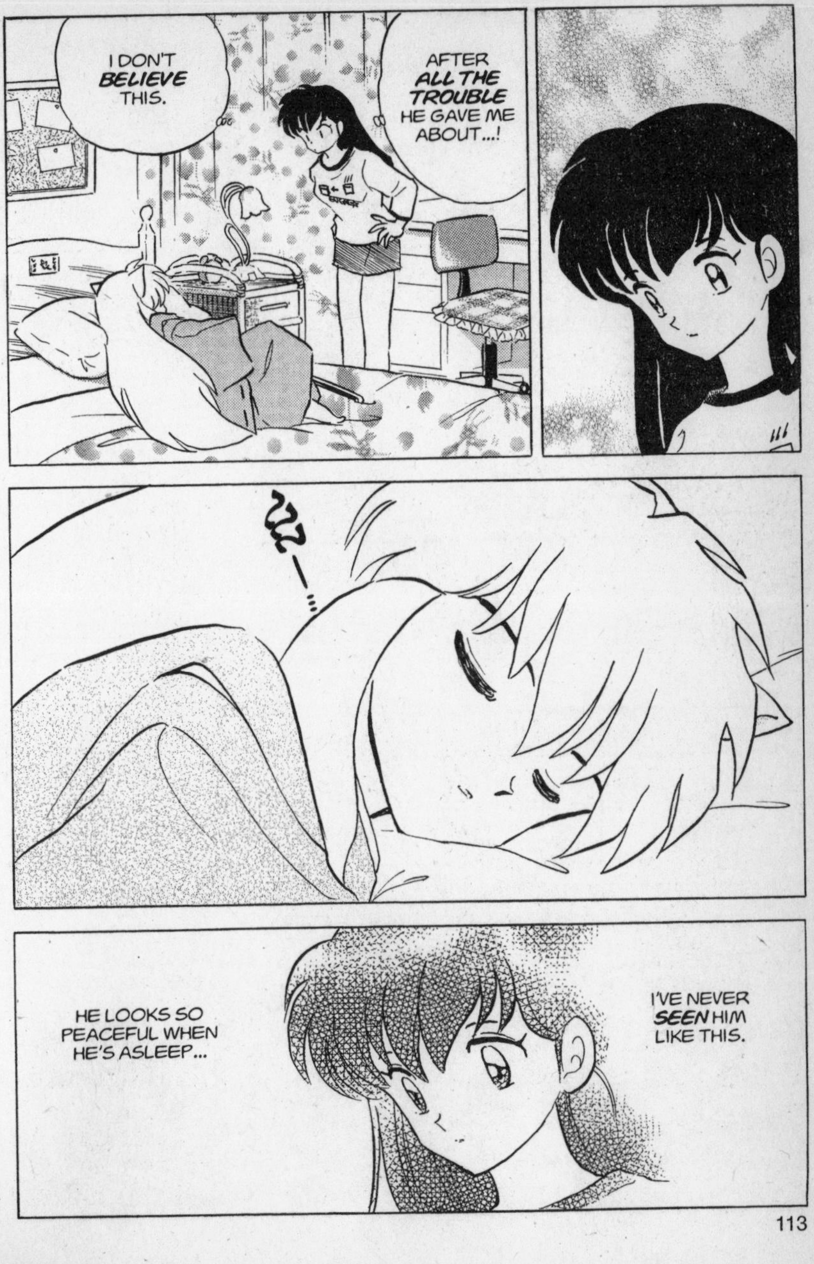
I DON'T **BELIEVE** THIS.
AFTER **ALL THE TROUBLE** HE GAVE ME ABOUT...!
ZZZ—...
HE LOOKS SO PEACEFUL WHEN HE'S ASLEEP...
I'VE NEVER **SEEN** HIM LIKE THIS.

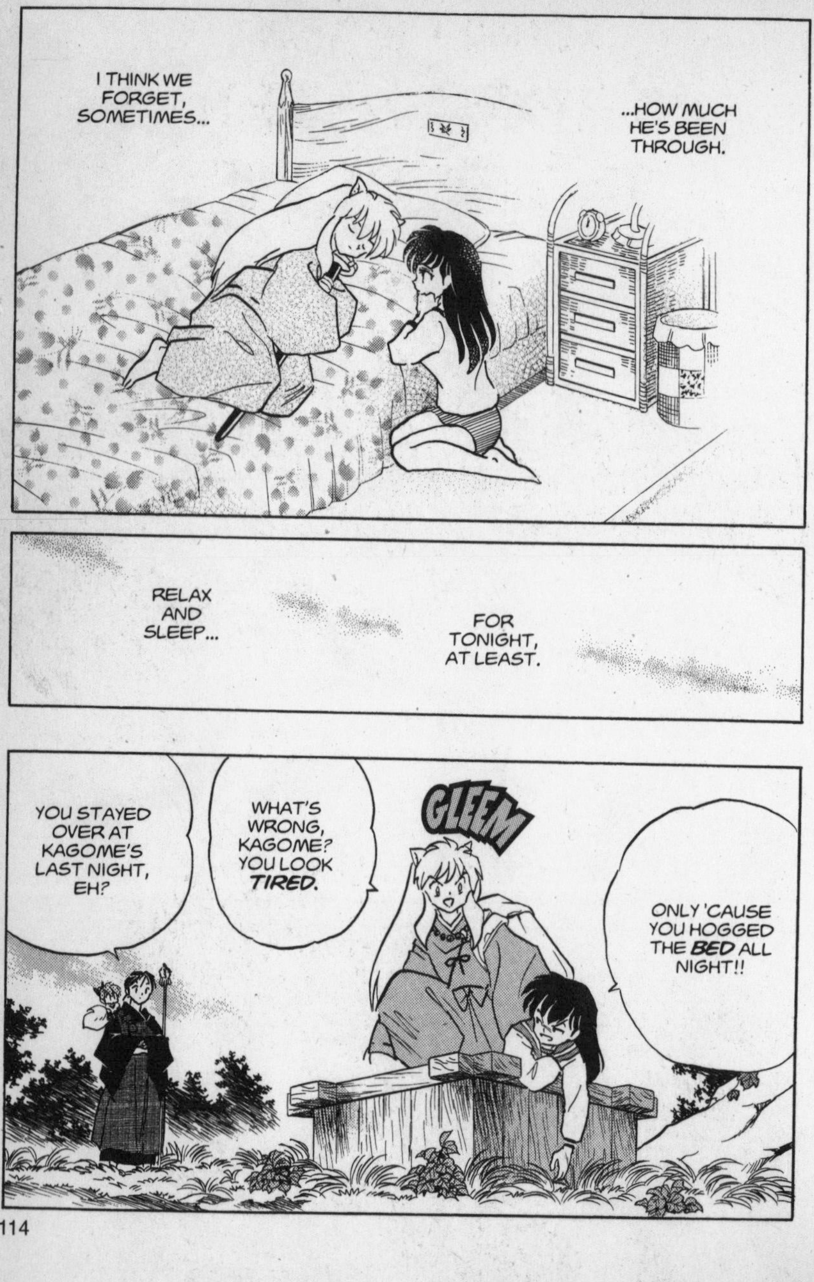
I THINK WE FORGET, SOMETIMES...
...HOW MUCH HE'S BEEN THROUGH.
RELAX AND SLEEP...
FOR TONIGHT, AT LEAST.
YOU STAYED OVER AT KAGOME'S LAST NIGHT, EH?
WHAT'S WRONG, KAGOME? YOU LOOK TIRED.
GLEEM
ONLY 'CAUSE YOU HOGGED THE BED ALL NIGHT!!

SCROLL SEVEN
THE MONSTER IN THE RUINS

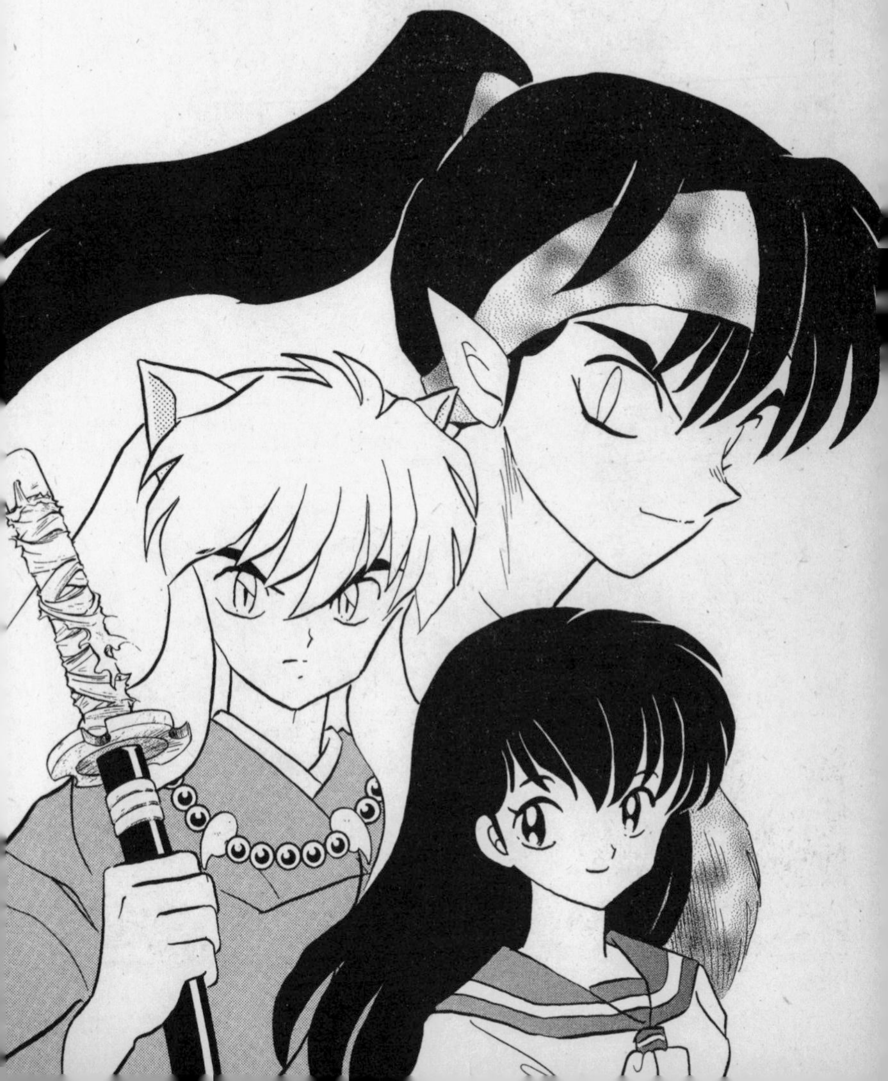

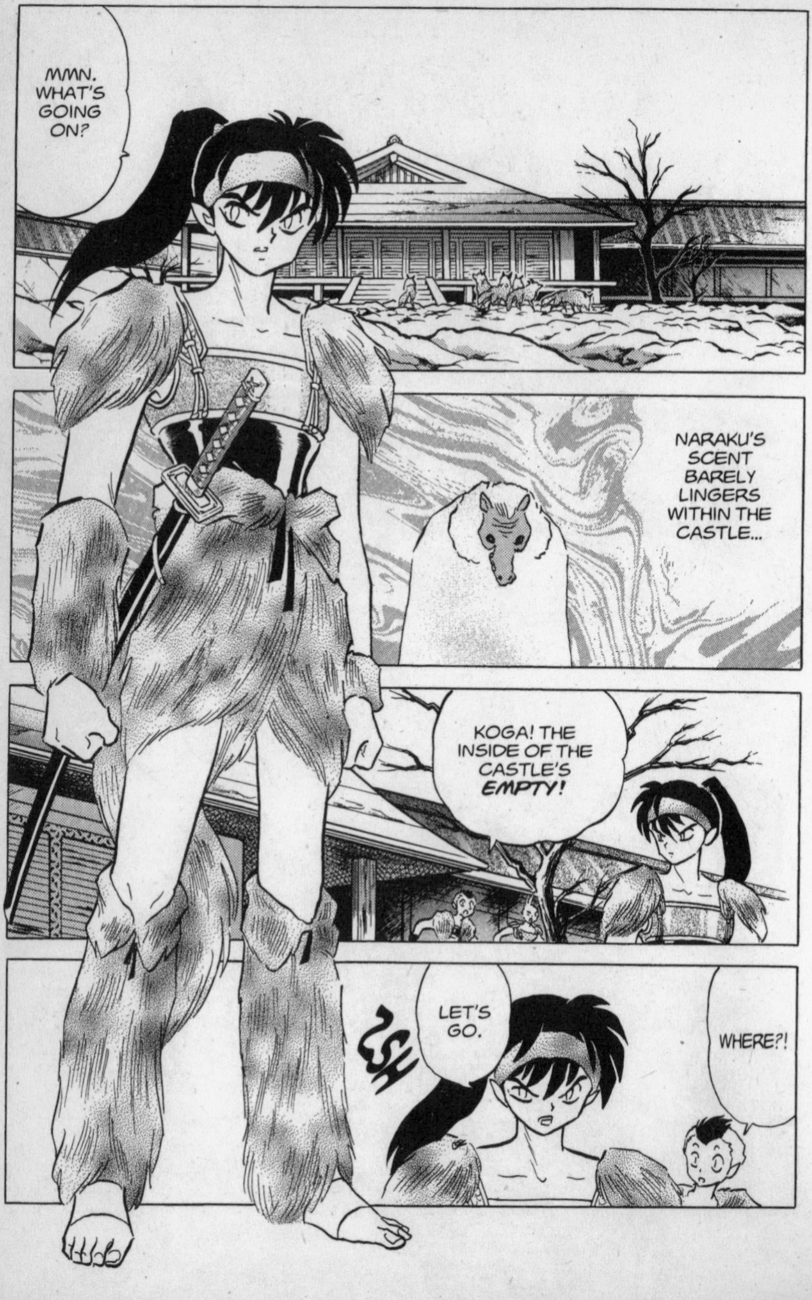
MMN. WHAT'S GOING ON?
NARAKU'S SCENT BARELY LINGERS WITHIN THE CASTLE...
KOGA! THE INSIDE OF THE CASTLE'S *EMPTY!*
ZSH
LET'S GO.
WHERE?!

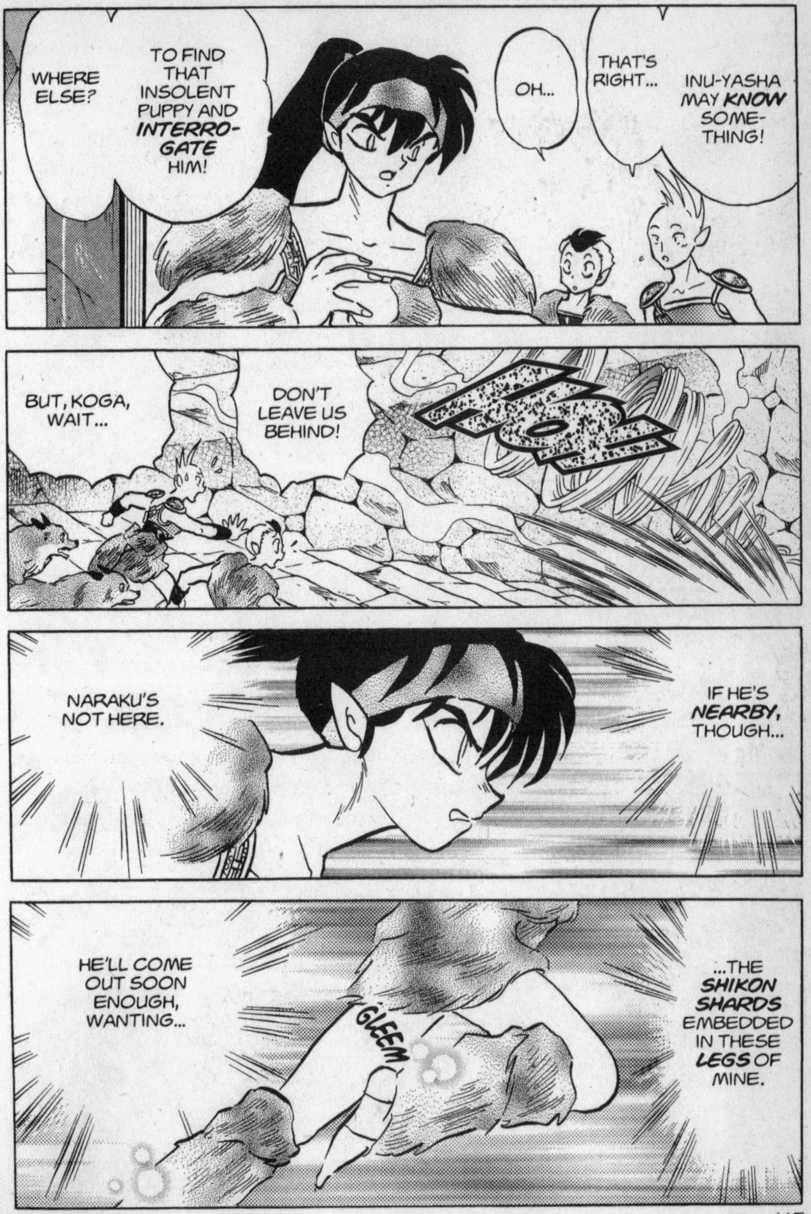
WHERE ELSE?
TO FIND THAT INSOLENT PUPPY AND INTERROGATE HIM!
OH...
THAT'S RIGHT...
INU-YASHA MAY KNOW SOMETHING!
BUT, KOGA, WAIT...
DON'T LEAVE US BEHIND!
HOP!
NARAKU'S NOT HERE.
IF HE'S NEARBY, THOUGH...
HE'LL COME OUT SOON ENOUGH, WANTING...
GLEEM
...THE SHIKON SHARDS EMBEDDED IN THESE LEGS OF MINE.

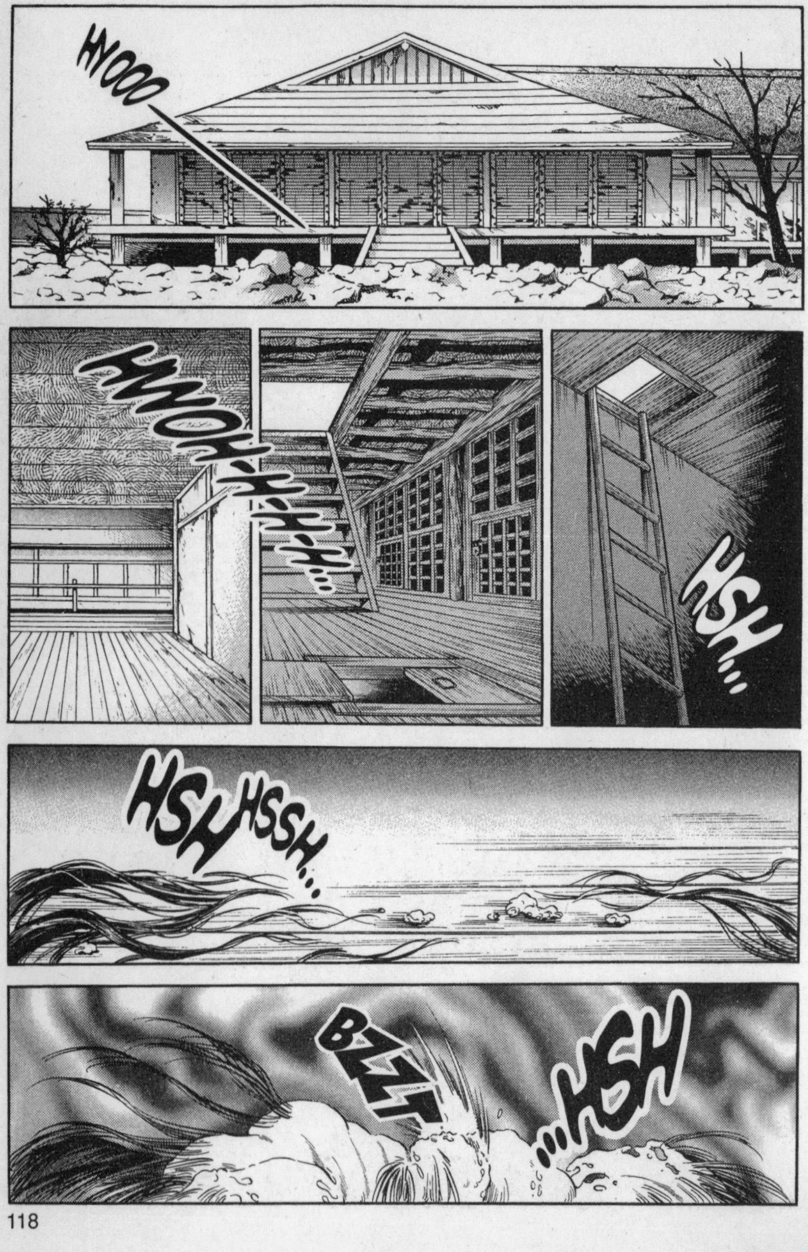
HYOOO—
HWOH-H-H-H...
HSH...
HSH HSSH...
BZZT
...HSH

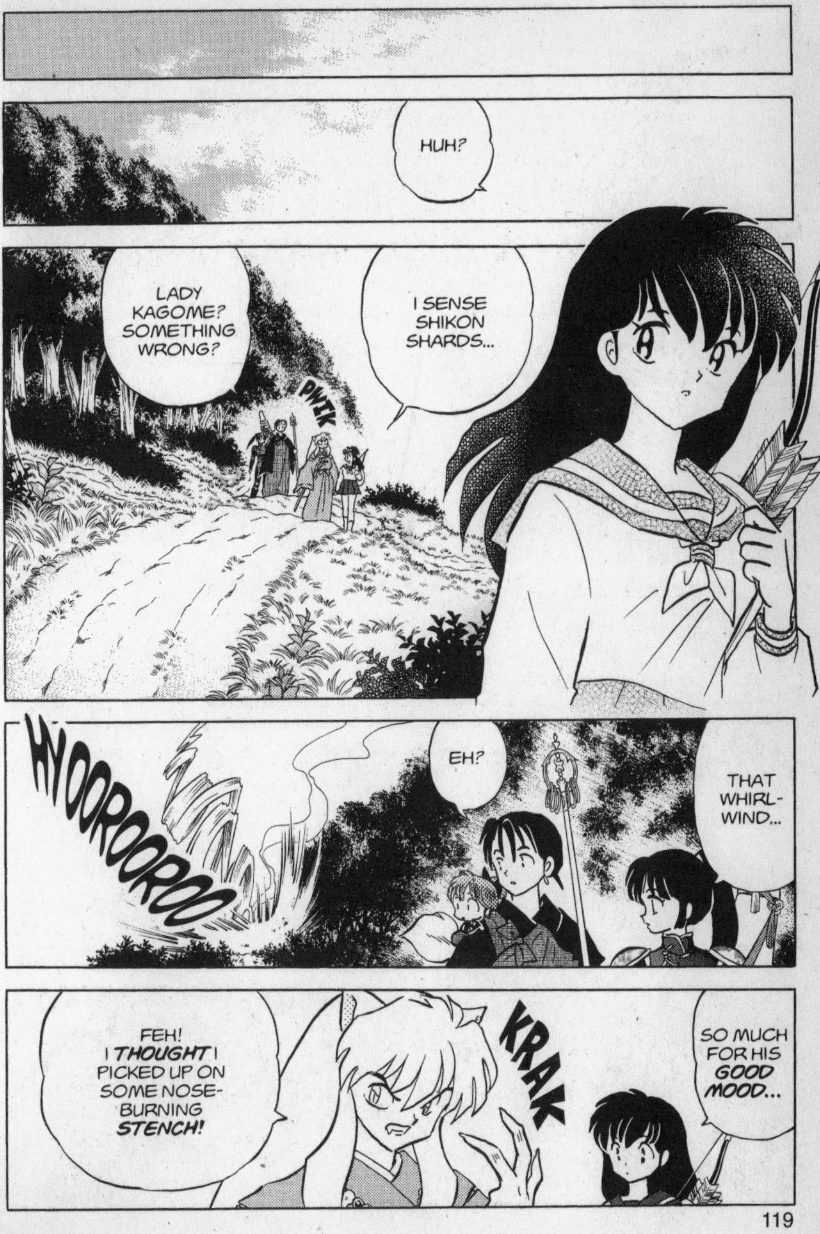

HUH?
LADY KAGOME? SOMETHING WRONG?
PWIK
I SENSE SHIKON SHARDS...
HYOOROOROO
EH?
THAT WHIRL-WIND...
FEH! I *THOUGHT* I PICKED UP ON SOME NOSE-BURNING *STENCH!*
KRAK
SO MUCH FOR HIS *GOOD MOOD*...

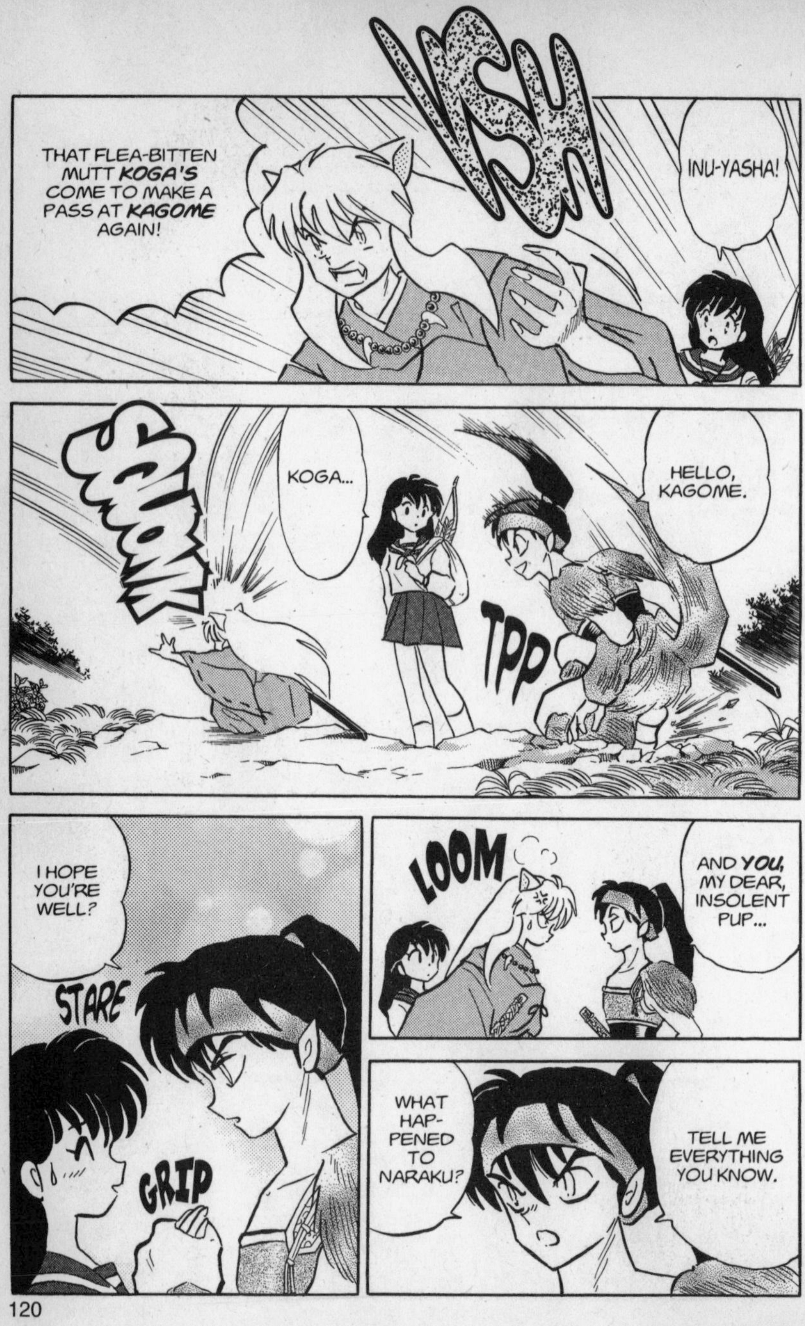
VYSH
THAT FLEA-BITTEN MUTT KOGA'S COME TO MAKE A PASS AT KAGOME AGAIN!
INU-YASHA!
SCHONK
KOGA...
HELLO, KAGOME.
TPP
I HOPE YOU'RE WELL?
STARE
GRIP
LOOM
AND YOU, MY DEAR, INSOLENT PUP...
WHAT HAP-PENED TO NARAKU?
TELL ME EVERYTHING YOU KNOW.

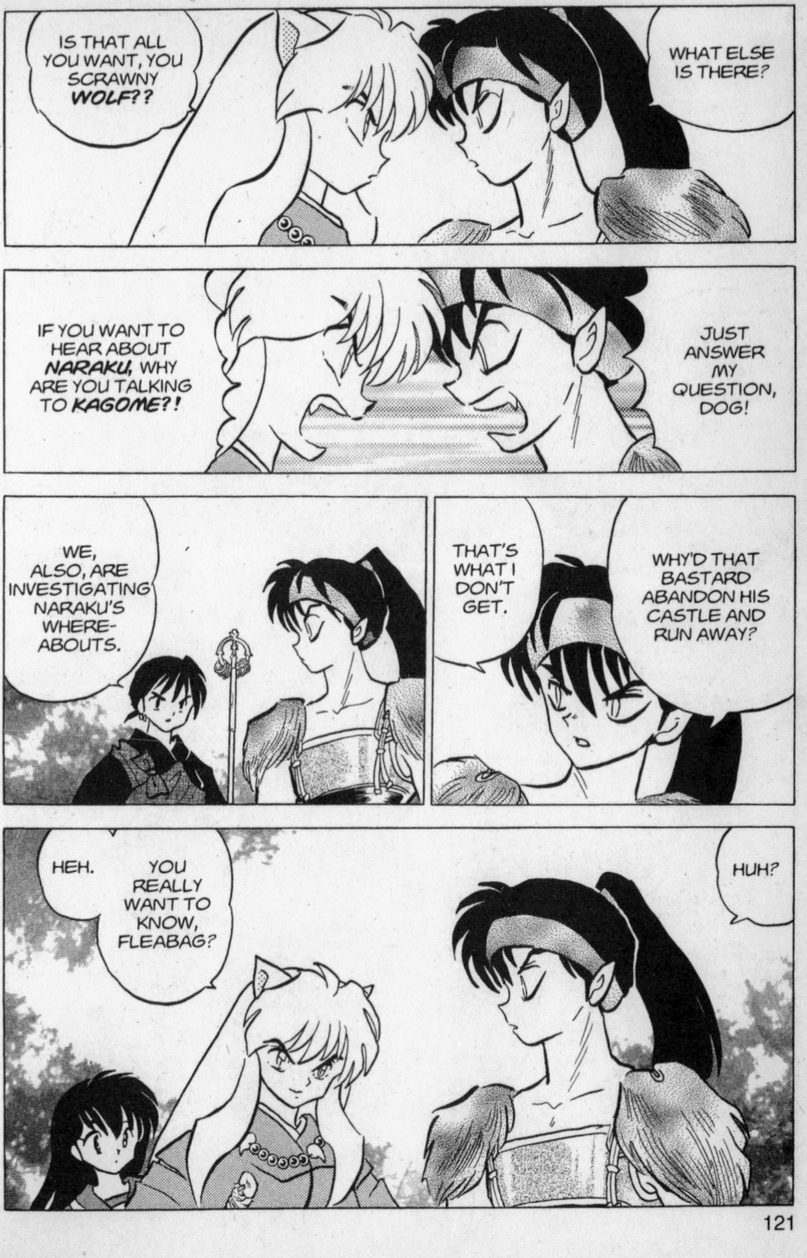
IS THAT ALL YOU WANT, YOU SCRAWNY **WOLF??**
WHAT ELSE IS THERE?
IF YOU WANT TO HEAR ABOUT **NARAKU,** WHY ARE YOU TALKING TO **KAGOME?!**
JUST ANSWER MY QUESTION, DOG!
WE, ALSO, ARE INVESTIGATING NARAKU'S WHERE-ABOUTS.
THAT'S WHAT I DON'T GET.
WHY'D THAT BASTARD ABANDON HIS CASTLE AND RUN AWAY?
HEH.
YOU REALLY WANT TO KNOW, FLEABAG?
HUH?

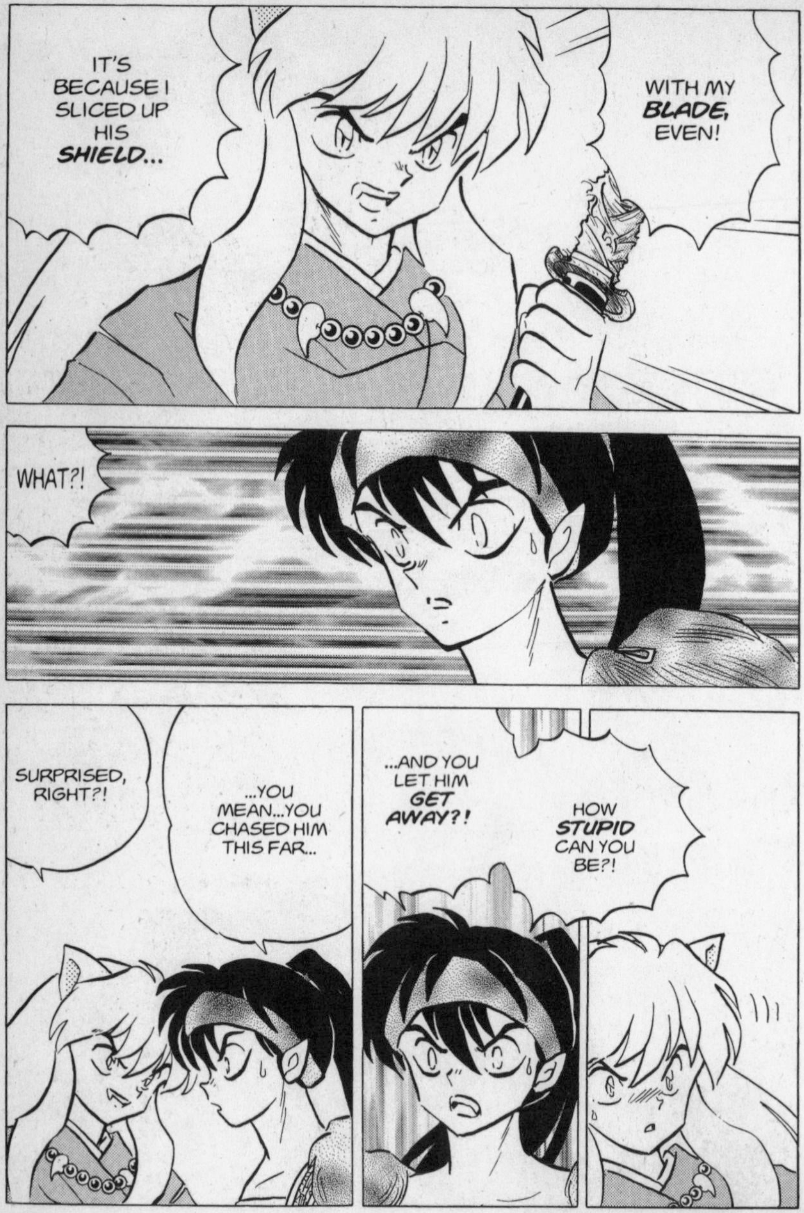
IT'S BECAUSE I SLICED UP HIS SHIELD...
WITH MY BLADE, EVEN!
WHAT?!
SURPRISED, RIGHT?!
...YOU MEAN...YOU CHASED HIM THIS FAR...
...AND YOU LET HIM GET AWAY?!
HOW STUPID CAN YOU BE?!

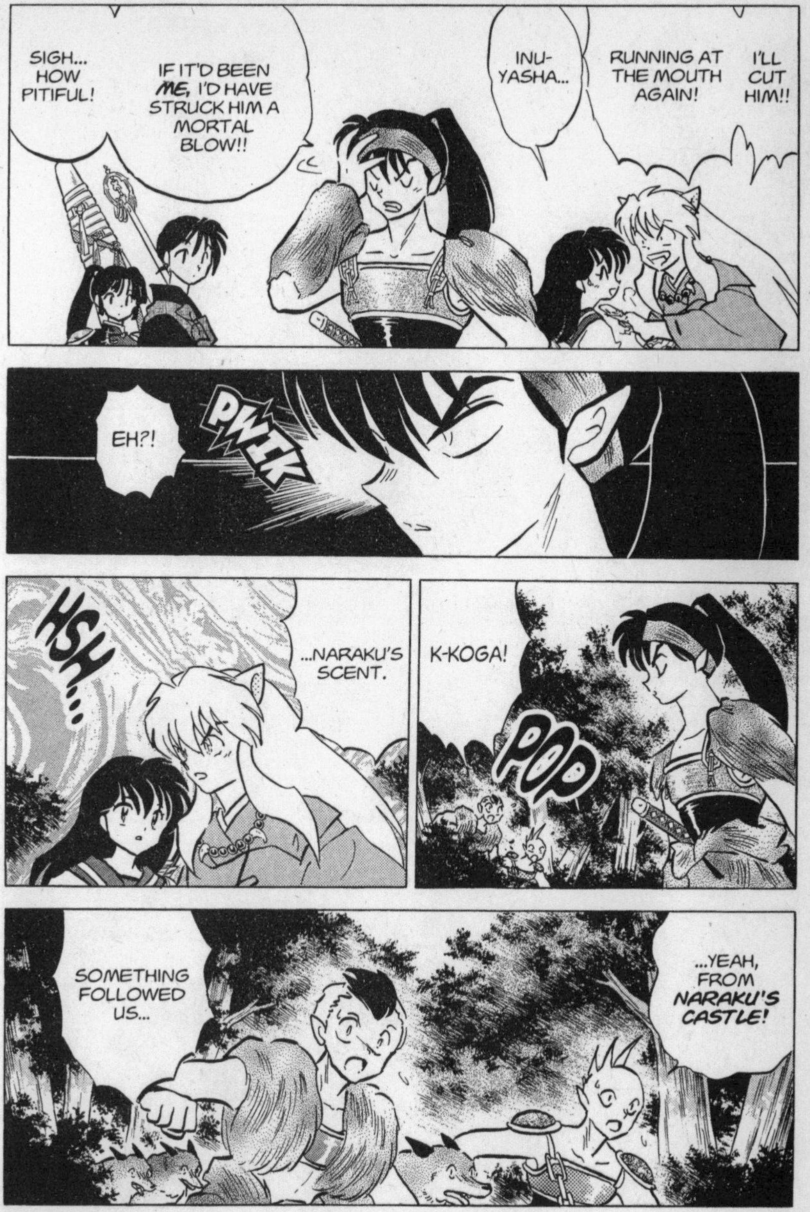
SIGH... HOW PITIFUL!
IF IT'D BEEN ME, I'D HAVE STRUCK HIM A MORTAL BLOW!!
INU-YASHA...
RUNNING AT THE MOUTH AGAIN!
I'LL CUT HIM!!
EH?!
PWIK
HSH...
...NARAKU'S SCENT.
K-KOGA!
POP
SOMETHING FOLLOWED US...
...YEAH, FROM NARAKU'S CASTLE!

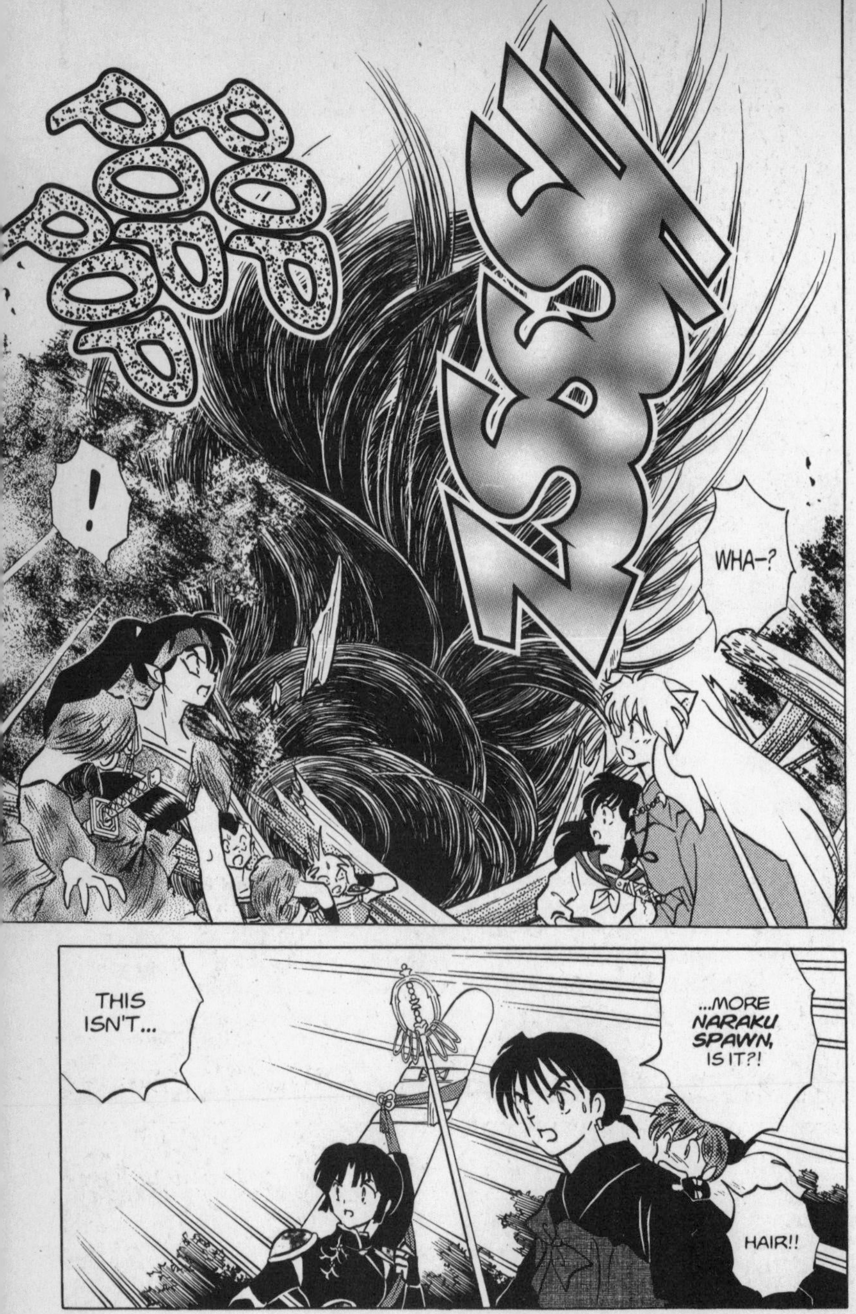
POP POP POP
!
WHA-?
THIS ISN'T...
...MORE NARAKU SPAWN, IS IT?!
HAIR!!

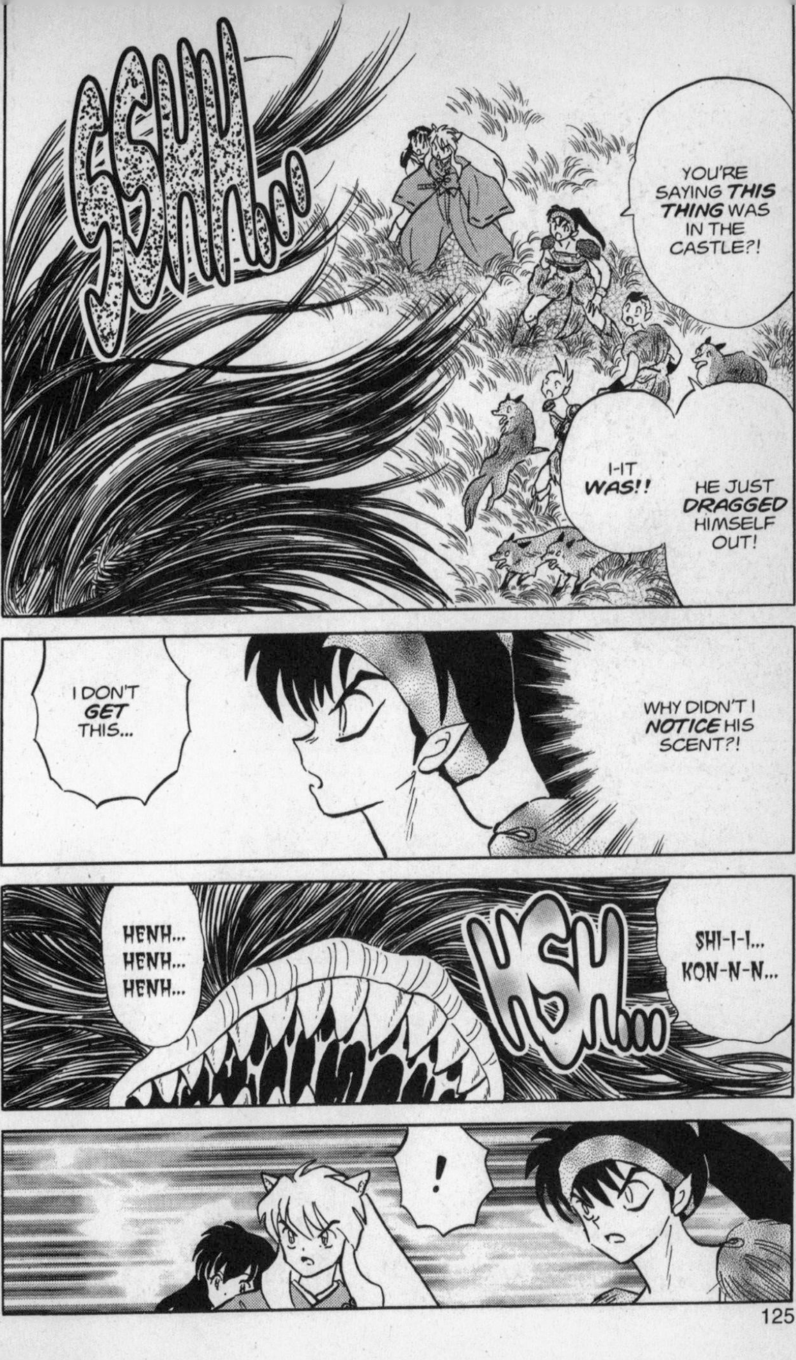
SSHH...
YOU'RE SAYING **THIS THING** WAS IN THE CASTLE?!
I-IT **WAS!!**
HE JUST **DRAGGED** HIMSELF OUT!
I DON'T **GET** THIS...
WHY DIDN'T I **NOTICE** HIS SCENT?!
HENH... HENH... HENH...
HSH...
SHI-I-I... KON-N-N...
!

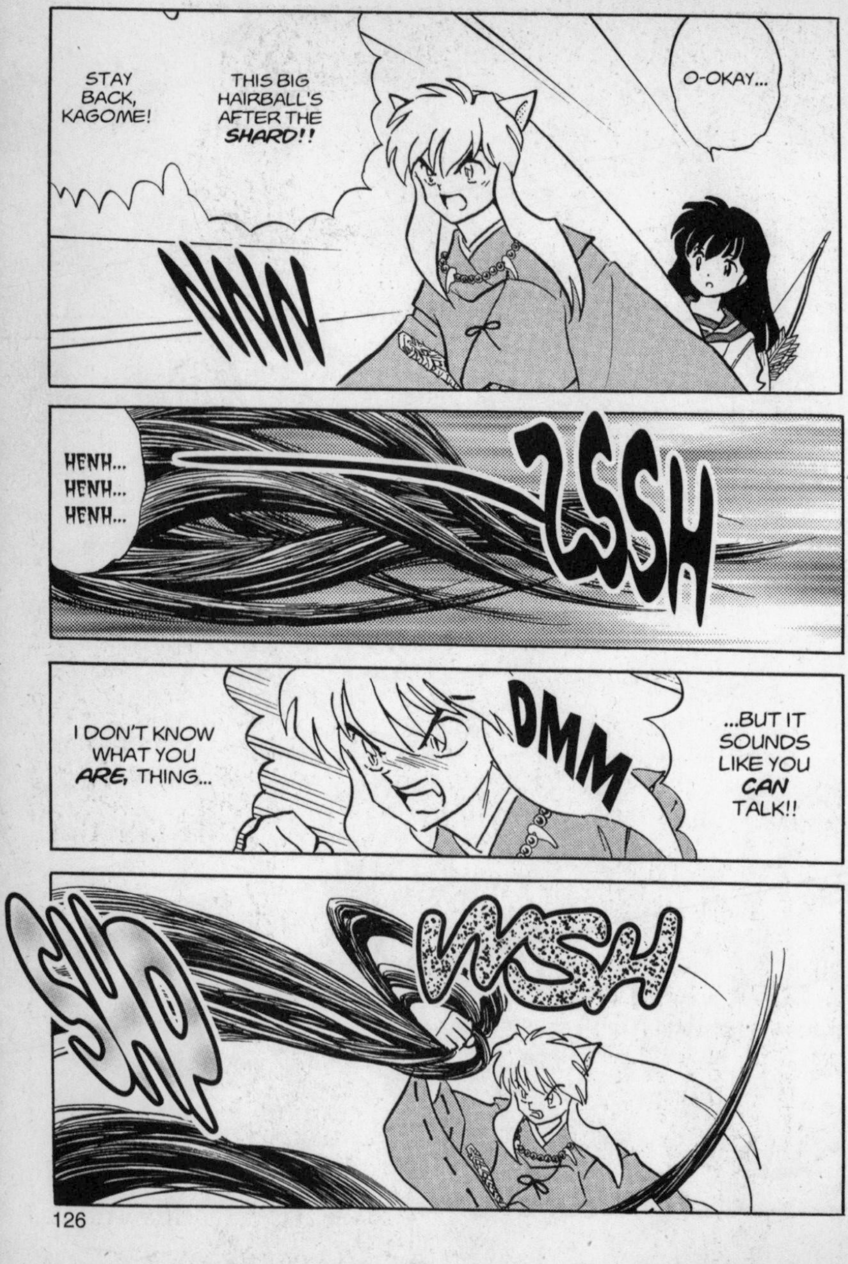
STAY BACK, KAGOME!
THIS BIG HAIRBALL'S AFTER THE ***SHARD!!***
O-OKAY...
NNN
HENH... HENH... HENH...
ZSSH
I DON'T KNOW WHAT YOU ***ARE,*** THING...
DMM
...BUT IT SOUNDS LIKE YOU ***CAN*** TALK!!
SHP
WSH

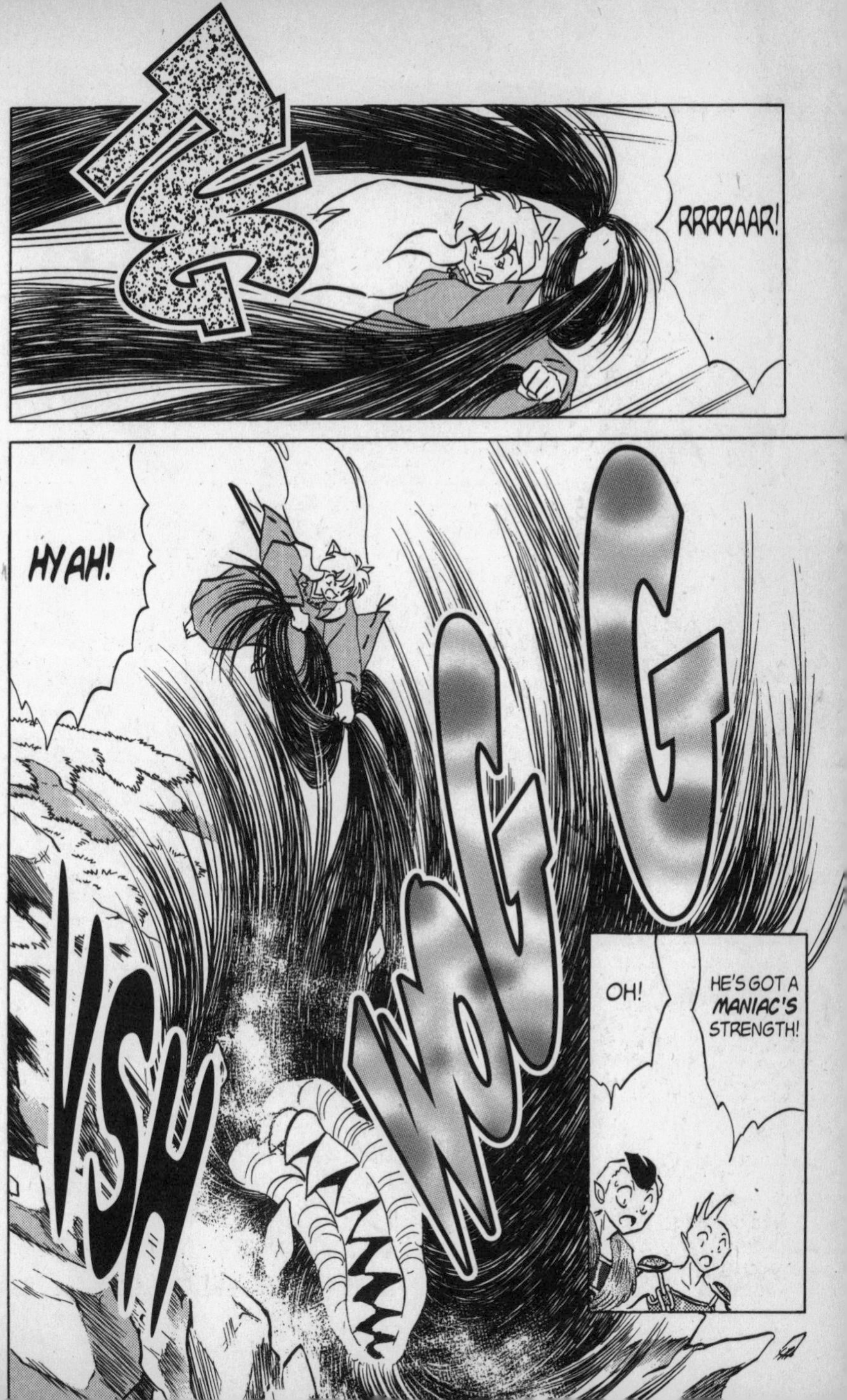
TUG
RRRRAAR!
HYAH!
OH!
HE'S GOT A MANIAC'S STRENGTH!

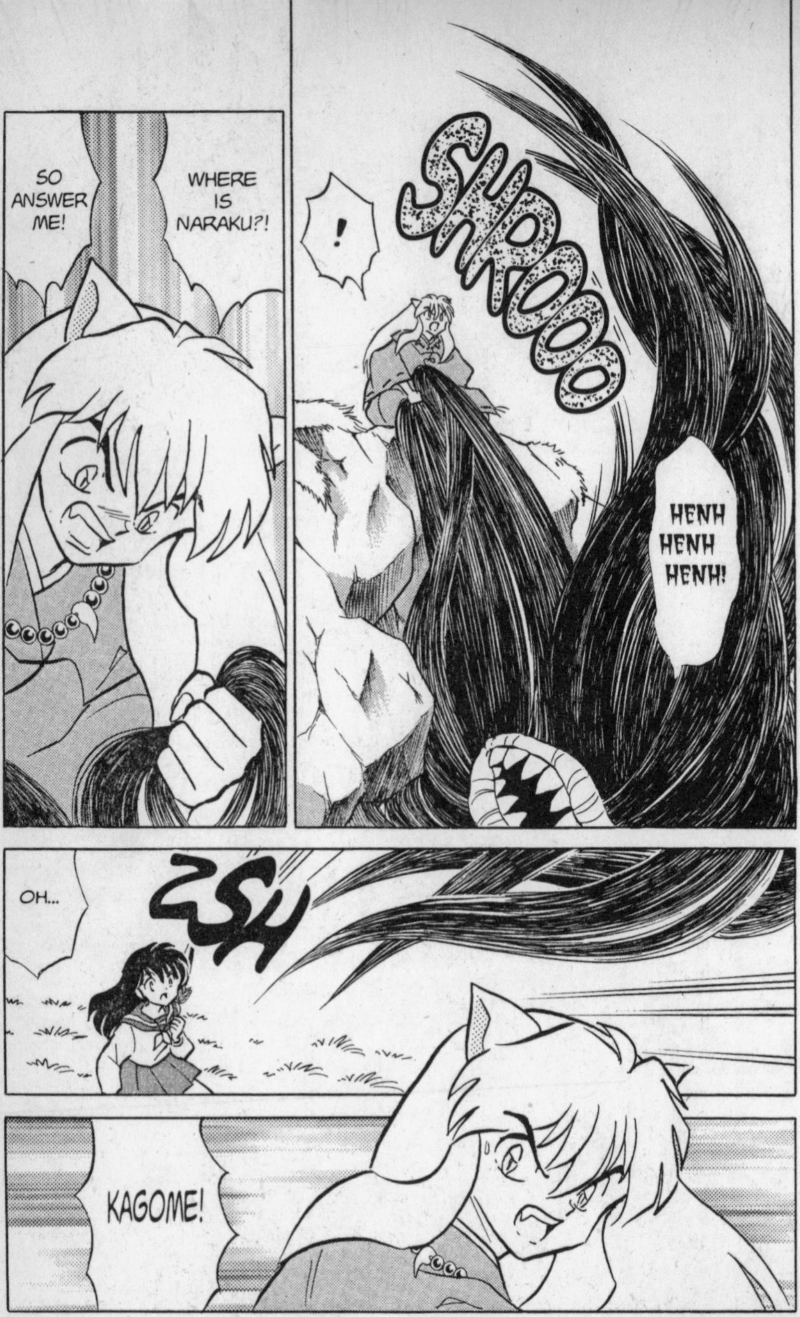

SO ANSWER ME!
WHERE IS NARAKU?!
!
SHROOOO
HENH HENH HENH!
OH...
ZSH
KAGOME!

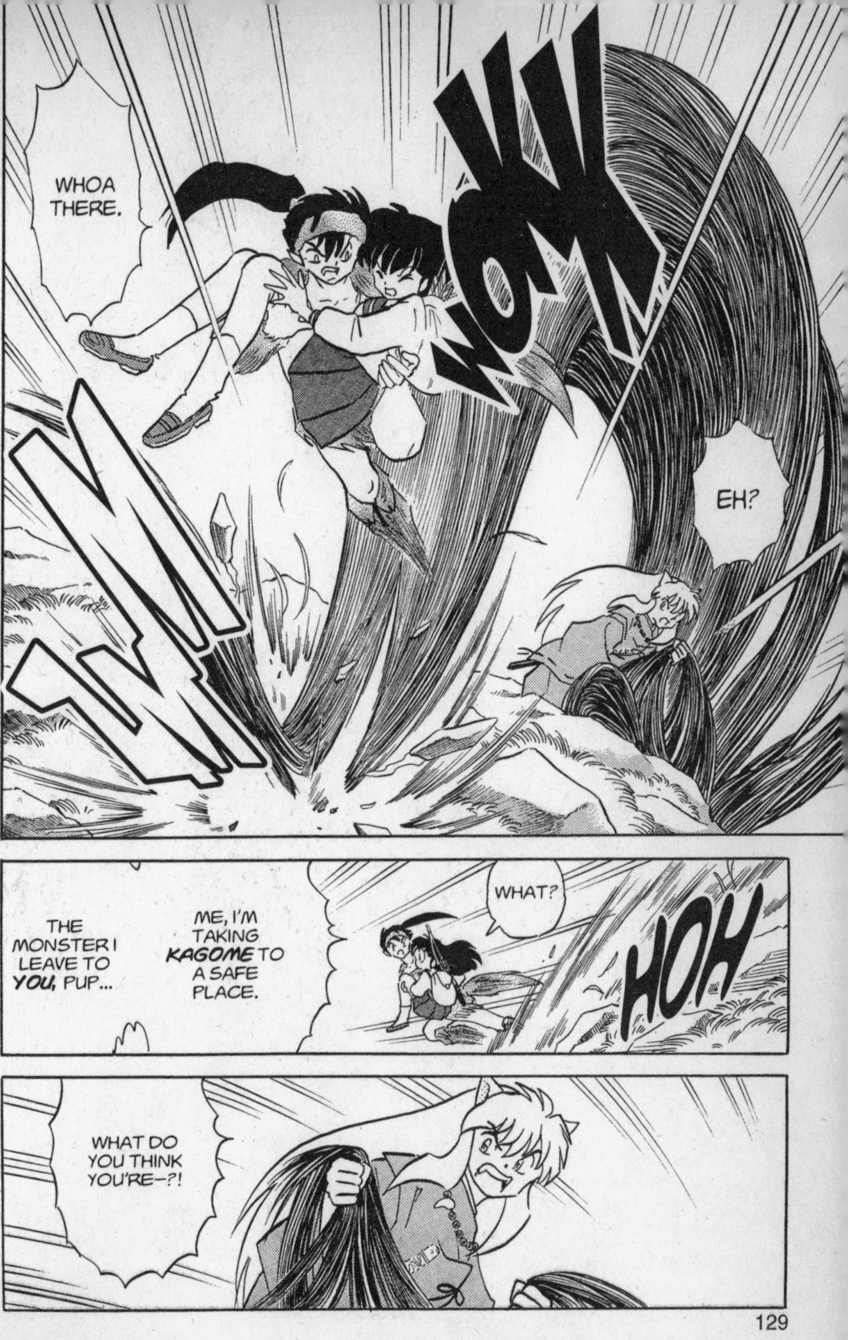
WHOA THERE.
WOMP
ZAM
EH?
THE MONSTER I LEAVE TO YOU, PUP...
ME, I'M TAKING KAGOME TO A SAFE PLACE.
WHAT?
HOH
WHAT DO YOU THINK YOU'RE--?!

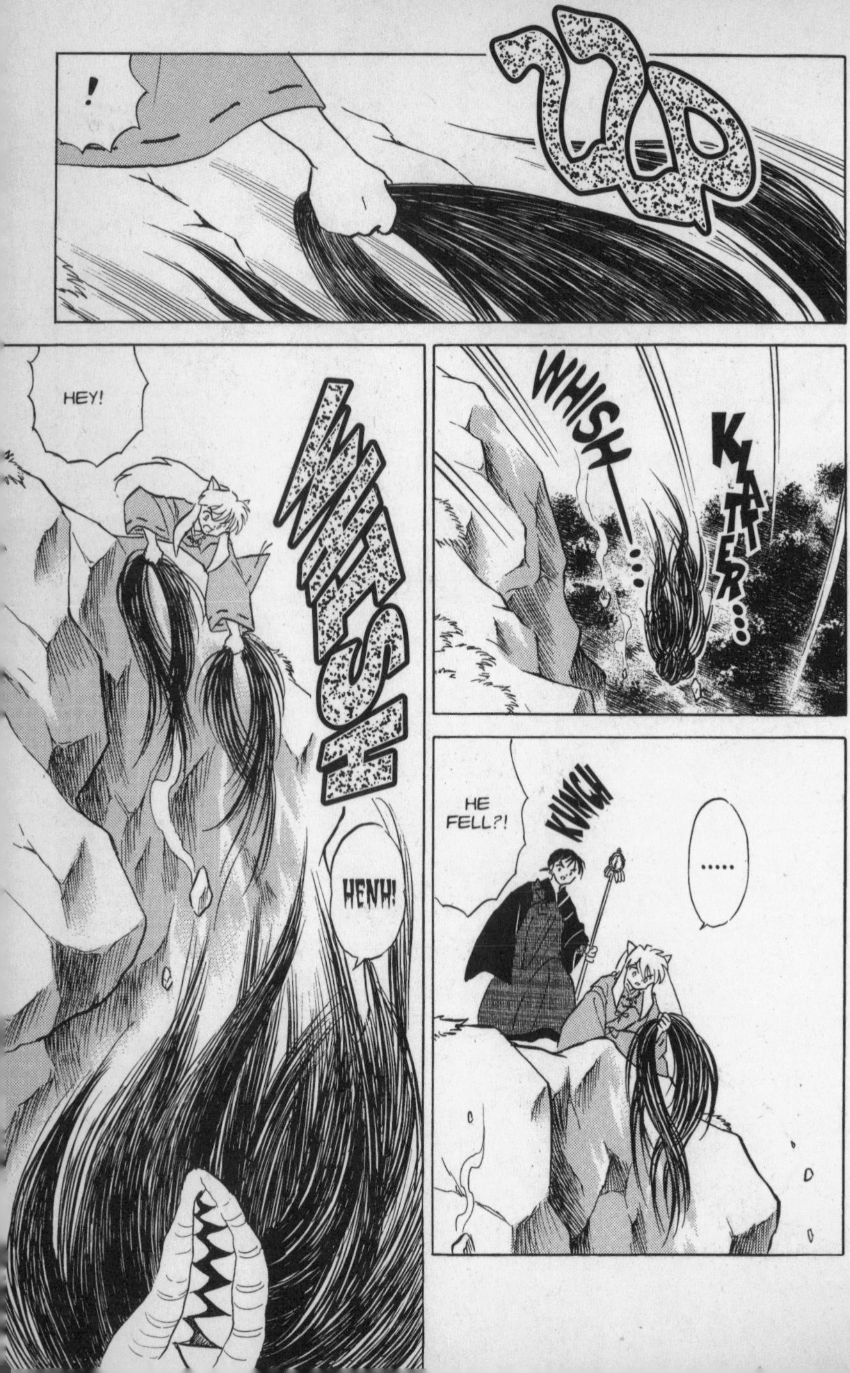

!
ZZAP
HEY!
WHISH
HENH!
WHISH—...
KLATTER...
HE FELL?!
KLUNCH
......

FOR *NARAKU SPAWN,* DIDN'T HE GO DOWN AWFUL *EASY?*

YEAH. *THAT* THING...

...FELL ON PURPOSE.

HIS TARGET IS THE SHIKON SHARDS.

DMM

WAIT, KOGA... PLEASE.

DMM

WHERE ARE WE GOING?

KAGOME...

IT SEEMS YOUR DIMWITTED FRIEND HAS LET THE MONSTER *GET AWAY.*

WHAT?

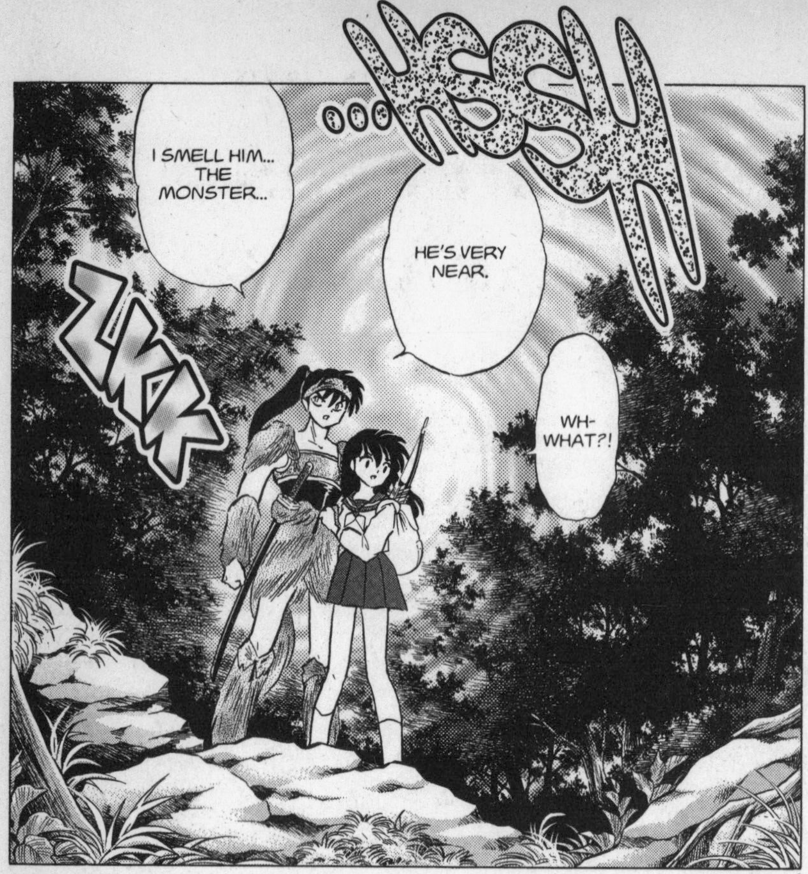
I SMELL HIM... THE MONSTER...
HE'S VERY NEAR.
WH- WHAT?!

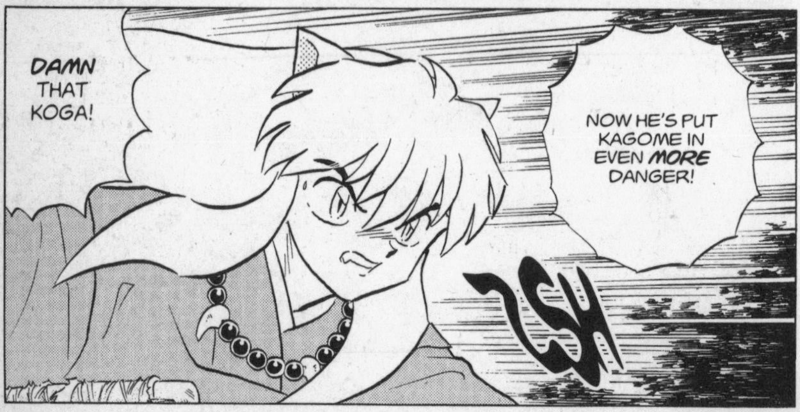
DAMN THAT KOGA!
NOW HE'S PUT KAGOME IN EVEN MORE DANGER!

SCROLL EIGHT
WHERE IS NARAKU?

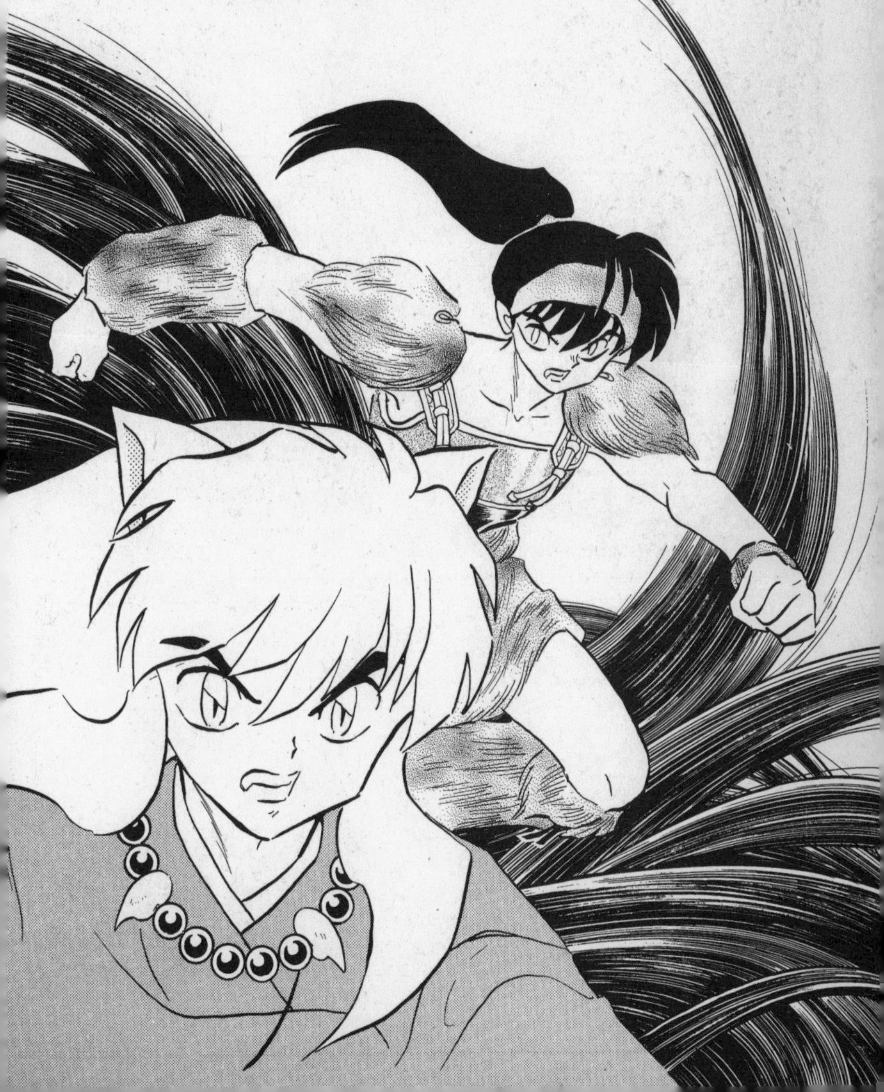

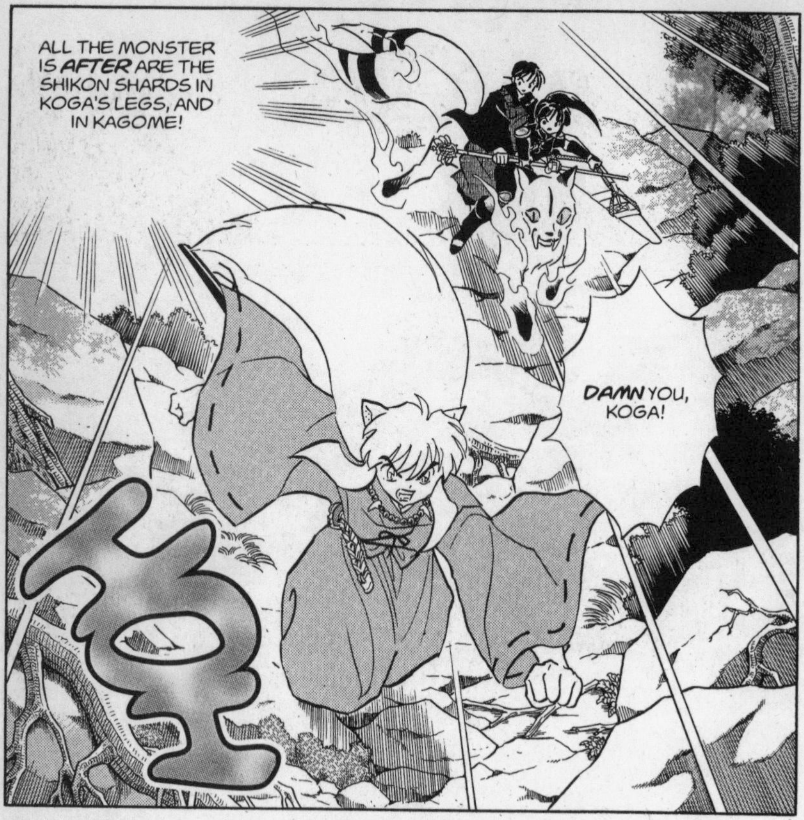
ALL THE MONSTER IS **AFTER** ARE THE SHIKON SHARDS IN KOGA'S LEGS, AND IN KAGOME!
DAMN YOU, KOGA!
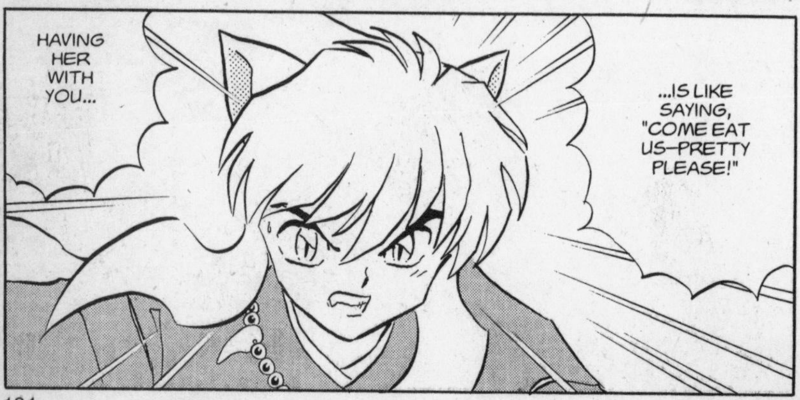
HAVING HER WITH YOU...
...IS LIKE SAYING, "COME EAT US—PRETTY PLEASE!"

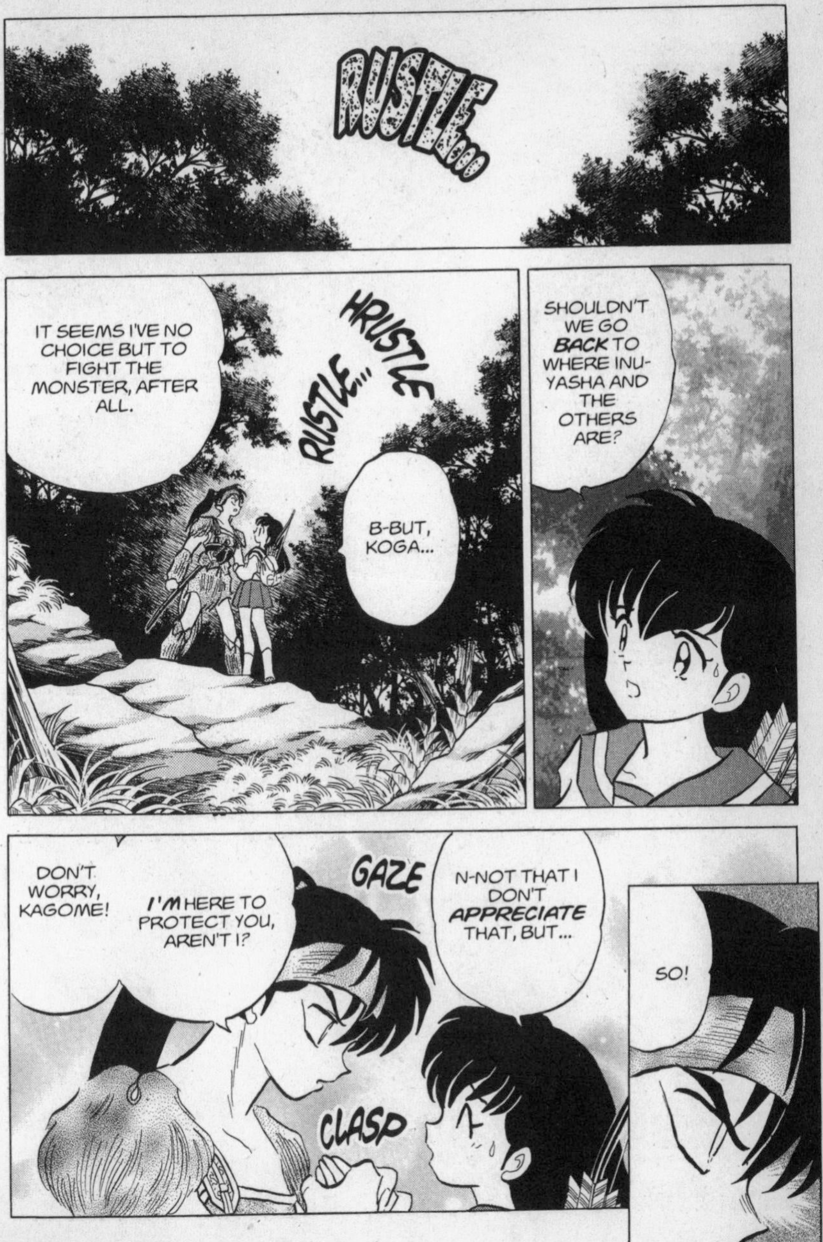
RUSTLE...
IT SEEMS I'VE NO CHOICE BUT TO FIGHT THE MONSTER, AFTER ALL.
HRUSTLE
RUSTLE...
B-BUT, KOGA...
SHOULDN'T WE GO BACK TO WHERE INU-YASHA AND THE OTHERS ARE?
DON'T WORRY, KAGOME!
I'M HERE TO PROTECT YOU, AREN'T I?
GAZE
N-NOT THAT I DON'T APPRECIATE THAT, BUT...
CLASP
SO!

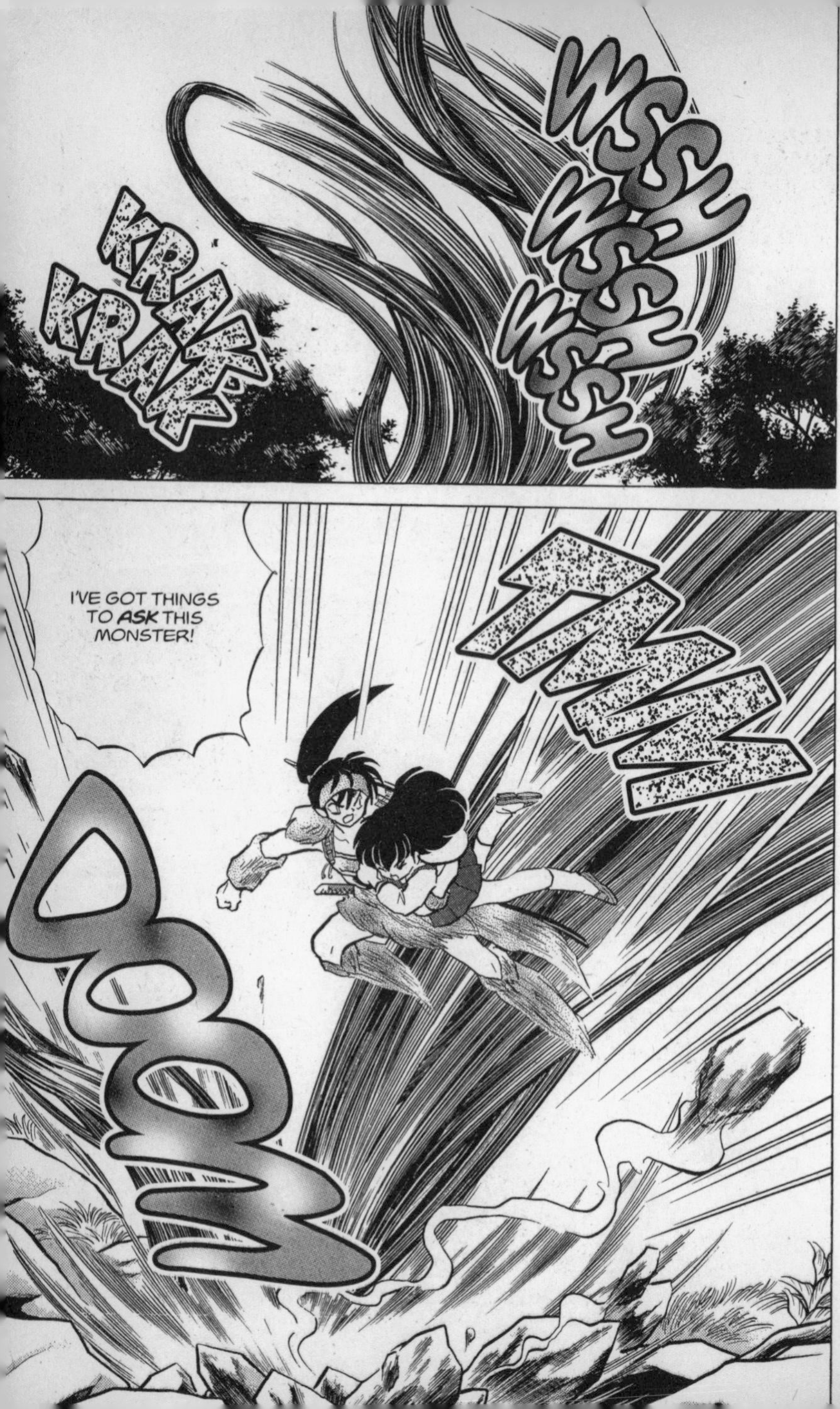
KRAK KRAK
WSSH WSSH WSSH
I'VE GOT THINGS TO ASK THIS MONSTER!
TMMM
DOOM

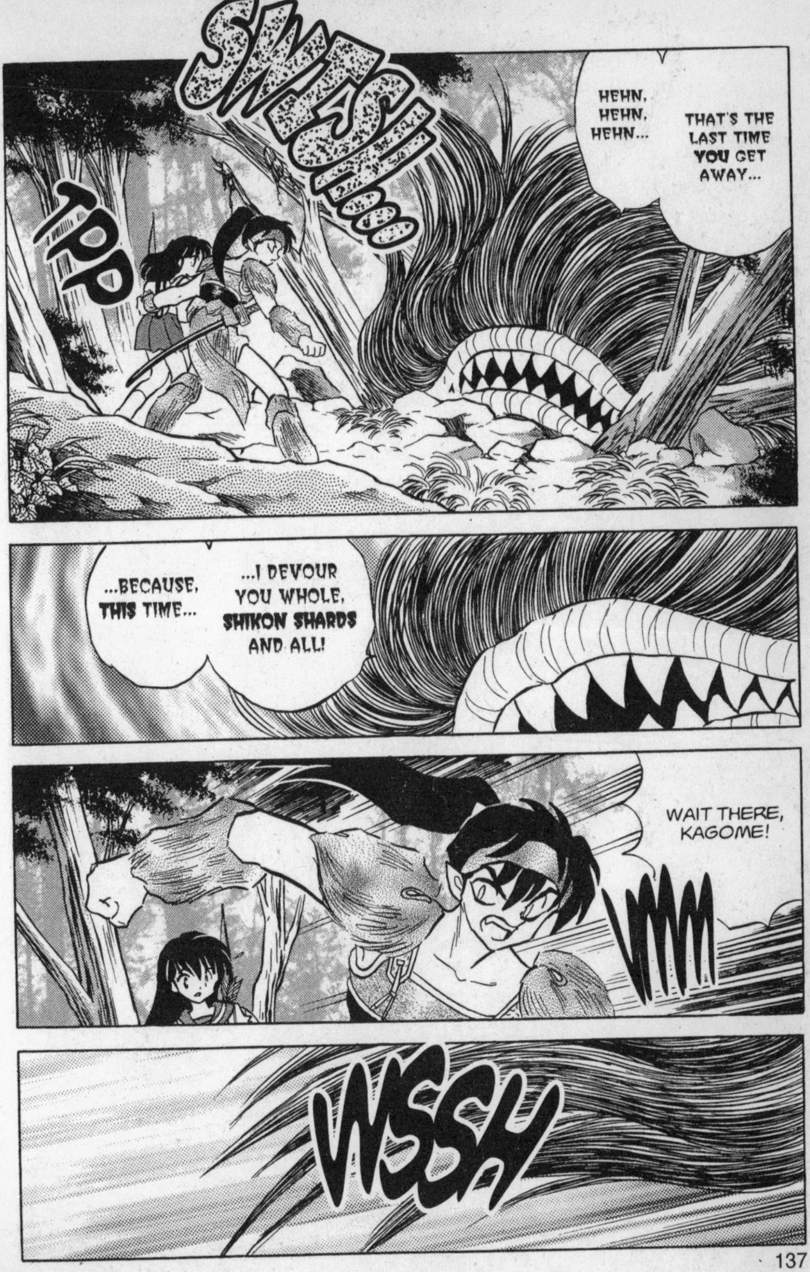
SWASH
TPP
HEHN, HEHN, HEHN...
THAT'S THE LAST TIME YOU GET AWAY...
...BECAUSE, THIS TIME...
...I DEVOUR YOU WHOLE, SHIKON SHARDS AND ALL!
WAIT THERE, KAGOME!
VMM
VSSH

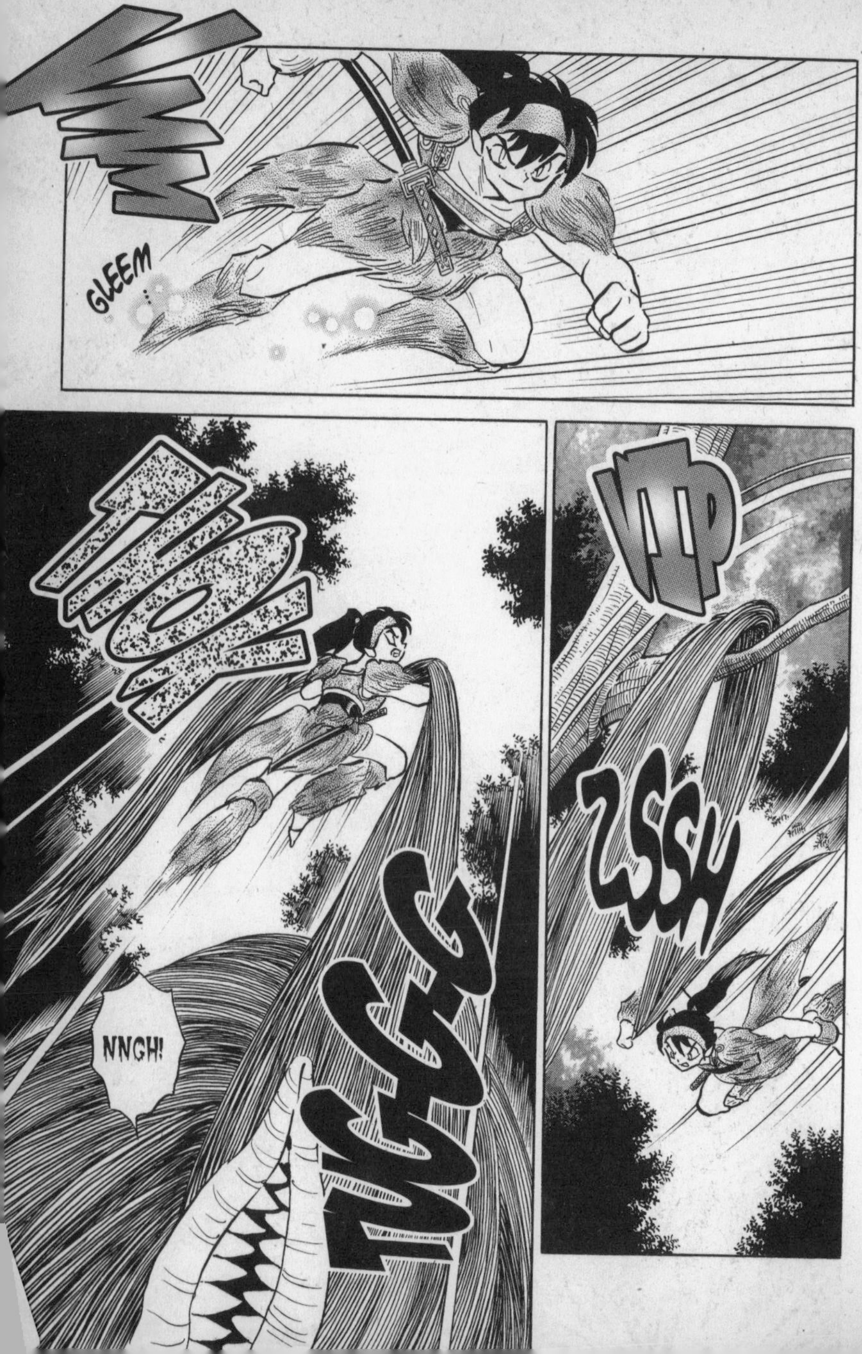
GLEEM
NNGH!
VIIP
ZSSH

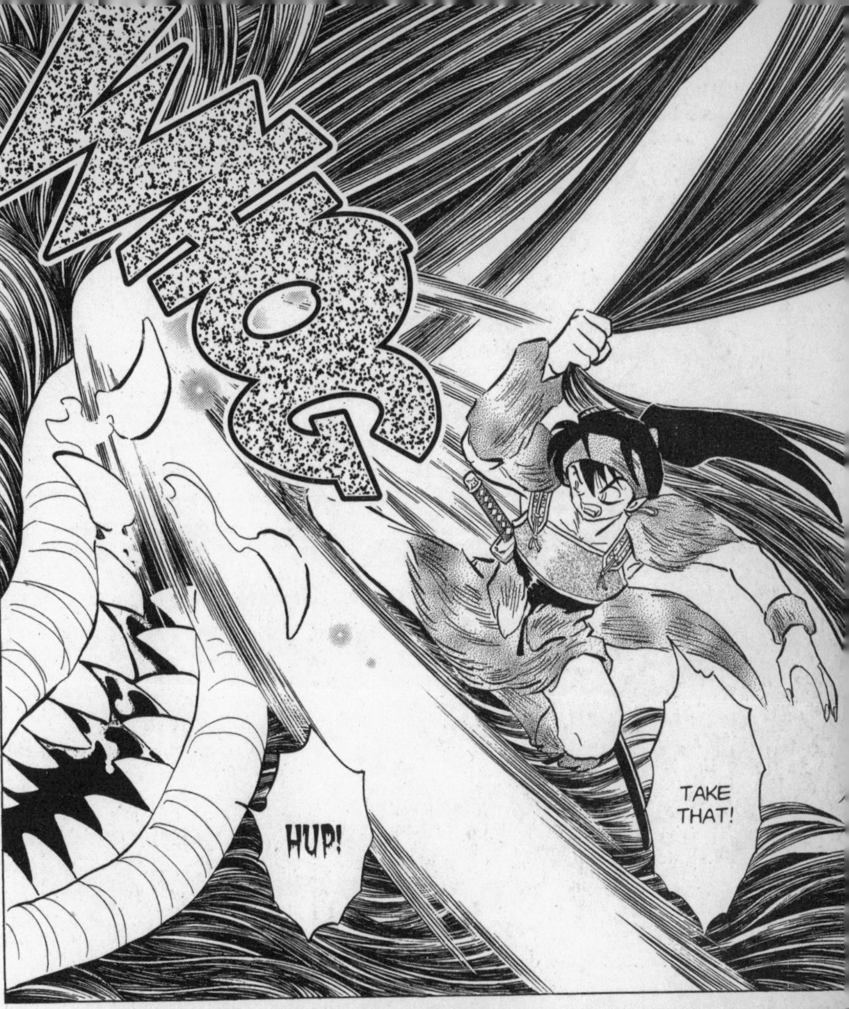
HUP!
TAKE THAT!
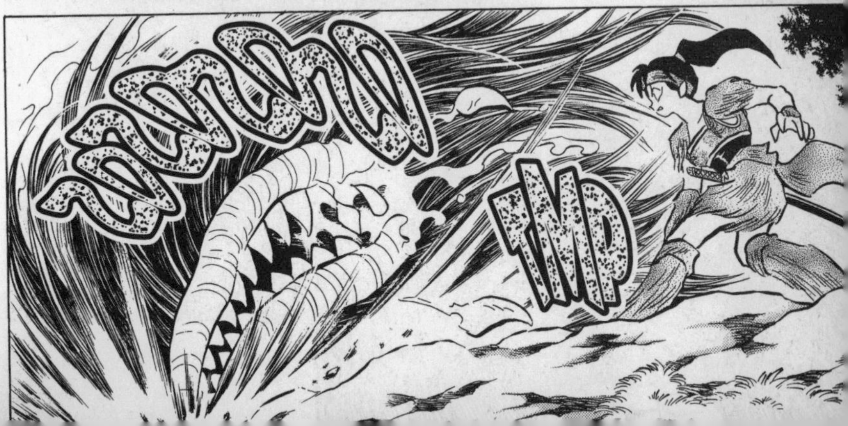
TMP

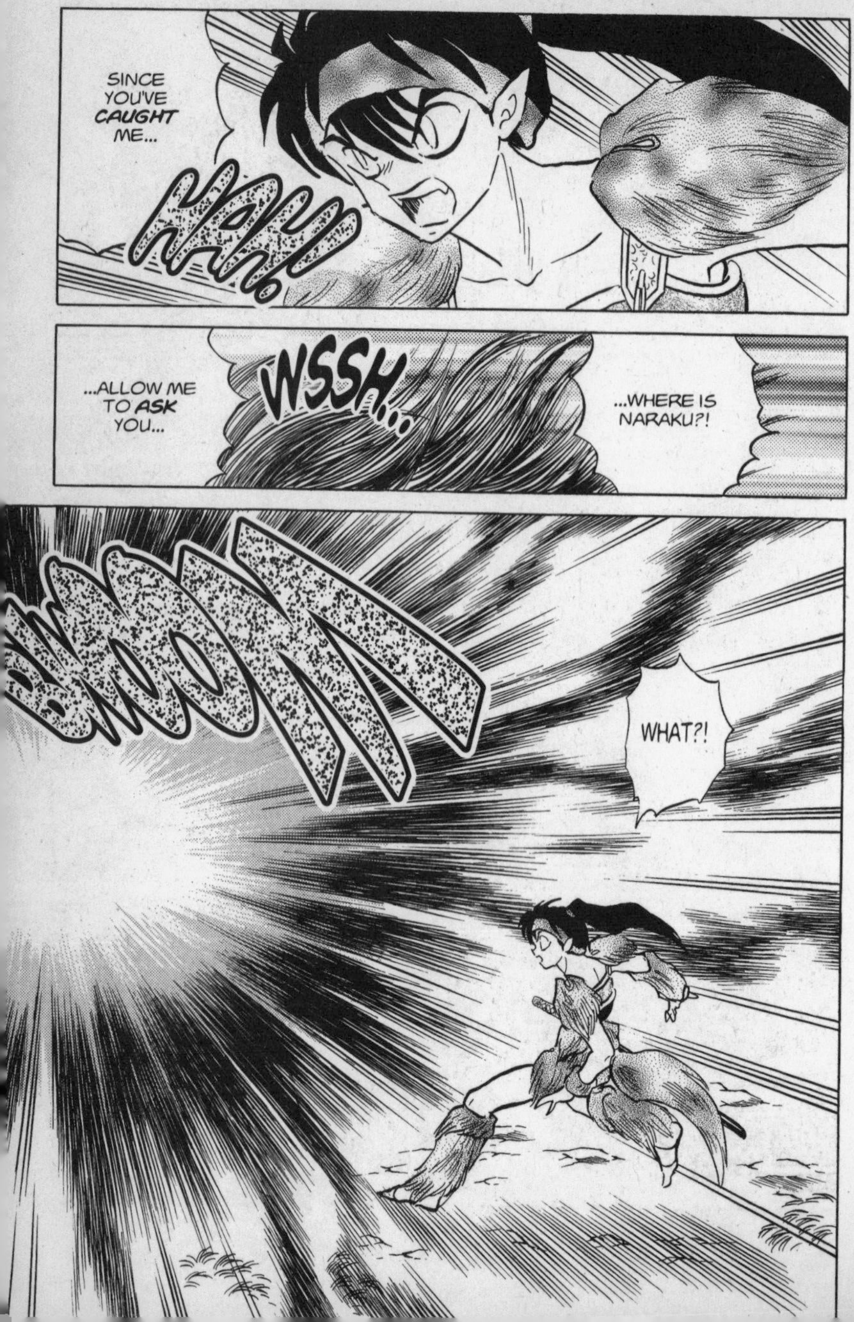
SINCE YOU'VE *CAUGHT* ME...
HAH!
...ALLOW ME TO *ASK* YOU...
WSSH...
...WHERE IS NARAKU?!
WHAT?!

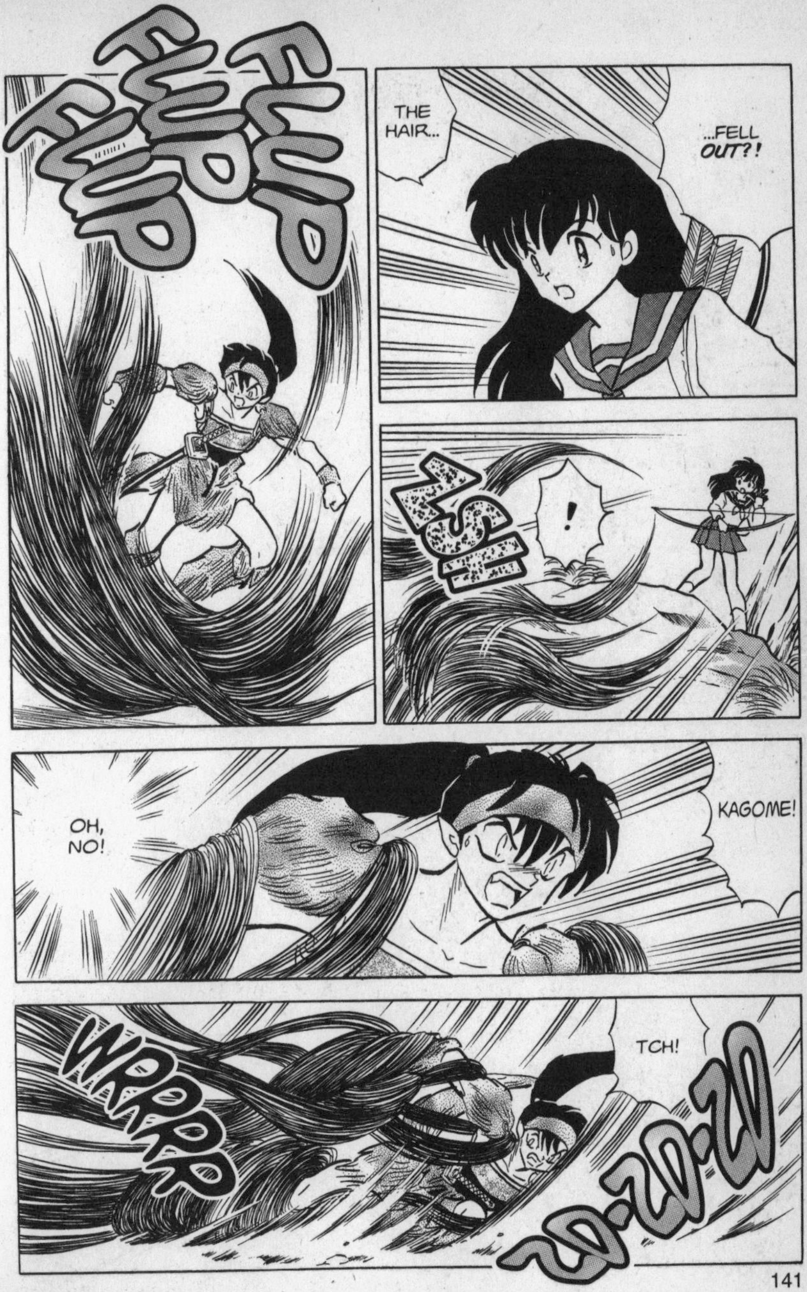
FLIP FLIP FLIP
THE HAIR...
...FELL OUT?!
ZSH!
!
OH, NO!
KAGOME!
WRRRR
TCH!
ZO-ZO-ZO-ZO

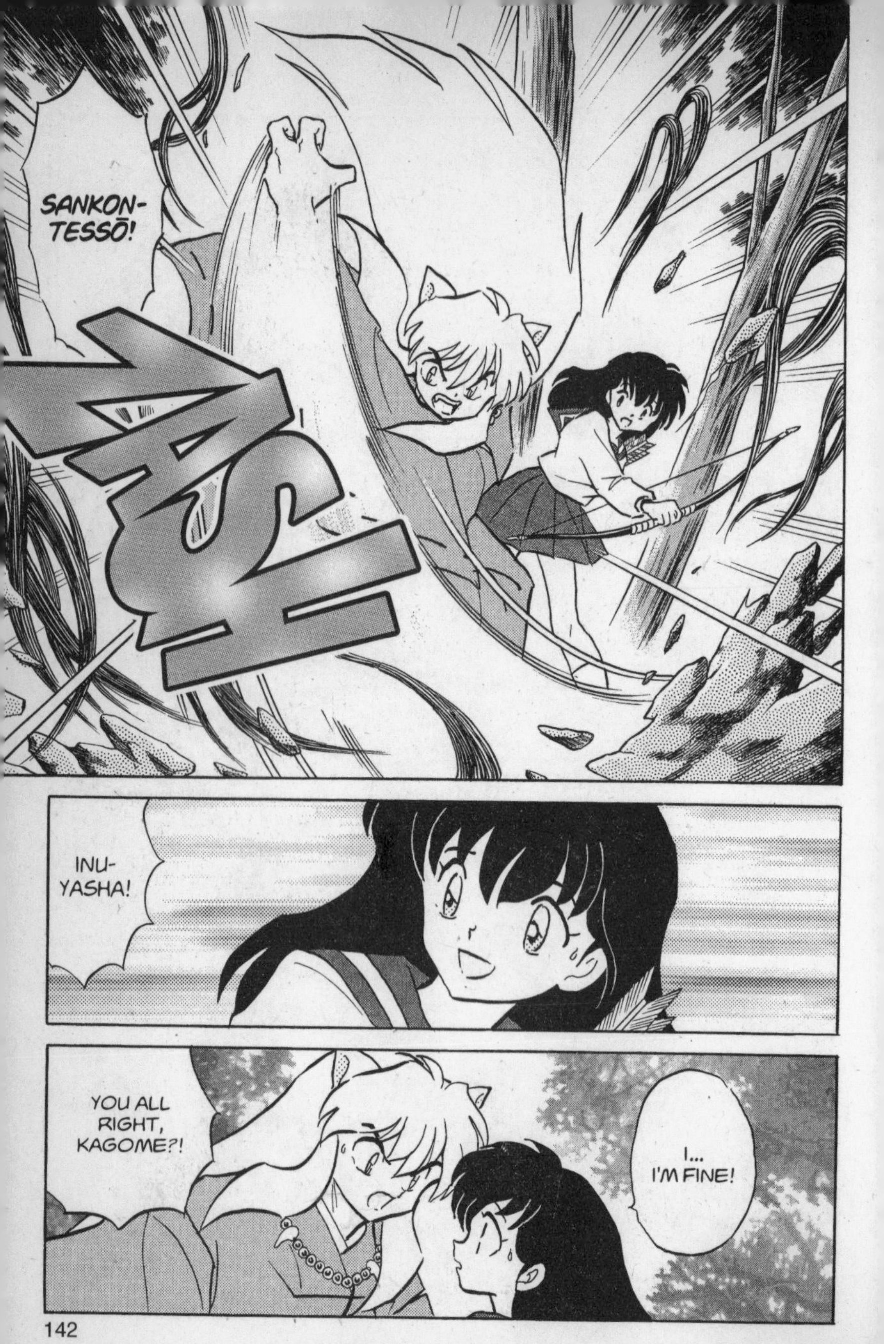
SANKON-TESSŌ!
ZASH
INU-YASHA!
YOU ALL RIGHT, KAGOME?!
I... I'M FINE!

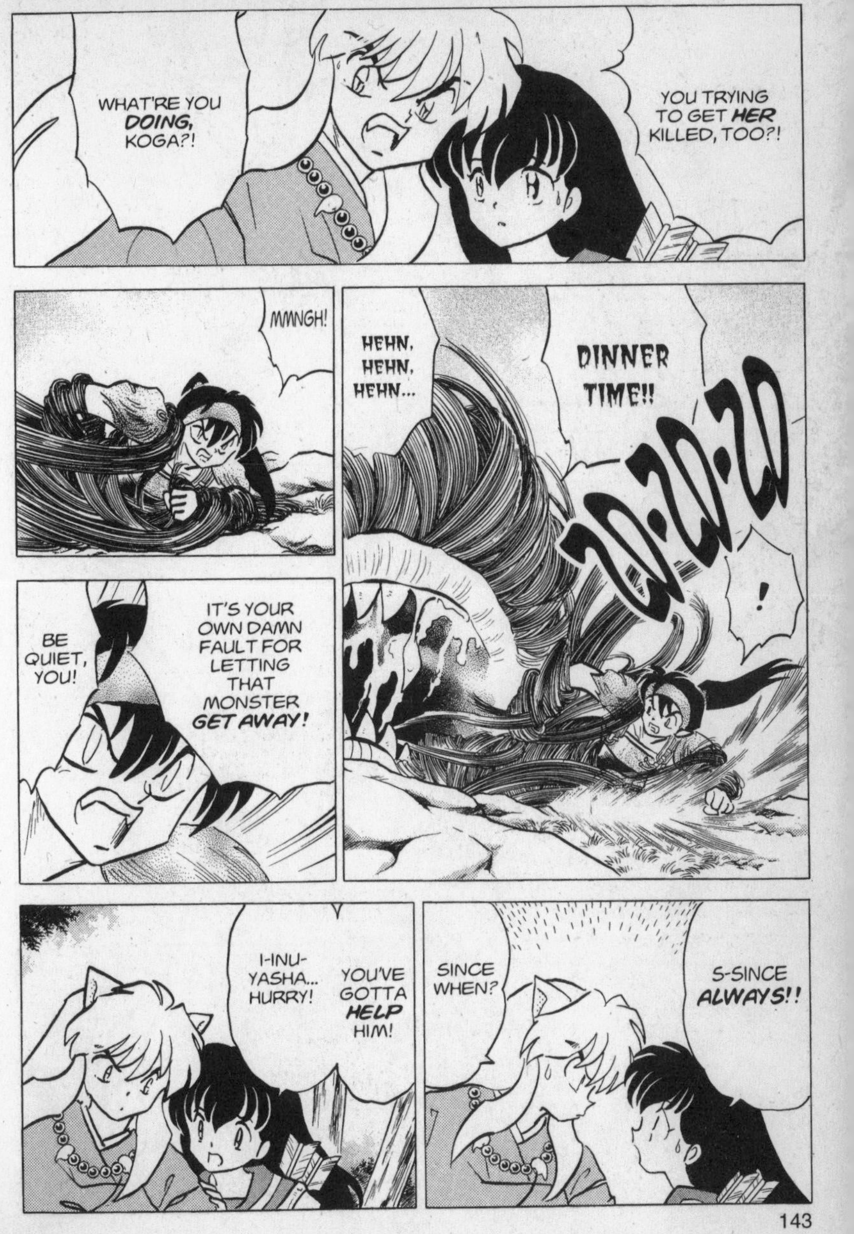
WHAT'RE YOU DOING, KOGA?!
YOU TRYING TO GET HER KILLED, TOO?!
MMNGH!
BE QUIET, YOU!
IT'S YOUR OWN DAMN FAULT FOR LETTING THAT MONSTER GET AWAY!
HEHN, HEHN, HEHN...
DINNER TIME!!
ZO-ZO-ZO
!
I-INU-YASHA... HURRY!
YOU'VE GOTTA HELP HIM!
SINCE WHEN?
S-SINCE ALWAYS!!

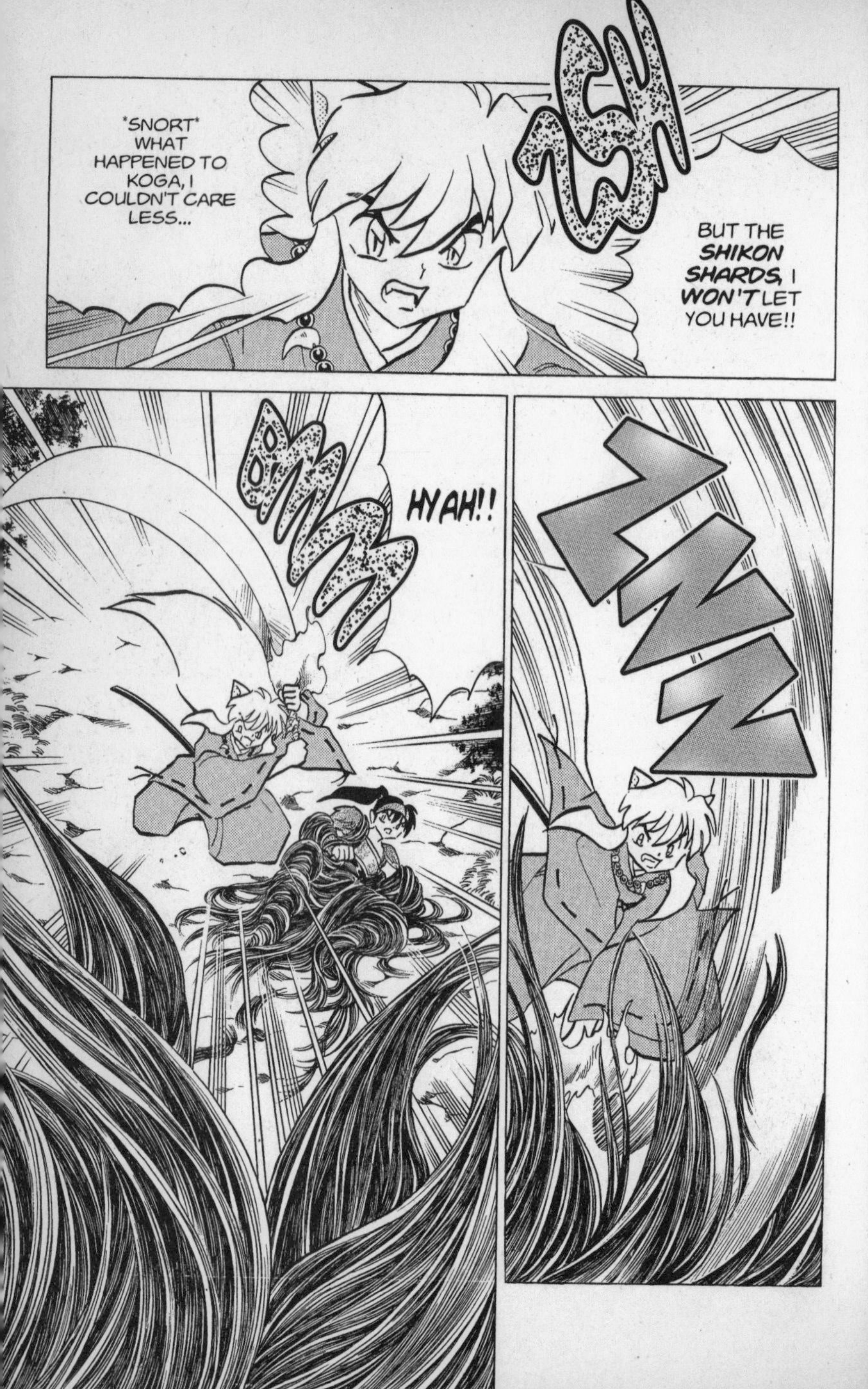
SNORT WHAT HAPPENED TO KOGA, I COULDN'T CARE LESS...
ZCH
BUT THE SHIKON SHARDS, I WON'T LET YOU HAVE!!
BOMM
HYAH!!
ZWNN

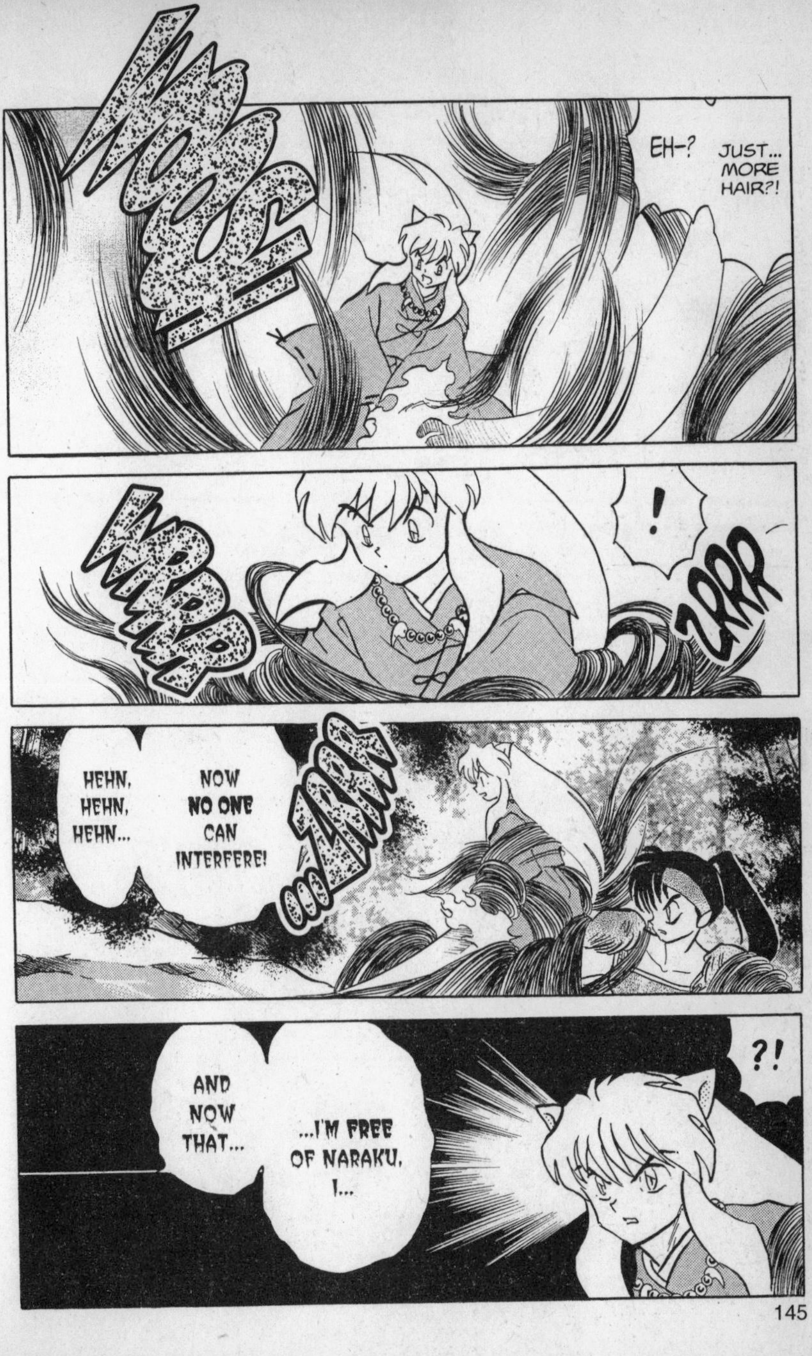
WOOSH
EH-?
JUST... MORE HAIR?!
WRRRP
!
ZRRR
HEHN, HEHN, HEHN...
NOW NO ONE CAN INTERFERE!
...ZRRR
AND NOW THAT...
...I'M FREE OF NARAKU, I...
?!

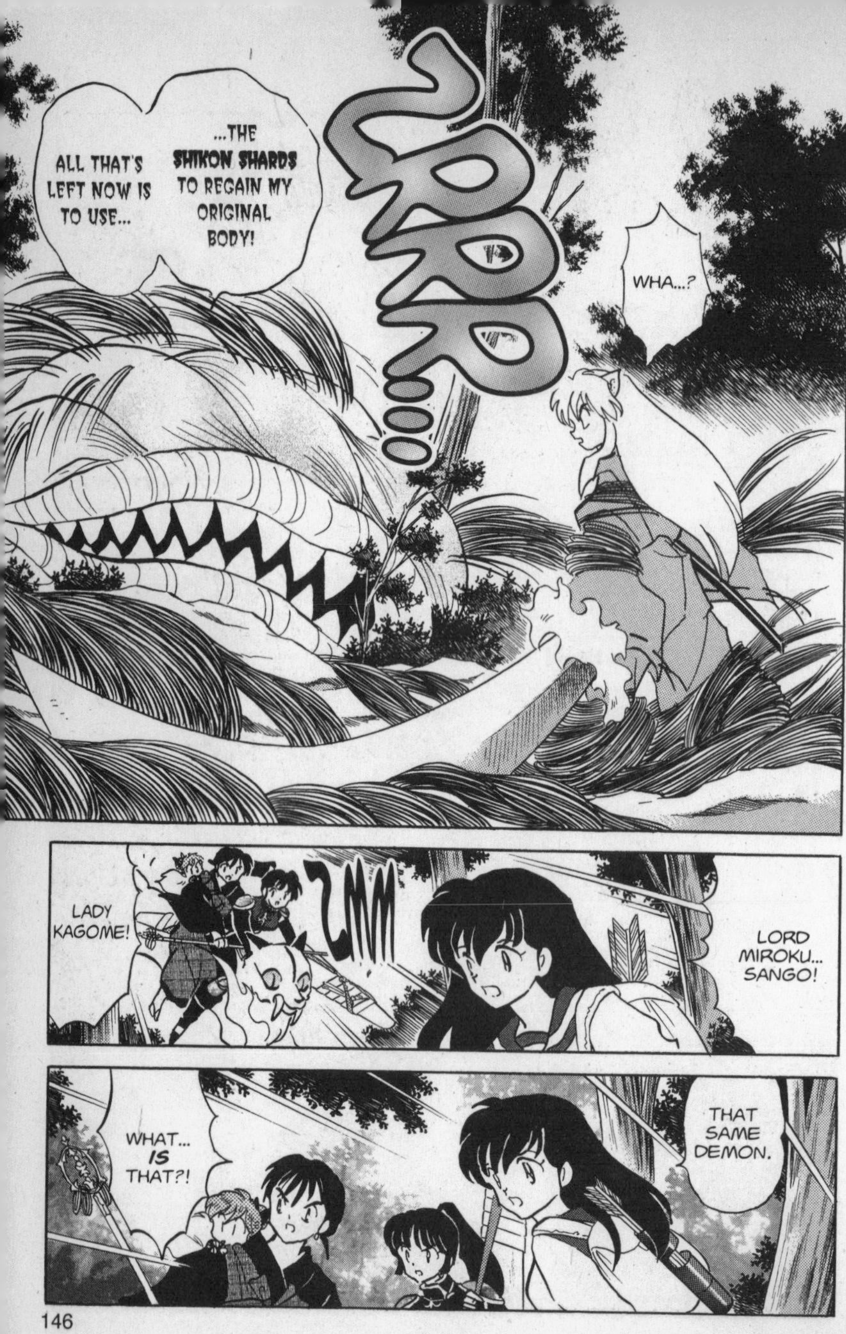
ALL THAT'S LEFT NOW IS TO USE...
...THE SHIKON SHARDS TO REGAIN MY ORIGINAL BODY!
ZRRR...
WHA...?
LADY KAGOME!
LORD MIROKU... SANGO!
WHAT... IS THAT?!
THAT SAME DEMON.

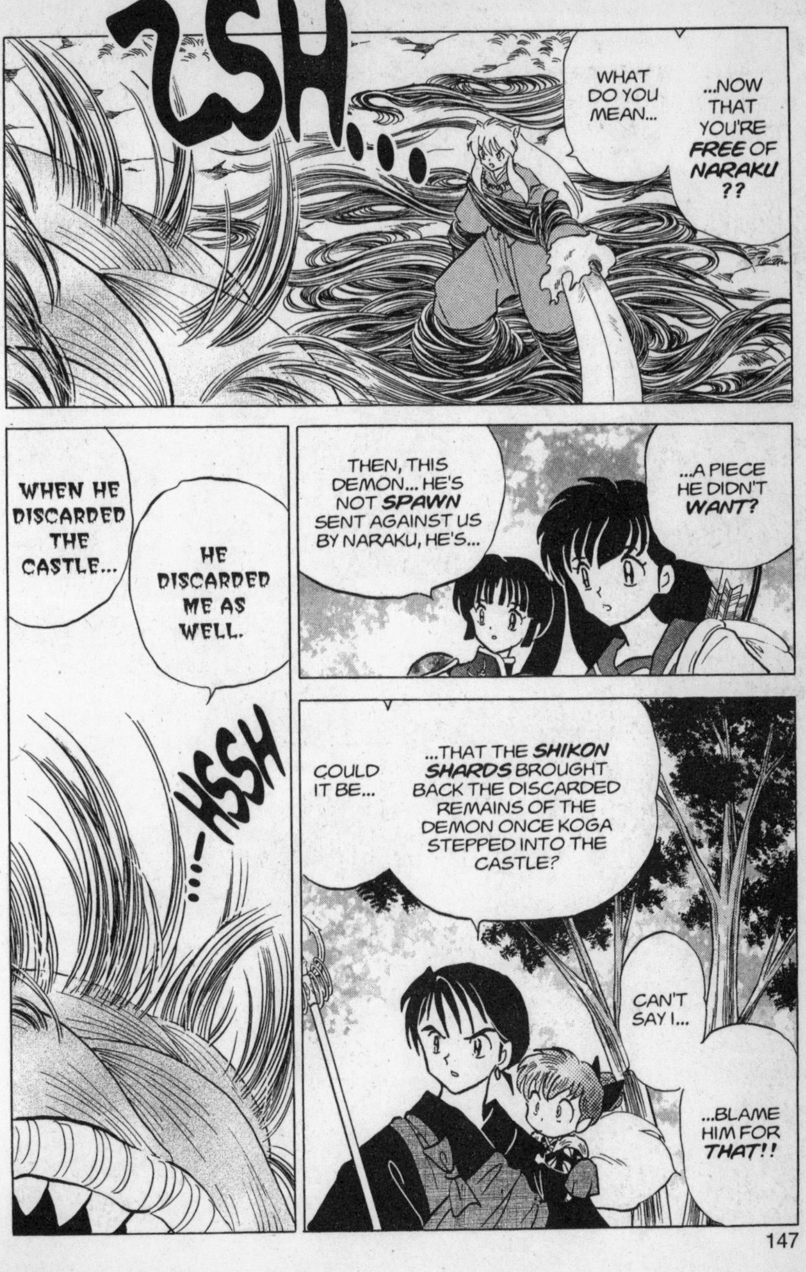
ZSH...
WHAT DO YOU MEAN...
...NOW THAT YOU'RE FREE OF NARAKU ??
WHEN HE DISCARDED THE CASTLE...
HE DISCARDED ME AS WELL.
HSSH...
THEN, THIS DEMON... HE'S NOT SPAWN SENT AGAINST US BY NARAKU, HE'S...
...A PIECE HE DIDN'T WANT?
COULD IT BE...
...THAT THE SHIKON SHARDS BROUGHT BACK THE DISCARDED REMAINS OF THE DEMON ONCE KOGA STEPPED INTO THE CASTLE?
CAN'T SAY I...
...BLAME HIM FOR THAT!!

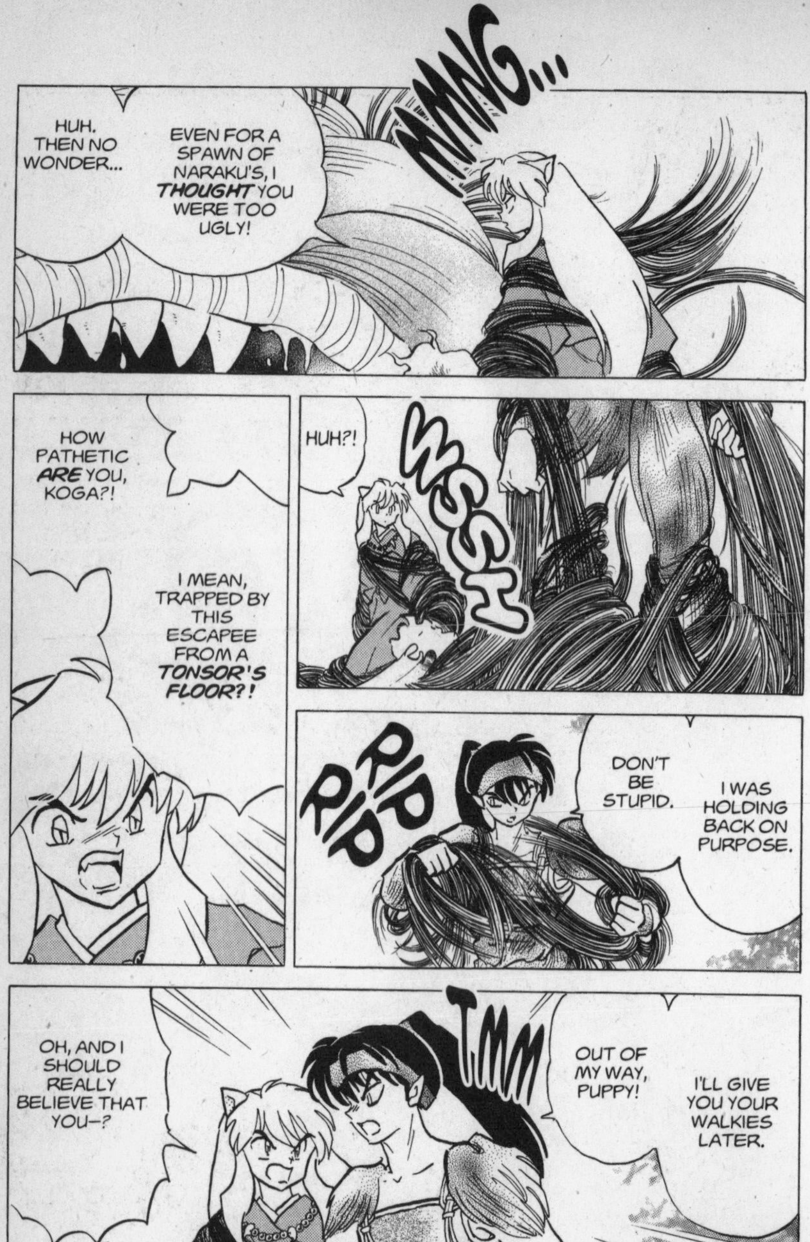
HUH. THEN NO WONDER...
EVEN FOR A SPAWN OF NARAKU'S, I **THOUGHT** YOU WERE TOO UGLY!
MMNG...
HOW PATHETIC **ARE** YOU, KOGA?!
I MEAN, TRAPPED BY THIS ESCAPEE FROM A **TONSOR'S FLOOR?!**
HUH?!
WSSH
RIP RIP
DON'T BE STUPID.
I WAS HOLDING BACK ON PURPOSE.
OH, AND I SHOULD REALLY BELIEVE THAT YOU–?
TMM
OUT OF MY WAY, PUPPY!
I'LL GIVE YOU YOUR WALKIES LATER.

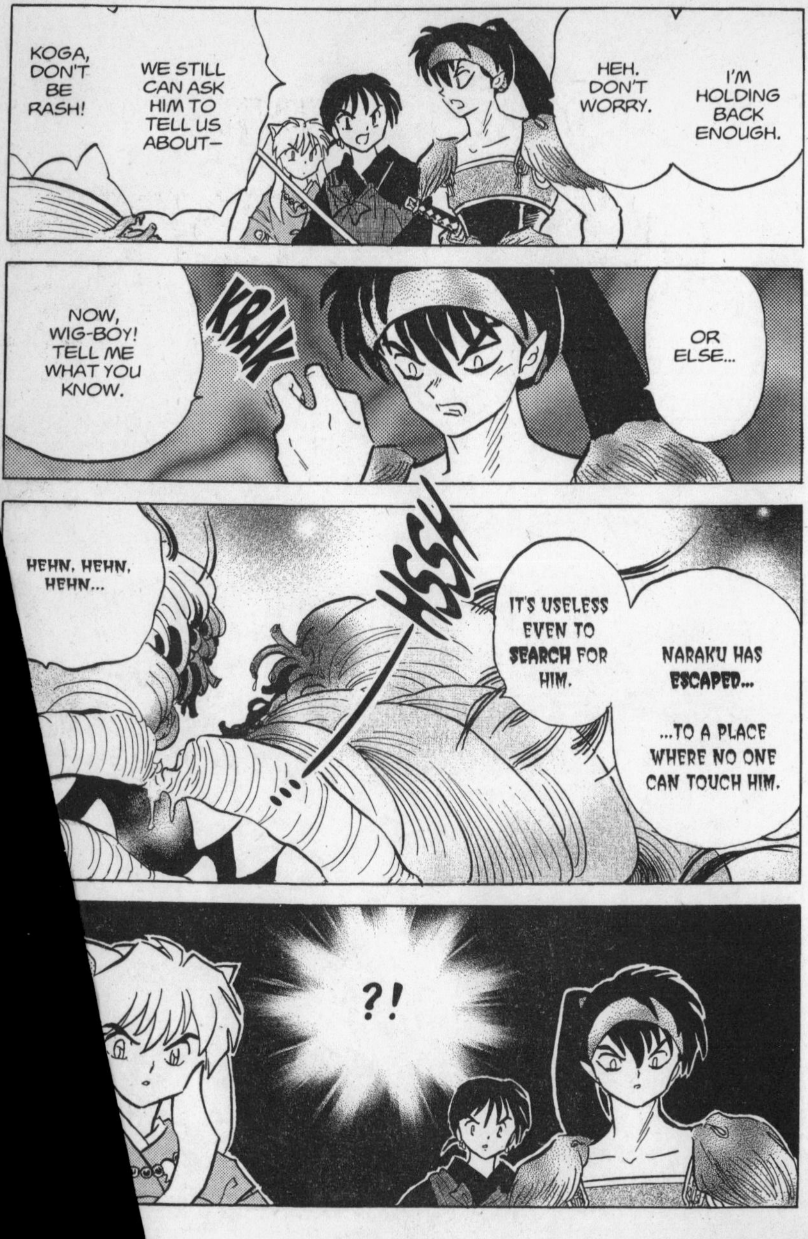
KOGA, DON'T BE RASH!
WE STILL CAN ASK HIM TO TELL US ABOUT—
HEH. DON'T WORRY.
I'M HOLDING BACK ENOUGH.
NOW, WIG-BOY! TELL ME WHAT YOU KNOW.
KRAK
OR ELSE...
HEHN, HEHN, HEHN...
...
HSSH
IT'S USELESS EVEN TO SEARCH FOR HIM.
NARAKU HAS ESCAPED...
...TO A PLACE WHERE NO ONE CAN TOUCH HIM.
?!

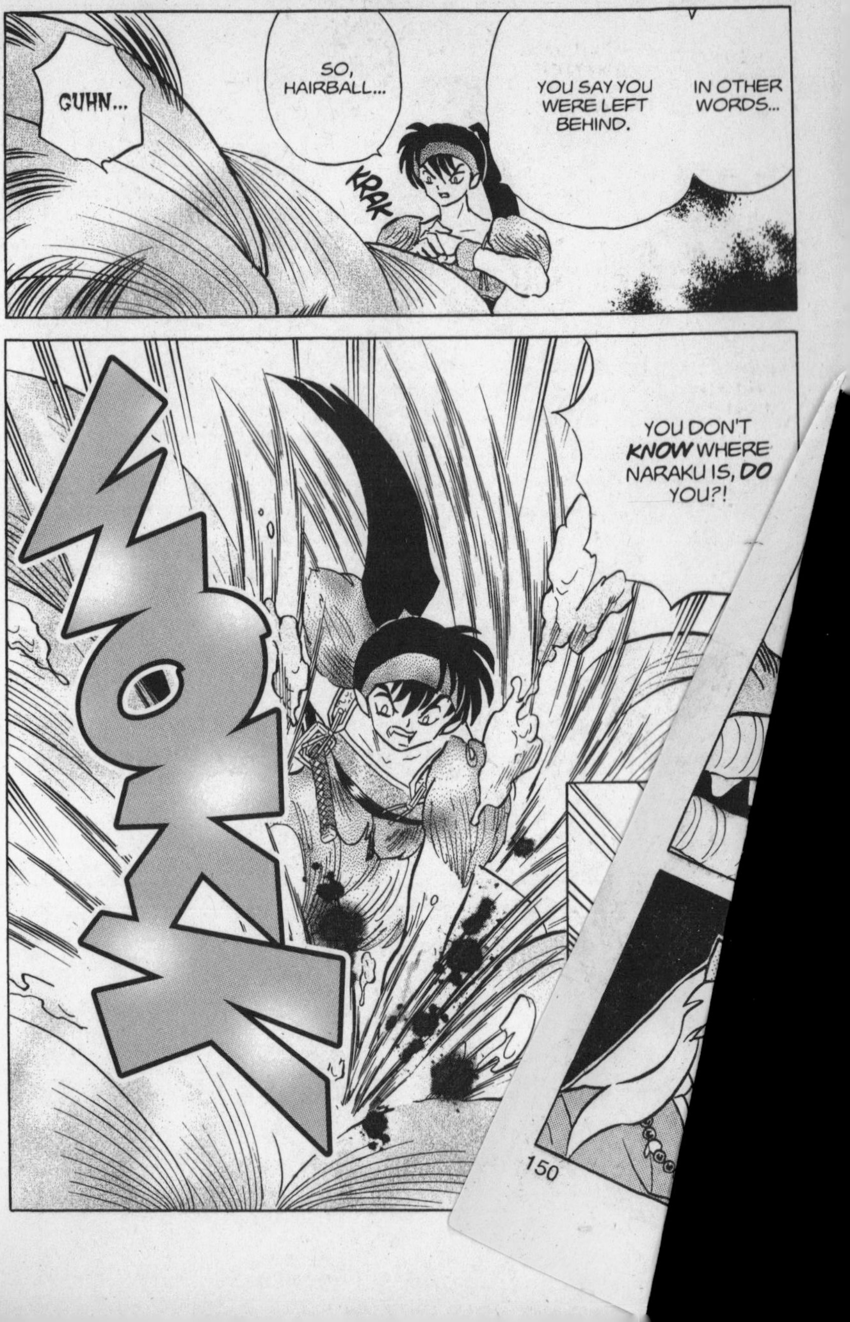
GUHN...
KRAK
SO, HAIRBALL...
YOU SAY YOU WERE LEFT BEHIND.
IN OTHER WORDS...
YOU DON'T KNOW WHERE NARAKU IS, DO YOU?!

SCROLL NINE
LOST SCENT

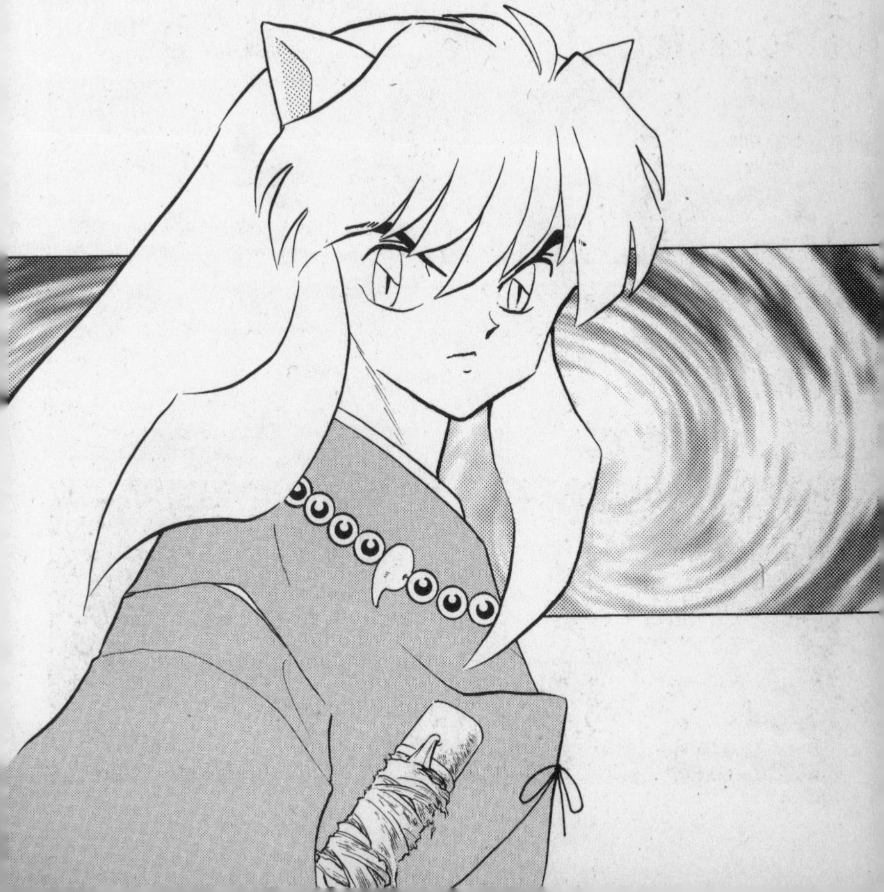

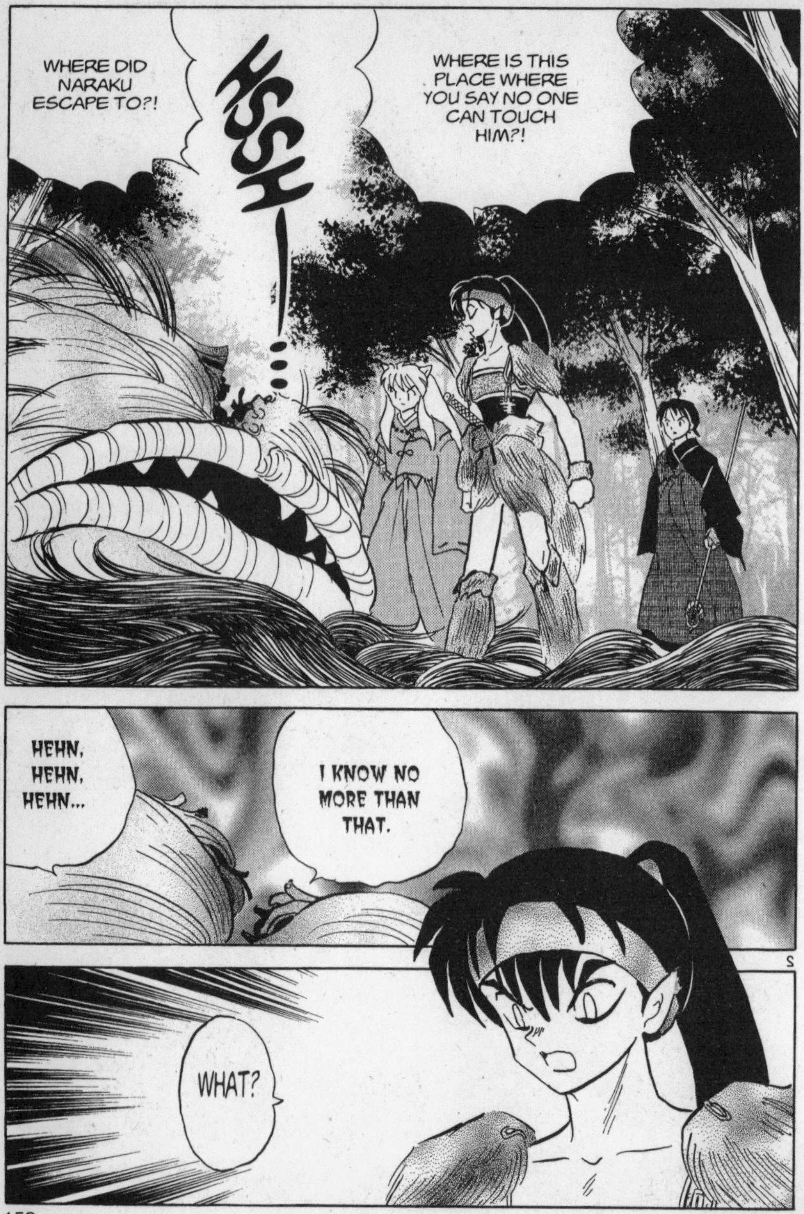
WHERE DID NARAKU ESCAPE TO?!
HSSH...
WHERE IS THIS PLACE WHERE YOU SAY NO ONE CAN TOUCH HIM?!
HEHN, HEHN, HEHN...
I KNOW NO MORE THAN THAT.
WHAT?

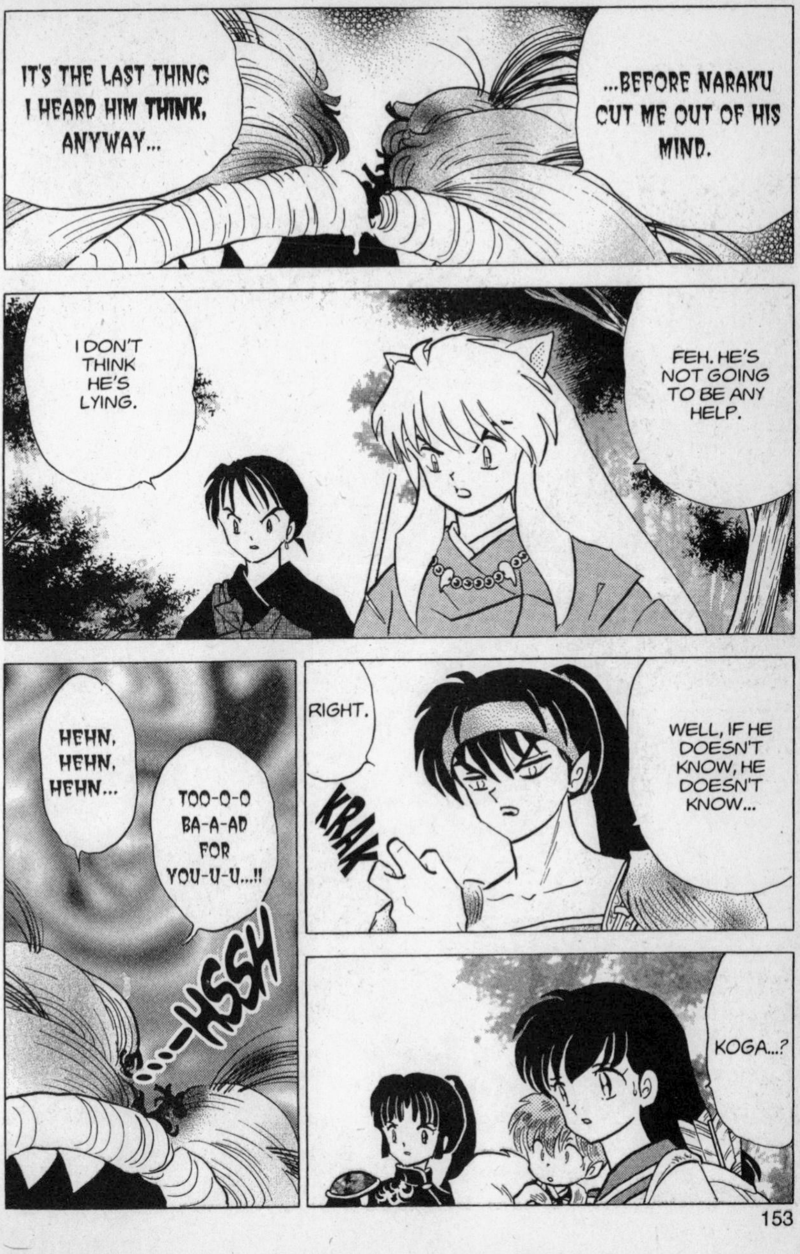
IT'S THE LAST THING I HEARD HIM THINK, ANYWAY...
...BEFORE NARAKU CUT ME OUT OF HIS MIND.
I DON'T THINK HE'S LYING.
FEH. HE'S NOT GOING TO BE ANY HELP.
HEHN, HEHN, HEHN...
TOO-O-O BA-A-AD FOR YOU-U-U...!!
HSSH
RIGHT.
WELL, IF HE DOESN'T KNOW, HE DOESN'T KNOW...
KRAK
KOGA...?

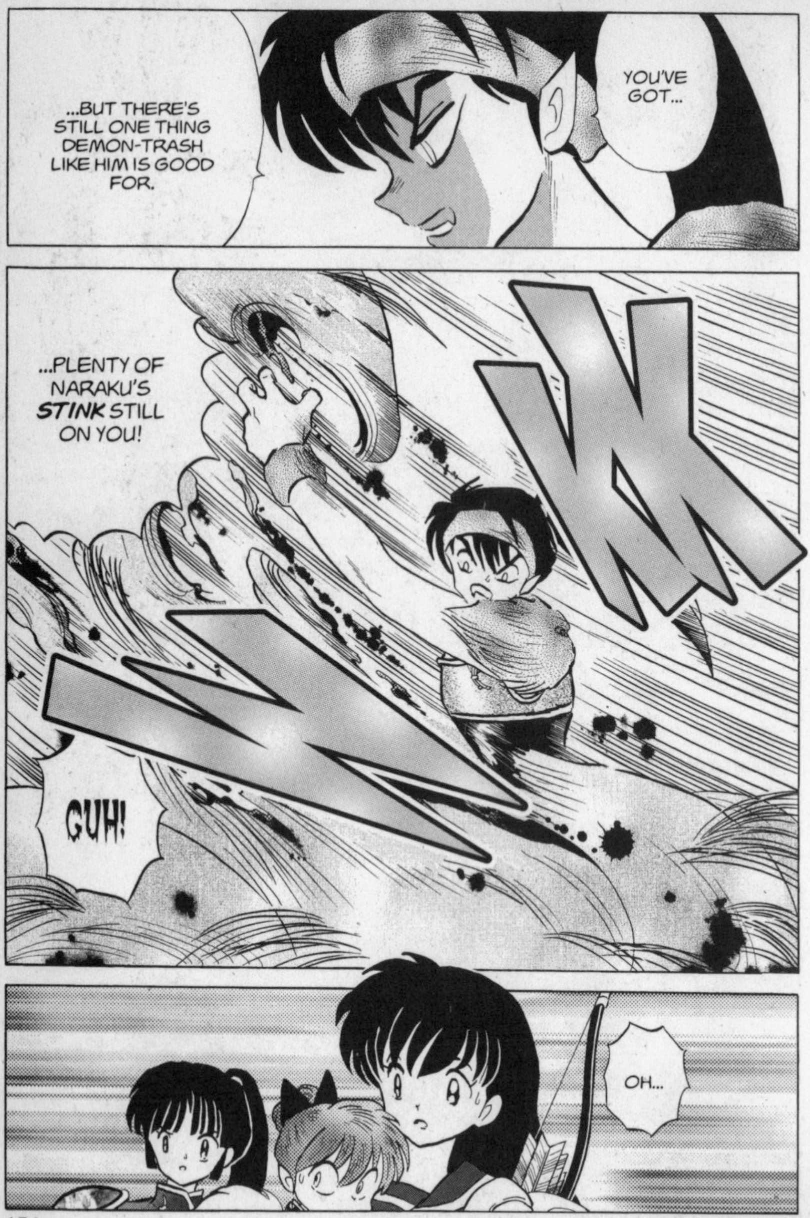
...BUT THERE'S STILL ONE THING DEMON-TRASH LIKE HIM IS GOOD FOR.
YOU'VE GOT...
...PLENTY OF NARAKU'S STINK STILL ON YOU!
GUH!
OH...

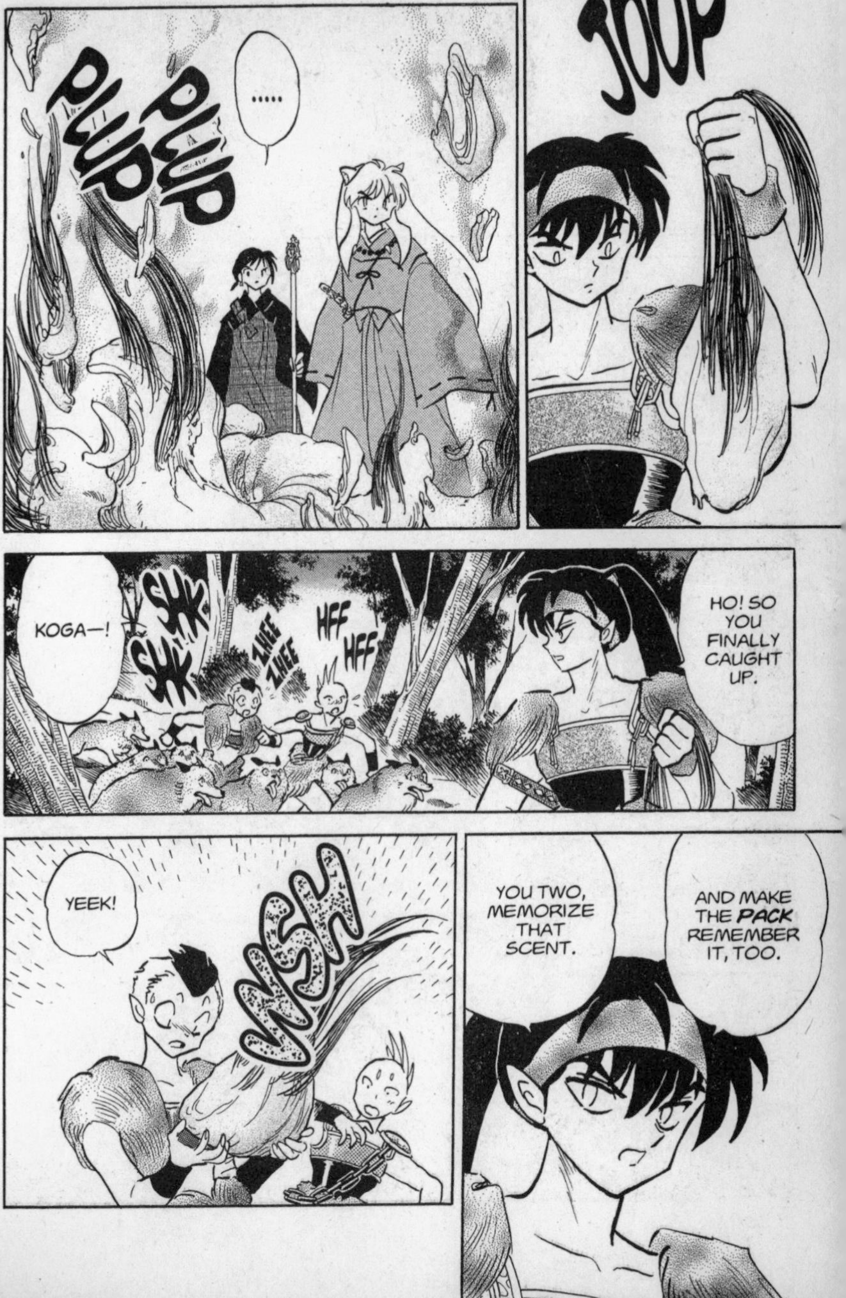
PLWIP
PLWIP
......
JOOP
KOGA—!
SHK
SHK
ZHEE
ZHEE
HFF
HFF
HO! SO YOU FINALLY CAUGHT UP.
YEEK!
WSH
YOU TWO, MEMORIZE THAT SCENT.
AND MAKE THE PACK REMEMBER IT, TOO.

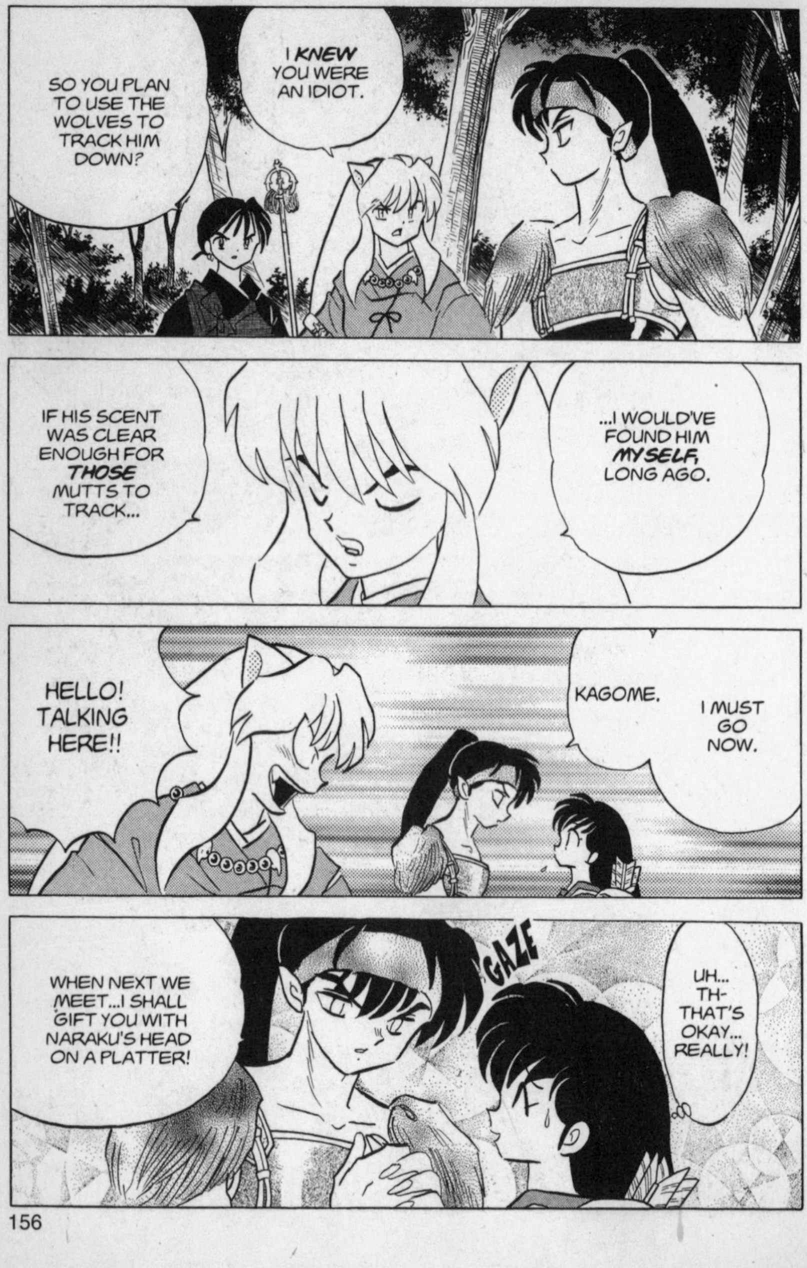
SO YOU PLAN TO USE THE WOLVES TO TRACK HIM DOWN?
I KNEW YOU WERE AN IDIOT.
IF HIS SCENT WAS CLEAR ENOUGH FOR THOSE MUTTS TO TRACK...
...I WOULD'VE FOUND HIM MYSELF, LONG AGO.
HELLO! TALKING HERE!!
KAGOME.
I MUST GO NOW.
WHEN NEXT WE MEET...I SHALL GIFT YOU WITH NARAKU'S HEAD ON A PLATTER!
GAZE
UH... TH- THAT'S OKAY... REALLY!

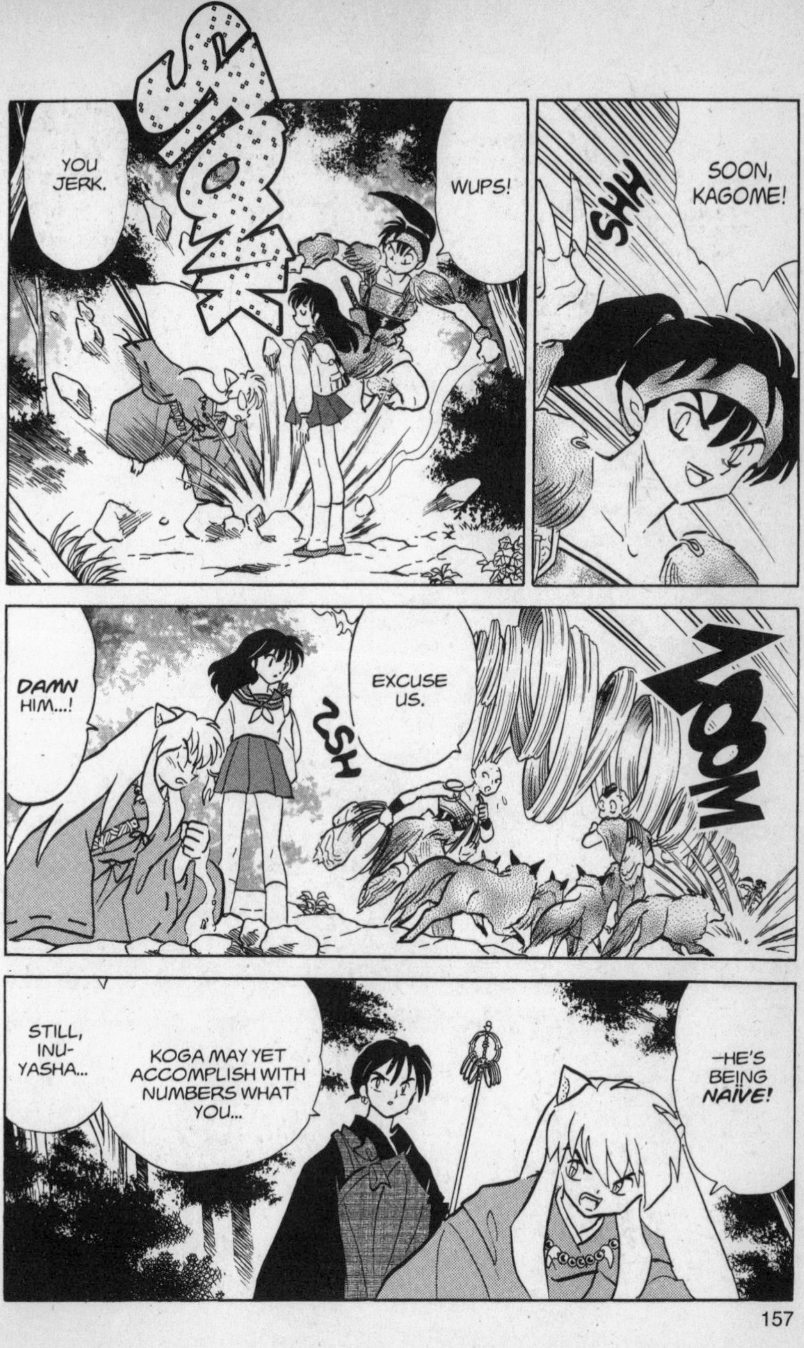
YOU JERK.
STONK
WUPS!
SHH
SOON, KAGOME!
DAMN HIM...!
EXCUSE US.
ZSH
ZOOM
STILL, INU-YASHA...
KOGA MAY YET ACCOMPLISH WITH NUMBERS WHAT YOU...
—HE'S BEING NAÏVE!

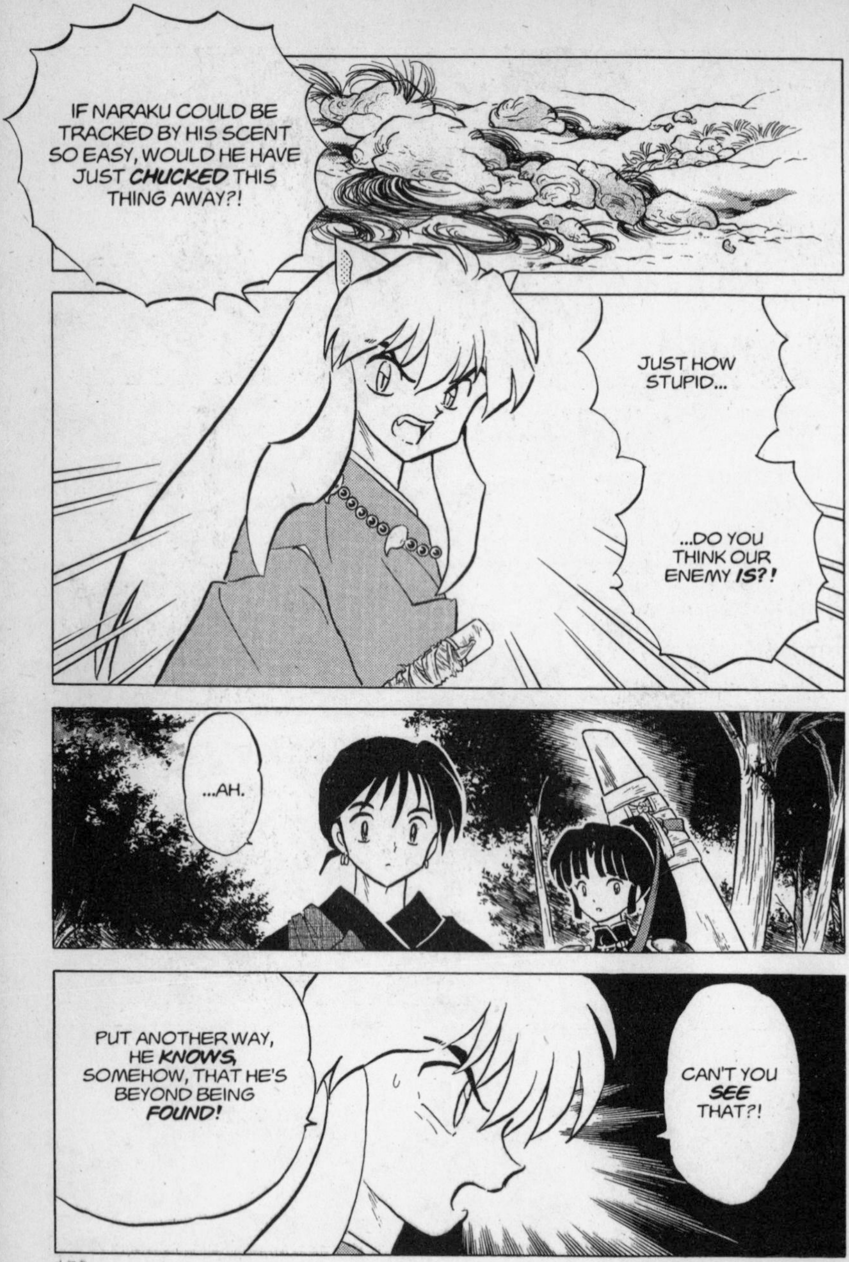
IF NARAKU COULD BE TRACKED BY HIS SCENT SO EASY, WOULD HE HAVE JUST CHUCKED THIS THING AWAY?!
JUST HOW STUPID...
...DO YOU THINK OUR ENEMY IS?!
...AH.
PUT ANOTHER WAY, HE KNOWS, SOMEHOW, THAT HE'S BEYOND BEING FOUND!
CAN'T YOU SEE THAT?!

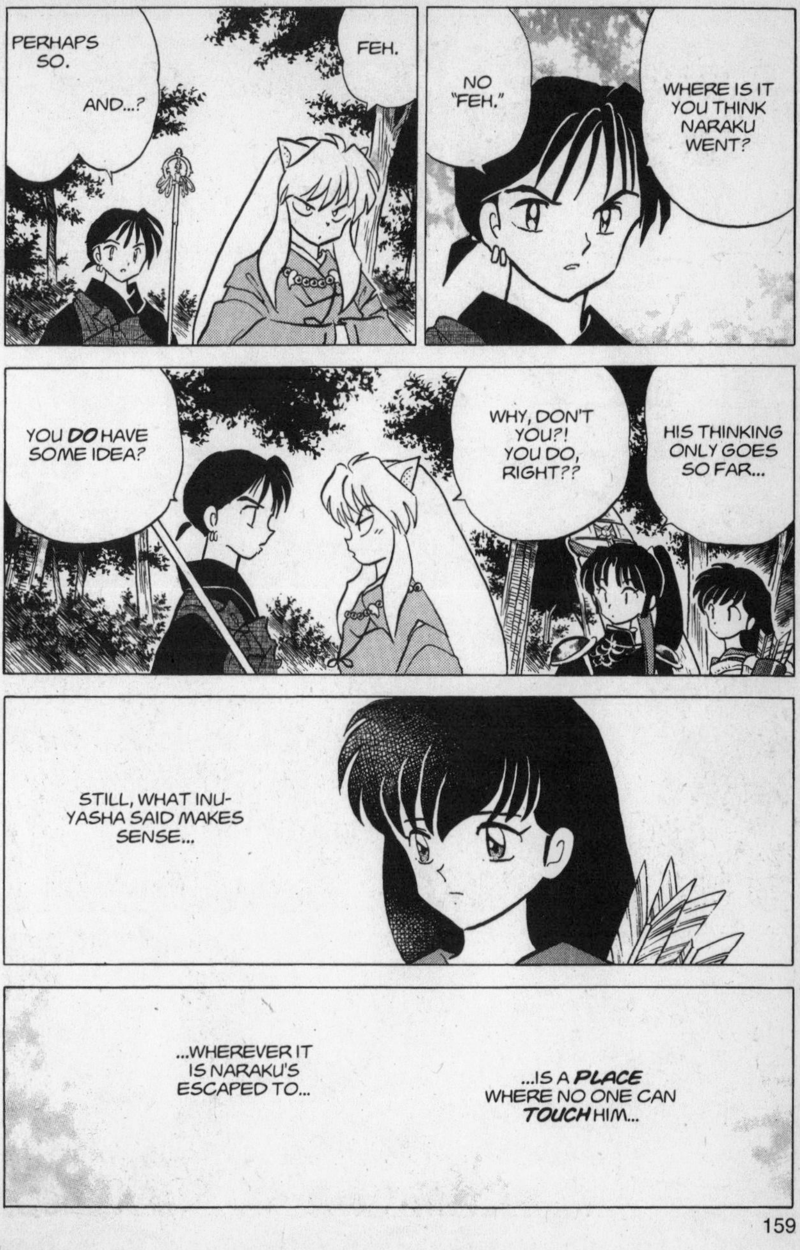
PERHAPS SO.
AND...?
FEH.
NO "FEH."
WHERE IS IT YOU THINK NARAKU WENT?
YOU **DO** HAVE SOME IDEA?
WHY, DON'T YOU?! YOU DO, RIGHT??
HIS THINKING ONLY GOES SO FAR...
STILL, WHAT INU-YASHA SAID MAKES SENSE...
...WHEREVER IT IS NARAKU'S ESCAPED TO...
...IS A ***PLACE*** WHERE NO ONE CAN ***TOUCH*** HIM...

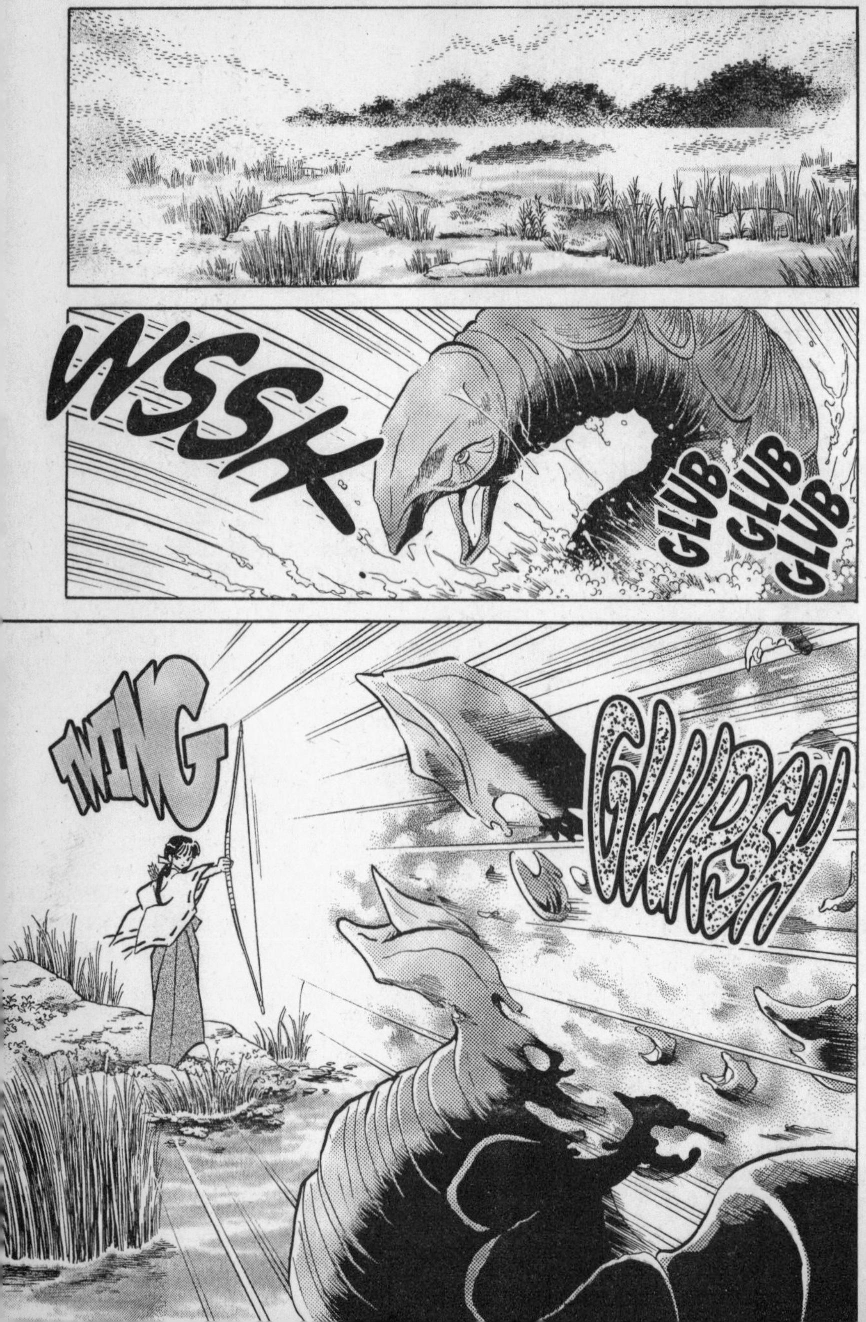
WSSK
GLUB GLUB GLUB
TWANG

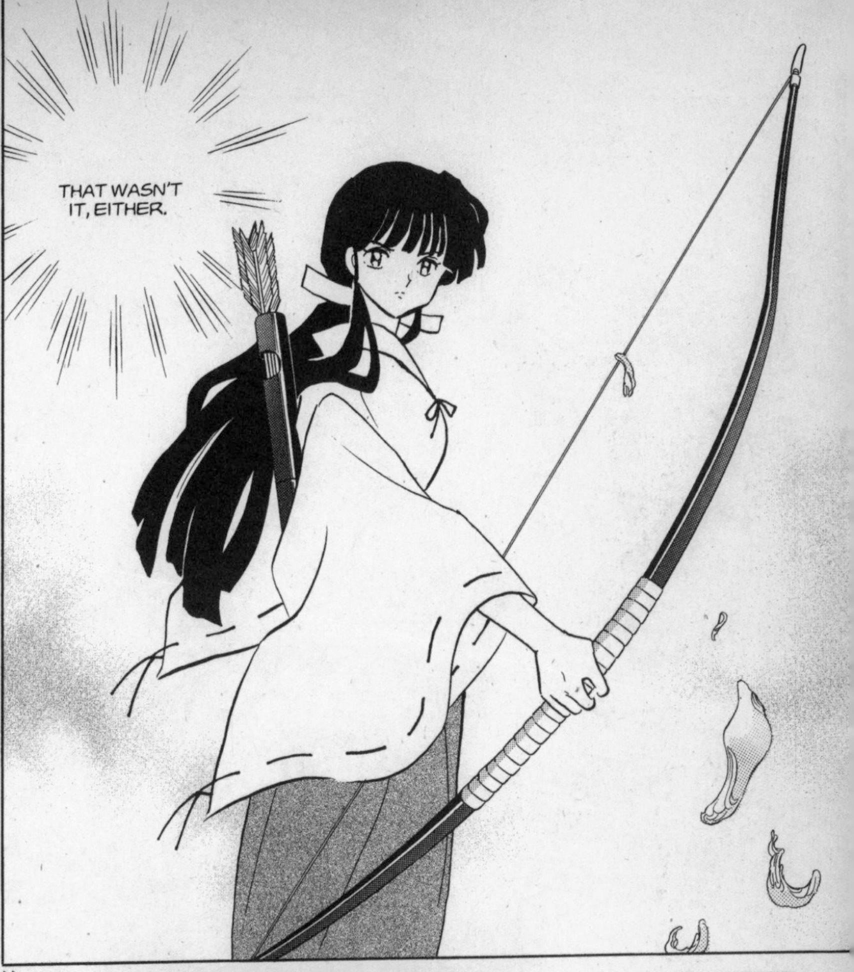
THAT WASN'T IT, EITHER.

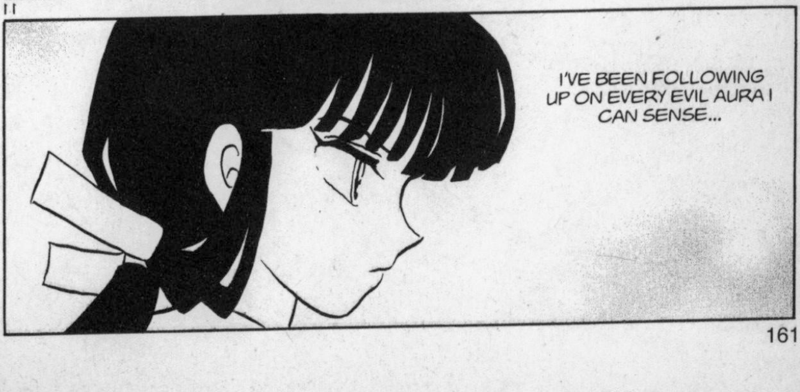
I'VE BEEN FOLLOWING UP ON EVERY EVIL AURA I CAN SENSE...

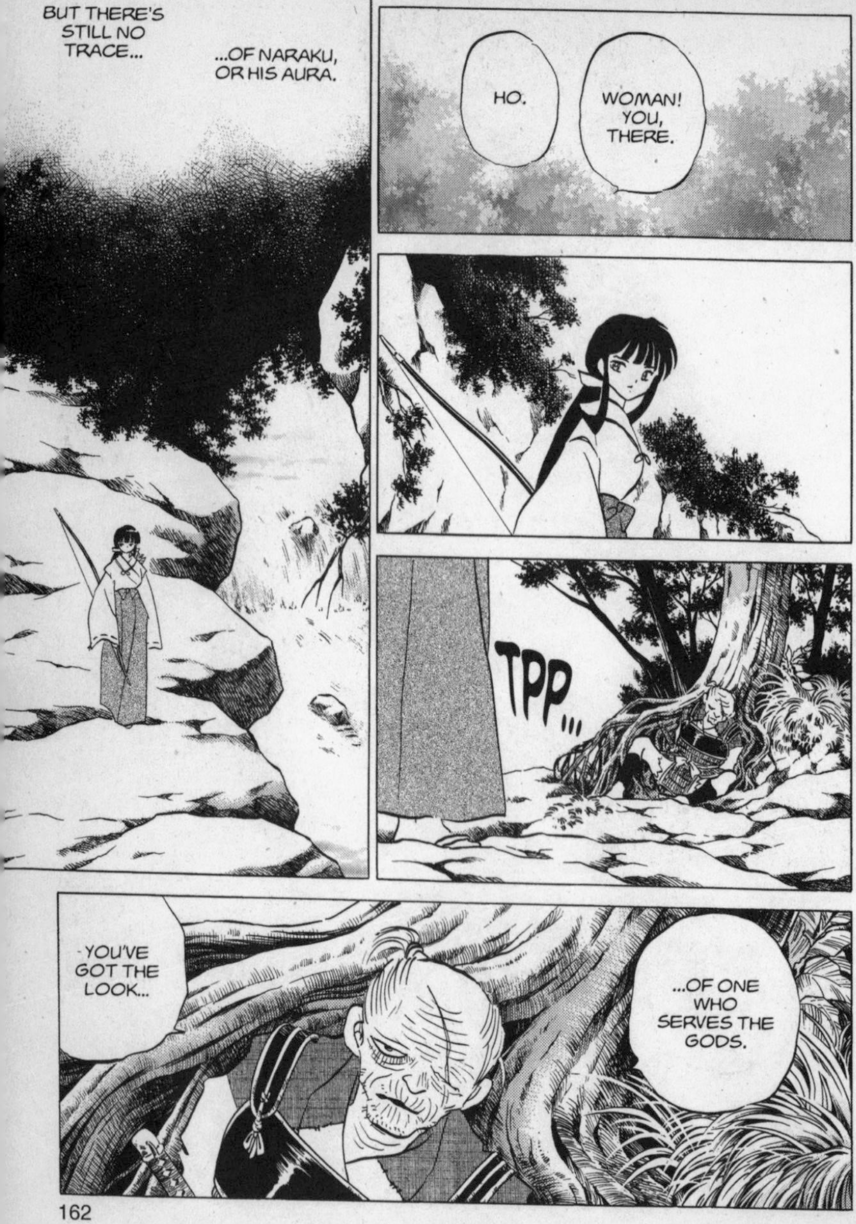
BUT THERE'S STILL NO TRACE...
...OF NARAKU, OR HIS AURA.
HO.
WOMAN! YOU, THERE.
TPP...
YOU'VE GOT THE LOOK...
...OF ONE WHO SERVES THE GODS.

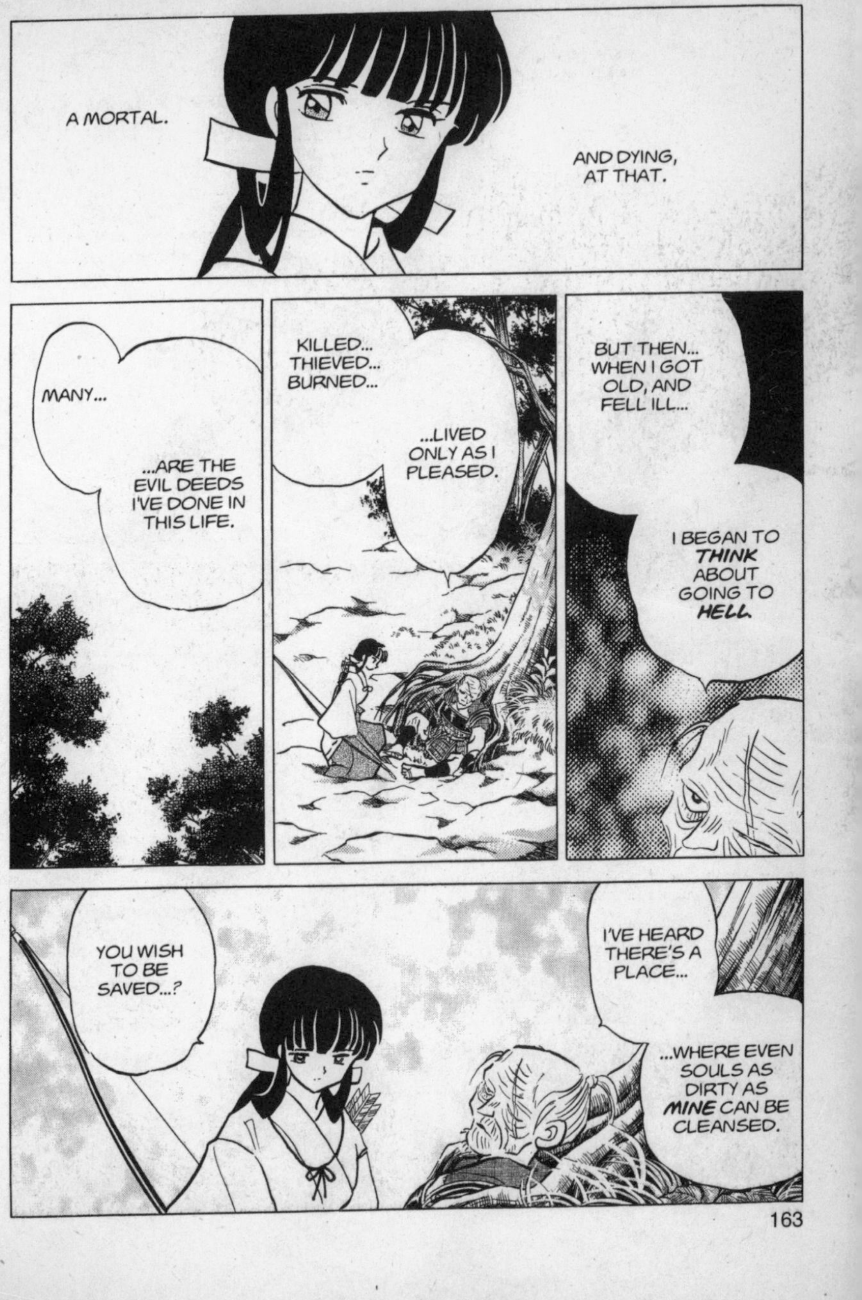
A MORTAL.
AND DYING, AT THAT.
MANY...
...ARE THE EVIL DEEDS I'VE DONE IN THIS LIFE.
KILLED... THIEVED... BURNED...
...LIVED ONLY AS I PLEASED.
BUT THEN... WHEN I GOT OLD, AND FELL ILL...
I BEGAN TO **THINK** ABOUT GOING TO **HELL**.
YOU WISH TO BE SAVED...?
I'VE HEARD THERE'S A PLACE...
...WHERE EVEN SOULS AS DIRTY AS **MINE** CAN BE CLEANSED.

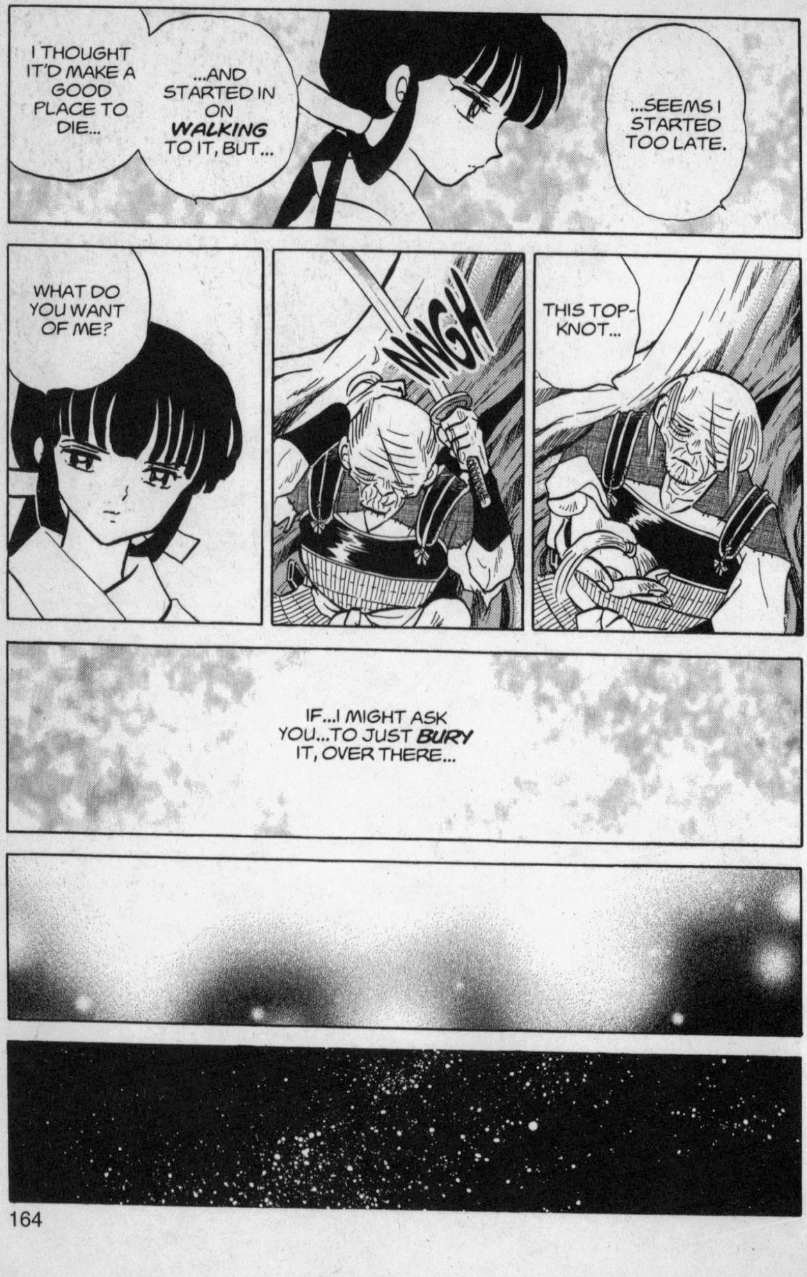
I THOUGHT IT'D MAKE A GOOD PLACE TO DIE...
...AND STARTED IN ON WALKING TO IT, BUT...
...SEEMS I STARTED TOO LATE.
WHAT DO YOU WANT OF ME?
NNGH
THIS TOP-KNOT...
IF...I MIGHT ASK YOU...TO JUST BURY IT, OVER THERE...

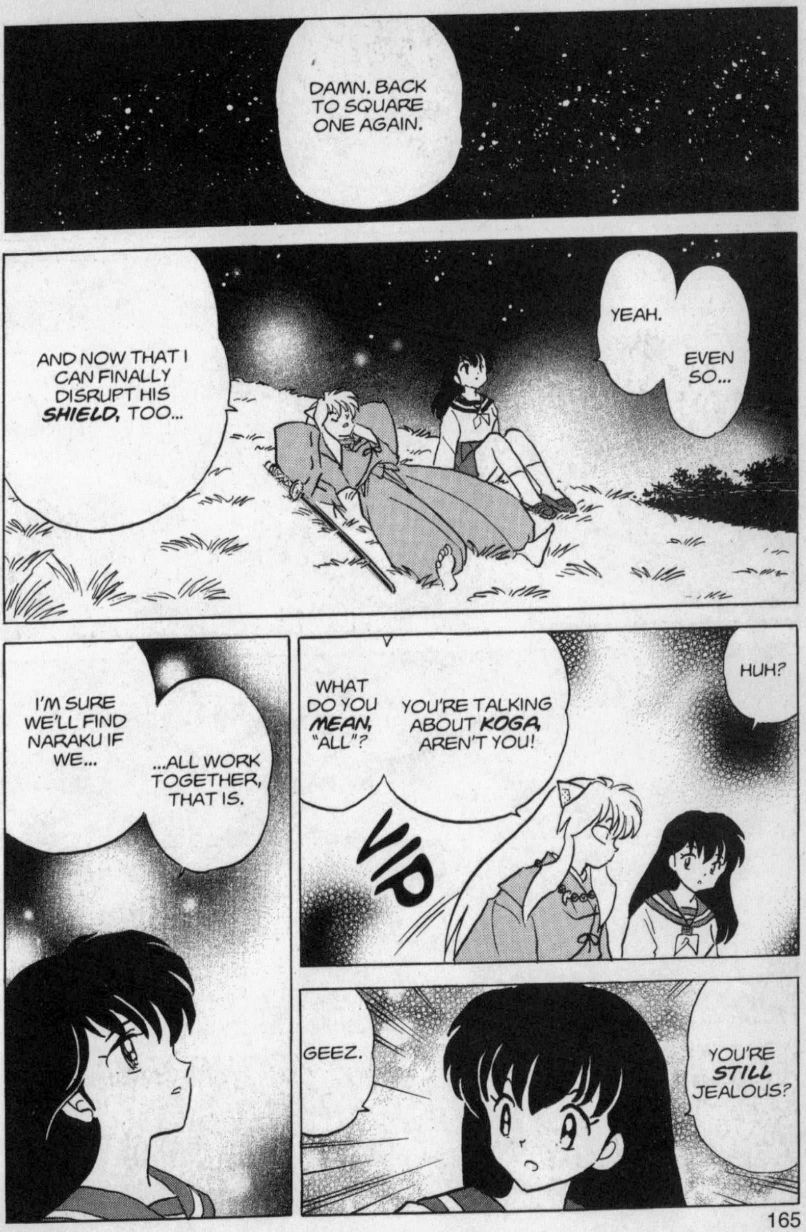
DAMN. BACK TO SQUARE ONE AGAIN.
AND NOW THAT I CAN FINALLY DISRUPT HIS **SHIELD**, TOO...
YEAH.
EVEN SO...
I'M SURE WE'LL FIND NARAKU IF WE...
...ALL WORK TOGETHER, THAT IS.
WHAT DO YOU **MEAN**, "ALL"?
YOU'RE TALKING ABOUT **KOGA**, AREN'T YOU!
HUH?
VIP
GEEZ.
YOU'RE **STILL** JEALOUS?

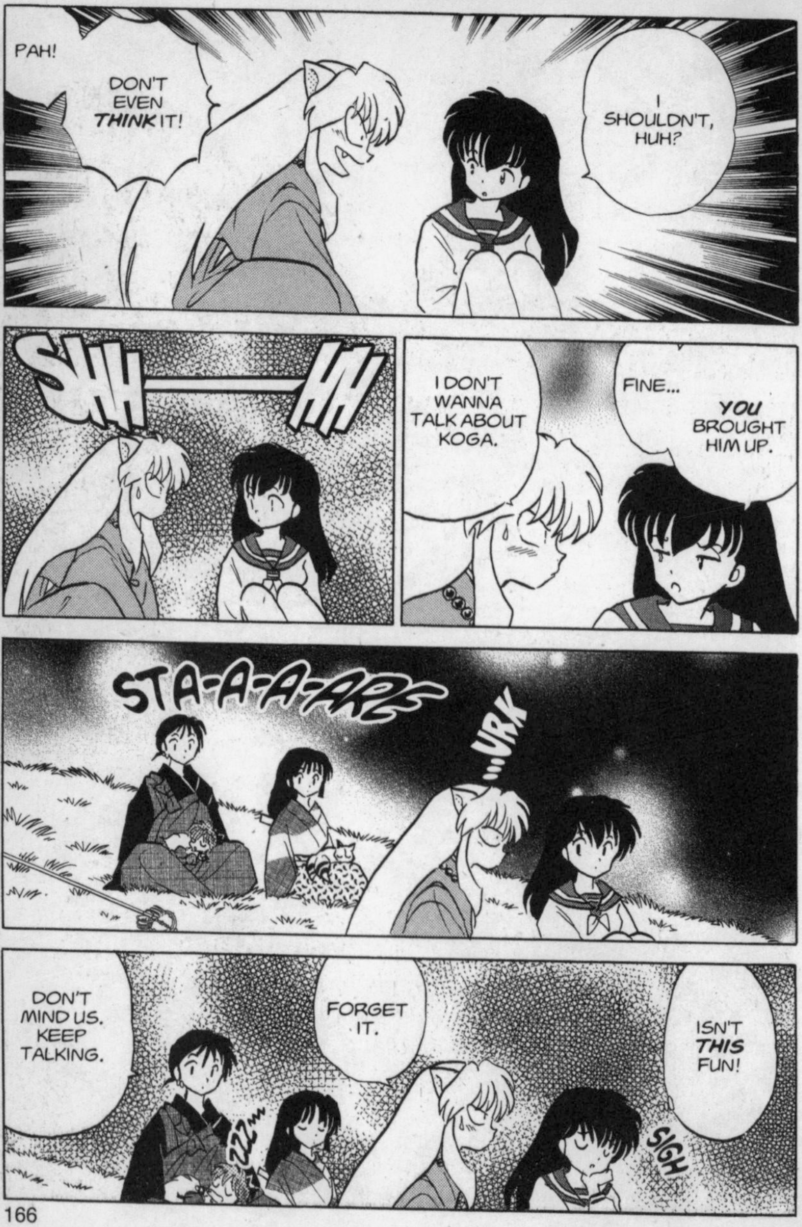

PAH!
DON'T EVEN **THINK** IT!
I SHOULDN'T, HUH?
SHHHH
I DON'T WANNA TALK ABOUT KOGA.
FINE... **YOU** BROUGHT HIM UP.
STA-A-A-ARE
...URK
DON'T MIND US. KEEP TALKING.
FORGET IT.
ISN'T **THIS** FUN!
SIGH

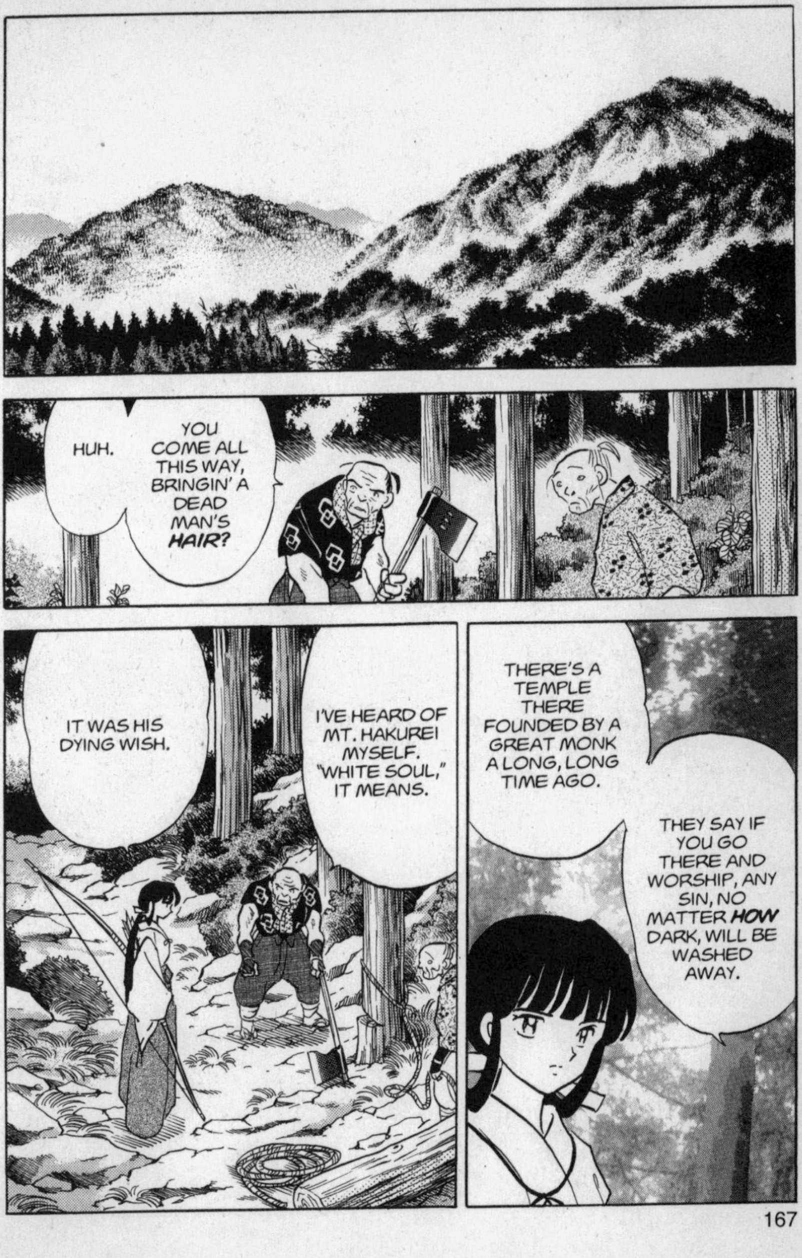
HUH.
YOU COME ALL THIS WAY, BRINGIN' A DEAD MAN'S *HAIR?*
IT WAS HIS DYING WISH.
I'VE HEARD OF MT. HAKUREI MYSELF. "WHITE SOUL," IT MEANS.
THERE'S A TEMPLE THERE FOUNDED BY A GREAT MONK A LONG, LONG TIME AGO.
THEY SAY IF YOU GO THERE AND WORSHIP, ANY SIN, NO MATTER *HOW* DARK, WILL BE WASHED AWAY.

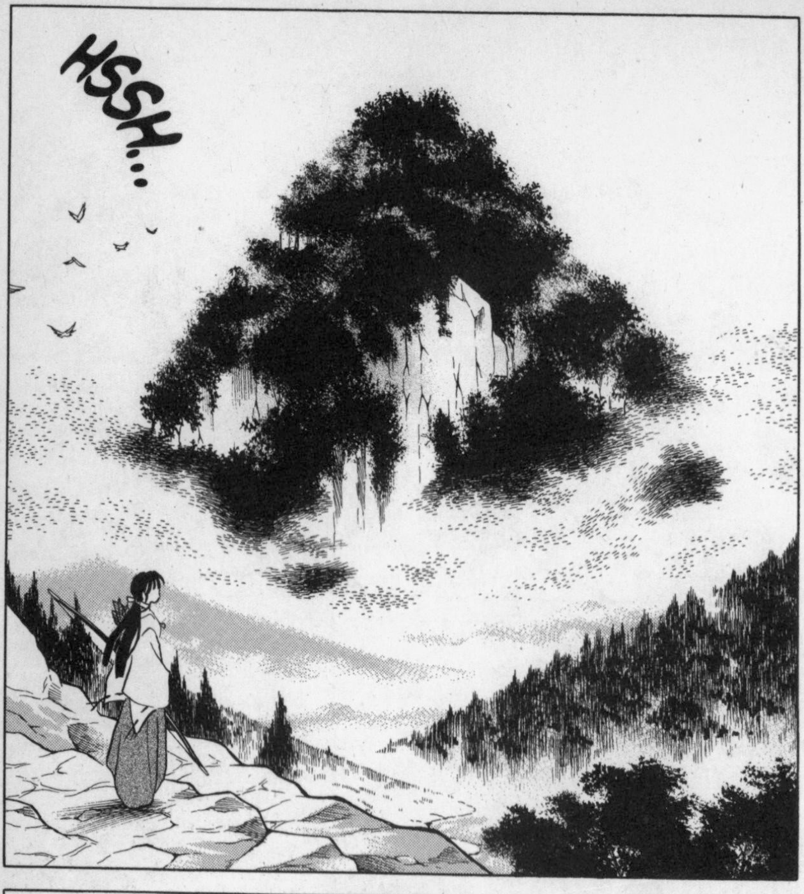
HSSH...

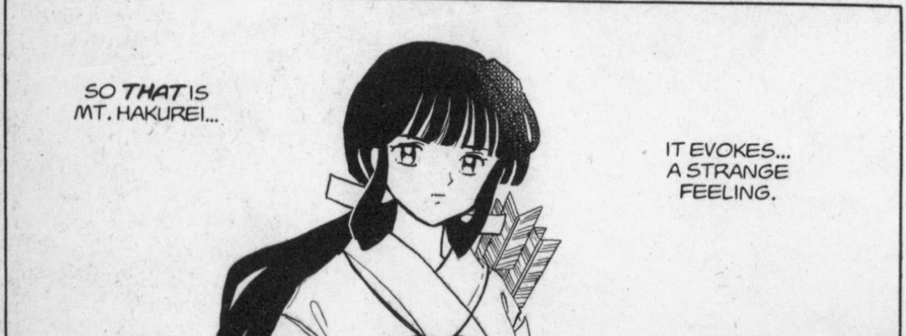
SO ***THAT*** IS MT. HAKUREI...
IT EVOKES... A STRANGE FEELING.

SCROLL TEN
THE OGRE'S HEAD

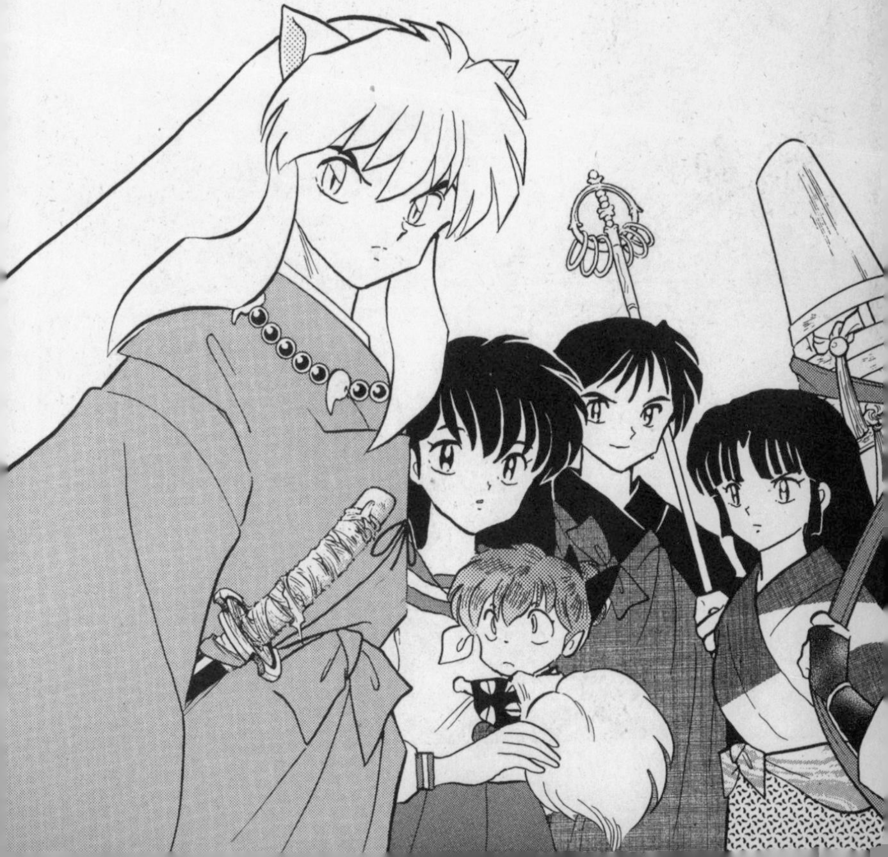

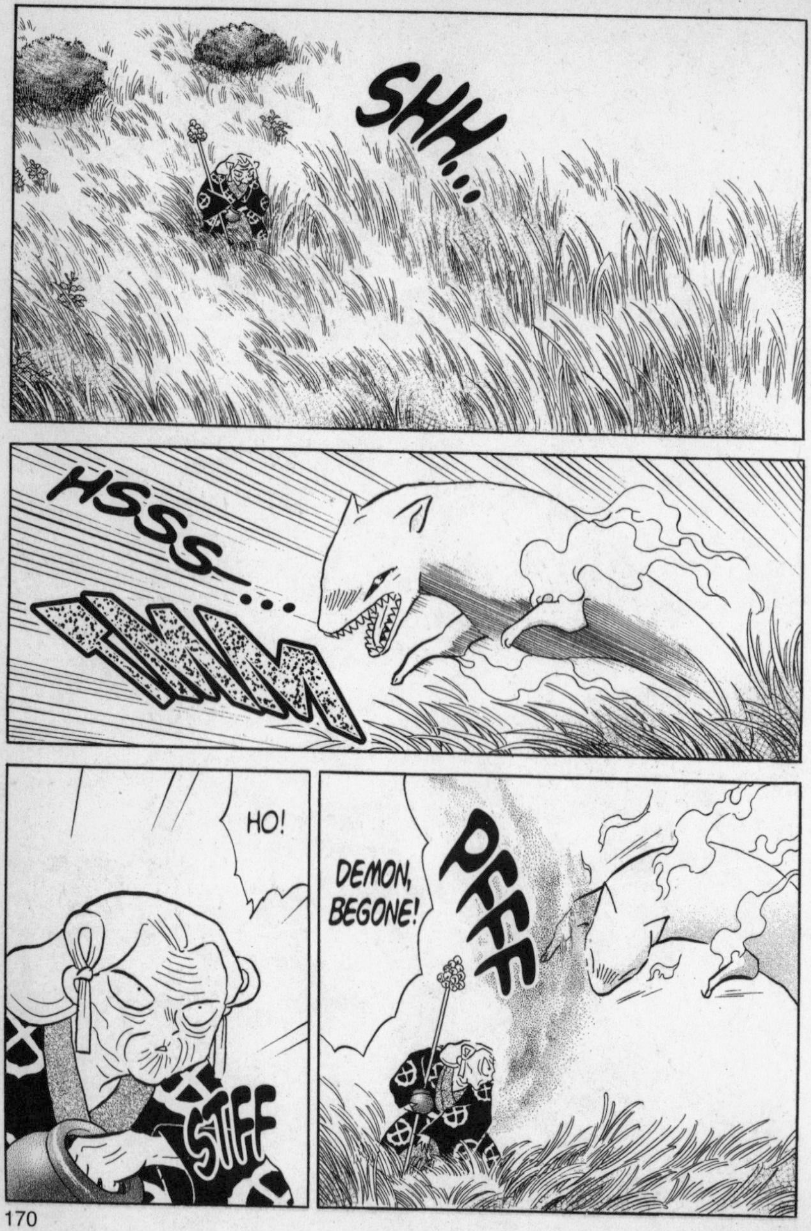
SHH...
HSSS...
FWM
HO!
STIFF
DEMON, BEGONE!
PFFF

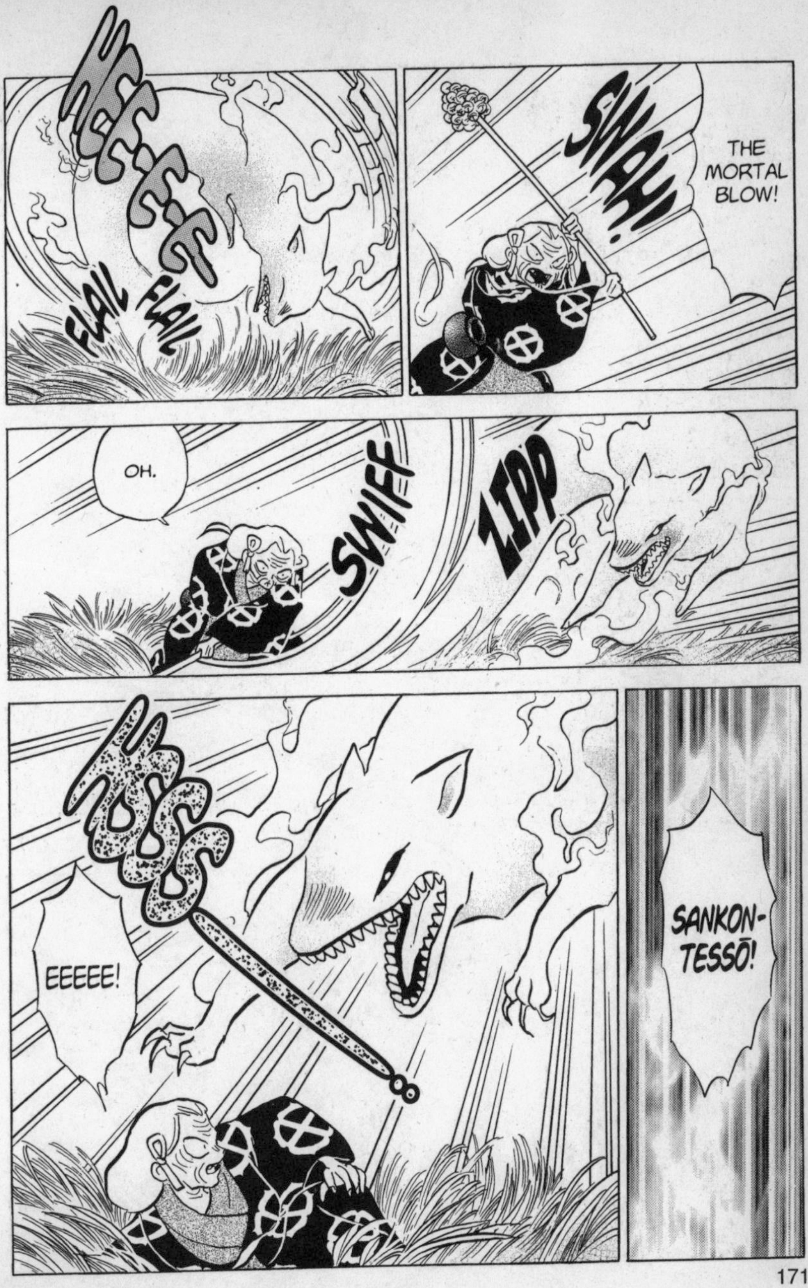
FLAIL FLAIL
SWAH!
THE MORTAL BLOW!
OH.
SWIFF
ZIPP
EEEEE!
SANKON-TESSŌ!

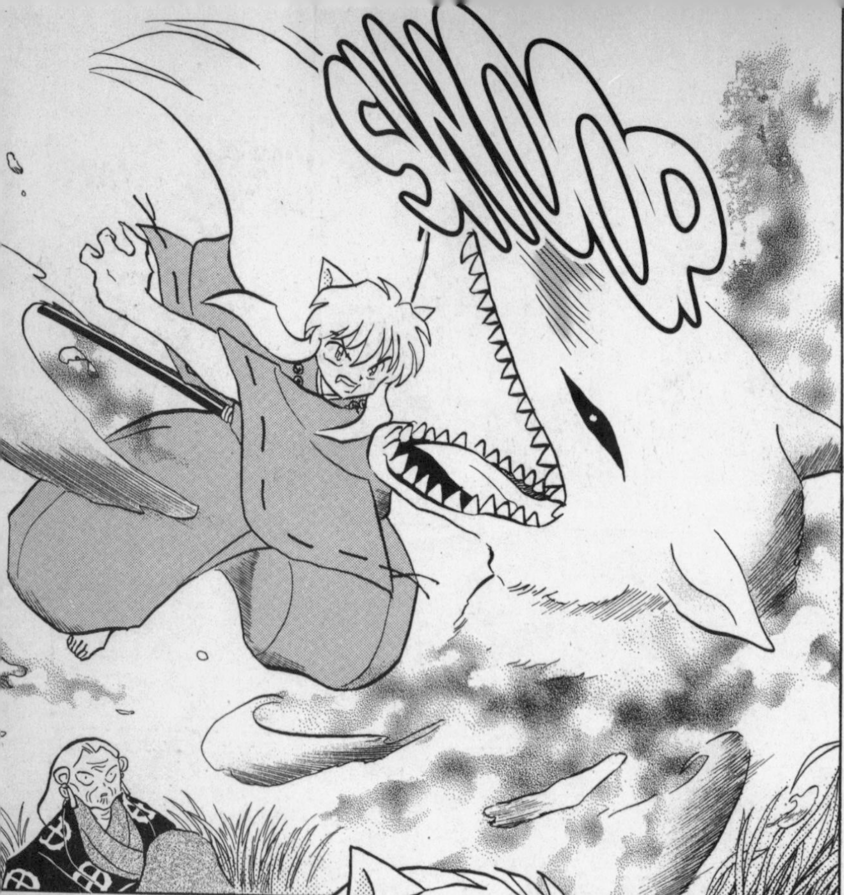
SWOOP

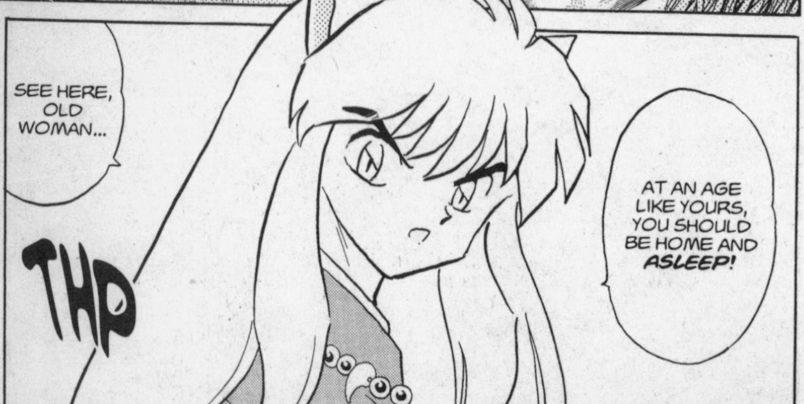
SEE HERE, OLD WOMAN...
AT AN AGE LIKE YOURS, YOU SHOULD BE HOME AND ***ASLEEP!***
THP

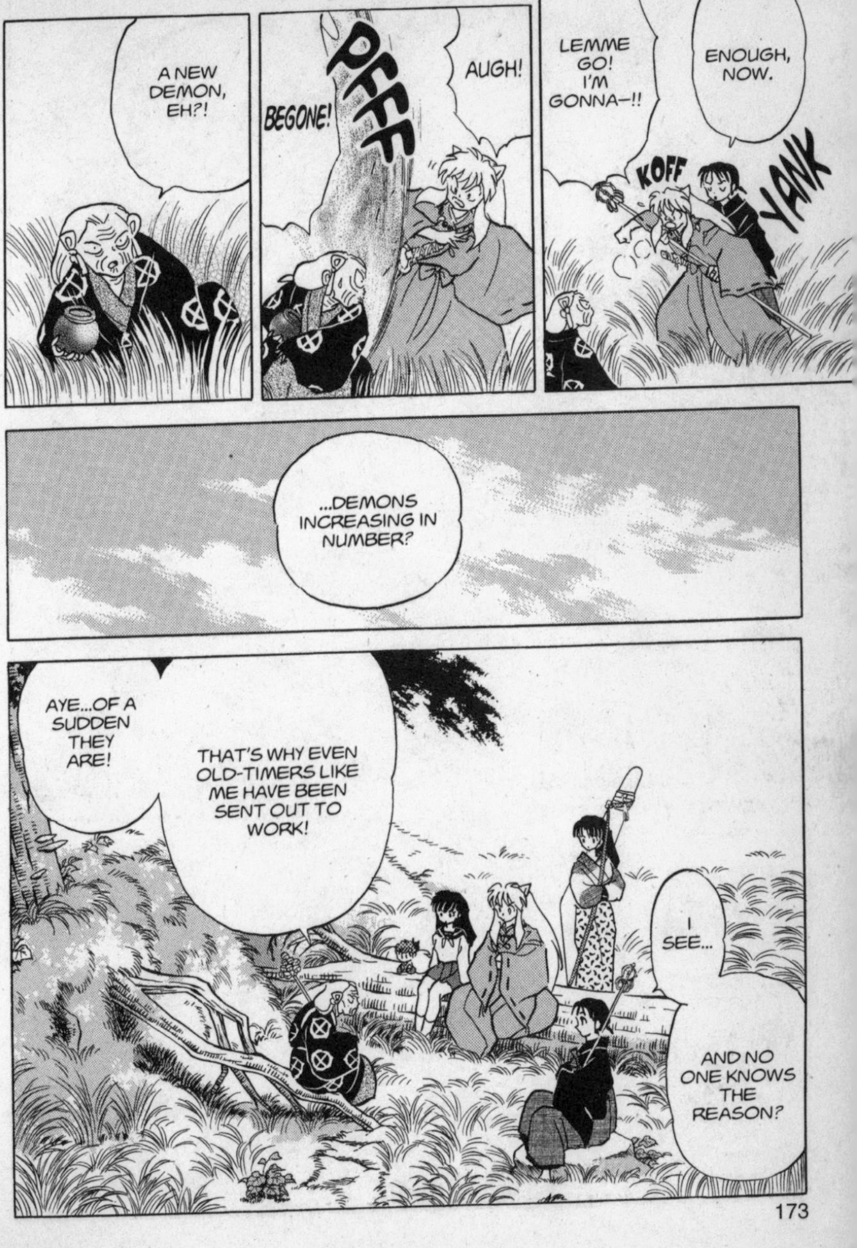
A NEW DEMON, EH?!
BEGONE!
PFFF
AUGH!
LEMME GO! I'M GONNA-!!
KOFF
ENOUGH, NOW.
YANK
...DEMONS INCREASING IN NUMBER?
AYE...OF A SUDDEN THEY ARE!
THAT'S WHY EVEN OLD-TIMERS LIKE ME HAVE BEEN SENT OUT TO WORK!
I SEE...
AND NO ONE KNOWS THE REASON?

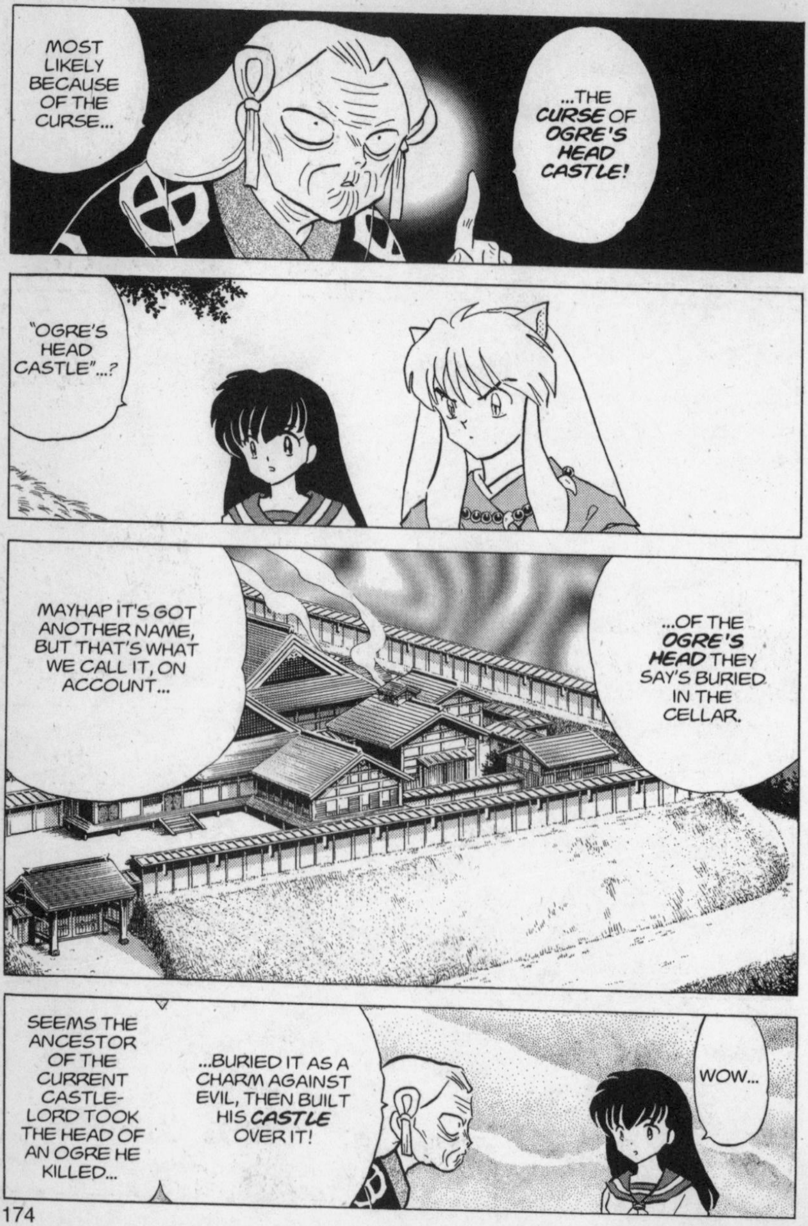
MOST LIKELY BECAUSE OF THE CURSE...
...THE CURSE OF OGRE'S HEAD CASTLE!
"OGRE'S HEAD CASTLE"...?
MAYHAP IT'S GOT ANOTHER NAME, BUT THAT'S WHAT WE CALL IT, ON ACCOUNT...
...OF THE OGRE'S HEAD THEY SAY'S BURIED IN THE CELLAR.
SEEMS THE ANCESTOR OF THE CURRENT CASTLE-LORD TOOK THE HEAD OF AN OGRE HE KILLED...
...BURIED IT AS A CHARM AGAINST EVIL, THEN BUILT HIS CASTLE OVER IT!
WOW...

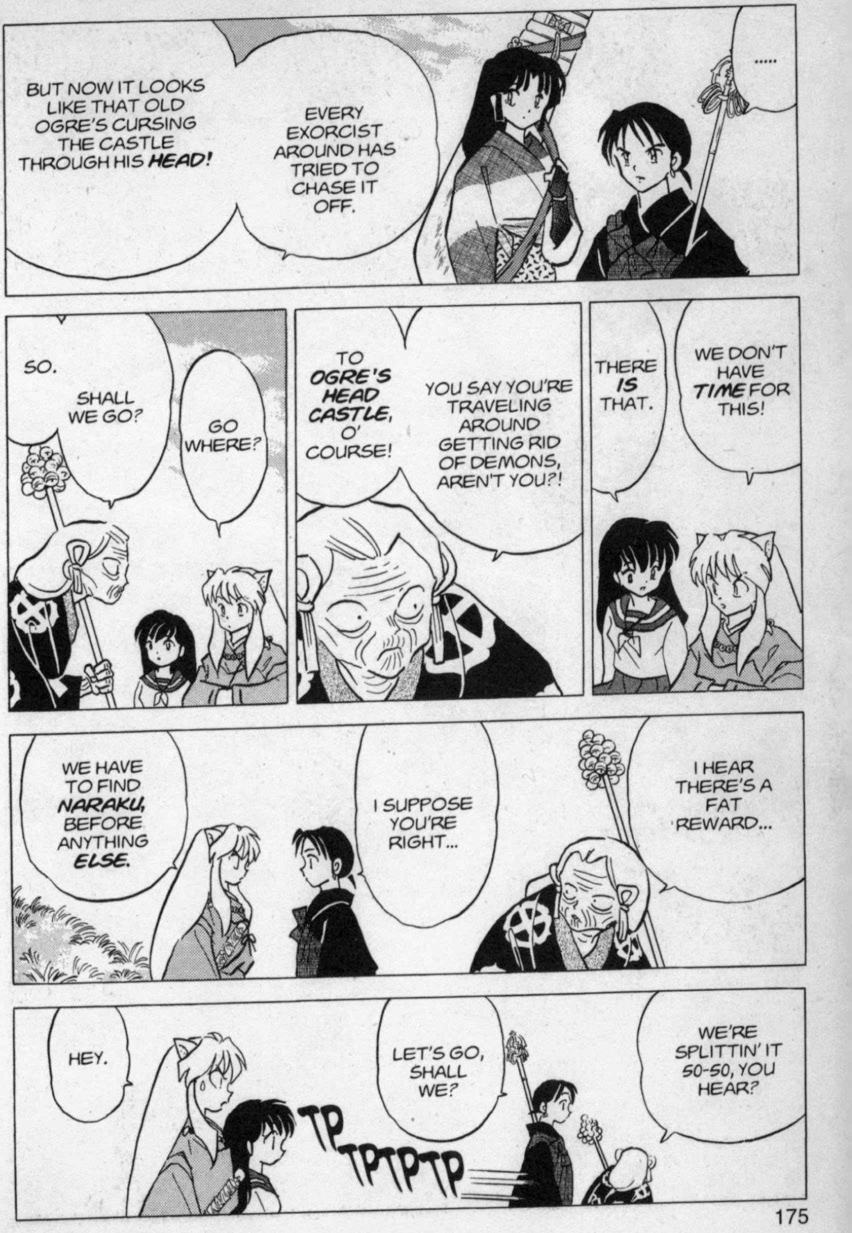
BUT NOW IT LOOKS LIKE THAT OLD OGRE'S CURSING THE CASTLE THROUGH HIS HEAD!
EVERY EXORCIST AROUND HAS TRIED TO CHASE IT OFF.
.....
SO.
SHALL WE GO?
GO WHERE?
TO OGRE'S HEAD CASTLE, O' COURSE!
YOU SAY YOU'RE TRAVELING AROUND GETTING RID OF DEMONS, AREN'T YOU?!
THERE IS THAT.
WE DON'T HAVE TIME FOR THIS!
WE HAVE TO FIND NARAKU, BEFORE ANYTHING ELSE.
I SUPPOSE YOU'RE RIGHT...
I HEAR THERE'S A FAT REWARD...
HEY.
TP TPTPTP
LET'S GO, SHALL WE?
WE'RE SPLITTIN' IT 50-50, YOU HEAR?

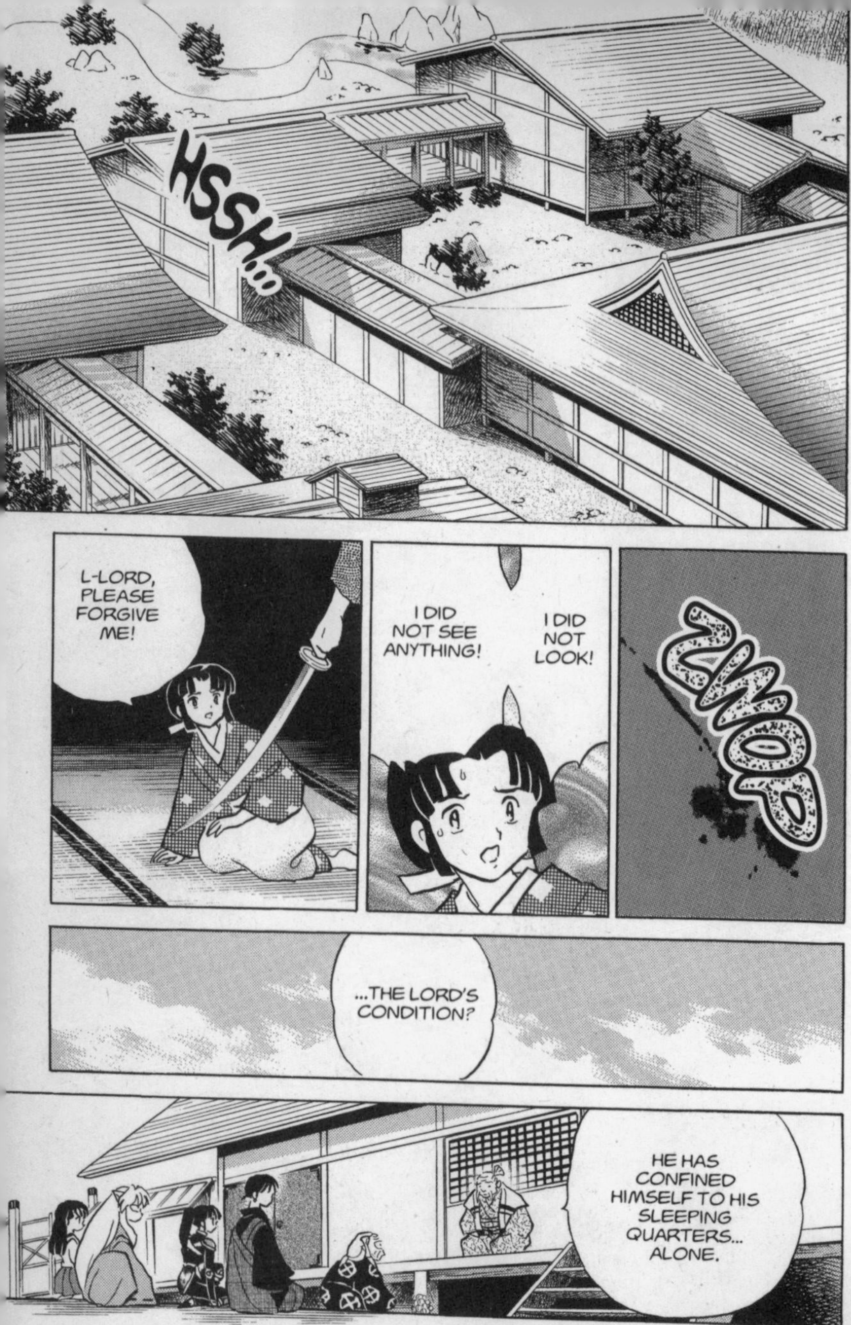
HSSH...
L-LORD, PLEASE FORGIVE ME!
I DID NOT SEE ANYTHING!
I DID NOT LOOK!
ZWOP
...THE LORD'S CONDITION?
HE HAS CONFINED HIMSELF TO HIS SLEEPING QUARTERS... ALONE.

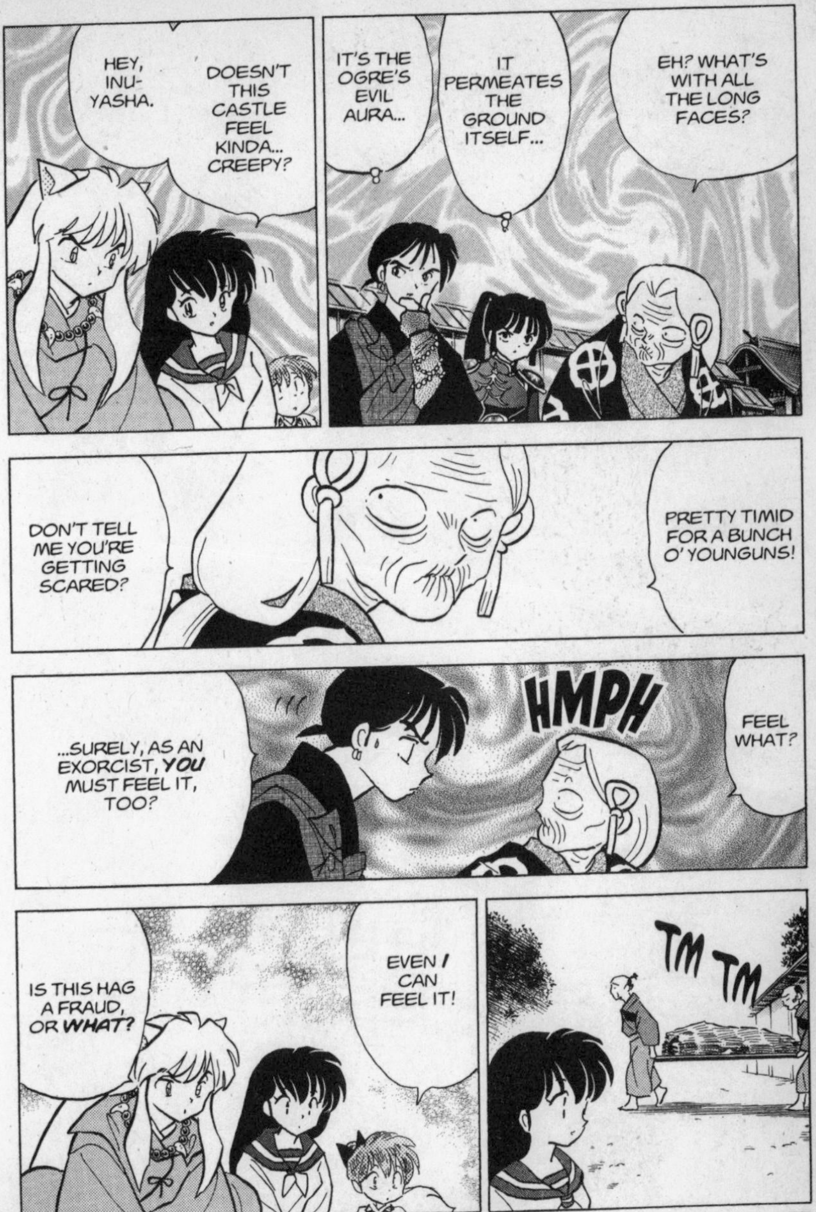
HEY, INU-YASHA.
DOESN'T THIS CASTLE FEEL KINDA... CREEPY?
IT'S THE OGRE'S EVIL AURA...
IT PERMEATES THE GROUND ITSELF...
EH? WHAT'S WITH ALL THE LONG FACES?
DON'T TELL ME YOU'RE GETTING SCARED?
PRETTY TIMID FOR A BUNCH O' YOUNGUNS!
...SURELY, AS AN EXORCIST, YOU MUST FEEL IT, TOO?
HMPH
FEEL WHAT?
IS THIS HAG A FRAUD, OR WHAT?
EVEN I CAN FEEL IT!
TM TM

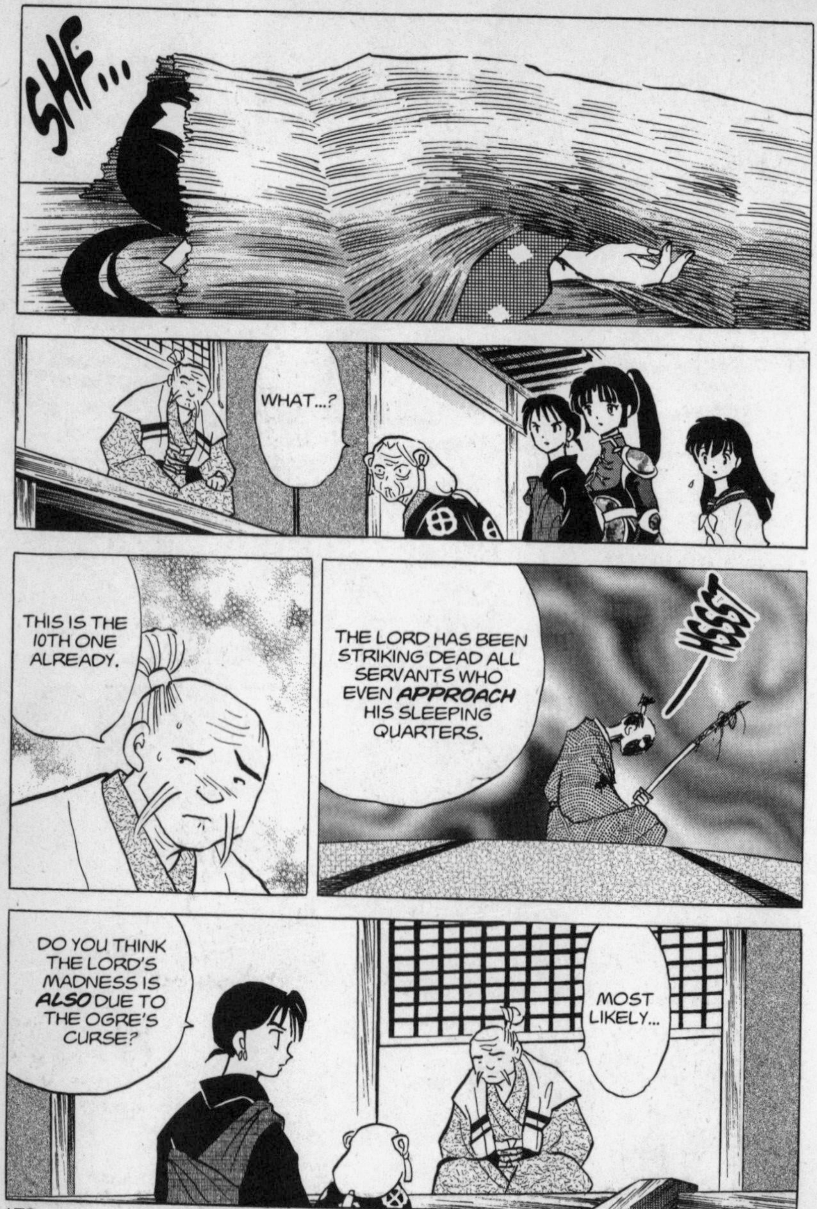
SHF...
WHAT...?
THIS IS THE 10TH ONE ALREADY.
THE LORD HAS BEEN STRIKING DEAD ALL SERVANTS WHO EVEN APPROACH HIS SLEEPING QUARTERS.
HSSST
DO YOU THINK THE LORD'S MADNESS IS ALSO DUE TO THE OGRE'S CURSE?
MOST LIKELY...

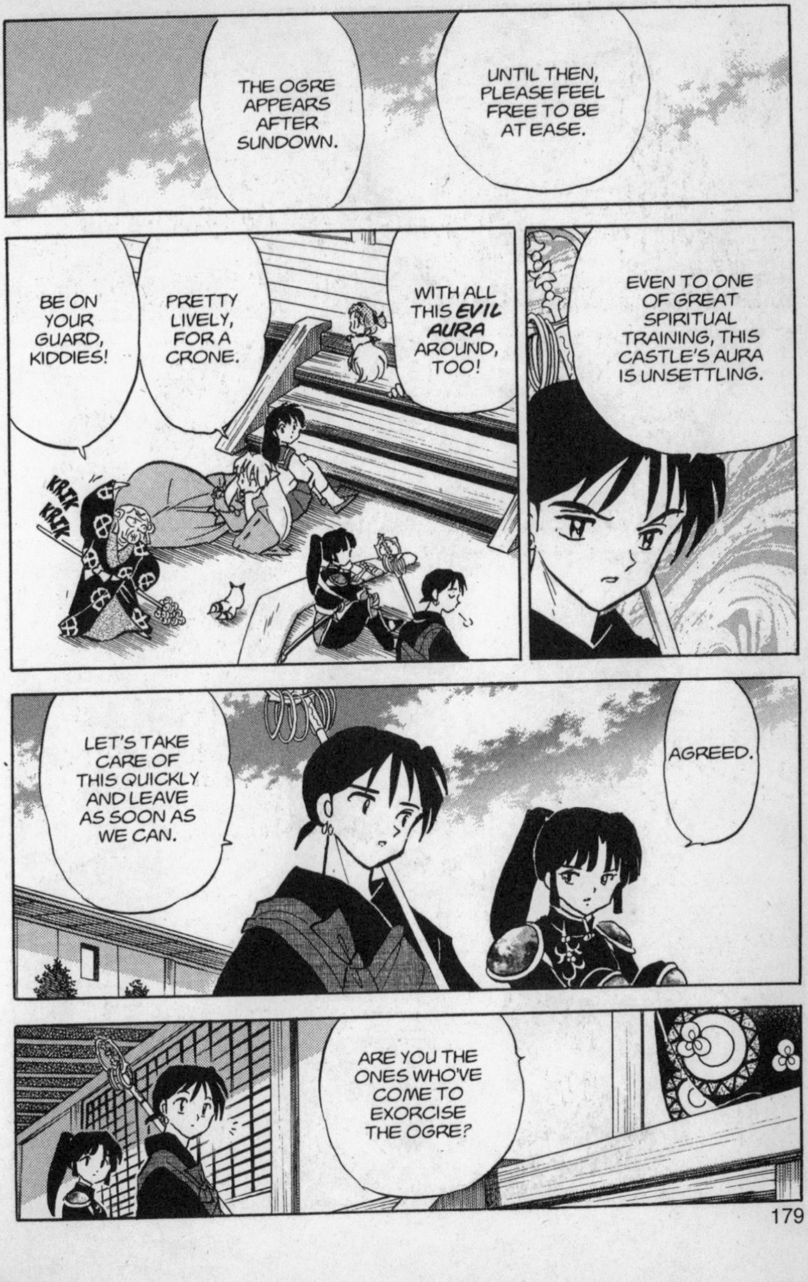
THE OGRE APPEARS AFTER SUNDOWN.
UNTIL THEN, PLEASE FEEL FREE TO BE AT EASE.
BE ON YOUR GUARD, KIDDIES!
KRIK KRIK
PRETTY LIVELY, FOR A CRONE.
WITH ALL THIS EVIL AURA AROUND, TOO!
EVEN TO ONE OF GREAT SPIRITUAL TRAINING, THIS CASTLE'S AURA IS UNSETTLING.
LET'S TAKE CARE OF THIS QUICKLY AND LEAVE AS SOON AS WE CAN.
AGREED.
ARE YOU THE ONES WHO'VE COME TO EXORCISE THE OGRE?

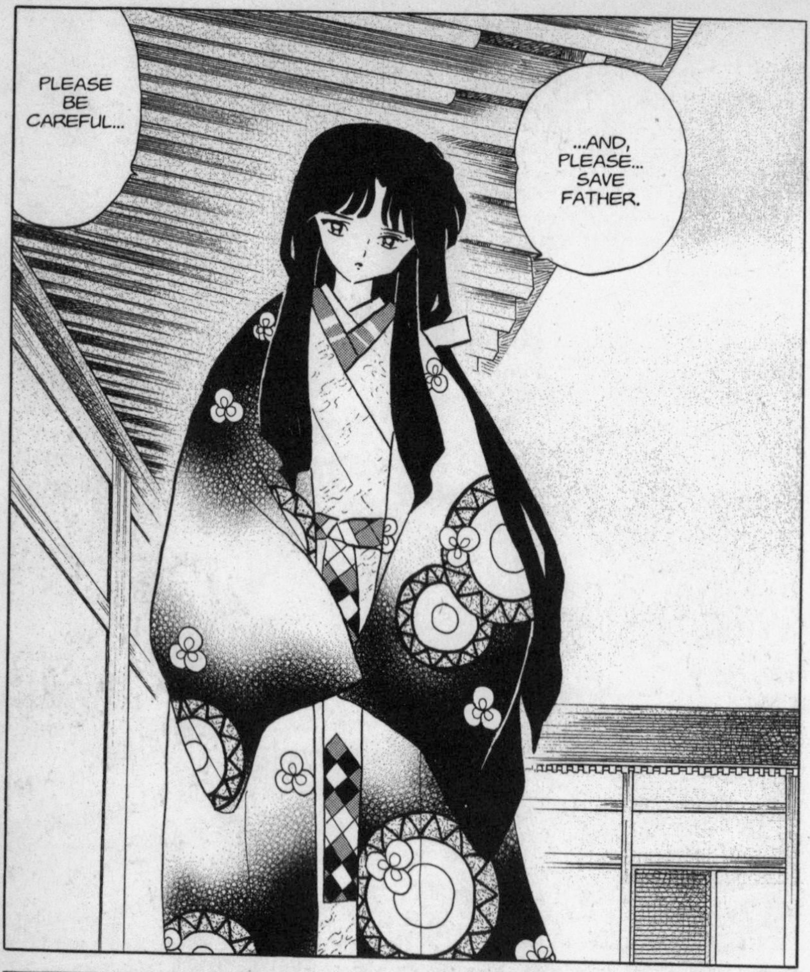
PLEASE BE CAREFUL...
...AND, PLEASE... SAVE FATHER.

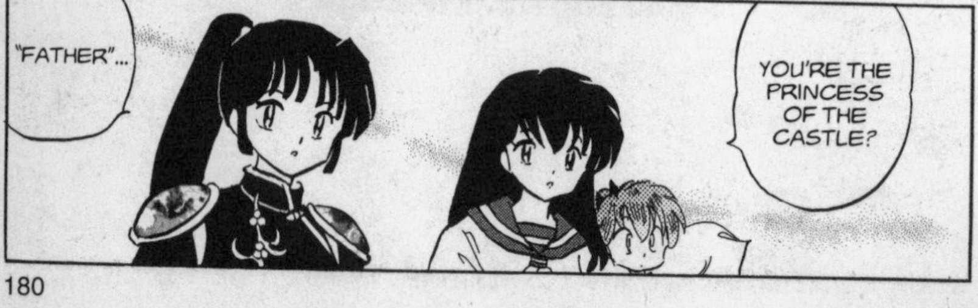
"FATHER"...
YOU'RE THE PRINCESS OF THE CASTLE?

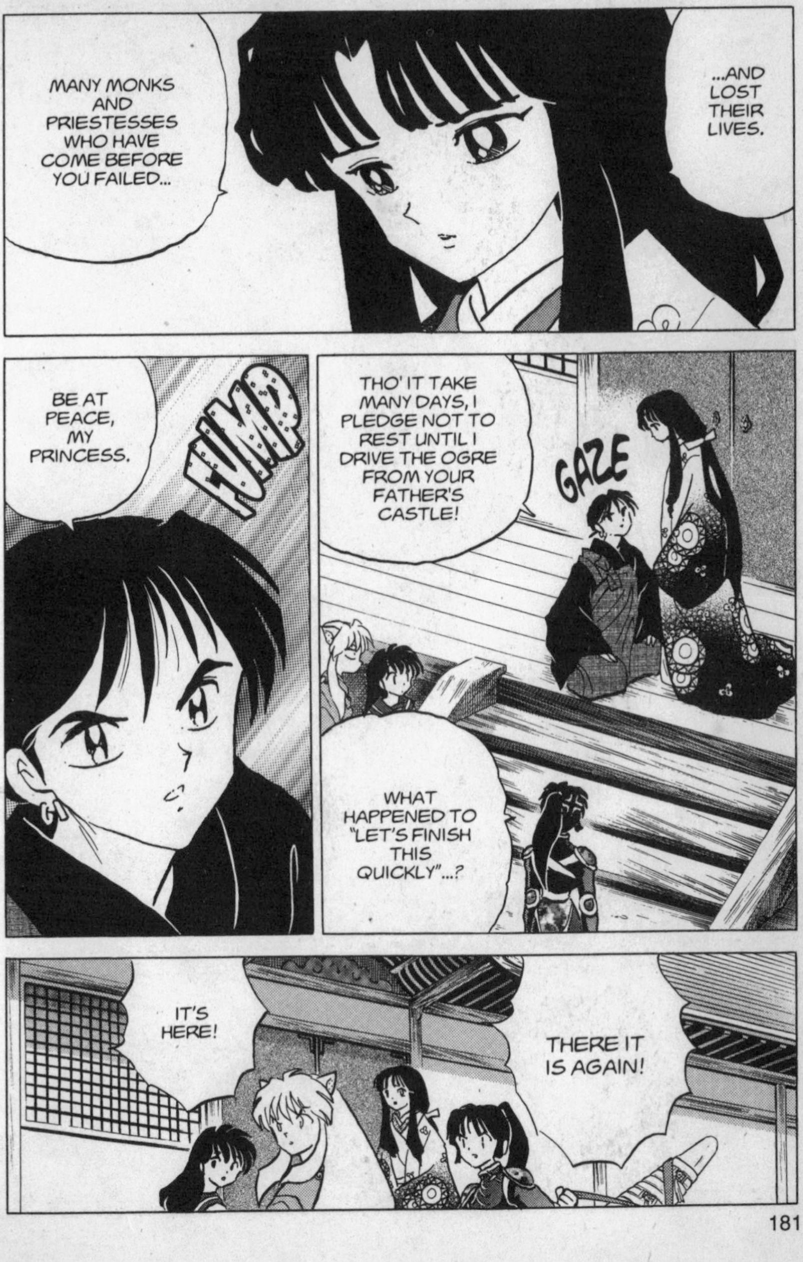
MANY MONKS AND PRIESTESSES WHO HAVE COME BEFORE YOU FAILED...
...AND LOST THEIR LIVES.
BE AT PEACE, MY PRINCESS.
THO' IT TAKE MANY DAYS, I PLEDGE NOT TO REST UNTIL I DRIVE THE OGRE FROM YOUR FATHER'S CASTLE!
GAZE
WHAT HAPPENED TO "LET'S FINISH THIS QUICKLY"...?
IT'S HERE!
THERE IT IS AGAIN!

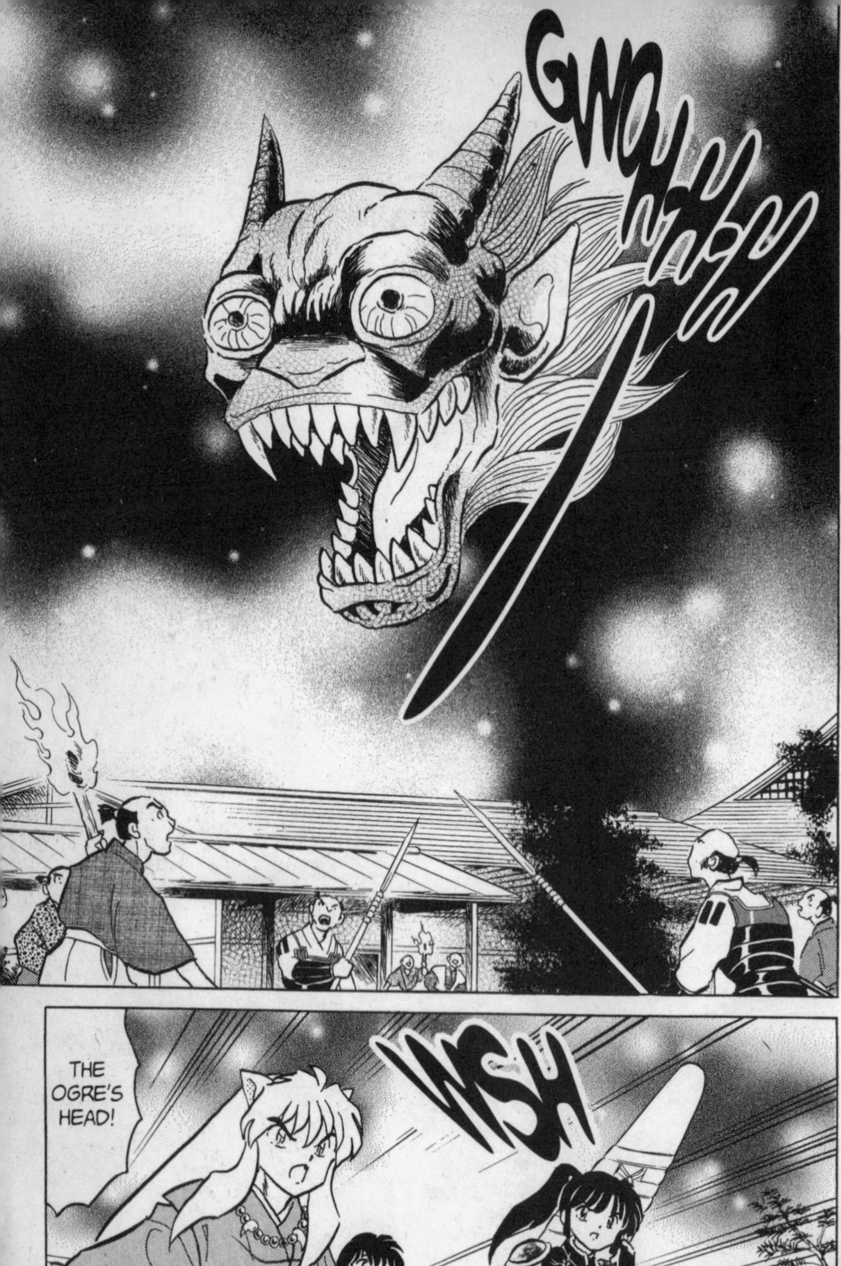
THE OGRE'S HEAD!
WSH

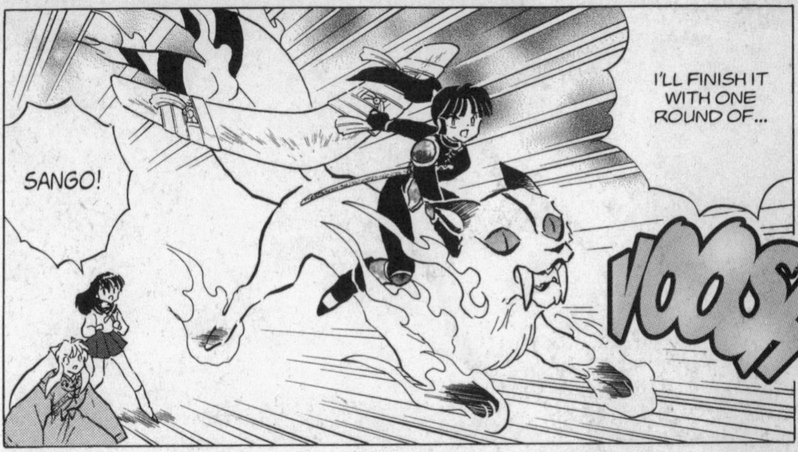
SANGO!
I'LL FINISH IT WITH ONE ROUND OF...
VOOSH
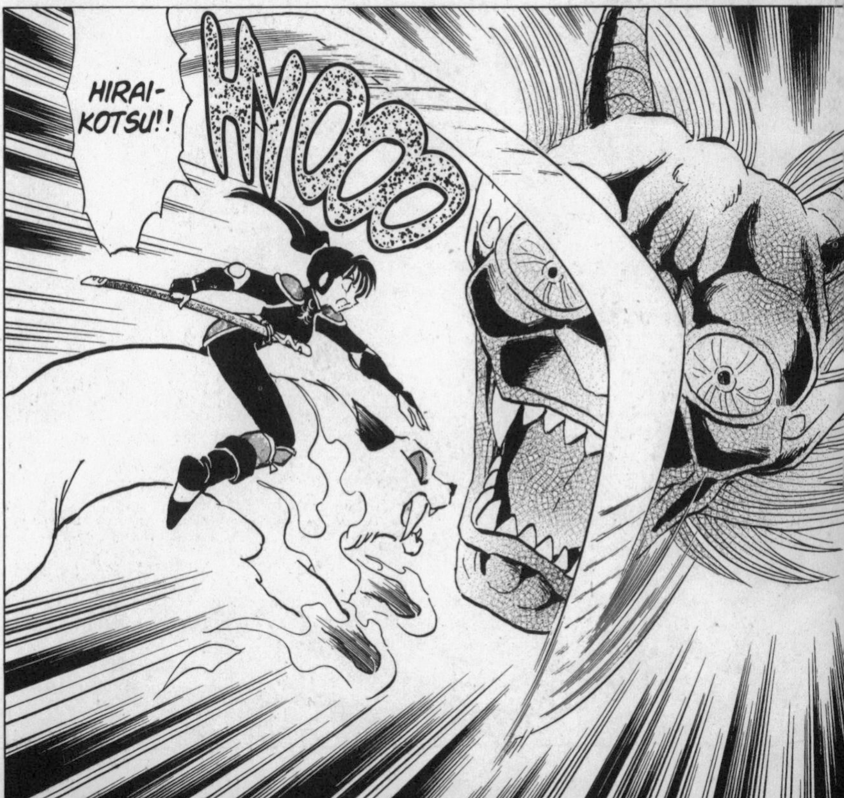
HIRAI-KOTSU!!
HYOOO

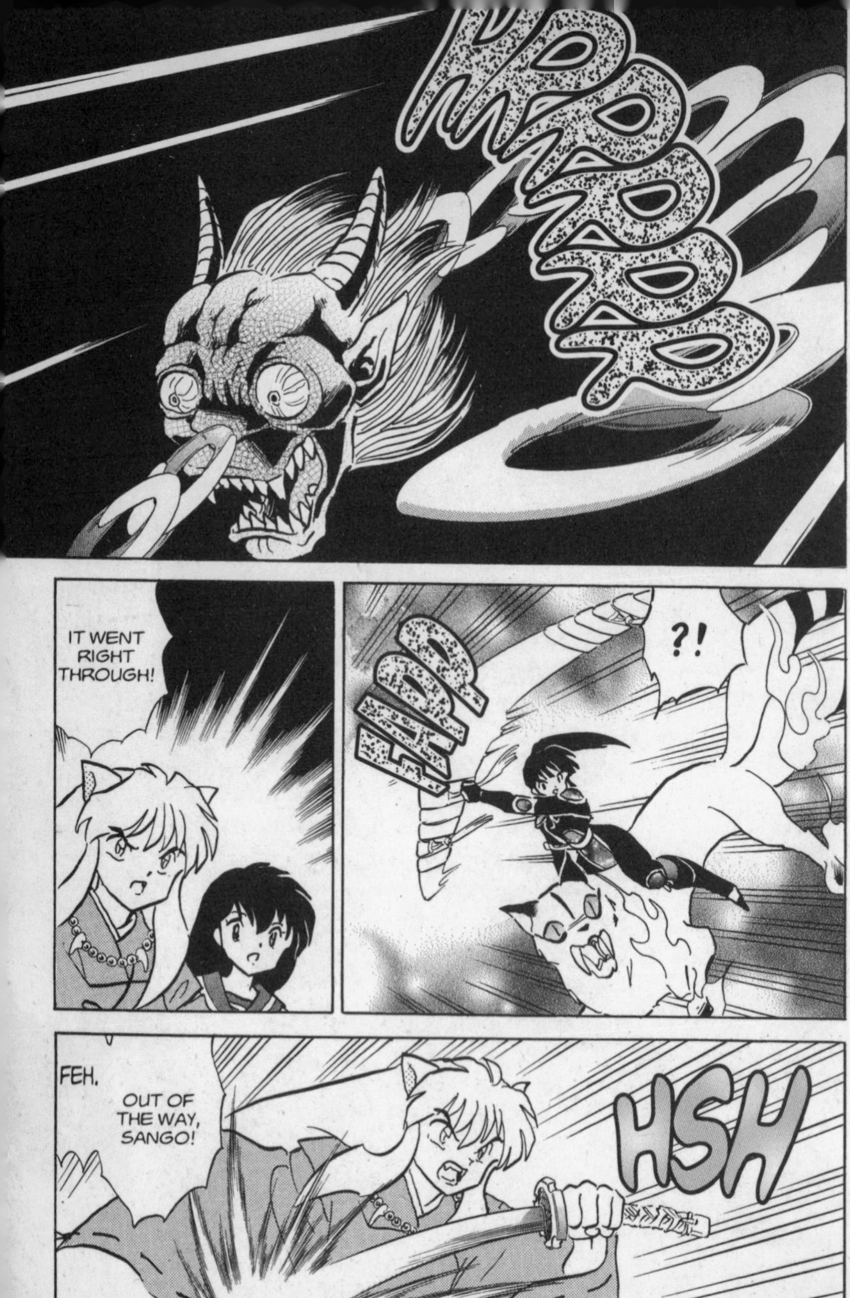
IT WENT RIGHT THROUGH!
?!
FEH.
OUT OF THE WAY, SANGO!
HSH

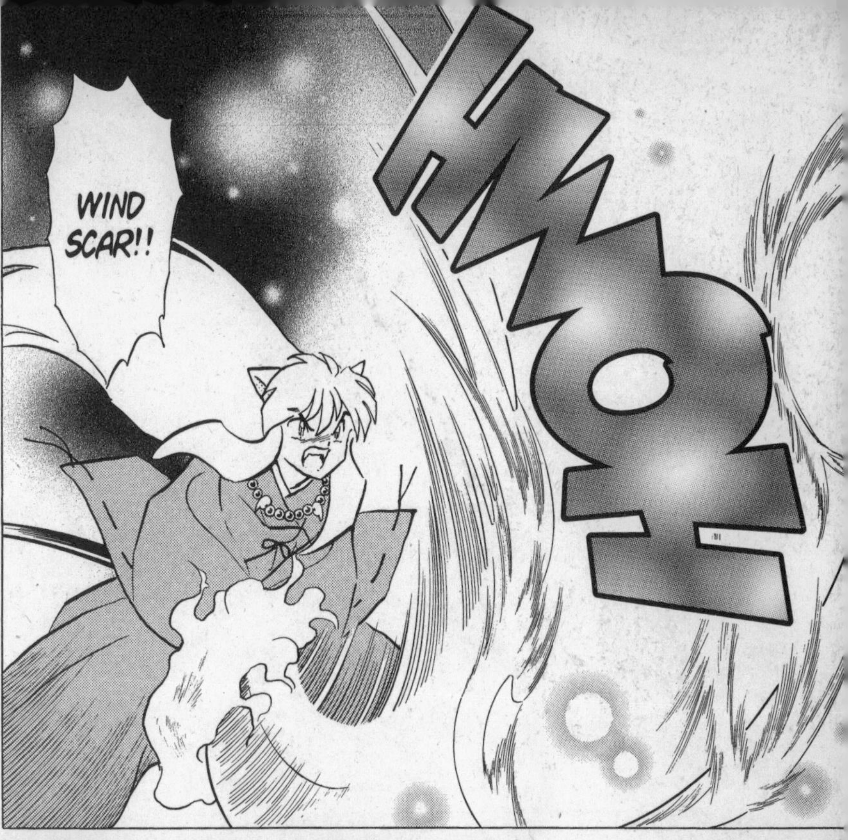
WIND
SCAR!!
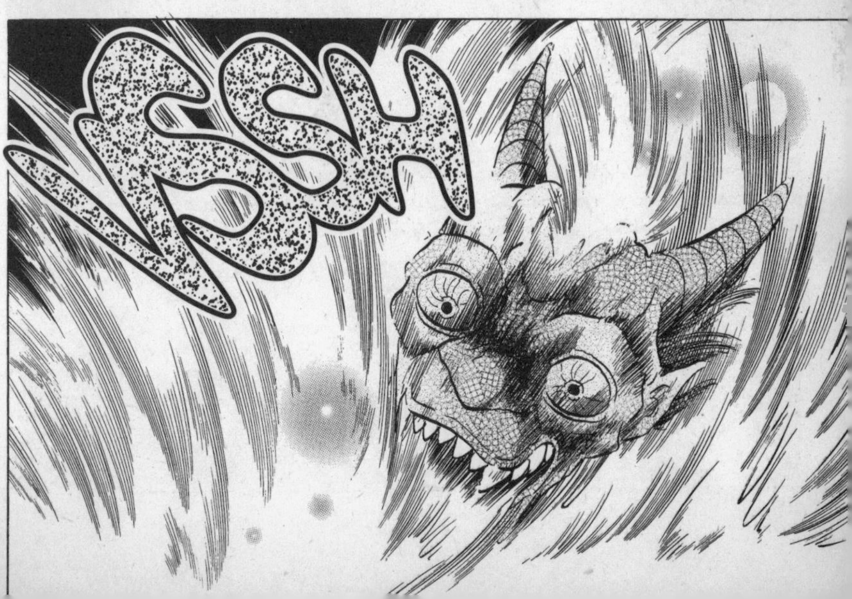
WSSH

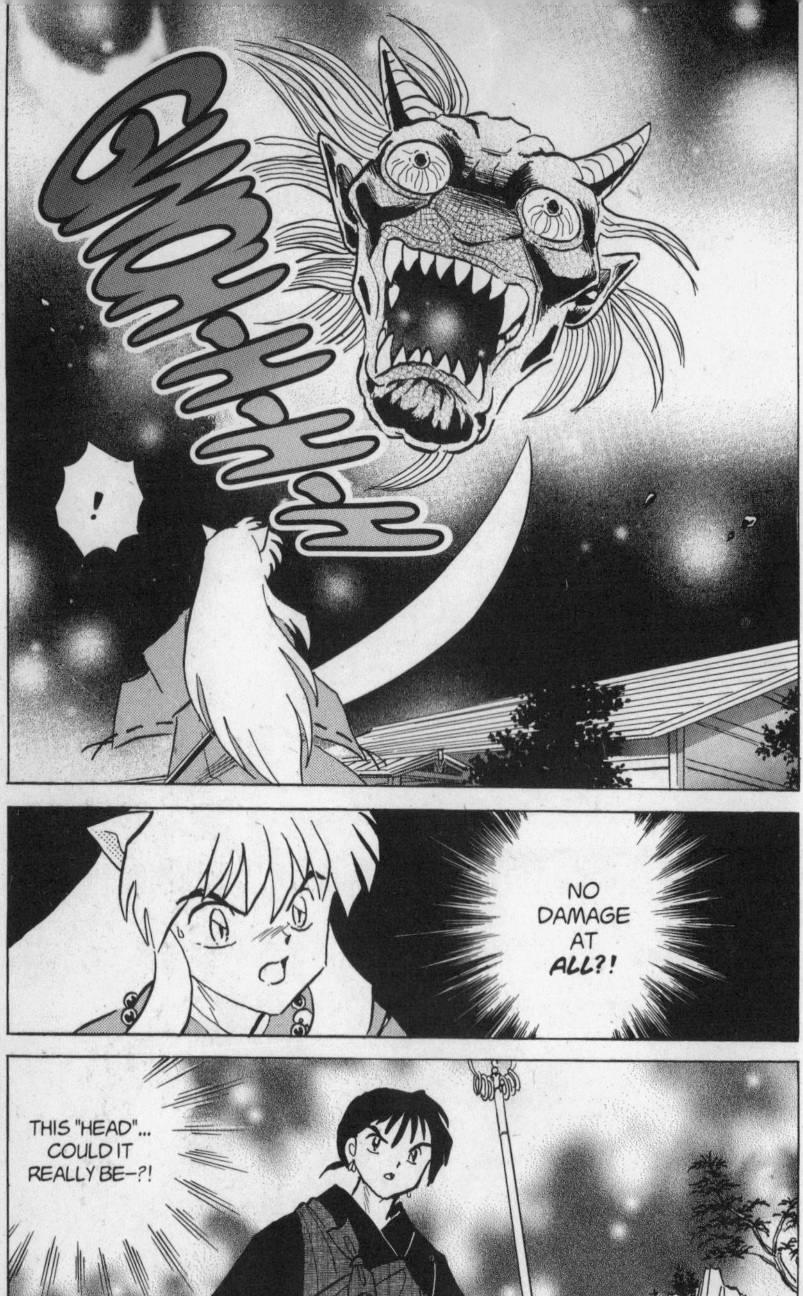
!
NO DAMAGE AT ALL?!
THIS "HEAD"... COULD IT REALLY BE-?!

TO BE CONTINUED...

About Rumiko Takahashi

Born in 1957 in Niigata, Japan, Rumiko Takahashi attended women's college in Tokyo, where she began studying comics with Kazuo Koike, author of *CRYING FREEMAN*. She later became an assistant to horror-manga artist Kazuo Umezu (*OROCHI*). In 1978, she won a prize in Shogakukan's annual "New Comic Artist Contest," and in that same year her boy-meets-alien comedy series *URUSEI YATSURA* began appearing in the weekly manga magazine *SHÔNEN SUNDAY*. This phenomenally successful series ran for nine years and sold over 22 million copies. Takahashi's later *RANMA 1/2* series enjoyed even greater popularity.

Takahashi is considered by many to be one of the world's most popular manga artists. With the publication of Volume 34 of her *RANMA 1/2* series in Japan, Takahashi's total sales passed *one hundred million* copies of her compiled works.

Takahashi's serial titles include *URUSEI YATSURA, RANMA 1/2, ONE-POUND GOSPEL, MAISON IKKOKU* and *INUYASHA*. Additionally, Takahashi has drawn many short stories which have been published in America under the title "Rumic Theater," and several installments of a saga known as her "Mermaid" series. Most of Takahashi's major stories have also been animated and are widely available in translation worldwide. *INUYASHA* is her most recent serial story, first published in *SHÔNEN SUNDAY* in 1996.

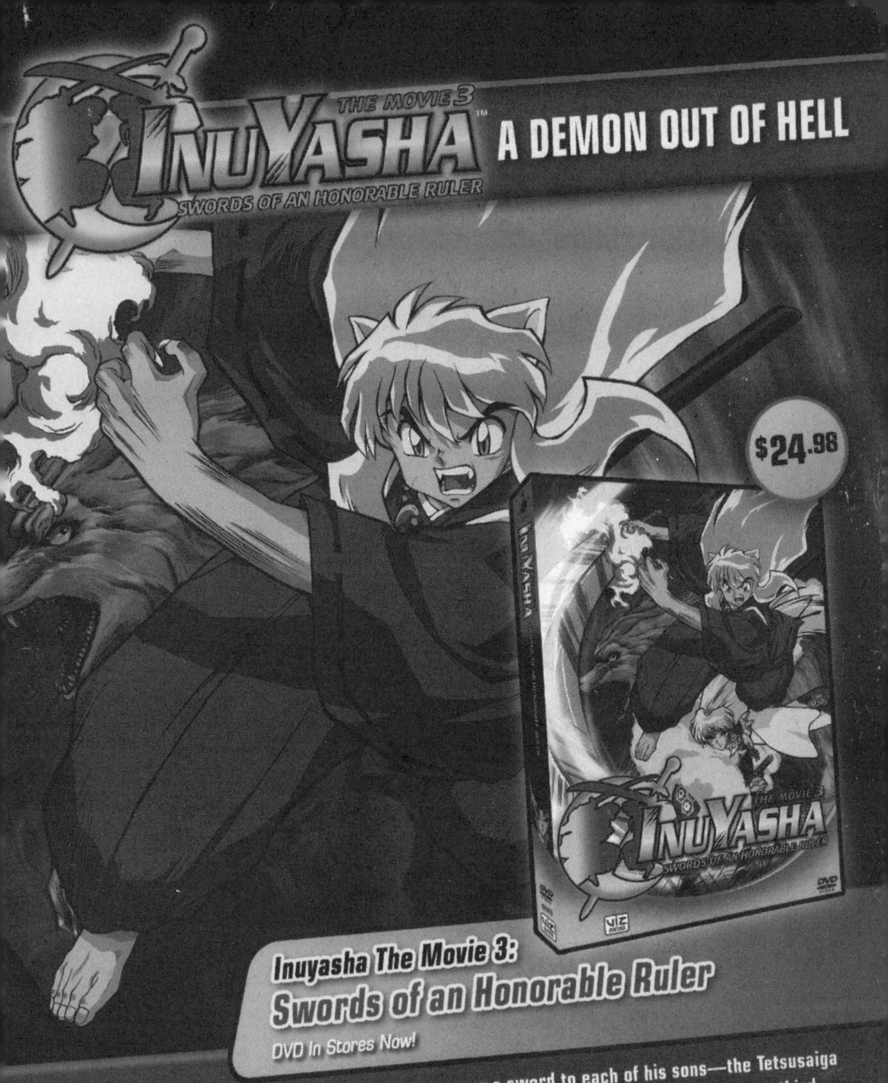
INUYASHA THE MOVIE 3
SWORDS OF AN HONORABLE RULER
A DEMON OUT OF HELL
$24.98
Inuyasha The Movie 3:
Swords of an Honorable Ruler
DVD In Stores Now!

LOVE MANGA? LET US KNOW!

☐ Please do NOT send me information about VIZ products, news and events, special offers, or other information.

☐ Please do NOT send me information from VIZ' trusted business partners.

Name: _____

Address: _____

City: _____ **State:** _____ **Zip:** _____

E-mail: _____

☐ Male ☐ Female **Date of Birth** (mm/dd/yyyy): ___/___/_____ (Under 13? Parental consent required)

What race/ethnicity do you consider yourself? (check all that apply)

☐ White/Caucasian   ☐ Black/African American   ☐ Hispanic/Latino

☐ Asian/Pacific Islander ☐ Native American/Alaskan Native ☐ Other: _____

What VIZ shojo title(s) did you purchase? (indicate title(s) purchased)

_____

_____

What other VIZ shojo titles do you own? _____

_____

Reason for purchase: (check all that apply)

☐ Special offer   ☐ Favorite title / author / artist / genre
☐ Gift   ☐ Recommendation   ☐ Collection
☐ Read excerpt in VIZ manga sampler   ☐ Other _____

Where did you make your purchase? (please check one)

☐ Comic store   ☐ Bookstore   ☐ Grocery Store
☐ Convention   ☐ Newsstand   ☐ Video Game Store
☐ Online (site:_____) ☐ Other _____

How many manga titles have you purchased in the last year? How many were VIZ titles?
(please check one from each column)

MANGA	VIZ
☐ None	☐ None
☐ 1 – 4	☐ 1 – 4
☐ 5 – 10	☐ 5 – 10
☐ 11+	☐ 11+

How much influence do special promotions and gifts-with-purchase have on the titles you buy?
(please circle, with 5 being great influence and 1 being none)

1 2 3 4 5

Do you purchase every volume of your favorite series?

☐ Yes! Gotta have 'em as my own ☐ No. Please explain: ______________________

What kind of manga storylines do you most enjoy? **(check all that apply)**

☐ Action / Adventure	☐ Science Fiction	☐ Horror
☐ Comedy	☐ Romance (shojo)	☐ Fantasy (shojo)
☐ Fighting	☐ Sports	☐ Historical
☐ Artistic / Alternative	☐ Other ______________________	

If you watch the anime or play a video or TCG game from a series, how likely are you to buy the manga? **(please circle, with 5 being very likely and 1 being unlikely)**

1 2 3 4 5

If unlikely, please explain: ______________________

Who are your favorite authors / artists? ______________________

____

What titles would like you translated and sold in English? ______________________

____

THANK YOU! Please send the completed form to:

NJW Research
42 Catharine Street
Poughkeepsie, NY 12601

Your privacy is very important to us. All information provided will be used for internal purposes only and will not be sold or otherwise divulged.